Transforming
Self and Others
Through Research

SUNY series in Transpersonal and Humanistic Psychology

Richard D. Mann, editor

Transforming Self and Others Through Research

Transpersonal Research Methods and Skills for the Human Sciences and Humanities

Rosemarie Anderson

and

William Braud

with a contribution by Jennifer Clements

State University of New York Press

Published by State University of New York Press, Albany

For information, contact State University of New York Press, Albany, NY
www.sunypress.edu

Production by Kelli W. LeRoux
Marketing by Michael Campochiaro

Library of Congress Cataloging-in-Publication Data

Anderson, Rosemarie.
   Transforming self and others through research : transpersonal research methods and skills for the human sciences and humanities / Rosemarie Anderson and William Braud.
       p. cm. — (Suny series in transpersonal and humanistic psychology)
   Includes bibliographical references and index.
   ISBN 978-1-4384-3672-2 (pbk. : alk. paper)
   ISBN 978-1-4384-3671-5 (hbk. : alk. paper)
   1. Psychology—Research—Methodology.   2. Transpersonal psychology—Research—Methodology.   3. Social sciences—Research—Methodology.
I. Braud, William.   II. Title.

   BF76.5.A68 2011
   150.19'87072—dc22   2011010372

We dedicate this book to our teachers and students.

Contents

List of Tables

List of Figures

Acknowledgments

The authors wish to explicitly acknowledge John Creswell and Robert Romanyshyn for their insightful comments on early portions of this book; Sonja Margulies and Miles Vich for information about the formative years of transpersonal psychology and for their own invaluable roles in helping frame and develop the "transpersonal orientation"; Jill Mellick and Nancy Rowe for their inspiring work in the area of creative expression and its applications to research; the Institute of Transpersonal Psychology (ITP) for its continuing support of transpersonal approaches to research, teaching, learning, professional practices, and the art of living; and to our ITP faculty colleagues and students in our ITP Residential and our Global Program cohorts for their contributions to the development of the approaches and skills treated in this volume. We are indebted to Jennifer Hill for her helpful assistance in the preparation of the final manuscript.

We thank the *Journal of Transpersonal Psychology* (JTP) for granting permission for us to include a modified and updated version of the following article as Chapter 3 of this book: J. Clements (2004), "Organic Inquiry: Toward Research in Partnership with Spirit." *Journal of Transpersonal Psychology, 36,* 26–49.

Preface

Throughout the human sciences and humanities, it is generally acknowledged that the major aim of research and academic pursuits is to expand the knowledge base of one's discipline—i.e., to provide further information about a topic of scientific or scholarly interest. What is not as frequently recognized is that, in addition to *information*, research can provide opportunities for *transformation* as well. Such transformation—in the form of important, meaningful, and sometimes profound changes in one's attitudes and views of oneself and of the world at large—can occur in the researcher or scholar; other participants, including colleagues and research participants; the readers or audience of the report; and even in the society or culture in which the researcher or scholar is situated. In the forms in which research typically is conducted, transformative changes sometimes may occur as spontaneous, unintended side effects or aftereffects of a research project. However, it is possible to deliberately increase the likelihood of transformative changes in all research personnel by choosing inquiry approaches and emphasizing research skills that involve the researcher to a much greater degree than usually is the case and that allow the researcher to actualize aspects of herself or himself that typically are ignored and remain untapped during the course of a research project. The purpose of this book is to describe some of these transformation-fostering approaches and skills and to suggest ways of using them in research and scholarly endeavors throughout the human sciences and humanities.

Since the authors themselves are human science researchers, this book primarily addresses scientific research in the human sciences. Nevertheless, the transformative methods and skills described in this book are equally applicable to scholarly inquiry in the humanities. More generally, the humanities and human sciences would also be enriched by more collaborative, multidisciplinary efforts on related topics, a theme detailed in the final section of Chapter 2 and in Chapter 9, A Transformative Vision for Research and Scholarship.

The term *transformative* already has been used in a research context to describe a particular way of understanding, acquiring, and applying knowledge. For example, in a well-regarded research textbook, Mertens (2009) presented a *transformative paradigm* as one of the four major paradigms that inform current research practices. Earlier, Guba and Lincoln (1994) had called this a *critical theory paradigm*, and Mertens (2009) herself previously had named this an *emancipatory paradigm*. Mertens (2009) used the rubric *transformative* to describe a family of views: critical theory, neo-Marxist, feminist, critical race theory, Freirean, participatory, and emancipator. Guba and Lincoln (1994) had concisely characterized the purpose of inquiry, for persons working within this paradigm, as follows:

> The aim of inquiry is the *critique and transformation* of the social, political, cultural, economic, ethnic, and gender structures that constrain and exploit humankind, by engagement in confrontation, even conflict. The criterion for progress is that over time, restitution and emancipation should occur and persist. Advocacy and activism are key concepts. The inquirer is cast in the role of instigator and facilitator, implying that the inquirer understands a priori that transformations are needed. But we should note that some of the more radical stances in the criticalist camp hold that judgment about needed transformations should be reserved to those whose lives are most affected by transformations: the inquiry participants themselves. (113)

In this book, we are not using the term *transformation* in the sense used by Guba and Lincoln and Mertens. Instead, we are emphasizing *individual and personal transformation*. We are suggesting that under certain conditions, planning, conducting, participating in, or learning about a research project can be accompanied by increased self-awareness, enhanced psycho-spiritual growth and development, and other personal changes of great consequence to the individuals involved. Of course, such personal transformations are not unrelated to the kinds of political, social, and cultural transformations mentioned earlier, but in this book we emphasize the former more than the latter.

Throughout this book, we provide detailed descriptions of ways in which self and others may be transformed through research. Here, we can briefly characterize the kinds of changes that can be expected and the nature of the conditions that can help bring about these changes.

Personal transformation involves a qualitative shift in one's lifeview and/or worldview. Such a shift may occur rapidly or gradually, dramatically or subtly. Transformative change tends to be *persistent* (not merely a temporary shift that reverts to an earlier condition), *pervasive* (not confined to isolated aspects of one's being or functioning), and *profound* (having an important life impact). Transformation may manifest as changes in one's perspective, understandings, attitudes, ways of knowing and doing, and way of being in the world. It may be recognized by changes in one's body, feelings and emotions, ways of thinking, forms of expression, and relationships with others and with the world.

We suggest that personal and communal transformation can be an accompaniment or outcome of research if (a) the research *project* has great personal meaning and is one in which the researcher can become intimately involved, (b) the chosen research *approach* is an expansive and inclusive one that allows the researcher to engage in a greater variety of ways of knowing than usually is the case, and (c) the researcher more fully prepares herself or himself (and prepares the research participants and even the expected audiences of the work) for the project at hand by identifying and improving a set of *additional research skills* that ordinarily are neglected. These three conditions allow the researcher to be personally and more fully engaged in all phases of a research project, thereby actualizing many of the researcher's latent potentials. The researcher may further activate these potentials by approaching a research project with explicit intentions for enhanced self-awareness and transformative changes in all research personnel, by reviving and holding those intentions throughout the project, and by explicitly reflecting, at the conclusion of the project, on whether and how those aims were realized.

The purpose of this book is to assist researchers—student beginners and already accomplished investigators—in realizing the conditions and outcomes just mentioned. The chapters describe techniques that can complement already familiar methods and procedures for planning a study, collecting and analyzing data, and reporting findings. Part 1 describes three recently developed research approaches—each informed by principles and practices from the growing field of transpersonal psychology—that emphasize personal involvement and transformative possibilities. Part 2 provides detailed instructions for identifying, practicing, and enhancing a variety of specific skills and applying these in any research context. Although these specific skills are commonly used in contexts of personal life, professional applications (counseling and clinical work, health care, educational and training contexts), and individual psycho-spiritual growth and development, their research relevance and actual use in research projects have rarely been treated. The most distinctive feature of Part 2—and, indeed, of the entire book—is the recognition that these personal skills and practices can be applied in the service of more effective research and in the service of transformative changes in self and others.

It is important to note what this book is not. This is not meant to be a complete, stand-alone treatment of well-established research methods, principles, and practices. There already exist many excellent texts that provide extensive coverage of quantitative, qualitative, and mixed research methods—Creswell (2006, 2009), Dooley (1995), Howell (2007, 2009), Mertens (2008, 2009), and Whitley (2003). The present book focuses on distinctive approaches and techniques that complement and supplement these more familiar methods and that will be of interest and use to those who value the transformative possibilities of research projects as much as their informational yields.

Transforming Self and Others Through Research is part of the ongoing development of a collaborative and engaged research praxis in the human sciences. The book can be used as a textbook in advanced undergraduate and graduate research courses in humanistic and transpersonal psychology *and* applied human science programs, such as professional schools of psychology, education, counseling, nursing, allied health, and public health. Throughout the book, we encourage a transformative approach to research that is inherently multi-methodological and responsive to our rapidly changing multicultural and global environment.

Our aim is to introduce transformative research practice to researchers in the human sciences for adaptation and assimilation into established methods. We discuss the origins of these research approaches within the field of transpersonal psychology and suggest how students and mature researchers can integrate these with established methods without compromising familiar approaches to research. Throughout the book, the transpersonal research approaches and skills are presented in a detailed, student-friendly manner so that instructors and students can blend these with the quantitative and qualitative methods they already may be using.

The book is most useful as a primary, supplemental, or paired text in transpersonal, humanistic, and complementary health-care research courses, as a primary, supplemental, or paired text in professionally-oriented and allied programs, and as a secondary text in conventional quantitative and qualitative research courses. The book's presentation style is student-friendly and includes step-by-step instructions, practical information, many experiential exercises, and many examples based on the authors' extensive research experience and their experience in teaching undergraduate and graduate research courses and supervising master's theses and doctoral dissertations. The experiential exercises that treat the individual research skills can be modified and adapted for personal use in individual research projects, undergraduate and graduate research, and classroom use. Both professional researchers and students can supplement the presented skills and exercises by adding other familiar skills or by developing creative variations of the skills treated in Part 2 of the book.

Besides its emphasis on transformation, another distinctive feature of this book is its inclusion of much more *content-related information and resources* than is typical for research methods books. Usually, research books are devoted almost entirely to descriptions of the methods themselves, with little added in the way of findings or theories that already exist in the discipline being treated. In the present research book, we include a great deal of substantive information about various topics and subject matter. This information is presented as contextualizations of the treated approaches and skills and also in the examples included to illustrate various principles and practices.

Note to Course Instructors, Students, and Researchers

Instructors can use the book as a whole or integrate selected chapters with other texts in order to effectively fulfill particular course objectives and to satisfy their own and their students' interests. Instructors will find the approaches of Part 1 and the skills of Part 2 most relevant for courses in transpersonal psychology, transpersonal studies, humanistic psychology, and the human sciences generally. The contents of both parts also have great applicability to courses in nursing, other health- and wellness-related areas, and education. Selected sections from both parts of this book can be assigned in conventional research courses in psychology programs, so that students may learn about approaches and skills that complement the already established methods treated in these courses. Instructors of courses in applied areas such as counseling or social work may wish to select the most relevant of the skills chapters in Part 2 (especially those of Chapters 4 and 6) and coordinate these with the primary texts they already are using. Instructors of spirituality courses may find the approaches of Chapters 1 and 3 and the skills of

Chapters 4, 5, and 7 quite useful. All of the skills of Part 2, especially those described in Chapters 5, 6, and 7, are relevant to courses in the creative arts and performing arts. The content of Chapter 9 is relevant to courses in areas of ecopsychology, ecospirituality, human ecology, and environmental and global studies. Our overarching advice is that instructors be creative in selecting and ordering the various sections of this book to fit their own needs and interests.

Students in any of the areas mentioned above can use aspects of the approaches treated in Part 1 and selected skills treated in Part 2 to complement the research methods they already know or are learning. Students and professional researchers alike also can use the many skills described in Part 2 for purposes other than research—in their professional work and as aids in their personal growth, development, and transformation.

About the Book Chapters

Chapters 1, 2, and 3 were written respectively by Rosemarie Anderson, William Braud, and Jennifer Clements. All other chapters and sections of this book (unattributed) were cowritten by Rosemarie Anderson and William Braud.

About Critiques

In the various chapters of Parts 1 and 2 of this book, we do not include separate sections devoted exclusively to critiques of the presented research approaches and skills. Instead, we have attempted to develop these approaches and skills while bearing possible critiques in mind, and address issues that seem most relevant to us in appropriate subsections of the chapters and address these, in context, as possible limitations and challenges to the use of these approaches and skills. Since the approaches and skills presented in this book can be used as complementary to other approaches and skills, we respect and encourage researchers and scholars to use them in ways appropriate to their disciplines and the purposes of a particular investigation. We acknowledge that larger critiques of the materials presented in this book are likely to emerge from researchers working within an exclusively positivistic paradigm. However, the approaches and the uses of the skills recommended in this book reside in a transformative paradigm that expands beyond the epistemologies and methodologies of positivism; therefore, such critiques have reduced relevance. Finally, the inclusion of additional sections devoted to critiques would have increased the length of this book unacceptably.

Introduction to Part 1

Transpersonal Research Methods

The transpersonal research methods presented in Part 1 invite transformation of self and others in all aspects of research praxis and application—from the investigator's conceptualization of a study through the consumers' appreciation of research as they read and apply findings to practical life problems. All three research approaches—namely intuitive inquiry, integral inquiry, and organic inquiry—seek to invite everyone involved in research to engage the possibility of being transformed in some way by their participation. In transpersonal research, researchers, participants, and the audience or readers of research reports often change or transform their understanding of the research topic, including self understanding in relationship to the topic. Researchers are invited to study topics about which they are passionate and likely to have experienced themselves. Researchers analyze, interpret, and present findings in ways that engage their own participation, attitudes, and life stories and prompt changes in the ways they feel and think about the topic, themselves, others, and the world. Research participants, too, are actively involved and encouraged to engage the topic in ways that enhance their life journeys and personal growth. The eventual readers and consumers of research reports and applications are also invited to integrate and apply research findings in ways that further their self understanding and the transformation of their communities. The transpersonal research approaches presented in Part 1 share these common end goals.

Intuitive inquiry, integral inquiry, and organic inquiry began their development within the field of transpersonal psychology in the mid-1990s. Rosemarie Anderson and William Braud, the developers of intuitive inquiry and integral inquiry respectively, were the principal facilitators of these emerging transpersonal approaches to research in the context of teaching research methods and supervising doctoral dissertations at the Institute of Transpersonal Psychology (ITP). In 1994 and 1995, a set of unexpected circumstances led to one of the most fruitful endeavors of our careers. We began teaching quantitative and qualitative research methods together. The course became a laboratory to expand and extend established research methods *transpersonally*. One afternoon, wanting "to set a field of intention," we practiced what we were asking our students to do. We timed ourselves. In eight minutes, we had articulated a comprehensive list of ways in which well-established research methods, both quantitative and qualitative, could be extended or expanded to make them more applicable to the exploration of transpersonal and spiritual experiences. Around the same time, Jennifer Clements and colleagues Dorothy Ettling, Dianne Jenett, and Lisa Shields (1999) began to develop organic inquiry at ITP.

Our ongoing conversations and interactions with students and colleagues led us to coauthor *Transpersonal Research Methods for the Social Sciences* (Braud and Anderson 1998), in which the three approaches were presented in the theoretical way they emerged at the time. Since the mid-1990s, our three approaches have been tested and refined in a large number of empirical studies, mostly conducted by ITP graduate students who were engaged in dissertation research (see Chapters 1, 2, and 3 for descriptions of these studies). In classroom applications and research supervision, we have also learned ways to apply and broaden our approaches, making them relevant to beginning and mature researchers and professional practitioners in the human sciences. The presentations of intuitive inquiry, integral inquiry, and organic inquiry in Part 1 represent our readiness to offer the fruits of our transpersonal research practices to the wider human science research community.

Intuitive inquiry, integral inquiry, and organic inquiry are applicable to research endeavors throughout the human sciences. Many fields of scholarship and science seek to explore the potential of human transformation in our engagement with one another and the world at large. Transpersonal psychology is in no way unique in its exploration of the "farther researches of human nature" as Abraham Maslow put it so well in the 1960s. These other fields of study include economics, education, educational psychology, counseling, environmental studies, nursing science, medicine, political science, public health, and others that we cannot now envision. These three research approaches share some common features with current, fast-paced developments in qualitative research methods as well, though it is beyond the scope of this book to make these comparisons (see the appendixes in Braud and Anderson 1998 for some of these comparisons).

In our deepest self understanding, we hope that human science researchers who seek transformation for themselves and others in the practice and applications of research will incorporate our transpersonal approaches and skills, or aspects of them, in ways that further the transformative end goals of their fields of inquiry. Nothing would please us more. In no way, do we consider our approaches fixed or immutable but rather as scholarly grist for the mill in scientific discourse and discovery. Use these approaches toward positive, transformative ends so that all of us as scholars and researchers may collaborate and contribute to a better world for everything that lives.

Rationale for the Development of Transpersonal Approaches to Research

Explicit in the early transpersonal conversations was a recognition that methods more fitting to the nature of transpersonal and spiritual phenomena would eventually have to be created, validated, and employed within the scientific community. That is, the definition of *empirical* must eventually be expanded to include inner experiences, which are private and therefore unobservable by an external observer. Of course, while the study of researchers' and participants' inner experience is relevant to a wide variety of topics and human experiences, inner-experience data are essential to the study of transpersonal and spiritual experiences. Our first book, *Transpersonal Research Methods for the Social Sciences* was the first book to explore such methods in detail.

In transpersonal research, the Renaissance view of the artist may present a more complete model for investigating human experience than that of the nineteenth century physical scientist. Evaluated candidly, the most eloquent speakers today on the human experience often seem to be poets, novelists, playwrights, film-makers, story-tellers, and theologians—and more *rarely* psychologists, anthropologists, sociologists, and other scientists. By copying the objectivist and positivist views of the physical scientists (who are now abandoning that model themselves) and owning radical positivism and psychological behaviorism as the epistemological imprimatur, psychologists and other human scientists have ignored and even trivialized vast realms of fascinating human experiences. A well-known existential clinical psychologist, James Bugental, puts the dilemma quite succinctly: "The objectivist view of psychology . . . regards all that is not familiar as dangerous, mythical, or nonexistent" (Valle and Halling 1989, ix). Even when investigating extraordinary human experiences, researchers often seem content with meaning-diminishing methodologies. Without supporting methodologies, rich topics such as the study of passion, making love, giving birth, grieving, ecstasy, quietude, and mystical experiences are too often neglected. So often our research methods fall flat before the fullness and extraordinary experience of being human day-to-day. Having ceded the exploration of the expansive nature of being human to others by default, it may be time to re-enchant our methods of inquiry and related epistemologies with the rigors and vigor of imagination and more fully dimensionalized concepts and theories. Instead of tightening controls, we propose the rigors of full disclosure and complexity.

The paradigms of science are shifting. The stage is set for change. To quote Adrienne Rich (1979), we must get beyond the "assumptions in which we are drenched" (35). Along with the theories and critiques proposed by transpersonal psychologists and scientists in related fields, other developments and critiques have loosened the exclusive hold on psychological research that the experimental method once enjoyed. Some of these alternative views stem from the counterculture of the 1960s and 1970s, feminist critique and theory, existential-phenomeno-logical theory and phenomenological methods, deconstructionism and the post-modern critique of culture, the epistemological insights of quantum and high-energy physics, parapsychological investigations, narrative methods and discourse analysis, in-depth case studies, heu-ristic methods, and the concerns about external and effectual validity taking place within experimental psychology. There has been a series of critiques within psychology itself, notably from Bruner (1990), in reconceptualizing cognitive psychology as folk psychology, and from recent developments in the human sciences in general. Once thought of as unassailable epistemologies, behaviorism and some aspects of cognitive science have been besieged by still more complete and far-reaching ideas and methodologies. In wave upon wave, these critiques have enlivened scientific discourse as academic disciplines once again search for more suitable epistemologies and methods of inquiry.

Along with these transpersonal research approaches, of course, conventional qualitative and quantitative methods also may be employed—depending on how well they, or a mix of methods, suit the topic of inquiry. By presenting these transpersonal approaches to research, we hope to enliven scholarly and scientific inquiry in many fields with transpersonal approaches to investigating the nature and potential of human experience and—more generally, to support renewed imagination, creativity, and wonder/wonderment throughout all scientific inquiry and discourse.

Overview of Intuitive Inquiry, Integral Inquiry, and Organic Inquiry

Intuitive inquiry, integral inquiry, and organic inquiry share many of the same common values and end goals regarding the importance of the transformation of the researcher and others. Because the three approaches were developed within transpersonal psychology, the approaches also share values and end goals widely held within the field of transpersonal psychology and related fields. A description and a history of transpersonal psychology are provided below to help orient readers to this movement within psychology and the human sciences in general. All three of these transformative approaches emphasize complementary or multiple ways of knowing, usually known in scholarly literature as "multiple intelligences." All three also emphasize the evolving and organic quality inherent to all good research; the researcher's willingness and preparation to engage research activities wholeheartedly and personally; the appropriateness of the approaches to the study of experientially-based topics; and an unequivocal invitation for researchers, participants, and eventual readers of research reports to have a rollicking good time while participating in research.

The ways in which the three approaches differ tends to reflect the theoretical traditions emphasized or the scope of the method. For example, intuitive inquiry has been influenced primarily by traditions of European hermeneutics (interpretation), and organic inquiry was influenced by Carl Jung's concepts of the transcendent function and the four typological functions of thinking, feeling, intuition, and sensation. Integral inquiry differs from both intuitive inquiry and organic inquiry in its comprehensive integration of quantitative and qualitative data collection, analysis, and interpretation, and its presentation of findings in ways aligned with mixed-method approaches to research (Creswell 2009; Creswell and Clark 2006; Tashakkori and Teddlie 1998; Tashakkori and Teddlie 2003) developed in the last decade. Intuitive inquiry and organic inquiry emphasize qualitative data collection and analysis. That said, the differences become much more obvious in the *doing* of these approaches, because the different traditions emphasized and the scope of the methods invite distinctive processes more easily felt than conceptualized.

Intuitive Inquiry

Intuitive inquiry invites intuitive processes and insights directly into research practice—in the formulation of a research topic or question; the reflection on pertinent theoretical and empirical literature; data collection, analysis, and interpretation; and the presentation of findings. Based on the classic hermeneutical understanding that interpretation is personal and cyclical rather than linear and procedural, the approach provides a series of cycles that carry the research process forward. Throughout intuitive inquiry, compassion toward self and others is considered central to understanding.

Integral Inquiry

Integral inquiry provides both a comprehensive overview of psychological research methods and a means to blend these methods and to apply them to a particular research topic. Affirming the view that human experience is multileveled and complex, integral inquiry is multifaceted and pluralistic. A key feature of the approach is the presentation of a continuum of qualitative and quantitative methods, both conventional and avant-garde, from which researchers may choose or mix approaches to best suit their research questions. An inclusive approach to research is fostered by encouraging the integral inquirer to address four types of research questions—what is the nature of an experience, how has the experience been conceptualized through history, what are the triggers and accompaniments of the experience, and what are the outcomes/fruits of the experience? The approach also emphasizes expanding the time frame for a literature review; letting one's research be informed by a variety of disciplines; expanding the ways of collecting, treating, and presenting one's data and findings; and appealing to a variety of audiences.

Organic Inquiry

The fundamental technique of organic inquiry is telling and listening to stories. The topic of an organic inquiry grows out of the researcher's own story, and the researcher writes his or her own story at the start of a study. Analysis involves a presentation of participants' stories using their own words as much as possible, a group story reflecting the shared meanings of the stories collected, and a report of the researcher's own transformative changes during the course of the study. At the core of organic inquiry is the transformative power of inviting, listening to, and presenting stories among research personnel and eventually the readers of a research report.

What is Transpersonal Psychology?

Initially, as a social movement and evolving perspective, transpersonal psychology was dedicated to the study and cultivation of the values and experiences that inform the highest potential in human nature (Braud and Anderson 1998; Grof 2008; Grof, Lukoff, Friedman, and Hartelius 2008; Maslow 1967: Maslow 1969; Maslow 1971; Sutich 1968; Sutich 1969; Sutich 1976a; Sutich 1976b). In an address at the San Francisco Unitarian Church on September 14, 1967—following closely behind its historical predecessors of psychoanalytic theory, behaviorism, and humanistic psychology— Abraham Maslow announced this "fourth force" within psychology. In June, 1969, the first issue of the *Journal of Transpersonal Psychology* was published with Maslow's (1969) address entitled "The Farther Reaches of Human Nature" as the opening article. About midway in that address, he states:

> The fully developed (and very fortunate) human being, working under the best conditions, tends to be motivated by values which transcend his self. They are not selfish anymore in the old sense of that term. Beauty is not within one's skin nor is justice or order. One can hardly class these desires as selfish in the sense that my desire for food might be. My satisfaction with achieving or allowing justice is not within my own skin; it does not lie along my arteries. It is equally outside and inside: therefore, it has transcended the geographical limitations of the self. Thus one begins to talk about transhumanistic [later transpersonal] psychology. (4)

In the first issue of the *Journal of Transpersonal Psychology* in 1969, Editor Anthony Sutich (1969) portrays the emerging field of transpersonal psychology as the study of "those *ultimate* human capacities and potentialities . . ." specifically the

> empirical, scientific study of, and responsible implementation of the findings relevant to, becoming, individual and species-wide meta-needs, ultimate values, unitive consciousness, peak experiences, B-values, ecstasy, mystical experiences, awe, being, self-actualization, essence, bliss,

wonder, ultimate meaning, transcendence of self, spirit, oneness, cosmic awareness, individual and species wide synergy, maximal interpersonal encounter, sacralization of everyday life, transcendental phenomena, cosmic self-humor and playfulness, maximal sensory awareness, responsiveness and expression; and related concepts, experiences and activities. (16)

In a letter in February 1968, from Maslow to Sutich (cited in Sutich 1976a), Maslow credits Stanislav Grof for suggesting the name *transpersonal* to replace the term *transhumanistic*, with which Maslow, Sutich, and others had become increasingly dissatisfied. The term *transpersonal* seemed familiar, perhaps reminiscent of the term *überpersonlich* (meaning more than or above the personal in German) used earlier in the century by Carl Jung. The word *transpersonal* has its etymological roots in two Latin words: *trans* meaning beyond, across, or through, and *personal* meaning mask or facade—in other words, beyond, across, or through the personally identified aspects of self.

After surveying the many definitions of transpersonal psychology proposed between 1968 and 1991, Lajoie and Shapiro (1992, 91) conclude by defining the field of transpersonal psychology as ". . . concerned with the study of humanity's highest potential, and with the recognition, understanding, and realization of unitive, spiritual, and transcendent states of consciousness." Shortly thereafter, Walsh and Vaughan (1993) emphasized the study of transpersonal experiences "in which the sense of identity or self extends beyond (*trans*) the individual or personal to encompass wider aspects of humankind, life, psyche or cosmos" (203).

Caplan, Hartelius, and Rardin (2003) updated and expanded our understanding of transpersonal psychology by surveying and presenting definitions of the field written between 1968 and 2003 by forty-one transpersonal professionals who were active in the field. Their survey revealed a rich diversity of views, especially as related to the value placed on the potential of transpersonal and spiritual experiences to support individual and communal transformation. Whereas the early years of transpersonal psychology emphasized individual experience, transpersonalists were beginning to explore the impact of transpersonal and spiritual experiences on communal and even global values and actions and apply them to practical ends, related to personal growth and in service to the environment and peace among nations and people. What also stands out among the definitions is the placement of the field's activities within the cosmic dimensions of experience. As cited by Caplan et al. (2003), Jack Kornfield describes transpersonal psychology as an exploration of our "sacred place in the cosmos" (150) and Richard Tarnas portrays transpersonal psychology as an "opening to a fuller participation in the divine creativity that *is* the human person and the ever unfolding cosmos" (156). A few years later, Hartelius, Caplan, and Rardin (2007) presented a thematic analysis of the definitions of transpersonal psychology published between 1969 and 2003, concluding that the field can be summed up in three themes: beyond-ego psychology, integrative or holistic psychology, and the psychology of transformation—ways that align with the three definitions of the Latin *trans* meaning beyond, across, and through. The beyond-ego theme concerns the *content* of transpersonal psychology and aligns with Sutich's initial definition of the field cited above. The integrative or holistic theme "provides a widened *context* for studying the whole of human experience." The psychology of transformation is the *"catalyst"* for change, which signals both personal and social transformation (Hartelius, Caplan, and Rardin 2007, 9-11). Laura Boggio Gilot (cited in Caplan, Hartelius, and Rardin 2003), portrays the hopes for change of many transpersonalists:

> Aiming to contribute to healing the pervasive disease affecting the life of the planet, from the more advanced lines of transpersonal psychology are growing people of wisdom and maturity, capable of acting with altruistic purposes, not only to relieve suffering, but also to awaken consciousness to the universal meanings of life, which can only lead to lasting peace and unity. (148)

Kaisa Puhakka (cited in Caplan, Hartelius, and Rardin 2003), states: "The best way to guard against [mistaking egoic functioning for something beyond it] and to ensure the continued vitality of inquiry in Transpersonal Psychology is to consider its theories, methods, and definitions . . . as provisional and open-ended" (153). We agree. Therefore, in the spirit of open-ended definitions of the field, we propose our own definition: Transpersonal psychology is the study and cultivation of the highest and most transformative human values and potentials—individual, communal, and global—that reflect the mystery and interconnectedness of life, including our human journey within the cosmos.

A Brief History of the Transpersonal Movement

Historically, the transpersonal movement emerged amid the cultural melee of the 1960s in the United States with the vanguard of the movement epicentered in Northern California. The challenges and eccentricities of the 1960s awakened so many, as though we had been sleeping while awake and listlessly unaware. The Vietnam War raged in Asia. Experimenting with psychedelics was commonplace. American culture rocked with voices of conflict and derision. Fresh perspectives rushed in, as if replacing a vacuum. Ancient spiritual lineages, especially from Asia, were openly discussed and explored, and young people went to Asia to explore these traditions for themselves. The ideological "shakes" of this era became a worldwide cultural phenomenon—impacting not only politics but the arts, music, interpersonal relations, and societal values. It is difficult to imagine how the emerging field of transpersonal psychology, with limited funds and few resources aside from dedicated volunteers, could have nurtured and sustained this movement without the high-voltage atmosphere of the San Francisco Bay Area and the expanding U. S. economy of the 1960s and 1970s.

As with so many things in this era, the context for this emerging field of transpersonal psychology began informally—friends gathered in their homes to talk, spiritual leaders came to North America to join the conversations and often stayed, up-and-coming transpersonalists met to chat while on the road lecturing, and many exchanged letters with like-minded scientists, scholars, and spiritual teachers around the world (Sutich 1968; Sutich 1976a; Sutich 1976b). Although the transpersonal movement has been housed within the field of psychology, a multidiscipline emphasis was present from the start. The two primary proponents of this transpersonal vanguard were Abraham Maslow and Anthony Sutich. Maslow was a well-known public figure and scientist, and traveled extensively. Due to his travel schedule and declining health, Maslow's influence on the new journal was mostly through his writing and lively correspondence with Sutich (excerpts from his letters in Sutich 1976a; Sutich 1976b). Sutich was a busy psychotherapist and organized his private practice and professional activities at his home in Palo Alto, California. As a result of an accident in a baseball game at age twelve that lead to progressive arthritis, Sutich was severely disabled and transacted all his activities while lying on a gurney. Like Maslow, Sutich was a big thinker and was always interested in being at the cutting edge. For years, he had used his home as a salon for innovative thinking and conversation. Joining these early transpersonal exchanges were James Fadiman, Stanislav Grof, Sonja Margulies, Michael Murphy, Frances (nee Clark) Vaughan, and Miles Vich. Eventually the salon become the editorial board for the new *Journal of Transpersonal Psychology* (JTP), meeting on Wednesday afternoons and into the evenings to discuss submitted manuscripts, the latest developments, and to converse with guests (Anderson 1996a).

Throughout the years, one of the distinguishing characteristics of the transpersonal movement has been the desire to integrate our understanding of human nature and behavior with the wisdom psychologies of the world's spiritual and religious traditions. From the beginning, Buddhism, Hinduism, and indigenous forms of shamanism were actively explored. Spiritual teachers Ram Dass, Chögyam Trungpa Rinpoche, Sensei Kobun Chino Otogawa, and others regularly joined the Wednesday meetings for conversation. In the last twenty years, the faith and mystical traditions of Judaism, Christianity, and Islam (especially Sufism) also have been influential in shaping the transpersonal orientation to understanding human experience. An excerpt from an article by Tarthang Tulku (1976) in the new journal provides a glimpse of what these early conversations might have entailed:

> According to Buddhist psychology, the mind manifests over fifty specific mental events and at least eight different states of consciousness, but even these comprise just the surface level of the mind. In the West, for example, it seems that when anyone talks about "mind," it is "mind-sensing" that is meant—relating mind to a series of perceptual processes such as seeing, hearing, smelling, tasting, touching, and conceptualizing. . . . Beyond this level of perceptual processes and interpretations . . . there is a more pervasive substratum of consciousness, termed *kun-gzhi* in Tibetan, which is a kind of intrinsic awareness which is not involved in any subject/object duality.
>
> Mind itself has no substance. It has no color and no shape. It has no form, no position, no characteristics, no beginning, no end. . . . When the mind becomes still, thoughts are like drawings on water—before you finish, they flow away. . . . (42–43)

In 1969, the Transpersonal Institute was founded to sponsor the JTP. In 1972, the Association for Transpersonal Psychology (ATP) was created as a membership association. By the mid-1970s, a second wave of scholars and researchers had joined the efforts and made important contributions to the JTP. These included Robert Frager, Alyce and Elmer Green, Daniel Goleman, Stanley Krippner, Charles Tart, Roger Walsh, John Welwood, and Ken Wilber. Over the years, many of them have made contributions in other fields as well. In 1975, Frager, as founding president, founded the (California) Institute of Transpersonal Psychology (ITP), dedicated to transpersonal theory, research, and graduate-level education. In 1978, Grof, as founding president, and Michael Murphy and Richard Price, co-founders of Esalen Institute, founded the International Transpersonal Association (ITA), which includes members and sponsors conferences representing a multidisciplinary spectrum of transpersonal interests. After a proposed new APA Division of Transpersonal Psychology failed to receive the requisite two-thirds vote from the APA Council of Representatives in 1984 and 1985 (Aanstoos, Serlin, and Greening, 2000), transpersonal psychologists, therapists, and practitioners renewed their efforts to support their own associations and conferences. Graduate programs and undergraduate courses in transpersonal psychology and related fields continue to grow in the United States (see the ATP directory, at www.atpweb.org, for a current listing).

In the last thirty years, in countries around the world, the transpersonal perspective took root with different research and application emphases. The *International Journal of Transpersonal Studies* (IJTS), representing a wide spectrum of transpersonal interests, theory, and applications, was founded as the *Australian Journal of Transpersonal Psychology* in 1981 with Don Diespecker at the University of Wollongong as the founding editor. IJTS is currently awaiting sponsorship as an official publication of ITA. The Japanese Association of Transpersonal Psychology/Psychiatry was formed in 1998 and has sponsored several conferences (www.soc.nii.ac.jp/jatp). After organizational meetings in Europe in the late 1990s and yearly conferences in Europe since 2000, the European Transpersonal Association (EUROTAS, www.eurotas.org) was incorporated in 2003. Currently, EUROTAS includes twenty-two national and regional transpersonal associations. In the United Kingdom, a Transpersonal Section (www.transpersonalpsychology.org.uk) of the British Psychological Society draws broadly upon the insights of Eastern psycho-spiritual traditions, the human sciences, and the humanities to provide a "much-needed impetus for research, as well as offering a forum in which ideas and initiatives can be exchanged and developed" (Fontana and Slack 1996, 269); the Section publishes its own journal, the *Transpersonal Psychology Review*. Since the early 2000s, several transpersonal related conferences that emphasize the field's common boundaries with Buddhist, Taoist, and Confucian traditions have been held in China. If the announcements we receive about transpersonal activities in our faculty mail and email inboxes is any indication, transpersonal professionals are located in most countries worldwide, at least in small numbers. What is still lacking in the transpersonal movement and associations is strong representation throughout Asia and the Southern Hemisphere generally (Hartelius, Caplan, Rardin 2007). The current reorganization of ITA seeks to engage greater worldwide participation and promote transpersonal dialogue and conferences among like-minded colleagues across many disciplines in the humanities and human sciences—people who seek to study and apply spiritual insights and orientations, when applicable, to modern culture (Grof, Lukoff, Friedman, and Hartelius 2008).

Details regarding the history of the early years of the transpersonal movement are not readily available in print, except as cited in the sources used in this Introduction to Part 1. In addition, the archives of the correspondence and production files of the first thirty years of the *Journal of Transpersonal Psychology* are located in the library of the Institute of Transpersonal Psychology (www.itp.edu). The authors acknowledge and thank Miles Vich and Sonja Margulies for providing important information about the transpersonal movement in 1960s and 1970s, especially as related to activities of JTP.

Suggestions for Using Transpersonal Research Approaches

Students and experienced researchers alike are encouraged to engage the three transpersonal research methods presented in Part 1 with *a beginner's mind* and a spirit of adventure. Some of the ideas contained in the approaches may seem familiar to you, and others may not. If you are experienced in meditation or well versed in the personal growth movement, aspects of the approaches and the experiential exercises of Part 1, and the transpersonal skills in Part 2, are more likely to seem familiar. Whether the approaches and exercises seem familiar, unfamiliar, inspiring, or challenging, we invite you to explore the three transpersonal approaches and try the experiential exercises with an exploratory mind and open heart.

The authors of this book were trained as experimental psychologists in the late 1960s and early 1970s, when the reigning research strategies were experimental design and statistical analyses. We know that some of the ideas represented by these three approaches are different than those we learned earlier because we have lived through the changes in human science research and methods ourselves. Depending on your research background, these new approaches may seem challenging. Know that the transpersonal approaches in Part 1 are invitations to explore and expand your research horizons and to practice these new approaches. You are invited to try them out and use and integrate these transpersonal approaches, or aspects of them, with other research approaches in ways that help you become a more accomplished and versatile researcher. Take what works for you and leave the rest—perhaps for another time or, more likely, for use with a research topic that might otherwise escape your understanding.

CHAPTER 1

Intuitive Inquiry

The Ways of the Heart
in Human Science Research

Rosemarie Anderson

The secret . . . is to regard . . . intelligence as a fertile field in which
seeds may be sown, to grow under the heat of flaming imagination.

—Maria Montessori (Montessori 1997)

An Introduction to Intuitive Inquiry

I am writing this chapter on intuitive inquiry (Anderson 1998; Anderson 2000; Anderson 2004a; Anderson 2004b; Anderson 2011) as the winter solstice draws near. In poetic terms, the impulse to conduct an intuitive inquiry begins like a light in the dark of winter because this impulse to explore a topic claims the researcher's imagination often in an unconscious and surreptitious way. She cannot stop thinking about the topic. Almost everything seems to remind her of it in some way. As the yearning forms to understand the topic fully, she begins to explore accounts of others who are informed about the topic. Everything related to the topic has meaning and significance, drawing the intuitive inquirer closer to understanding. She yearns to know more and more. Named or unnamed, conscious or unconscious, an intuitive inquiry has begun. What matters to the researcher may be an ordinary experience latent with symbolic meaning, a transformative or peak experience, or a communal or interpersonal phenomenon that invites inquiry for reasons that only she may apprehend, albeit vaguely, at the start. Intuitive inquiry cultivates the ways of the heart in human science research.

"Beloveds" are not only intimates but those occurrences, places, and curiosities in life that claim a person *before* he even knows them well. This yearning to understand is Eros or love in pure form because the intuitive inquirer wants to know his beloved topic fully. Probably all great research is compelled by such an ardor that invites disclosure of events, objects, and others. In intuitive inquiry, the researcher studies the fine points of a research account in a manner not unlike a lover exploring a beloved's hand. Details matter. Secrets matter. The ordinary is extraordinary. The particular is favored. In 1890, William James (1950) put the matter as follows:

> Why, from Plato and Aristotle downwards, philosophers should have vied with each other in scorn of the knowledge of the particular, and in adoration of that of the general, is hard to understand, seeing that the more adorable knowledge ought to be that of the more adorable things, and that the "things" of worth are all concretes and singulars. The only value of universal characters is that they help us, by reasoning, to know new truths about individual things. The restriction of one's meaning, moreover, to an individual thing, probably requires even more complicated brain-processes than its extension to all the instances of a kind; and the mere mystery, as such, of the knowledge, is equally great, whether generals or singulars of the things known. In sum, therefore the traditional Universal-worship can only be called a bit of perverse sentimentalism, a philosophic "idol of the cave." (479–80)

In attending to the particulars of data, intuitive inquiry joins intuitive and compassionate ways of knowing to the intellectual rigor of human science research. Methodologically, intuitive inquiry does not replace linear, left-brain attributes with imaginal, right-brain attributes. Rather, "in the union of [conventional] masculine and feminine perspectives, the method seeks to balance structure and flexibility, exterior and interior, reason and emotion, thinking and feeling, discernment and holism" (Dorit Netzer, pers. comm.).

I have been developing intuitive inquiry as a research method since 1995, exploring my initial impulses in a doctoral-level research course that emphasized the particularity of feminist approaches to research (Houston and Davis 2001; Nielsen 1990; Reinharz 1992) and heuristic research (Moustakas, 1990). My early notes on intuitive inquiry have a lively quality to them, including phrases such as *rigor without dogma, breaking set in concept making, compassion as value and principle, state-specific access to experience, contemplative conversations,* and *engaging the psyche in research.* Over time, I have been inspired by the biblical hermeneutics of Friedrich Schleiermacher (1977), the philosophic hermeneutics of Hans-Georg Gadamer (Bruns 1992; Gadamer 1976; Gadamer 1998a: Gadamer 1998b; Packer and Addison 1989), the embodied phenomenology of Maurice Merleau-Ponty (1962, 1968); Eugene Gendlin's (1991, 1992, 1997) "thinking beyond patterns"; and many scholars describing intuitive and embodied practices among indigenous peoples (Abram 1996; Luna and Amaringo 1991; Sheridan and Pineault 1997).

The first version of intuitive inquiry incorporated intuitive and compassionate ways of knowing in the selection of a research topic, data analysis, and presentation of findings in what might be described as a qualitative research approach emphasizing intuitive ways of knowing (Anderson 1998). Later, I added a hermeneutic process composed of iterative cycles of interpretation to give intuitive inquiry a soft structure that invites both freedom of expression and intellectual thoroughness throughout the method (Anderson 2000). The version of intuitive inquiry presented in this chapter and elsewhere (Anderson 2004a; Anderson 2004b; Esbjörn-Hargens and Anderson 2005; Anderson 2011) represents a further integration of these resources and my experience in supervising intuitive inquiry studies over the last fifteen years.

Like all empirical research methods, intuitive inquiry provides ways to collect, analyze, and interpret data. In addition, intuitive inquiry seeks to speculate about the possibilities implicit in the data that intimate new ways of being human in the world. In honoring the archetypal, symbolic, imaginal, and the possible latent in all human experience, the analyses and interpretations provided by an intuitive inquiry tend toward wholeness and wellness, regardless of the topic chosen. Often, intuitive inquirers explore topics that require attention by the culture at large, as though they are called to envision anew. What may seem like a researcher's zeal for a topic may be the tip of an iceberg of a call for change from the culture at large.

Epistemologically, intuitive inquiry is a search for new understandings through the focused attention of one researcher's passion and compassion for her- or himself, others, and the world. In so doing, intuitive inquiry affirms a world reality in flux and mutable and, therefore, challenges conventional notions of a static worldview that is separate and distinguishable from the knower, the lover. The intuitive inquirer may feel like she is chasing a moving target and that she is likely to wonder if she is or the data are changing before her eyes. Both are changing because insight changes what can be seen and what is seen changes understanding in an ongoing ebb and flow. Therefore, it is not unusual for intuitive inquirers to cultivate insights that may "break set" with established theory and scholarship. In research reports, the tale of an intuitive inquiry is reported fully *and* projected toward the future as an impetus for individual, ethical, moral, and collective change.

Methodologically, intuitive inquiry contains five iterative cycles that form a complete hermeneutic circle of interpretation. These cycles are described later in this chapter. Within the five cycles, analysis and interpretation pivot around the researcher's intuition. Active imagination, creative expression, and a variety of intuitive styles are encouraged in all five cycles in order to (a) move the research process forward when stuck (b) discern understandings both explicit and implicit in the data, and (c) cultivate deeper and speculative insights suggested in the data about the potential "farther reaches of human nature" (Maslow 1971). This interpretive and interactive dynamic of intuitive inquiry tends to transform both the researcher's understanding of the topic studied and his personal life—sometimes profoundly so. This transformation is structurally contained by the five cycles of interpretation—each inviting the researcher's psyche to roam freely within its boundaries, each containing specific and unique activities. Several of my dissertation students refer to the five cycles as a "sacred" container because each cycle gives directions on what is and what is *not* needed to complete that portion of the method and move the study forward successfully. Therefore, the researcher's psyche roams freely but not aimlessly so. Tangents are useful, but aimless meandering generates fatigue or depression. The procedural containment of intuitive inquiry provides the opportunity to meander safely, rather like good psychotherapy. The concrete tasks set by each cycle help to stabilize the intuitive inquirer's emotional and imaginal world, giving forward movement even in those times when progress seems incredibly slow, as happens from time to time in most studies. Again and again, I tell my dissertation students, "When in doubt, go back and reread the directions for the cycle in which you are engaged and do precisely what it says to do."

Intuitive inquiry is *not* for every researcher or every topic. Not every researcher wants or needs to explore the spontaneous and startling nature of the psyche, as so often happens in the course of an intuitive inquiry. Many topics in the human sciences do not require the in-depth, reflective process required by intuitive inquiry. Of course, aspects of intuitive inquiry can be used in any study or combined with other qualitative and quantitative research methods. However, as presented in this chapter, an ideal intuitive inquiry employs all five cycles of intuitive inquiry, the five cycles providing a complete hermeneutic circle suitable for the analysis and interpretation of complex human experiences.

From the start, I developed intuitive inquiry in response to the challenges posed by my dissertation students who studied topics in the field of transpersonal psychology. "Right body size" for women (Coleman 2000), the healing presence of a psychotherapist (Phelon 2001), grief and other deep emotions in response to nature (Dufrechou 2002), true joy in union with God in mystical Christianity (Carlock 2003), storytelling and compassionate connection (Hoffman 2003), and the dialectics of embodiment among contemporary female mystics (Esbjörn 2003) are among initial topics studied. I supervised these dissertations and most of the intuitive inquiries cited in this chapter, covering nearly thirty topics related to personal and communal transformation. Therefore, I write and speak with assurance and nuance about the possibilities of the method in generating insights and theory about human experience and the potential of cultivating intuition as a research praxis within scientific discourse. When research is infused with the imaginal and intuitive, science is imbued with a renewed ethical and compassionate dimension. Our times are needy. Let us begin.

What Is Intuition?

In Latin, *intuitus* refers to the direct perception of knowledge. Jeremy Hayward (1997) defines intuition "as the direct perception of things as they are," suggesting that when "we experience the world directly, beyond the filter of conception, we *live* that world" (ix). I agree with Hayward's comprehensive definition for intuition because it allows for direct and embodied ways of knowing prior to conceptual or psychological interpretation. Intuitions often feel palpable as distinct perceptions into the nature of things, even as these perceptions vanish into the background of awareness when the focused, rational mind kicks in, searching for meaning. From a Jungian psychological perspective, Marie Louise von Franz (1971) described intuition as "as a kind of sense perception via the unconscious or a subliminal sense perception" (37) that expands upon what is ordinarily sensed. The individual often feels as though he or she is tapping into a collective or unconscious source of knowing. In order to capture the meaning of intuitive perceptions, intuitives usually learn unique—and sometimes idiosyncratic—means to navigate between the often diffuse or dreamlike states that accompany intuitions and analytical reason and reflection. With practice, individuals can learn to witness their intuitive perceptions and integrate them with other ways of knowing. Often intuitive insights build upon and integrate knowledge gained from analytic reason and the conventional five human senses toward higher levels of understanding.

In terms of psychological typology, Carl Jung (1933) presents intuition as an irrational function because intuition eludes attempts to understand its character. We may notice our intuitions and discern their triggers. We can often describe how intuitive insights assist or confound life decisions. Sometimes the meaning of an intuition is immediately interpretable. But, often, its meaning is elusive, unrepeatable by will, and understandable via rational thought only after a period of reflection and discernment. Intuition appears more akin to those unique moments—while playing a musical instrument, touching a lover, or writing a poem—when impulses "fly" from the fingertips of our bodymind. Moments such as these have a fleeting and sometimes marvelous quality. They may pass quickly in seconds or prevail for hours or even days. Spanish poet Frederico Garcia Lorca (1992) describes music, dance, and spoken poetry as arts particularly mysterious and grand "because they are forms that perpetually live and die, their contours are raised upon an exact presence" (165). In one moment, intuition seems vibrant and breathtaking to behold—and then it disappears. To be sure, much of the attraction of intuition is its numinous and even whimsical character. On speaking of intuitive insights, Emily Dickinson instructs us, "Tell all the truth but tell it slant (Franklin 1999, 494), reflecting the surprise and sometimes enigmatic character of perceiving things directly.

Bastick (1982) conducted extensive research on the nature of intuition, asking participants to describe their experiences in depth. Bastick concluded that intuitive experiences generally have nine common characteristics:

1. Confidence in the intuitive process itself
2. a sense of certainty about the insights derived
3. sudden or immediate appearance in awareness

4. accompanying feelings of wonder or numinosity
5. gestalt and nonrational character of the insights derived
6. accompanying feelings of empathy
7. a sense of the ineffability of the intuitive experience
8. intrinsic relationship of intuition to creativity
9. a sense that insights derived may prove to be incorrect

In a phenomenological investigation of the intuition experience, Claire Petitmengin-Peugeot (1999) has described four "interior gestures" that were strikingly similar from interview to interview despite the differences in the context and content of intuitive insights: (a) the gesture of letting go, slowing down, and of interior self-collection; (b) the gesture of connection with a person, object, problem, or situation; (c) the gesture of listening with senses and awareness open and attentive; and (d) the intuition itself. Intuitions surged forth in many forms, as "an image, a kinesthetic feeling, a sound or word, even a taste or an odor, most of the time in several simultaneous or successive sensorial forms" (69). Often, intuitions are accompanied by feelings of certitude, coherence, meaningfulness, wholeness, harmony, and unpredictability. Petitimengin-Peugot concludes:

> This study confirms our hypothesis at the starting point: intuition does correspond to an experience, that is, a set of interior gestures which involve the entire being. Even if intuition keeps an unpredictable, capricious character, it is possible to encourage its appearing, and to accompany its unfolding, by a very meticulous interior preparation. This preparation does not consist in learning, in progressively accumulating knowledge. It consists in emptying out, in giving up our habits of representation, of categorization, and of abstraction. This casting off enables us to find spontaneity, the real immediacy of our relation to the world. (76)

In a current study of multicultural expressions of intuition, together with graduate students from around the world, I am collecting in-depth interviews with individuals who are known in their own communities as highly intuitive. The sample includes individuals in both industrialized First World and indigenous First Nation countries. Initial observations reveal that intuition seems a capacity of the human heart and psyche to experience the wholeness, goodness, or rightness of things in any situation—whether the situation is good or bad in a conventional sense. Intuitions seem to see beneath the surface of things and experience directly the force of love within every thing. While intuition has value in circumstances both practical (finding one's car keys) and sublime (understanding the nature of reality), intuition seemed aligned with the direct experience of creation itself that ever seeks wholeness and completion. Reflecting the perception of things as they are, intuitive insights often seem natural, not *extra*-ordinary.

Five Types of Intuition

Roberto Assagioli (1990), Arthur Deikman (1982), Peter Goldberg (1983), Carl Jung (1933), Arthur Koestler (1976), Frances Vaughan (1979), and others have explored the nature of intuition and described various expressive forms. The typology of different types of intuition presented below describes how I have come to understand the various ways in which intuitions express themselves in lived experience. Experiences typical to one type often blend with experiences particular to other types in everyday experience. Many of these intuitive types listed below are explored in depth as research skills in the Transpersonal Research Skills section of this book.

    1. *Unconscious, symbolic, and imaginal processes.* Unconscious, symbolic, and imaginal processes have been explored in depth in visionary experiences (Hildegard von Bingen 1954; Chicago 1985; Cirker 1982; Luna and Amaringo 1991), Jungian and archetypal psychology (Burneko 1997; Edinger 1972; Edinger 1975; Jung 1959; Jung 1973) and more recently in imaginal psychology (Romanyshyn 2002; Romanyshyn 2007). Individuals who experience such intuitive processes tend to have active symbolic lives, often accompanied by numinous dreams, active imagination, archetypal experiences, and the like. Helen Luke (1995) writes of the emergence of new cultural images in what she describes as the "perennial feminine" in all of us:

> Each of us has a well of images within, which are the saving reality and from which may be born the individual myth carrying the meaning of a life. That new images are now emerging in the tales and poetry of our time is now beyond doubt. But any truly valid "new myth" cannot be rationally invented. It must be born out of the crucible of our own struggles and suffering. . . . Therefore, every individual woman who is capable of reflection and discrimination, and

who lays claim to freedom, carries a responsibility to ask
herself, "What kind of free spirit is it that breaths through
me . . . ?" (9, 30)

In indigenous cultures, what Westerners in industrialized countries
describe as unconscious, symbolic, and imaginal processes tend to
be embedded in the sensorium of the Earth, experienced as patterns,
symbols, and visions that are felt and seen directly in nature and
especially in the wilderness. In some indigenous traditions, such
imaginal processes are commonplace (Luna and Amaringo 1991;
Sheridan and Pineault 1997). In industrialized countries, people
commonly experience imaginal processes as embedded within the
human collective psyche in the play of symbols and archetypes. In
indigenous cultures, people often experience these processes in the
activities or movements of the natural environment, in animals and
plants, and everyday events—with or without the aid of hallucino-
genic plants. Air, earth, fire, and water are interactive with humans.
Plants, animals, and humans converse through their common elements.
Human activity takes place within these forces, life taking place in a
web of interdependence. Even within industrialized countries, nature
mystic John Muir, poet Emily Dickinson, photographer Ansel Adams,
painter Georgia O'Keeffe, and nature artist Andy Goldsworthy have
established worldwide reputations by making explicit the timeless,
spiritual forces in the patterns of nature.

2. *Psychic or parapsychological experiences.* Despite their rather
common occurrence for some people, psychic and parapsychological
phenomena typically are unacknowledged in furthering the insights
of scientific research. Such direct and unmediated experiences include
telepathy, clairvoyance, and precognitive experiences that take place
at a distance (in space or time). These experiences are aspects of
what have been called "exceptional human experiences" (EHEs) by
researcher Rhea White (1997). Recently, William Braud (2002b, 2003a)
has detailed a full range of such experiences that have been the subject
of experimental research, along with the physical, physiological, and
psychological conditions that can influence their occurrence. Since
such experiences are typically encouraged by our heartfelt feelings
of connection with others and specific circumstances, the researcher's
personal connection to a topic and to the research participants is likely
to encourage such experiences:

The fact that we are able to access information at a distance, through space and through time, suggests that in

some subtle and profound manner, we are interconnected with . . . those remote places, times, and their content. These potentials and abilities already suggest that we are More than we might previously have thought. In addition to providing access to known realms of information and events in novel ways, perhaps these same additional modes of knowing can provide access to *different realms*, as well. Such possibilities have scarcely been explored by contemporary researchers. . . . This can be an exciting and fruitful field for future research. (Braud 2003b, 8)

3. *Sensory modes of intuition.* In addition to the five special senses of sight, hearing, smell, taste, and touch; kinesthesia (sense of movement in space); proprioception (sense of orientation in space); and a visceral sense arising from sense receptors in the organs and tissues of the body may serve as intuitive receptors, conveying subtle forms of information usually unavailable to the thinking mind. Typically, information from receptors in joints, ligaments, muscles, and viscera are subliminal to human awareness (Olsen 2002). Yet, these subliminal senses, the five sense perceptions, and their patterning sensorium can both signal danger, beauty, and novelty and serve intuition and imagination. Moreover, indigenous traditions commonly describe sense perceptions deeper than mental chatter, which provide direct perception into things as they are (Abram 1996; Luna and Amaringo 1991; Sheridan and Pineault 1997). In addition, Sri Aurobindo's companion, called the "Mother," provides extended examples of how the human body itself may become fully conscious (Satprem 1981).

Awareness of proprioceptive and kinesthetic signals can be enhanced through attention and specialized training, by techniques such as Focusing developed by psychologist Eugene Gendlin (1978, 1991, 1992, 1997), Authentic Movement developed by body practitioners Mary Whitehouse, Janet Adler, and Joan Chodorow (Adler 2002; Pallaro 1999), and many other practices. In my own work, I have sought to cultivate enhanced body awareness through embodied writing, a research technique that records the finely textured nuances of lived experience, awakening the senses in the writer and inviting a kindred resonance in readers (Anderson 2001; Anderson 2002a; Anderson 2002b).

4. *Empathic identification.* Through compassionate knowing or empathic identification, writers, actors, psychotherapists, and scientists inhabit the lived world of another person or object of study. In a seamless display of gesture and timbre of voice, a fine actor convinces an audience that Macbeth is present. Psychotherapists attend to the

life of their clients, seeing the world through their eyes, helping them see possibilities they cannot see for themselves. Similarly, biochemist Jonas Salk (1983) trained himself in what he called an "inverted perspective." He would imagine himself as a virus or cancer cell and ask how he would act if he were that virus or cancer cell. Similarly, geneticist Barbara McClintock spoke about looking through a microscope at corn fungus and found herself viewing the chromosomes as though she were "down there and these were my friends" (quoted in Keller 1983, 117). An extensive discussion of empathic identification as used by great artists and scientists can be found in *Sparks of Genius* (Root-Bernstein and Root-Bernstein 1999).

In my own experiences, empathic identification has a softness, as though what is observed yields itself to our knowing. There is no intrusion, no object, and no subject. Aspects of the experience studied that do not belong to the depth of the experience fall away. Those aspects that give amplitude and fullness to the experience studied begin to cohere in their complexity and interrelatedness. By loving, and through living thoroughly the experience studied, the researcher looks around from inside the experience and witnesses the essential qualities of the other come to life as the researcher's own experience. Gradually, the entire panorama of other comes more clearly into view.

Along with a full spectrum of sensory awareness, empathic identification also tends to evoke feelings of compassion. Allow me to give an example. During the initial stages of identifying a research topic, Cycle 1, I often lead an experiential exercise designed to facilitate the researcher's empathic identification with an object strongly associated with a research focus. (See Cycle 1, Experiential Exercise #1: Selecting a Text or Image That Claims Your Imagination.) During one such exercise, dissertation researcher Merry Coburn (2005), who was studying the psychological and transformative effects of long-distance hiking, chose to "identify" with her own well-used, hiking boots. In doing so, she discovered physical and emotional properties of long-distance hiking, which she had not been consciously aware before.

5. *Through our wounds.* Having conducted and supervised research for over thirty years, I am poignantly aware that a researcher's intuitive style tends to settle along the "fault lines" or wounds in the personality of the researcher in a manner akin to the concept of the wounded healer described by Catholic priest and contemplative Henri Nouwen (1990) and Roshi Joan Halifax (1983). For Nouwen, our human wounds are sites of both suffering and hospitality to the divine. From a spiritual perspective, these wounds are also openings to the world, enabling personal and research explorations along the

fault lines of the personality to invite change that transforms these wounds to sources of inspiration for others.

Lama Chögyam Trungpa (Gimian 1999) describes the open wound of compassion and understanding as follows:

> Compassion is based on some sense of the "soft spot" in us. It is as if we had a pimple on our body that was very sore—so sore that we do not want to rub it or scratch it. . . . That sore spot on our body is an analogy for compassion. Why? Because even in the midst of immense aggression, insensitivity in our life, or laziness, we always have a soft spot, some point we can cultivate—or at least not bruise. Every human has that kind of basic sore spot, including animals. . . . An open wound, which might be a more vivid analogy, is always there. That open wound is usually very inconvenient and problematic. We don't like it. . . . Sometimes people translate that sore spot or open wound as "religious conviction" or "mystical experience." But let us give that up. It has nothing to do with Buddhism, nothing to do with Christianity, and moreover, nothing to do with anything else at all. It is just an open wound, a very simple open wound. That is very nice—at least we are accessible somewhere. We are not completely covered with a suit of armor all the time. We have a sore spot somewhere, some open wound somewhere. (118–19)

So often the topics my doctoral students choose to explore in research are those aspects of their personalities that seek healing either within themselves or within the culture at large, or both. The topics seem to mark places in their own psyches or the culture at large that burn brightly. In turn, the findings of their studies tend to illuminate this realm of human struggle for us all. Often these researchers are distressed, embarrassed, and surprised to find that the very aspect of their personal history that they have been avoiding for years is a primary source of insight and delight. Some regress to childhood behaviors, bringing them slowly into the light of awareness is a manner not unlike the course of psychotherapy. Sometimes these processes and insights are uniquely personal and sometimes they shed light directly on the topic of inquiry, or both. As a research supervisor, I help researchers to distinguish the difference between personal and research insights and occasionally suggest that they seek professional assistance from a therapist or spiritual guide.

Robert Romanyshyn in a recent book entitled *"The Wounded Researcher"* (2007) strikes a similar theme. For Romanyshyn, the wounded researcher is claimed by the work of research, which in time invites the researcher to relinquish the claim she has upon it so that the work itself can speak. Since alchemical hermeneutics invites and engages the researcher's unconscious processes, the "wounded researcher . . . is meant to go down into the terrain beneath the bridge, into that abyss that the vulnerable observer attempts to bridge. The difference is that while the vulnerable observer includes only those subjective factors that she is conscious of, the wounded researcher delves into her unconscious complexes, which she then strives to make conscious" (108). From this perspective, re-search is soul work or spiritual work because in relinquishing one's claims upon the work and the narrow perspectives with which one began, re-search again takes on a lively character all its own. The past that claims the researcher speaks through us to the future in language transformed by the act of searching again. The researcher begins to ask, "Who's doing this work after all?" begging the question even of authorship. Romanyshyn describes this process eloquently:

> The work that the researcher is called to do makes sense of the researcher as much as he or she makes sense of it. Indeed, before we understand the work we do, it stands under us. Research as a vocation, then, puts one in service to those unfinished stories that weigh down upon us individually and collectively as the wait and weight of history. As a vocation, research is what the work indicates. It is re-search, a searching again of what has already made its claim upon us and is making its claim upon the future. (113)

Five Cycles of Hermeneutic Interpretation

Intuitive inquiry is a hermeneutic approach to research that employs five iterative cycles of interpretation. In Cycle 1, the researcher clarifies the research topic via a creative process described below and articulates a precise statement of the research topic. In Cycle 2, the intuitive researcher reflects upon her own understanding of the topic in light of specific texts found in extant literature about the topic *and* prepares a list of preliminary interpretative lenses based on these reflections. These Cycle 2 lenses describe the researcher's understanding of the topic *prior* to data collection. In Cycle 3, the researcher gathers original or archival data *and* presents descriptive findings that invite readers to come to their own conclusions about them before they read the researcher's interpretations in Cycles 4 and 5. In Cycle 4, the researcher presents a set of interpretative lenses *and* provides a lens-by-lens comparison of Cycle 2 and Cycle 4 lenses. These Cycle 4 lenses have been refined and transformed in light of researcher's personal engagement with the data gathered in Cycle 3. In Cycle 5, the researcher presents an integration of the Cycle 4 lenses with the empirical and theoretical literature of the topic *and* discusses the implications.

The five cycles of intuitive inquiry are illustrated in Figure 1.1. Based on my own experience in conducting and supervising intuitive

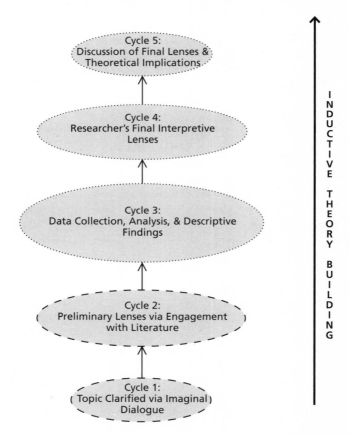

Figure 1.1. Intuitive inquiry: Five cycles of interpretation and forward-and-return arcs. Dashed oval outlines indicate the forward arc of Cycles 1 and 2; dotted oval outlines indicate the return arc of Cycles 3, 4, and 5.

inquiries, the size of the ovals for each cycle indicates the amount of time and effort each cycle typically requires relative to the others.

In hermeneutics, interpretation requires a back-and-forth, iterative process between parts and the whole of the text(s) known as the *hermeneutic circle*. While hermeneutic philosophers offer various definitions for the hermeneutic circle, the most basic involves an interpretative process between the parts and the whole (Ramberg and Gjesdal 2005). Intuitive inquiry invariability involves many hermeneutic circles as the researcher compares various texts and parts of texts to arrive at a final interpretation in Cycle 5.

One aspect of the hermeneutic circle central to hermeneutic analysis is known as the *forward-and-return arcs* (Packer and Addison 1989). The forward arc articulates the researcher's understanding of the topic prior to careful examination and reflection on the texts studied. In the return arc, this careful examination and reflection on the texts' examined questions and transforms the researcher's pre-understanding. In intuitive inquiry, Cycles 1 and 2 represent the forward arc in a process of identifying the topic and clarifying pre-understandings respectively. Cycles 3, 4, and 5 represent the return arc in a process of transforming pre-understanding via the understandings of others. The number of these interpretative cycles may increase if the researcher wishes to supplement the research endeavor with resonance panels, as described in Braud and Anderson (1998), and the validity chapter (Chapter 8) of this volume. Each iterative cycle changes, refines, and amplifies the researcher's interpretation of the experience studied. Both internal data known only to the researcher *and* externally verifiable data are documented in each cycle.

For readers familiar with my first presentation of intuitive inquiry as a hermeneutic process of inquiry (Anderson 2000), I have made three significant changes to the sequence of iterative cycles. First, I have discovered that many researchers need to prepare a summary of descriptive findings prior to the development of their final set of interpretative lenses in order to organize the data gathered, honor the individual voices of the research participants, and allow readers to explore the data for themselves prior to the researcher's interpretation presented in Cycle 4. Cycle 3 findings should be as descriptive and non-interpretative as is possible and reasonable. The second change moves the presentation of the researcher's final interpretative lenses from what was formerly called "Cycle 3" to Cycle 4, as a logical consequence of adding a more conventional presentation of data as Cycle 3. The third change adds an additional cycle, Cycle 5, a formal presentation that integrates the researcher's interpretative lenses in light of the theoretical and empirical literature, as suggested by my colleague William Braud some years ago. I have added this cycle to clarify and emphasize the importance of integrating research findings and prior research and theory, though doing so is conventional for the discussion section of any scientific report.

Given the circles of interpretation implicit in intuitive inquiry, it is not always clear where to present the five cycles of intuitive inquiry in research reports. Conventionally, in theses and dissertations, chapter titles are called the "Introduction," "Literature Review," "Methods," "Results," and "Discussion." Unfortunately, the five cycles do not fit naturally into these chapter names. Therefore, I recommend the intuitive inquirers use each of the five cycles as chapter titles in research reports. If conventional chapter titles are preferred and Cycle 1 can be relayed briefly, the clearest presentation is to report Cycle 1 in the Introduction and the interpretative lenses of Cycle 2 at the end of a traditional Literature Review. If the presentation of Cycle 1 is lengthy, report Cycle 1 at the start of the Methods or at the start of the Results. Cycle 3's descriptive findings are always reported as part of the Results. Cycle 4 lenses and Cycle 5 are always reported in the discussion, honoring the clearly interpretative nature of Cycles 4 and 5. When comparing Cycle 2 and 4 lenses, repeat the Cycle 2 lenses briefly or direct the reader to the location of the Cycle 2 lenses—whichever is easier for the reader. The discussion of the changes between Cycle 2 and Cycle 4 lenses is ordinarily detailed and lengthy. Label each of the five cycles in the table of contents, so they can be clearly identified by readers unfamiliar with the procedural requirements of intuitive inquiry. Dissertation and thesis research proposals might simply include a presentation of Cycle 1 only along with a clear statement of the research topic in the Introduction or Methods.

Several years ago, I guest edited an issue of *The Humanistic Psychologist* on intuitive inquiry (Anderson 2004a). The issue reviews and updates intuitive inquiry (Anderson 2004b) as a hermeneutic approach applicable to research the human sciences and gives case examples of intuitive inquiries, based on dissertation research by Jay Dufrechou (2004), Vipassana Esbjörn-Hargens (2004), Sharon Hoffman (2004), and Cortney Phelon (2004). These case examples also illustrate a streamlined report-writing style for intuitive inquiries appropriate for journal articles.

Cycle 1: Clarifying the Research Topic

In established research practice, a researcher typically chooses a research topic based on current research in an area of scholarly interest. In other words, the researcher reviews the extant empirical and theoretical literature in the specialized area and attempts to identify a relevant next study. In contrast, in the three transpersonal methods presented in this book, a researcher identifies a topic based on his unique interests and passions. In intuitive inquiry, in order to clarify and refine the identification of a topic of study, the intuitive inquirer selects a text or image that repeatedly attracts or claims his attention and relates in a general—and sometimes initially ambiguous way—to his research interests. A thorough examination of the extant literature follows but only after the researcher's topic or question has been precisely stated at the end of Cycle 1.

When teaching intuitive inquiry, I begin the first class by leading an experiential exercise, entitled "Selecting a Text or Image That Claims Your Imagination," that helps doctoral students to find a text or image that claims their attention around their general research interests. Students are often surprised by what appears in their imagination during these experiential exercises. For example, in a study of true joy among Christian mystics, Susan Carlock (2003) was surprised to see a clear, visual image of the Michelangelo's *Pieta* during this experiential exercise. Only later in her study did she discover that the joyful Christian mystics in her study identified the element of suffering as essential to true joy because joy was understood in contrast to the experience of human suffering. Texts and images for Cycle 1 have included photographs, paintings, mandalas, collages, sketches, symbols, sculptures, song lyrics, movies, poems, sacred texts or scripture, interview transcripts, recorded dreams, and accounts of a meaningful transformative experience.

Basic Instructions for All Experiential Exercises

Preparation

Step 1. Chose a time and place wherein you will be free from external distractions.

Step 2. Gather or purchase a notebook or journal to record your thoughts and art supplies to express images and symbols that occur spontaneously during the exercises. Art supplies might include white butcher paper, colored papers, sketch pad, glue stick, good scissors, water-based pastels, watercolor paint set, magic markers, crayons, copies of favorite photographs, and old magazines with pictures and colors that can be used for collages.

Step 3. Prepare a space for yourself that is clean and orderly for quiet reflection.

Step 4. Read through each experiential exercise before beginning. Alternatively, you might make an audio tape recording of these instructions to yourself, in your own voice, leaving adequate pauses and times for the experiences to occur. Then play the created instruction tape, as you follow the instructions, with your eyes closed.

Concentration

Step 1. Sit in a comfortable position with your back straight. Let your eyes close, and allow your body to become relaxed and quiet. Take a few deep breaths and notice the exhalations and inhalations. Continue watching your breathing for a while, as you allow you body to relax more and more deeply. Don't try to change or control your breathing; just direct your attention to it, notice it. Allow yourself to become very comfortable, very much at peace. Let all of your muscles relax. Let your mind become peaceful, quiet, and tranquil.

Step 2. With each exhalation, imagine that you are letting go of tensions, distractions, doubts, and self-judgment. With each inhalation, imagine that you are breathing in increased well-being, confidence, ability to accomplish the task at hand, ability to imagine and visualize desired and useful outcomes.

Step 3. Consider smiling ever so slightly—not a great big toothy grin but a half smile—as not to take yourself too seriously. After all, quieting down, relaxation, and mindfulness are not accomplishments but for delight!

Step 4. Once your body relaxes and mental chatter and emotions quiet down, allow your awareness to expand naturally. Sometimes you may feel as though opening to a vast internal space. Sometimes you will feel as though aligned with all the elements of space converging with all that lives and all of nature. Sometimes you may simply feel quiet or silent within. Allow yourself some time to rest in your expanded awareness.

Cycle 1, Experiential Exercise #1:
Selecting a Text That Claims Your Imagination

Step 1. Complete the Basic Instructions for All Experiential Exercises, described above.

Step 2. When your awareness feels relaxed and alert, scan your awareness for a research topic that you find most inspiring now. Perhaps your research topic has changed in the last few days or weeks, and you have not noticed.

Step 3. Then, scan your life for an experience that exemplifies that research topic. With your imagination, recall the experience with as much sensorial, cognitive, and emotional detail as possible. Remember what you were seeing, smelling, tasting, hearing, and sensing through touch and pressure during that experience.

Step 4. Once you have your research topic clearly in mind and have relived the experience through recall, invite your imagination to spontaneously evoke a "text" in the form of an art object, sculpture, painting, photo, poem, reading from scripture or prose, movie, statistical equation, or graph—anything at all—that represents your topic to you in some way. Do not censor what your imagination evokes. The text may not make rational sense. If you get more than one object, image, or graph, choose the one that seems most evocative of your topic at this time. If you have the object of art or text in your home, get it and place it in front of you. Spend some time exploring the impressions received.

Step 5. Begin an imaginary dialogue with the object of art or text, allowing it to inform you about your topic. Invite a part of your awareness to witness the dialogue so you will remember it later.

Step 6. Using your art supplies, continue your dialogue with your art object or text by drawing, painting, or expressing yourself in words, song, or movement. Spend about fifteen minutes in this imaginary dialogue.

Step 7. Once you have completed the dialogue return to ordinary awareness slowly and write down thoughts, insights, and impressions in your journal or portfolio. If you danced or sang during this exercise, try to capture the experience in words or images as best you can.

Step 8. Continue your imaginal dialogue with the text frequently for several weeks, recording your impressions in a notebook, sketchbook, computer file, etc., that is dedicated to your ongoing imaginal dialogue.

In a study by Katherine Unthank (2007) on the deep structure of trauma survival, Unthank chanced upon a Rembrandt sketch entitled *"Jesus Saves Peter from Drowning"* (1632) as her Cycle 1 image. Unthank describes her experience of viewing the sketch and how she came to understand shame specific to profound trauma among survivors that shaped her research question:

> I entered the horrified silence of a visual experience . . . that propelled me into the overwhelming, wordless experience of drowning. . . . I discovered that my focus was on the space between Peter's clutched hands and Jesus' outstretched hand. I saw the contrast between Peter's desperate powerlessness and the relaxed elegant presence of Jesus in this moment of choice. . . . I looked at [the sketch] every day for weeks . . . asking myself what secret it stubbornly held inside. . . . Day after day with the image of Peter drowning, with the image of Jesus so close and yet so far from him trapped there in indecision, my unconscious need to have . . . the people, who say "I love you," reject me the way shame causes me to reject myself slowly came to light. (83–85)

Similarly, Diane Rickards (2006) discovered her topic of the feminine cultural shadow when a friend lent her a recently published book by Marcus Binney (2002) about British espionage agents in World War II. Published in the United Kingdom, the book was based on recently declassified information. The book lay idle on a table in her bedroom. After weeks in search of a satisfying dissertation topic, she gave up trying. Soon after, she picked up and opened the book. Her eyes fell on these words, "Agents were flown into France during moon periods—one week on either side of the full moon, when there was sufficient light for night flying" (22). Rickards had found her topic:

> I was compelled and . . . turned toward the subject that had
> found me, had been waiting patiently for me. . . . My chest
> felt gripped. I held my breath. My imagination began to
> sweep about—the moon . . . dark and white, shadow and
> light, waving and waxing, the feminine, cycles, creation,
> *herstory.* (45)

Theoretically, a statistical analysis, graph, or figure based on statistical analysis might be suitable as a text for Cycle 1, but to date no
intuitive inquirer has focused on such a text. Possible texts for Cycle
1 are listed in Table 1.1. At John Creswell's suggestion (pers. comm.),
I have added the option of a quantitative text for Cycle 1 in order to
invite quantitative and mixed-methods applications of intuitive inquiry.
In my own research as an experimental social psychologist, I often
intuited ideas and conceptual relationships after staring at graphs and
computer printouts. I would tape printouts up on the wall of my office.
Usually while waiting around for someone to show up, eureka!, I saw
the latent pattern and knew the answer. In agreement with Creswell's
suggestion, statistical texts might suffice as Cycle 1 texts.

Once the text (broadly defined) is identified, the intuitive
researcher enters Cycle 1 interpretation by engaging with the art object
or text daily and recording insights. Researchers should spend at least
twenty minutes a day (or approximately forty minutes every other

Table 1.1. Types of Possible Texts in Cycle 1 or Cycle 2

- statistical analyses, graphs, and figures from quantitative studies
- mathematical equations and formulas
- descriptive accounts from qualitative studies
- summaries of research findings
- theoretical or philosophic writings
- historical accounts or archival data
- literary accounts
- sacred texts, scripture, and mystical accounts
- paintings, sculpture, photos, images, drawings, mandalas, symbols, etc.
- combinations of the above

day) reading, listening to, or viewing the identified text. Thoughts, ideas, daydreams, conversations, impressions, visions, and intuitions occurring during sessions and at other times, are recorded in a non-invasive manner so as not to disrupt the stream of consciousness that often accompanies intuition. Notebooks, hand-held voice recorders, and art supplies should be readily available to support recording of thoughts, memories, images, and impressions. This process of engagement with the art object or text should be continued until the creative tension between the intuitive inquirer and the text or image feels resolved and complete.

By repeatedly engaging with a potential text in this dialectic process, impressions and insights converge into a focused research topic. As described in Table 1.2, a suitable topic for intuitive inquiry is compelling, manageable, clear, focused, concrete, researchable, and promising. Note that these criteria for a suitable research topic apply to most studies regardless of method.

To give further clarity to the statement of a research topic, I recommend identifying the intended audience (or audiences) at the start of the research project; doing this gives an overall direction and intention to the research. As a result, the stated topic is often more precise, and the research design follows closely upon the intention of the project. Necessary decisions and changes made during the course of any research project are easier to make because the long-term direction of the research endeavor is clear.

In intuitive inquiry, identifying the intended audience also helps to give the writing of research reports a lively quality. I learned the importance of understanding one's audience some years ago when I was learning to preach in my first parish job as an Episcopal priest. The quality of my sermons improved appreciably when I stopped worrying about my performance and conversed with people I loved. I was no longer nervous. My focus was on them, not me. My sole purpose was to reflect on the scripture of the day in whatever way it might be useful to my listening congregation. Because I knew the joys and sufferings in their lives, I spoke to their joy and challenges as I preached in scriptural and pastoral terms. Some years later, I learned that celebrated writers of poetry and fiction often use a similar technique. When writing, they address their writing to a real or imaginary reader who becomes their conversational focus in writing. They write to a specific person, real or imaginary, and their writing takes on the lively character of conversation.

The experiential exercise entitled "Identifying Your Intended Audience" can be used to provide the intuitive inquirer with an

Table 1.2. Does Your Topic Meet the Criteria for a
Suitable Research Topic?

Criterion	Suitability Consideration
Compelling	For a research topic to sustain the researcher's interest and energy, it should inspire the motivations and intellectual passions of the researcher.
Manageable	If the researcher is a thesis or dissertation student, once the research proposal is complete, the topic should be potentially doable in one year for fulltime graduate students, including time for rest and relaxation. Of course, as most researchers know only too well, personal life events and research logistics can complicate and delay any research study.
Clear	Good research topics can be expressed easily in one sentence. The more a researcher understands a research topic the simpler the basic statement of intent becomes.
Focused	A simple and focused topic with significant implications for human experience is preferable to a diffuse, ambiguously defined topic.
Concrete	The research topic should be directly related to specific behaviors, experiences, or phenomena.
Researchable	Some topics are too grand or do not (yet) lend themselves to scientific inquiry.
Promising	A topic is promising when it signifies an experience of something that is still unknown or appears to beg understanding. Since the topics pursued in intuitive inquiry tend to be at the growing tip of cultural understanding, it is often the case that only the intuitive inquirer herself can evaluate the potential importance of a given topic at the start of the inquiry.

imaginary audience for creative dialogue. Doing this exercise early in a research project, and from time to time as the research unfolds, helps to give research a specific intention and the final reports a lively literary character.

Cycle 1, Experiential Exercise #2: Identifying Your Intended Audience

Step 1. Complete the Basic Instructions for All Experiential Exercises (described earlier in this chapter).

Step 2. When your awareness feels relaxed and alert, let your research topic surface in awareness. Let your sense of the topic come alive by thinking of a concrete personal example of the experience you wish to study. As in the first experiential exercise in this chapter, recreate that experience in your imagination using all your senses,.

Step 3. Once the experience seems vivid and alive, imagine the intended (or anticipated) audience for the fruits of your dissertation or research project. Whom do you wish to serve in the study of this research topic at the conclusion of your study? Are you hoping you will gain information or insights that may benefit specific individuals? Or groups? Try to be concrete by imagining precisely what these individuals or groups look like. As best you can, focus on one individual and imagine what he looks like. Imagine his facial features, eye color, the quality of his voice, etc.

Step 4. Once you have a clear sense of a person or group as your intended audience, begin an imaginary dialogue with him, her, or them. Notice what he, she, or they have to say to you. If the intended audience includes animals or aspects of nature, adapt your imaginal dialogue accordingly.

Step 5. Return to ordinary awareness in your own timing. Try doing this experiential exercise at least twice during the week. Record your insights and reactions in a journal or portfolio.

Step 6. By doing this exercise often throughout the course of your research project, you may discover several audiences claiming your attention or that your audience changes or shifts over time.

Cycle 2: Developing the Preliminary Interpretive Lenses

The goal of Cycle 2 of intuitive inquiry is the articulation in words of the researcher's personal values, assumptions, and understanding of the research topic as preliminary interpretive lenses *prior* to data gathering. By comparing Cycle 2 and Cycle 4 lenses, the reader of the final research report can evaluate the course of change and transformation that has taken place in the researcher's understanding of the topic over the course of the study.

In order to articulate these lenses, the researcher again engages the research topic via imaginal dialogues with another set of text(s), uniquely selected to help the researcher discern the values, assumptions, and understanding she brings to the topic at the start of the study. Texts are chosen from the extant research and literature directly related to the topic of study. This imaginal dialogue of Cycle 2 is similar to the imaginal dialogue in Cycle 1. However, in Cycle 2, the researcher's reflections and notes become more conceptual and intellectual in relationship to the topic over time. Cycle 2, Experiential Exercise, Selecting Theoretical, Empirical, Literary, or Historical Texts, found below supports the choice of texts for the Cycle 2's imaginal dialogues.

Cycle 2, Experiential Exercise: Selecting Theoretical, Empirical, Literary, or Historical Texts to Clarify your Pre-understanding of the Topic

Note: Before doing this experiential exercise, acquaint yourself with the empirical, theoretical, historical, and literary texts directly relevant to your topic.

Step 1. Complete the Basic Instructions for All Experiential Exercises.

Step 2. When you feel relaxed and alert, let your research topic surface into awareness. Allow your sense of the topic to come alive by thinking of a concrete personal example of the experience you wish to study. Recreate that experience in your imagination using all your senses, as in the first experiential exercise in this chapter.

Step 3. Once the experience seems vivid and alive, mentally review the many texts that are relevant to your research topic. Imagine that the possible choices are arrayed visually before you.

Step 4. Once you can visualize the possible choices, invite the texts to signal their importance to your study in some obvious way. Some texts might light up in your imagination or become animate by moving around and sorting themselves visually. Some texts might become larger in your imagination. Or, nothing may happen. If so, try this experiential exercise another time.

Step 5. Once the texts are prioritized in your imagination, notice their relative importance or sequence carefully so you will remember this later.

Step 6. Return to ordinary awareness slowly and write down the information you discovered through this experiential exercise. If you danced or sang during this exercise, try to capture the experience in words or images as best you can.

Step 7. Use the texts from this experiential exercise for the imaginal dialogues of Cycle 2 to help you explore your current understanding of your topic prior to data collection and generate preliminary interpretative lenses.

Structurally, Cycle 2 involves a three-part process. First, the intuitive inquirer familiarizes herself with the empirical findings—theoretical, empirical, historical, and literary texts relevant to her topic—and chooses a unique set of texts that are directly related to the topic from among these varied texts. Empirical literature might include both quantitative and qualitative studies. Second, the researcher identifies from among the literature and research on the topic, a unique set of texts for her Cycle 2 imaginal dialogue. Third, based on ongoing imaginal dialogue with these newly selected texts, the researcher prepares a list of preliminary interpretative lenses that express her understanding of the topic prior to data collection.

Usually, selecting appropriate texts for the imaginal dialogue of Cycle 2 takes place at the same time as the researcher writes a review of the theoretical and research literature on the topic, as is conventional in research reports. As in Cycle 1, Cycle 2 texts are broadly defined.

These texts may include findings from quantitative and qualitative studies, theoretical writings, and historical, archival, literary, art, symbols, music, etc. For example, in Susan Carlock's (2003) study of true joy among Christian mystics, Carlock reflected on the writings and lives of four Christian mystics. She chose to engage specific texts on joy written by Christian mystics who met three criteria: (a) The mystics were described by contemporaries as overflowing with joy, (b) they wrote about their experiences of joy, and (c) their writings were available in English. The four mystics chosen for Cycle 2 were Francis of Assisi, Clare of Assisi, Mechthild of Magdeburg, and Brother Lawrence. While Carlock's literature review included many other sources, both empirical and literary, the texts chosen for Cycle 2 were uniquely compelling and informative regarding the nature of true joy among Christian mystics. In a study of healing presence in a psychotherapist, for Cycle 2, Cortney Phelon (2001, 2004) chose a variety of theoretical and empirical texts describing presence. These texts included philosophical writings by European phenomenologists, spiritual discourses by Zen Buddhist teachers, clinical writings by existential and transpersonal psychotherapists, and research findings from the fields of nursing and pastoral care that described dimensions of presence in the care of patients and in the context of pastoral counseling. Among this wide range of sources, Phelon chose texts that offered (a) a novel perspective on healing presence, (b) variety in content, and (c) a vividly communicated presence. In additional to scholarly texts, in a study of the relationship between nondualism and manifest reality, Carol Schopfer (2010) used three collages that she had created in response to specific questions regarding her topic. By engaging in imaginal dialogue with the scholarly texts and the three collages, Schopfer generated four sets of preliminary lenses that expressed both conscious and unconscious processes related to her understanding of the topic prior to data collection.

After choosing the texts for Cycle 2, the researcher engages in imaginal dialogue with selected texts and records insights in a journal or portfolio as he did in Cycle 1. This process of engagement with the texts continues for several weeks until the researcher feels ready to generate an initial list of preliminary lenses.

After what can feel like a long period of imaginal dialogue with the selected texts for Cycle 2, the identification of preliminary interpretative lenses is usually quick and easy, feeling more like creative imagination or brainstorming than a formal process. At a certain point, the researcher knows that she has integrated the Cycle 2 texts sufficiently and sits down with pen and paper or with fingers at the keyboard and roughs them out. Often the generation of Cycle 2 lenses occurs in an hour or two of intense concentration. However, the style in which these lenses are generated seems to vary a great deal. I tend to sketch them out as key words and word pictures on paper until the list feels complete. Later, I organize and phrase the lenses so they communicate well to others. I have students who see interpretive lenses as scenes, images, or symbols while musing during the day, in dreams, or during focused reflection on the topic. Others may hear key words or thoughts that cannot be easily ignored. Sometimes, the preliminary list of lenses includes several dozen statements, seemingly a list of everything the researcher feels and thinks about the topic in no particular order. After generating such a list, the researcher prioritizes the list and identifies patterns or clusters of ideas. Through a process of combining, reorganizing, and identifying emerging patterns, the list of preliminary lenses typically shortens to less than a dozen. Typically, ten to twelve preliminary lenses are sufficient to capture the nuance and range of most research topics.

Three examples of Cycle 2 lenses from intuitive inquiries illustrate what is intended by Cycle 2 lenses:

1. Kelly Sue Lynch (2002) studied Emily Dickinson's creative process. After a close reading of Dickinson's life, poems, and letters, she generated four hermeneutic lenses as a way of understanding Dickinson's life and texts. The four lenses were (a) recognition through one's body, (b) compassionate listening, (c) a relational reading, and (d) the hermeneutics of creative expression.

2. Susan Carlock (2003) studied true joy among historical Christian mystics. She initially brainstormed thirty-three lenses. After a period of resting and withdrawal from focused attention on the writings, Carlock distilled a list of thirty-three lenses down to six final Cycle 2 lenses: (a) inward providence in the giving up of pleasures of the world, (b) imitation of the life and character of Christ, (c) willing surrender of the self to God, (d) the love of God for sake of God alone, (e) desire for the direct presence of God, and (f) openness to God's love even amid God's apparent absence.

3. Catherine Manos (2007) studied the creative expression of women artists working in nature, interviewing contem-

porary women artists whose artistic expression cultivates an ongoing connection with the natural environment. Her texts for developing Cycle 2 lenses were the art and writings of two "nature artists, namely Hildegard of Bingen and Georgia O'Keeffe. After visiting museum collections of their work and reviewing their art weekly for several months, Manos identified fifteen preliminary lenses. Among these lenses were the following: (a) nature artists are aware of the flows and nuances in nature that often go unnoticed, (b) sensitivity to the natural world increases with time spent in nature while working artistically, (c) nature artists are aware of simulacra, aspects of nature that appear to have animal or human characteristics, and (d) the artists' spiritual lives and creativity are closely related and enhance one another.

Although imaginal dialogue with another set of texts, as described above, is currently the most developed procedure for Cycle 2, future intuitive inquirers might consider other more socially engaged activities for this dialectic process. For example, clarifying the researcher's values and assumptions and understanding about the topic might be accomplished through engagement in psychodrama or social action that is directly related to the topic and that is videotaped, and analyzed later. Another option might be a series of focused interviews of the researcher by others who are also knowledgeable about the topic. For example, one intuitive inquirer, Sharon Hoffman (2003, 2004), felt stymied in articulating lenses despite her best efforts dialoguing with her Cycle 2 texts. Finally, she asked a friend who was knowledgeable about her topic to interview her. She recorded the interview and easily brainstormed her lenses thereafter. Many excellent interview procedures are available in the field of qualitative research methods. In particular, procedures from Focus Group research (Fern 2001; Morgan 1988; Morgan 1993; Stewart and Shamdasani 1990) or Action Inquiry (Fisher, Rooke, and Torbert 2000; Reason 1988; Reason 1994) could easily be adapted for this purpose. Dialogal Approach (Halling, Rowe, and Laufer 2005) and Insight Dialogic Inquiry (O'Fallon and Kramer 1998) are two research approaches that capitalize on dialogue as a source of insight about a topic. Whatever the dialectic activities chosen for Cycle 2, they should be recorded and used as sources of reflection for the preparation of interpretive lenses of Cycle 2.

In intuitive inquiry, lenses are *both* a way of viewing a topic and what is seen. We all wear lenses all the time. Typically, often for the sake of healthy functioning, we ignore or are unaware of the many ways our personal histories, biology, and culture shape how we perceive and understand our life worlds. In intuitive inquiry, the researcher attempts to discern and acknowledge these lenses as best he can by becoming aware of them in relationship to the research topic. Of course, many of our values and assumptions are so deeply embedded in our biology, personalities, and cultures that identifying and articulating them may be difficult. Note that in intuitive inquiry, the articulation of lenses is not intended to identify and separate pre-understandings from influencing the research process. Rather, the method is boldly hermeneutic in nature. Lenses are articulated in order to track and record how they change and transform in the course of the study. In articulating Cycle 2 lenses, the intuitive researcher places these lenses in full scrutiny and invites their transformation, revision, removal, amplification, and refinement as the cycles of interpretation move forward. Again and again, when colleagues contact me about intuitive inquiry (presumably because they like it), they say something like "Intuitive inquiry is so honest!" with a tone of incredulity.

Based on my experience in working with microscopes in a human cytology lab during my graduate school training in my late twenties, I have chosen the words *lens* and *lenses* to describe this process. I was astonished by the levels of organization revealed by different levels of magnification on a single slide preparation. By flipping the lenses on my high-power microscope, "worlds" were revealed at different levels of magnification. My conventional level of understanding was shattered because I became increasingly aware that what I see and apprehend is uniquely shaped by who I am biologically, technologically, intellectually, historically, and culturally. This understanding humbles and haunts still. These experiences in microscopy led me to use optical words to describe the perceptual assumptions essential to human understanding and interpretation. However, the use of optical terms reflects my personal history and does not imply a preference for visual perception within intuitive inquiry itself.

The articulation of Cycle 2 interpretive lenses completes the forward arc of the hermeneutic circle during which the intuitive inquirer seeks to identify the topic clearly and express his pre-understanding of the topic. With data collection in Cycle 3, the return arc of the hermeneutic circle begins and the researcher's focus shifts to understanding the topic in light of the experiences of others. The forward arc (Cycle 1 and 2) focuses inwardly and the return arc (Cycles 3 and 4) focuses on the experiences reported by others, often research participants. Cycle 5 completes the hermeneutic circle by discussing the relevance of the final Cycle 4 lenses on extant research and theory on the topic.

After concentration on inner processes, the interpretive shift from the forward arc to the return arc usually feels refreshing and more active and socially engaged. It is extremely important to articulate Cycle 2 lenses *before* collecting data. Once data collection begins, there is no turning back to reclaim the researcher's pre-understanding of the topic because engagement in data collection propels the intuitive inquirer into a different mode of engagement and perception. The primary mode of activity in the forward arc of Cycles 1 and 2 is inward and reflective. In contrast, the primary mode of activity in the return arc of Cycles 3 and 4 is outwardly engaged in order to reimagine and reinterpret one's own understanding in light of the experiences of others. The affective and intellectual sensibilities between the forward and return arcs of intuitive inquiry are illustrated in Table 1.3.

Cycle 3: Collecting Data and Preparing Summary Data Reports

In Cycle 3, the researcher (a) identifies the best source(s) of data for the research topic, (b) develops criteria for the selection of data from among these sources, (c) collects the data, and (d) presents a summary report of data in as descriptive manner as possible. While researchers may be tempted to choose data that are conveniently available, rarely does any study profit from this approach—far less for the in-depth, intuitive processes invited by intuitive inquiry. Therefore, choose the data sources that best suit the researcher's unique and focused interests in the topic of study. Follow your enthusiasm and intuition.

Table 1.3. Perceptual Style Differences between Intuitive Inquiry's Forward and Return Arcs

Forward Arc (Cycles 1 and 2)	Return Arc (Cycles 2, 3, and 4)
Reflective	Engaged With Others
Introverted	Extraverted
Self-critical and Discerning	Discerning of Others
Clarification of Self	Synthesis of Others
Imaginal Dialogue	Imagining the Possible

Notice data sources that attract your attention again and again. Choose inviting, challenging, or even provocative data sources even if you do not always know why that data source attracts. Empirical research on intuition (Bastick 1982; Petitmengin-Peugeot 1999) has consistently shown that intuitive processes tend to convey an impression of certainty even when the intuitive insight proves later to be incorrect. Therefore, intuitive inquirers might consider collecting among data sources that intentionally challenge their Cycle 2 interpretative lenses.

Qualitative, quantitative, or a mix of qualitative and quantitative data can be used in a study using intuitive inquiry. As both a quantitative and qualitative researcher, I am aware that the distinction between quantitative and qualitative data is somewhat arbitrary and often exaggerated. Qualitative data is usually sorted and analyzed by the number of meaning units, types of narrative accounts, and the like. Quantitative data, especially when subjected to multivariate or factor analysis, requires many qualitative or subjective judgments on the part of the researcher. In other words, qualitative researchers sort and number, and quantitative researchers qualify what they count. Interpreting quantitative and qualitative data involves inference and intuition. The experiential exercise entitled "Identifying the Best Data Source(s) for Your Study" can be used to help you select the empirical data most suitable and relevant to your study.

Cycle 3, Experiential Exercise: Identifying the Best Data Source(s) for Your Study

Note: In intuitive inquiry, data may be collected by the researcher specifically for the study, usually known as original data, or collected by others for non-research purposes, usually known as historical or archival data. Data may be qualitative or quantitative or a mix of both. Before doing this experiential exercise, explore your access to and the availability of research participants who are uniquely informed about your topic, usually because they identify themselves as having experienced the phenomenon you wish to study. Also, explore the availability of archival or historical data relevant to your study, such as song lyrics, art, public and civic records, newspaper and broadcasting interviews, Internet accounts, memories and journal entries, etc. that are directly related to your topic.

Step 1. Complete the Basic Instructions for All Experiential Exercises.

Step 2. When you feel relaxed and alert, let your research topic surface into awareness. Allow your sense of the topic to come alive by thinking of a concrete personal example of the experience you wish to study. Recreate that experience in your imagination using all your senses, as in the first experiential exercise in this chapter.

Step 3. Once the experience seems vivid and alive, mentally review the availability of research participants who are informed about your topic and archival and historical data to which you have or can gain access. Consider many data sources, without assuming that one is more important than another. Be open to surprise about what data sources and combination of data sources might best inform you now about your topic.

Step 4. Once you can visualize the possible choices, invite the various sources of data to signal their importance to your study in some obvious way. Some data sources might "light up" in your imagination or become animate by moving around and sorting themselves visually. Some might become "larger" in your imagination, prioritizing themselves in terms of size or color. Some might "line up" together, signally that they are most important sources of data. Or, nothing may happen. If so, try this experiential exercise again another time.

Step 5. Once the potential data sources are prioritized in your imagination, notice their relative importance or combinations carefully so you will remember this later.

Step 6. Return to ordinary awareness slowly and write down the information you intuited through this experiential exercise. If you danced or sang, try to capture the experience in words or images as best you can.

Step 7. After capturing your experience in words, images, or sketches, reflect on the possibilities they present for data collection in Cycle 3.

To date, most researchers using intuitive inquiry have collected original empirical data in the form of interviews or stories from research participants who meet specific criteria as informants relevant to the topic of study (Coleman 2000; Dufrechou 2002; Dufrechou 2004; Esbjörn-Hargens 2004; Manos 2007; Phelon 2004; Rickards 2006, Shepperd 2006; and Unthank 2007). However, in a study of true joy among Christian mystics, Carlock (2003) chose an additional set of writings from historical mystics related for Cycle 3, rather than collect data from contemporary Christian mystics, because of the spiritual depth of the historical mystical sources. In addition to interviews, Rickards (2006) made use of extensive historical narratives about and journal accounts by former espionage agents, and Unthank (2007) recorded observations of body language while interviewing her trauma survivors to supplement her qualitative data. Several researchers have used embodied writing (Anderson 2001; Anderson 2002a; Anderson 2002b) collected from participants (Dufrechou 2004; Shepperd 2006; Netzer 2008) or provided examples of participants' artistic expression (Hill 2005; Hoffman 2003; Hoffman 2004; Manos 2007; Rickards 2006). I hope that future intuitive inquirers will incorporate both qualitative and quantitative sources into the five cycles in order to refine, expand, and clarify the method.

For descriptive analysis and presentation of data in Cycle 3 be creative. Possibilities for descriptive modes of analysis and presentation of findings are listed in Table 1.4. Until now, these summary data reports have included:

> edited interview transcripts (Esbjörn 2003; Esbjörn-Hargens 2004; Esbjörn-Hargens and Anderson 2005)
> portraits of participants (Coleman 2000; Rickards 2006)
> using the procedures developed within heuristic research by Moustakas (1990)
> historical portraits (Carlock 2003)
> portraits accompanied by illustrative examples of participants' art (Manos 2007)
> aspects of discourse analysis developed by Potter and Wetherell (1995)
> plus interviewee stories (Unthank 2007)
> portraits plus common themes in interviews (Brandt 2007)
> common themes in interviews plus artistic expression (Perry 2009),
> a series of participants' embodied writings (Dufrechou 2004; Shepperd 2006)
> participants' stories accompanied by excerpts of embodied writing by participants (Netzer 2008)
> and common themes plus integral mandala artwork (Cervelli, 2010)

Table 1.4. Descriptive Modes of Analysis and Presentation of Data in Cycle 3

- written depictions and portraits of participants (Moustakas,1990)
- participant stories or narrative accounts
- Thematic Content Analyses (TCA) of texts or interviews (available at www.rosemarieanderson.com)
- embodied writing excerpts oganized by themes
- summary and inferential statistics without interpretation
- textual or statistical summaries presented systematically
- graphic or artistic presentation of participant stories, portraits, etc.
- participants' creative expression presented systematically with text or narration
- summaries (as above) accompanied by quotes, poetry, embodied writings, art, photography
- combinations of the above

Prepare these summary accounts of the data in as descriptive a manner as possible, allowing that some measure of interpretation is implicit in any analytic procedure. When I am teaching intuitive inquiry, a metaphor that seems to communicate the descriptive presentation of findings in Cycle 3 is that of "low-hovering" over the data and relaying what you see from that vantage point. If quantitative data are presented, prepare a presentation of means, modes, standard deviations, ranges, and other basic statistics for Cycle 3 and present inferential statistical analyses in Cycle 4. For the descriptive analysis and presentation of qualitative data in Cycle 3, summarize and present the data gathered but refrain from interpretation as much as possible, remembering that the purpose of Cycle 3 is to invite readers to come their own conclusions about the data prior to reading the researcher's interpretations presented in Cycle 4.

In order to encourage variety in data collection and descriptive presentations of data in Cycle 3, five examples from intuitive inquiries follow:

1. Jay Dufrechou (2002, 2004) gathered stories from forty research participants, primarily through back-and-forth email communication with participants in a study on grief, weeping, and other deep emotions in response to nature.

The majority of his participants were recruited through email exchanges with members of the Institute of Noetic Sciences (IONS). Dufrechou mentored participants to write in the style of embodied writing (see Chapter 7), a style intended to portray life experiences in a lived, embodied way full of sensory, visceral, and kinesthetic detail (Anderson 2001; Anderson 2002a; Anderson 2002b). In Cycle 3, he presented a thematic content analysis of the stories as well as a descriptive summary of the data with extended quotes from the participants' embodied writings, in order to invite readers to respond and resonate to the writing before reading his interpretations presented in Cycle 4. The themes presented were ecological grief, healing, feelings of insignificance, sustenance, longing for deep sensory connection or harmony with nature, experience of God through deep sensory connection with nature, awareness of brokenness or loss of source, and a return to experiencing oneself as part of nature.

2. Sharon Hoffman (2003, 2004) studied personal storytelling as a mode of compassionate connection. The initial part of the study involved an artistic collaboration with a woman who told her story of living with breast cancer that included photographing the woman's journey through breast-cancer treatment and the telling of her story through photos and narrative. In Cycle 3, the woman's story was presented to ninety-five individuals who participated in an interactive, mixed media gallery exhibition in San Francisco. Participants were either invited by the researcher or walked into the exhibit off the street. The exhibition featured photography before and after chemotherapy, poetry, painting, narrative, a breast casting, an audio recording of the teller, and music directly related to the story. Critical design features of the exhibit included (a) a ritual entry into the space, (b) an aesthetically pleasing space, (c) the positioning of stations for private reflection and creative expression by participants, (d) near museum-quality story materials, and (e) opportunities to physically engage with the materials. The latter included an opportunity to try on hats worn by the storyteller after receiving chemotherapy and losing her hair. Stations near each display invited participants to give written feedback or draw. After leaving the exhibit area,

participants were asked to fill out a questionnaire about the exhibit and their responses. The researcher's aesthetic responses to the participants' creative expressions were also included in the data. Data presentation was mostly narrative in style.

3. Aurora Hill (2005) studied the experience of joy as remembered in a circle of twelve Native American women. Supported by tribal leader Grandmother Doris Riverbird, Hill invited women of the Turtle Island Chautauqua and Eastern Lenape Nation of Pennsylvania to a joy-memory-telling ritual. In a ceremonial circle, women told and shared their memories of joy. The ritual and stories were witnessed and recorded by a nonnative, professional caption transcriber. Hill's data consisted of interviews with Doris Riverbird, transcripts of the women's circle, and an interview with the caption transcriber. Much of Hill's descriptive analysis and presentation of data were presented graphically, in order to honor the holism implicit in the women's circle and their remembrance of joy along with extended quotes from participants.

4. Diane Rickards (2006) interviewed Belgian, Dutch, French, Irish, Polish, Turkish, and American-born women who volunteered for espionage activities such as couriers, weapons specialists, informants, and saboteurs in the Second World War. Her work grew out of her interest in understanding the feminine nature traditionally attributed to the feminine shadow in Western culture through the authentic stories of women who worked undercover in enemy territory. Her recruitment of these women, in their eighties and nineties at the time of the study, took many forms: Internet sources, newspaper articles, networking, word of mouth, archives, and military contacts. Rickards chose and interviewed women who met the following criteria: (a) they had worked undercover in dangerous territory in the WW II era for a Resistance group or military organization and (b) they were able to respond to the interview questions clearly and confidently. Confidentiality was strictly observed, including the shredding of some of Rickards' contact records at the end of the inquiry. Data collection has taken the form of in-depth interviews, often including or responsive to

the women's photos, art, memorabilia, and writings and letters about or from the war era. Rickards also collected demographic and historical data, when appropriate. Using procedures developed by Moustakas (1990), Rickards' Cycle 3 descriptive analysis and presentation of data offered literary portraits of each woman. In addition, one of the portraits was a composite of actual details from several of the participants' interviews that were too sensitive or might jeopardize confidentiality, if included along with the individual women's portraits.

5. Dorit Netzer (2008) studied the potential of the imaginal character of mystical poetry to inspire an awareness of spiritual freedom. She conducted five group sessions in which twenty-eight participants listened to selected mystical poetry and then engaged in a process of imaginal resonance with the poems. The group sessions consisted of an opening ritual, listening to a mystical poem, group reporting of their initial mental image, creative expression and embodied writing in response to the poem, and closure. Each participant was contacted at least once following the session for recollections about their reactions to the poem. Cycle 3 descriptive findings included aspects of phenomenological and hermeneutic analyses and the researcher's intuitive synthesis of her own imaginal resonance to the participants' oral reports, embodied writing, and artwork produced in response to the poems.

While many qualitative approaches require specific forms of data analyses, a wide variety of analytic procedures can be used as the basis for data analysis and presentation of data in Cycle 3 of intuitive inquiry. To date, many intuitive inquirers have relied primarily on participant portraits of various types, edited interview transcripts, and thematic content analysis (Anderson 2007) for Cycle 3 analysis and presentation. However, many qualitative analytic procedures—including those of action research, case study, focus group, ethnographic, grounded theory, heuristic, narrative, and empirical phenomenological research—could be used to describe and present data in Cycle 3 of intuitive inquiry. Recently, in a study that explored the nature of personal self and no-self, Laurel McCormick (2010) has used the coding, categorizing, and theorizing procedures of constructivist grounded theory (Charmaz 2006) in Cycles 3 and 4. In Anderson

(2011), I have used what I call "an intuitively derived form of thematic content analysis," which might be used as one model for elaborating thematic content analysis in ways appropriate to intuitive inquiry. Because these choices among analytic approaches for Cycle 3 should reflect the nature of the topic and be chosen to suit the purposes of a study, I do not prescribe a particular form of descriptive analysis or a presentation of data for Cycle 3 but encourage a wide variety of approaches. Sometimes, participant portraits and other narrative forms best represent a topic. At other times, detailed examination of content is required, suggesting the analytic procedures of grounded theory or empirical phenomenology.

Cycle 4: Transforming and Refining Interpretive Lenses

In Cycle 4, the intuitive inquirer refines and transforms the preliminary interpretive lenses developed in Cycle 2 in light of his engagement with the data gathered in Cycle 3. Cycle 2 lenses are modified, removed, rewritten, expanded, etc.—reflecting the researchers more developed and nuanced understanding of the topic at the conclusion of the study. Expanding and refining understanding of a topic is the purpose of research; therefore, researchers are advised to anticipate significant changes in lenses between Cycle 2 and Cycle 4 lenses and to elaborate the changes in detail.

In intuitive inquiry, two-fold articulation of lenses in Cycle 2 and again in Cycle 4 mitigates against circularity, that is, reiterating what the researcher believed from the start. The degree of change between Cycle 2 and Cycle 4 lenses is in part a measure of the researcher's willingness to be influenced by data and to modify his understanding of a topic. Some changes are likely to be major, others minor. In Cycle 4, the researcher prepares a lens-by-lens comparison of the Cycle 2 and Cycle 4 lenses in order to make the changes obvious to the reader. By comparing Cycle 2 and Cycle 4 lenses, the reader of an intuitive inquiry can evaluate what changed in the researcher's understanding of the research topic during the course of the study. The new, change, and seed lenses proposed by Esbjörn (2003) and her nuanced discussion of changes and emerging insights provide a reader-friendly way to make substantive and subtle changes obvious to the reader in Cycle 4. Similarly, in a study that explored the vision quest experiences of modern wilderness rites of passage, Robert Wood (2010) provides an extensive discussion of strengthened, expanded, changed, and new lenses that could also be used a model for lens-by-lens comparisons.

Given their interpretive nature, Cycles 4 and Cycles 5 are presented in the discussion section of a research report.

Perhaps more than in any of the other cycles of intuitive inquiry, the researcher's familiarity with his own intuitive style is key to the success of Cycle 4. Knowing how one's intuitive process works makes it is easier to cultivate and invite breakthrough insights. Over the years, I have been so impressed by the variety of intuitive styles that I am beginning to believe that there are as many of styles as there are people. As I indicated in the earlier section on intuition types, intuitive style tends to blend our unique personalities, histories, and talents and even capitalize on what the researcher considers his worst qualities. For example, I am unusually sensitive to changes in communication patterns between individuals and groups, probably because I grew up in an ethnic and sometimes conflict-ridden neighborhood outside New York City. Other researchers trained in Aikido seem unusually adept at kinesthetic and proprioceptive modes of intuition, reflecting their own interests and abilities. Researchers who have experienced trauma and abuse seem remarkably adept at noticing nonverbal signals during interviews and tracking the emotional content of interviews. Intuition takes many forms.

In an earlier section of this chapter entitled "What is Intuition?," I identified five general types of intuition. The experiential exercise entitled "What is Your Intuitive Style?" invites you to explore and identify your own intuitive style.

Cycle 4, Experiential Exercise: What Is Your Intuitive Style?

Note: Before doing this experiential exercise, you might generally review the moments in your life when you sensed that you were unusually creative, perceptive within concrete situations or of future events, able to make really good decisions even when the relevant facts were not available, or other personal responses that might be considered intuitive.

Step 1. Complete the Basic Instructions for All Experiential Exercises.

Step 2. When you feel relaxed and alert, review occasions in which you felt particularly intuitive in your creative activities, perceptions, or able to make decisions without all the facts. In your imagination, try to relive the details of these occurrences that seem to draw your attention and seem vivid to you now. Recall the experience with as much sensorial, cognitive, and emotional detail as possible. Remember what you were seeing, smelling, tasting, hearing, and sensing through touch and pressure during these experiences. Take time to remember the many times you felt intuitive. If there are too many for one session of this experiential exercise, repeat this step of this experiential exercise until you feel that you have reviewed them all.

Step 3. After you feel that you have reviewed each intuitive occasion in your imagination, imagine all of them in your visual field as though they were spread out before you in a vast array. Notice similarities and patterns between these intuitive occurrences. Are there common events, people, or situations that trigger your intuitions? Are your intuitions seen or heard? Are there smells or tastes associated with them? Are your intuitions felt in your body or in movements? Continue to review the array of intuitive occurrences until similarities and patterns stand out to you in some way.

Step 4. Return to ordinary awareness slowly and write down the insights you discovered about your intuitive style through this experiential exercise. If you danced or sang during the exercise, try to capture the experience in words or images as best you can.

Step 5. Use your insights from this experiential exercise to help you focus your activities while analyzing and interpreting your data from Cycle 3. You might also repeat it from time to time as you continue with your study to explore your intuitive style more fully.

Throughout an intuitive inquiry, the most important feature of interpreting data is intuitive breakthroughs, illuminating moments when the data begin to shape themselves in the eyes of the researcher. Generally speaking, feelings of confusion and bewilderment are indications that a researcher is encountering what he does not know and yet seeks to understand. There is no need to worry as patterns will reveal themselves with time and reflection. When the researcher begins to see patterns in the data, interpretation in the form of Cycle 4 lenses has begun.

My own process of generating Cycle 4 interpretive lenses is usually visual. I work with a paper and pencil, drawing small and large circles—representing themes or ideas—and shifting the patterns and modifying the relationships and size of the circles, rather like a mobile Venn diagram. I know other researchers who work in a more narrative or auditory style as though talking to themselves. Again and again, they bring ideas together in an array of interrelated concepts, themes, narratives, sequences, or irreducible features of the experience studied. Sometimes, intuitive inquirers start dreaming about the final lenses or envisioning them as symbols or images. Document your insights along the way. This interpretative process may go on for several days or weeks with rest or incubation periods between work sessions.

To illustrate Cycle 4 lenses, four examples from intuitive inquiries follow:

1. Vipassana Esbjörn-Hargens (2003, 2004) studied the role of the body in the psycho-spiritual development of contemporary women mystics. In order to clearly identify changes between Cycle 2 and 4 lenses, she developed three categories for her presentation of Cycle 4 lenses: (a) new, (b) change, and (c) seed lenses. New lenses signify breakthroughs in understanding that were entirely new and unexpected; change lenses signify a significant progression of change from lenses presented in Cycle 2; and seed lenses signify lenses that were nascent in the lenses of Cycle 2 but greatly nuanced and developed in the course of the intuitive inquiry. This tripart formulation for the presentation of Cycle 4 lenses spares readers the time and effort necessary to make in-depth comparisons between the lenses in Cycle 2 and Cycle 4. Esbjörn-Hargens identified four new lenses: (a) childhood experiences, from visions to trauma, serve as catalysts for spiritual sensitivity in the body; (b) the body serves as a barometer, where intuitions become physicalized; (c) transformation of the body occurs on a cellular level; and (d) being embodied is a deliberate choice. Her change lenses included her "central interpretation" that women devoted to a spiritual path "tend to go through a process of disidentification and re-identification with the body." Two subsidiary change lenses included (a) sexuality is integral to embodiment and (b) bringing spirit into matter is purposeful. Her six seed lenses included (a) spiritual maturation includes an energetic awakening of the body; (b) boundaries—between you and me, world and self—are experienced as permeable; (c) self reference, or awareness of "I," is fluid and flexible and is not fixed in the body; (d) the

contemplation of death brings into focus the immediacy of life; (e) women are teachers of conscious embodiment; and (f) inquiring into the relationship between body and spirit deepens and enlivens one's experience of living as a body.

2. Aurora Hill (2005) studied the experience of joy in a storytelling circle of Native Americans recounting and sharing moments of joy in their lives. Her Cycle 4 lenses described joy as a multifaceted experience, often like an event or state of being accompanied by strong feelings. Characteristics of joy were: (a) a truth quality expressed in the presence of goodness and beauty; (b) a mysterious quality expressed in a sense of the magical, transitory, and elusive; (c) a somatic quality expressed in proprioceptive and kinesthetic language among the women; (d) a positive quality expressed as gratitude and appreciation; (e) a spiritual quality expressed through Native American teachings and practices; (f) a life-affirming quality expressed in a sense of unconditional acceptance and being blessed; (g) a cocreative quality expressed through shared life in community; (h) a felt sense of energy and presence; (i) an awareness of loss when joy is not present in their life; (j) a noticeable increase in the range and variety of states of consciousness during storytelling; (k) specific time and place associations; and (l) strong associations of joy with light in its many nuances.

3. Cortney Phelon (2001, 2004) studied the healing presence of the psychotherapist. In individual and group interviews, Phelon gathered accounts from advanced psychotherapists about their experiences of the healing presence of their own psychotherapists in the context of psychotherapy. The Cycle 2 lenses included (a) alignment with the client, (b) attentional ability, (c) integration and congruence, (d) inner awareness, (e) spiritual practice and belief, and (f) receptivity. These Cycle 2 lenses were nuanced and expanded in Cycle 4. In addition, three new lenses emerged in Cycle 4: (a) commitment to personal growth, (b) kinesthetic aspects of presence, and (c) the seasoning of a mature psychotherapist through years of practice.

4. Patricia Brandt (2007) studied the spiritual meaning of birth for doulas who attend to the psychological and

spiritual needs of women during childbirth. Brandt interviewed fourteen female doulas and presented a portrait of each doula and a thematic content analysis of the interview transcripts in Cycle 3. Brandt's admiration of the work of the doulas allowed her to portray and analyze the interview data easily. However, the shift in perspective from describing the interviews in Cycle 3 to interpreting the interviews in Cycle 4 was challenging to her. In an email exchange, Brandt expressed her struggle like this:

I felt such empathy with, and honor for, the doulas in my study that I was inclined to list the themes that emerged from their interviews as Cycle 4 lenses. You (R. A.) kept saying Cycle 4 was a chance to state what I learned, what I believed [emphasis hers]. I struggled with this for quite a while. One day, I sat down at the computer stymied. I put on Missa Gaia (Earth Mass) and turned up the volume. I sang and moved with the music. I began to type the lyrics from Mystery [by Paul Winter] repeatedly. I had listened to this music often throughout the project, but I had not realized I was engaging with Missa Gaia in much the same way I had engaged with Leonardo da Vinci's painting The Virgin and Child with St. Anne during Cycle 1. (pers. comm.)

In so doing, Brandt shifted her perspective from what the doulas had said to what she felt and knew about this topic from having integrated their experiences into her own. Therefore, she was ready to begin her interpretation of their experience in her own terms. Brandt's Cycle 4 lenses affirm the mystery felt in (a) "a woman as she gives birth to a child," (b) "intuitions that emerge during childbirth," (c) "the innate ability of women to nurture and support other women," and (d) "the calling of women to become doulas" and sacrifice on behalf of others (184–202). These final lenses read with a tone of clarity and vitality not present in the Cycle 3 analyses.

Cycle 5: Integration of Findings and Literature Review

Based on working the hermeneutic process of Cycles 1 through 4, in Cycle 5, the intuitive inquirer presents authoritative theoretical speculations and theory related to the topic of study. As in all research reports, at the end of the study, the researcher returns to the literature review done prior to data collection and reevaluates that theoretical and empirical literature in light of her findings. In other words, the researcher must determine what is valuable about the study and what is not—sorting through the assets and liabilities of the interpretative cycles—and determine what can now be said about the research topic, including what she feels is still undisclosed. In a sense, the researcher stands back from the entire research process to date and takes into consideration all aspects of the study anew—as though drawing a large hermeneutic circle around the hermeneutic circle prescribed by the forward and return arcs of the study itself.

Intuitive inquiry also requires telling the entire truth about the course of the research project—including (a) mistakes made, (b) procedures and plans that did not work, (c) the researcher's apprehensions and puzzlements about the study and findings, (d) the style of intuitive interpretation used, and (e) what remains unresolved or problematic about the topic or the method. A successful intuitive inquiry invites the reader of the research report to understand the researcher's style of intuitive processing and the manner in which intuitions manifested in the course of the interpretative cycles—including the twists, slow downs, dead ends, and flow of the unconscious journey. The most straightforward way to reveal the researcher's intuitive process is to provide an example of how an important intuition informed a study (Esbjörn-Hargens 2004).

In addition, rather unique to intuitive inquiry and fully aligned with its transformative perspective, the intuitive inquirer attempts to imagine the possible, as though seeking to find trajectories for new and more refined ways of being human in the world. Therefore, unapologetically, intuitive inquirers speculate about the possibilities implicit in the data that draw us closer to understanding the deeper and more restorative and transformative elements of human experience. Implicit in intuitive inquiry is the hope that researchers are called to explore topics that require attention by the culture at large and that the researcher's personal exploration of the topic will envision human experience with fresh eyes. In this sense, intuitive inquiry is both practical and visionary, allowing that research findings can provide new options for the world that is changing and manifesting anew all the time. In so doing, intuition and vision are joined to established scientific discourse. More discussion on the visionary aspects of intuitive inquiry follows in the final section of this chapter that discusses future directions for the method. The experiential exercise entitled "What Is Left Unsaid? Possibilities Unimagined? Visionary Trajectories Based on This Study?" may help you explore possible interpretations implicit in your findings that have not been explicitly expressed.

Cycle 5, Experiential Exercise:
What Is Left Unsaid? Possibilities Unimagined?
Visionary Trajectories Based on This Study?

Note: Review your Cycle 4 interpretative lenses before beginning this experiential exercise.

Step 1. Complete the Basic Instructions for All Experiential Exercises.

Step 2. When you feel relaxed and alert, invite the findings of your study to rise to the surface of your awareness. In your imagination, explore them as completely as you can, noticing what attracts your attention. If you find you wish to focus on a specific aspect of the study and its findings, explore this first and return to a complete review of your findings or other aspects of the study in further sessions based on this experiential exercise. Continue this process of review until you feel that you are able to retain the complexity of your findings in your imagination as through in a vast array.

Step 3. Once you are able to fully imagine the various components of your findings to date in your imagination, notice relationships and patterns between findings in a manner similar to creating your Cycle 4 interpretive lenses. Repeat this process of looking for similarities in this way in order to notice whether you have missed something important. Note any previously unrecognized relationships and patterns in your findings.

Step 4. Then, still retaining your findings in active imagination, invite your attention to the spaces between findings rather than the findings and their interrelationships. Consider the findings and their interrelationships as analogous to the furniture in a room and the spaces between the furniture. Instead of attending to the findings and their interrelationships, attend to the spaces created between the findings in the way the findings are arrayed in your imagination. Note the size and shape of these in-between spaces. Note in-between spaces that seem important, drawing your attention by their color, brightness, density, movement, etc.

Step 5. Once the in-between spaces are vivid to you, begin an imaginal dialogue with those that seem important. Ask each one, if they have something to say to the present or the future. Continue this process until you have explored all the important in-between spaces, returning to the experiential exercise again and again until you feel complete.

Step 6. Return to ordinary awareness slowly and write down the information you intuited through this experiential exercise. If you danced or sang, try to capture the experience in words or image as best you can.

Step 7. Reflect on the insights derived from this experiential exercise over time expressing in writing subtle interpretations implicit in the findings. Give special attention to visionary trajectories that pose new possibilities for being more truly human in the world.

Four Distinctive Features of Intuitive Inquiry

Transformative Potential for Researcher and Others

Through an intersubjective engagement with self and the understandings of others, the intuitive inquirer invites transformation into her life and the lives of those in the study and those who read the findings. Perhaps it is possible to conduct an intuitive inquiry in a superficial way. However, having supervised or advised some thirty intuitive inquiries to date, I have not encountered an intuitive inquirer who has not been significantly changed by the process personally and often professionally.

In intuitive inquiry, the process of transformation is supported by the researcher's intention toward transformation and the dialectic process of each of the five cycles. Each cycle of intuitive inquiry is explicitly dialectic, requiring ongoing reflection and engagement with either texts or data. In Cycles 1 and 2, the researcher is required to engage in an active dialectic process with a text or texts, broadly defined, related to the topic. In Cycles 3 and 4, the researcher dialectically engages the data. In Cycle 5, drawing a still larger hermeneutic circle around the entire study, the researcher reinterprets the empirical and theoretical literature on the topic in light of the data and the Cycle 4 lenses. As in all transformative processes, this back-and-forth dialectic is often fun, delightful, confusing, and unsettling—sometimes simultaneously. One of my dissertation students, Diane Rickards (pers. comm.) told me that, when engaged in the generation of her Cycle 4 lenses, her dialectic process prompted sporadic patterns of rapid-eye movements that she related to higher-level integration of complex material.

While all three transpersonal methods and procedures presented in this book support the personal transformation of the researcher, the dialectic required in intuitive inquiry may be a unique impetus for personal transformation. Esbjörn (2003) describes her experience of the dialectic in this way:

> Intuitive inquiry is a method which models a dialectic, which in turn, invites the researcher into the process of "holding" or entering into that dialectic. Psychotherapists might recognize here the transformational possibilities inherent in a process which invites the researcher to hold a dialectic, which by its nature requires one to resist the ever-so-common human tendency to "split" (between good and bad, love and hate, subject and object, spirit and flesh). . . . If we assume, then, that part of the intuitive inquiry process for the researcher might include practice in holding a dialectic, this also suggests that by doing this, the researcher is strengthening her capacity for what Object Relationalists call a whole object relationship (Ogden 1990; Winnicot 1992). For the purposes of this discussion, the aspect of a whole object relationship that is being considered here, is the capacity to tolerate opposing forces within oneself. A number of developmentalists point to this stage of being and knowing through a variety of names including Robert Kegan's (1994) fourth order of consciousness, Ken Wilber's (1995) vision logic stage, and Jean Gebser's (1986) integral-aperspectival stage of development. As these theorists suggest, it is no small developmental task to tolerate opposing forces within oneself. (282–83)

Auspicious Bewilderment

When I first introduced intuitive inquiry (Anderson 1998), I created the term *auspicious bewilderment* to describe my own research experience of being completely taken by surprise by insights I did not anticipate. When deeply engaged in understanding a research topic, I often felt like a trickster had stepped on to my path. In indigenous cultures worldwide, tricksters are playful, mischievous, and outrageous characters who take one on a merry or dangerous chase, but often open gateways of awareness and insight along the way. Particular to the culture, coyotes, ravens, fairies, leprechauns, and pookas (a very Irish goblin) gift humans with insight—usually in the context of making us feel ridiculous or foolish, but nonetheless jarring us out of our usual way of understanding. Coyotes play tricks. Ravens steal and turn the stolen goods into something else. Fairies appear as lovers. Leprechauns give us gold that vanishes on touch. Pookas gleefully take us for a rowdy ride. Intuitive inquiries tend to be full of such auspicious bewilderments!

Typically, such auspicious bewilderments signal renewed understanding. Contradictory stories, interviews, data, and reflections move us deeper into the intricacies of the topic of inquiry. Nuances that do not fit generate new insights. Confusion takes us in an unanticipated direction. Paradox challenges our assumptions and so on. Methodologically, the nature of intuitive inquiry sets the stage for new ideas to happen. They often do. The research project will take longer, require more work, and probably cost more money, and it will also be more complete and useful in the end. Weeks, even months, of feeling auspiciously bewildered is not unusual for an intuitive inquirer. While bewildered, keep records and stay with the process as it is. If it gets to be too much, rest, sleep, take a break, or gently put the research project on the back burner for a while. Return to the project again when feeling refreshed.

More dangerous to intuitive inquiry is thinking we know what we are doing, being confident that we are on top of it all, or having fixed ideas about the findings before we have finished collecting, analyzing, and interpreting the full complement of data. The nature of transformative experience often demands periods of confusion to be more fully understood. If you go for long periods of not being surprised, beware. Something might be wrong. Is the topic so well understood that there is nothing new to say? What is happening to contradictory information? Are you bored? Exhausted? Otherwise preoccupied? In denial? Avoiding the inevitable move to the heart of the topic? If so, do not panic. Rest and come back when feeling refreshed and unwilling to spend energy going in the wrong direction.

The procedural containment of intuitive inquiry's five cycles seems to abet surprising insights. In a certain way, the five cycles provide boundaries and safety not unlike good psychotherapy.

Methodologically, intuitive inquiry sets the stage for new ideas to happen. They often do.

Writing in Your Own Voice

Scientific reports are easier to read and understand and more interesting when researchers write in their own distinctive writers' voice. When I was trained as an experimental social psychologist in the early 1970s, it was the case then, as now, that scientific reports were expected to be emotionally flat in style, resulting in an affective sameness from report to report. Researchers were often so intent on separating the personal from scientific inquiry that they often fail to render candid opinions, even at the conclusion of their research reports. The values of logical positivism that inform scientific report writing disguises the subjectivity of the researcher in the exactness of what can be observed behaviorally from the outside. Fortunately, rich descriptive reports from participants and in report writing are now favored by qualitative researchers (Denzin and Lincoln 2003).

Intuitive inquiry is a postmodern method averring the constructed nature of reality. Conventional reality is not just objectively present but rather constructed by the biological, cognitive, and cultural structures and habits we inhabit (Johnson 1987; Varela, Thompson, and Rosch 1991). Reality does not exist apart from the embodied participation of being a specific human being with a particular physiology, history, personality, and culture but is interpretative and intersubjective. Human subjectivity is a source of knowing, not dismissible as solipsistic expression or opinion.

Intuitive inquiry invites authenticity. If the authentic voice of the mind, body, and spirit of the inquirer is not revealed in the report, the study is not interpretable by others and, therefore, not valid as an intuitive inquiry. The success of the method depends on the researcher's ability and willingness to express himself uniquely and courageously. While technology is changing the presentation of scientific reports, these reports are still primarily written texts. Therefore, intuitive inquirers are expected to write compassionately and vividly, bringing emotional honesty to the fore. Research reports should (a) impart the distinctive feelings and experiences that the researcher brought to the topic, (b) convey what she feels important and inspiring about the findings, (c) speculate about the possibilities and visions for future implicit in her findings, and (d) be written in a manner that invites sympathetic resonance (Anderson 1998; Anderson, 2000) in readers as they read. Writing styles such as embodied writing (Anderson

2001; Anderson 2002a; Anderson 2002b) and autoethnography (Ellis 2003) offer researchers options for the presentation of findings that are evocative and engaging to readers. (See Chapter 8, An Expanded View of Validity, for a thorough discussion of sympathetic resonance and its applications in the evaluation of validity.) The experiential exercise entitled "Finding Voice" can help you present your research findings in a manner that engages the intended audience—personally, professionally, or spiritually—depending on their needs.

Experiential Exercise: Finding Voice

Note: This experiential exercise is related to an earlier experiential exercise in this chapter entitled "Identifying Your Intended Audience." Because of unanticipated findings or new insights, the intended audience for your research report may have changed in the course of the study. Therefore, a portion of the earlier experiential exercise is repeated in the experiential exercise below.

Step 1. Complete the Basic Instructions for All Experiential Exercises.

Step 2. When your awareness feels relaxed and alert, let your research topic surface in awareness. Let your sense of the topic come alive by thinking of a concrete personal example of the experience you wish to study. Recreate that experience in your imagination using all your senses, as in the first experiential exercise in this chapter.

Step 3. Once the experience seems vivid and alive, imagine the intended (or anticipated) audience for the fruits of your dissertation or research project. Whom do you wish to serve in studying this research topic at the conclusion of your study? Are you hoping you will gain information or insights that may benefit specific individuals? Or groups? Try to be concrete by imagining precisely what these individuals or groups look like. As best you can, focus on one individual and imagine what he looks like. Imagine his facial features, eye color, the quality of his voice, etc.

Step 4. Once you have a clear sense of a person or group as your intended audience, begin an imaginary dialogue with him, her, or them. In your natural conversational voice, begin to converse about your research findings in Cycle 4 and 5. Invite your audience to ask questions and make comments about the findings. Notice what he, she, or they have to say to you. Notice any nonverbal communications you sense in your visual imagination as well. If the intended audience includes animals or aspects of nature, adapt your imaginal dialogue accordingly.

Step 5. Once you have established an ongoing dialogue with the audience, explore various ways to present your findings with them. Notice how your audience responds to your presentations. Take special notice of presentation styles or particular findings that attract their attention and response. Continue this imaginary dialogue until it feels complete to you or your audience stops interacting with you.

Step 6. Return to ordinary awareness slowly and write down the information you intuited through this experiential exercise. If you danced or sang, try to capture the experience in words or image as best you can.

Step 7. Use the information and insights from this experiential exercise to refine, expand, and streamline your presentation of findings. For further suggestions and experiential exercises related to using embodied writing in research reports, see Chapter 7 of this volume.

Theory-Building Potential of Intuitive Inquiry

A promising aspect of intuitive inquiry is its potential to synthesize prior theory and research on a topic and render theoretical integrations in Cycles 4 and Cycles 5. Much like Grounded Theory (Strauss and Corbin 1990), the method allows for inductive theory building on the topic of study. Frankly, it is not possible to do intuitive inquiry well without maintaining a big-picture perspective throughout the research process. Rather outmanuevered by spontaneity and intuition insights, reductive processes do not fit the method. To date, two intuitive inquirers (Phelon 2001; Phelon 2004; Unthank 2007) have actively engaged the method's potential to generate theory inductively based on the development of their understanding of the topic in Cycle 1 through Cycle 5.

At the conclusion of her study, Phelon (2001, 2004) developed a theoretical model for understanding the embodied healing presence of a psychotherapist along with recommendations for the training of clinicians, as summarized earlier in this chapter in the section on Cycle 4. Unthank began her study of trauma survival with an implicit theory based on years of clinical practice as a therapist specializing in trauma recovery. By her own account, her study "brought her face to face with her own embodied shame and with survival habits of security in having [perceived] control" (Unthank 2007, 226). At the end of the study, she arrived at the following conclusions: (a) the deep structure of survival is a learned functional neurosis, specifically a double approach-avoidance complex with vulnerability associated with intolerable fear and safety and security associated with maladaptive guilt, (b) shame-fused guilt is the empowerment core of posttrauma survival that generates a world of perceived safety at the expense of maladaptive guilt, i.e., being chronically at fault. As with all emerging theories, further investigation is required.

Challenges and Limitations of Intuitive Inquiry

I have embedded caveats about intuitive inquiry throughout this chapter. At this point, I wish only to emphasize two general challenges or limitations to the method.

First, intuitive inquiry is often intellectual, emotionally, and spiritually demanding. The method requires a great deal of maturity to do the dance of balancing right- and left-brain processes. On the one hand, an intuitive inquirer is encouraged to use right-brain processes, such as intuitive, artistic, and imaginal processes, in all five cycles. On the other, articulating a clear research topic in Cycle 1, preparing a literature review along with Cycle 2, articulating lenses in Cycles 2 and 4, collecting and analyzing data in Cycle 3, and the integrating of findings with previous empirical and theoretical literature in Cycle 4 are challenging traditional intellectual tasks, usually thought of as linear tasks associated with left-brain processes. Anyone taking on an intuitive inquiry is forewarned that the dance is not easy. In some ways, while psycho-spiritual maturity can facilitate the integration of right- and left-brain processes, the quality of right- and left-brain functioning itself may also deepen or expand, requiring greater and greater levels of integration to manage the extremity of the swings from one type of processing to another.

Second, intuitive inquiry may not be suitable for use with data that are inherently narrative in form. The requirement in intuitive inquiry to create lenses can disrupt the structure of data that requires story or narrative for meaning. Therefore, in such cases, I recommend researchers use a form of narrative research (Josselson 1996; Mishler 1991; Mishler 2000).

Intuitive Inquiry, Hermeneutics, and Other Hermeneutic Approaches to Research

Intuitive inquiry employs terms and concepts used in philosophical hermeneutics, primarily those used by Friedrich Schleiermacher (1768–1834) and Hans-Georg Gadamer (1900–2002). As a theologian and philosopher, Schleiermacher was concerned with the interpretation and translation of ancient texts, both biblical and secular (Schleiermacher 1977, 1998). At stake in the interpretation of a text is a comprehensive scrutiny of its linguistic and cultural elements, and the author's use of these elements as compared with other texts of the same time and place. Schleiemacher locates the intent of interpretation as understanding the meaning of the text for the original author, a process that is likely to sound familiar to contemporary qualitative researchers attempting to discern the meaning of participants' words and use of words. Schleiermacher encourages both analytic and intuitive processes, acknowledging that understanding may never be final or fully satisfying because understanding the others' intent and other cultures is not something we can take for granted. In contrast to Schleiermacher, Gadamer (1998b) understood interpretation as a dialogue between the past and the present. The past is represented by the text, which makes a claim upon the interpreter (Bruns 1992). The texts address us, and we enter into a dialogical relationship to the past through them. In so doing, we gain a better understanding of both the text and ourselves (Bruns 1992; Ramberg and Gjesdal 2005).

There are many other hermeneutic approaches of qualitative research in addition to intuitive inquiry (Denzin 2001a; Moustakas 1990; Packer and Addison 1989; Romanyshyn 2007; Smith 2004; Smith 2007; van Manen 1990; van Manen 2002) and many researchers who have reflected on the application of philosophic hermeneutics to human science research, especially in recent years (Josselson 2004; Rennie 2007). While a thorough exploration of the relationship of intuitive inquiry to each of the methodological hermeneutics represented by these researchers goes beyond the purposes of this chapter, the hermeneutic approach that seems most aligned with intuitive inquiry is interpretive phenomenological analysis (IPA) developed by Jonathan Smith (2004, 2007). Both IPA and intuitive inquiry aver dynamic and inductive approaches to interpretation that invite nuanced interpretation of qualitative data and share similar applications of Schleiermacher's and Gadamer's hermeneutics.

Future Directions for Intuitive Inquiry

I created intuitive inquiry in order to carve creative space or capacity within scientific inquiry for the active contributions of intuitive insights. With the cycles of intuitive inquiry evaluated and clarified, the methodological formation of intuitive inquiry is complete, and I feel like a parent watching a child graduate from high school. It is now time for me to let go and watch how intuitive inquiry is used and shaped by others.

Although the method has been only twelve years in formal development, the seeds for intuitive inquiry were sown over fifty years ago when I as a gymnast learned that having a net and a spotter helped me to risk. I was a better gymnast for the help of the net and spotters that caught me when I missed the bar or slipped off the balance beam. In like manner, the five interpretative cycles of intuitive inquiry represent the supportive structures that guide and hold the creative research process of intuitive inquiry and move it forward progressively. The cycles invite researchers and research participants—and eventually users of the research findings—to confidently inhabit their intuitive ways of knowing and to interpret for themselves the visionary perspectives suggested by the data and the researcher's interpretations. Within a positivistic paradigm of modern science, conducting research outside the established culture feels risky and requires a sense of safety and permission from someone who has traveled this path before them. Based on my experience of conducting research from an intuitive perspective from since the early 1990s, I developed intuitive inquiry to help fill that need. Each interpretative cycle has a unique purpose in advancing the intuitive inquirer's understanding. I hope that future intuitive researchers do *not* skip any of the cycles in the interests of time and expediency. That said, I also hope that researchers will adapt the method and procedures to optimize their own intuitive styles, blend the procedures with both qualitative and quantitative methods, expand procedures to new applications, and evolve it further than I have taken intuitive inquiry thus far.

In many ways, the development of intuitive inquiry has been an intuitive inquiry in its own right, cycling in and out of my own research entanglements and those of my dissertation supervisees—and it has been great, good fun. It has been full of spontaneity, serendipity, and auspicious bewilderment. I never quite knew what would come next—and, frankly, I enjoyed the surprises the most. I hope that every intuitive inquirer has as much fun as I have had in the development of the method.

I believe that the greatest potential of intuitive inquiry is its capacity as a method to inspire vision in new ways of being human in a troubled world. The insistence of the five cycles to stay close to intuitive promptings is not an easy path to travel. Too often, the scientific discourse of Euro-America tends to suppress and discourage intuitive processes, especially body-based knowings such as proprioception and kinesthesia. This deep listening to intuition in research has a greater capacity to unfold into new ways of theorizing and envisioning that are closer to lived experience than do the rationalistic styles that dominate much of world culture and scientific discourse. The iterative cycles of deep listening and witnessing expand into theoretical formulations over time in a manner akin to Eugene Gendlin's (1991, 1992, 1997) descriptions of "thinking beyond patterns." Specifically, the spaciousness and permission given by intuitive inquiry invites a discourse in science that positions researchers, together with others, at the leading edge of that which is visionary, inspiring, and new in the realms of ideas and theory. Our world needs new vision. Be brave!

In the late 1960s, Abraham Maslow (1968, 1971) recommended that we explore the farther reaches of human experience by studying those individuals who had self-actualized their potential the most. Similarly, intuitive inquiry invites researchers to envision creative possibilities that are nascent in their creative exchanges with others in both the conduct of research and in their everyday lives. In Anderson (2011), I call this invitation "a hermeneutics of potential."

CHAPTER 2

Integral Inquiry

The Principles and Practices of an Inclusive and Integrated Research Approach

William Braud

Ultimate truth, if there be such a thing, demands the concert of many voices.

—Carl Jung 1993, xiv

An Introduction to Integral Inquiry

Overview of This Approach

This approach includes and integrates aspects of the research enterprise that conventional research approaches deliberately keep separate. Inclusion and integration take place in three major areas. First, a research session may simultaneously provide opportunities for knowledge gain for the discipline; clinical, educational, and other benefits for the research participants; and psycho-spiritual growth and the possibility of transformative change for the researcher (and also for the research participants and for the eventual readers of the research report). Second, a greater understanding of the topic of inquiry is made possible through attention to the nature of experiences, their history and conceptualization, their dynamic unfolding and the processes that facilitate or inhibit them, and their outcomes or fruits. Third, in the course of

[handwritten: Class Note]

[handwritten: The sixth sense   feeling connected]

71

Class intention

the investigation, the integral inquirer practices many complementary forms of knowing, being, and doing—including conventional, tacit, intuitive, body-based, feelings-based, and direct forms of knowing; ordinary and nonordinary states of consciousness; analytical/linear and nonanalytical/nonlinear ways of working with data; and alternative ways of expressing findings (themes, narratives, metaphors, similes, symbols, and nonverbal creative expressions).

In this chapter, each aspect of the integral inquiry approach is explained, along with examples of how each facet can be used in the data planning and collection, data treatment and interpretation, and findings presentation and communication stages of a research project. Experiential exercises are provided for each of the major components of the approach, allowing both experienced researchers and students to learn the components easily. From this chapter, the reader can learn integral inquiry's essential aspects and appropriate uses, and can develop expertise in applying the components and the approach as a whole to selected research questions and topics.

The present research approach is *integral* (i.e., *inclusive* and *integrated*) in terms of the following features:

> the involvement of the researcher's whole person
> the variety of functions and benefits of a research session
> the wide range of the researcher's sources of inspiration
> the researcher's, participants', and audience's alternative modes of knowing
> the nature of the research questions explored
> the variety of ways of collecting, working with, and presenting data and findings

These features are elaborated in later sections of this chapter.

Origin and Development of This Approach

Integral Inquiry had its genesis in two experiences in the early 1990s. The first of these was a meeting with two other faculty members. We were discussing the way the Institute of Transpersonal Psychology's (ITP's) curriculum and pedagogy addressed six facets of human functioning (intellectual, somatic, emotional, spiritual, relational, and creative expression) and what might be the nature of the ideal ITP dissertation, were it to honor all of those facets. I suggested that such a dissertation would involve not only collecting the usual data in the usual ways (gathering words and numbers through conventional interviews and assessments), working with data in the usual analytical manner, and presenting one's findings in the usual way—i.e., using linear prose. In addition, a variety of alternative modes of knowing, being, and doing would be used in the three major research stages. I suggested the metaphor of conducting a dissertation project using "multiple eyes" (ways of knowing), "multiple brains" (ways of working with and understanding one's data), and "multiple mouths" (ways of expressing and communicating one's findings), rather than the using the conventional, one-dimensional approach of using only "one eye, one brain, and one mouth."

The second experience took place during the Second International Symposium on Science and Consciousness, which I attended in Athens, Greece in 1992 (see Athenian Society for Science and Human Development and the Brahma Kumaris World Spiritual University 1992). As part of that meeting, the invited researchers, working in small groups, were asked to consider the question, "What is consciousness?" After I sat in silence for a while, pondering that question, these thoughts arose: Consciousness is an *experience*, consciousness is a *conceptualization*, consciousness is a *process* with an atmosphere, and consciousness has consequences or *fruits*—all occurring, all interacting, all changing, all to be honored, each incomplete without the others, all contributing to the whole. Later, I recognized that this fourfold consideration could be applied not only to consciousness but also to any topic or experience that one wished to study. Any experience could be approached in terms of the nature of the experience itself; how it might be conceptualized and how those conceptualizations may have changed through time; how the experience might unfold and develop, what might accompany the experience, and which conditions might facilitate or impede the experience (its process and atmosphere); and what might be the experience's outcomes or fruits.

In the development of this research approach, the first experience suggested *how* to study one's topic, and the second experience suggested *what* might be studied. Pluralistic approaches to both method and content could be introduced, leading to more complete and satisfying projects and findings. I chose the name *Integral Inquiry* in order to honor the inclusive and integrated nature of the approach. When this approach was being developed in the early 1990s, the term *integral* already was being used—in the Integral Yoga and Integral Yoga Psychology of Sri Aurobindo (2000), and in the integral structure of consciousness described by Jean Gebser (1986)—and later would be used for the Integral Psychology of Ken Wilber (2000). The naming of Integral Inquiry was not inspired by any of these three uses;

however, the approach does have considerable overlaps with these other views.

The Integral Inquiry approach was described in preliminary form in a 1994 working Paper (Braud 1994b) and further developed in a series of articles and book chapters (Braud 1998a; Braud 1998b; Braud 1998c; Braud 2002c; Braud 2006; Braud 2010; Braud 2008). Through the years, the approach has been modified and expanded on the basis of inputs from my own thinking and research, my teaching in various graduate research courses, and my supervision of thesis and dissertation projects. This present chapter can be viewed as the most current status report on the nature and uses of this research approach.

Most Suitable Topics

Although Integral Inquiry can be used in the study of nearly any topic, some topics are especially well-suited for this kind of approach. These are topics that have great personal meaning for the researcher, topics that one wishes to understand deeply, and topics that are highly experiential—especially those that involve exceptional, transpersonal, and spiritual experiences.

The integral inquirer can carefully consider a potential research project to determine whether it is likely to meet the following criteria for a meaningful and satisfying project.

A satisfying research project . . .

> is meaningful to the *researcher*: It addresses issues important to the investigator; ideally, the topic arises out of the researcher's personal experiences and interests;

> is meaningful to the *research participants*: It helps them learn more about, assimilate, and understand important issues in their lives;

> is meaningful to the *reader* (the audience) of the final research report: The future reader can identify with the participants, the researcher, and the issues explored and can benefit personally from the findings of the study;

> addresses a topic of *great relevance* to the preferred area of study: It contributes to a gain in knowledge and possible practical application in the specific chosen area of one's discipline;

can provide, in addition to new information, the opportunity for *transformation* for those involved in the project (researcher, participants), the reader (audience), one's field of study, and society as a whole;

is rich in *implications* for our understanding of human nature and the nature of the world;

contributes to the *professional growth* and development of the researcher: The project may build upon and extend present strengths and skills, as well as provide opportunities to acquire and develop new skills and abilities. The project also can serve as a stepping stone for follow-up studies.

As a potential integral inquirer, you can ask yourself the following specific questions to determine whether a potential project meets the criteria mentioned above and whether it fits your unique characteristics, aims, and circumstances:

Does the topic have heart and meaning for you, personally? Is it sufficiently close to you that it will sustain your interest, but not so close to unfinished issues that these could overwhelm you and divert you from the research itself?

Do you think exploring this topic will help you move ahead in your own psycho-spiritual development? As researcher, be prepared to experience important changes and even transformation in pursuing a meaningful topic.

Know that, as you work with a meaningful topic, you will confront all of your own issues during the course of the work; you will become what you study; and you will experience the complementary parts of all aspects of your work. Are you prepared for this, and able to pick a topic accordingly?

Is the topic one that can be beneficial to your research participants (coresearchers)? In exploring the research topic with you, participants will deal with issues that are meaningful to them and that can help in their own working through, assimilation, and integration of important issues.

Do you think the topic can help advance the specific area of the discipline in which you are working? A useful topic is one that can help fill a need or gap in knowledge, resolve conceptual issues, further theoretical development, lead to potential applications, and/or suggest important implications for the field.

Does the topic match or overlap the research interests of persons you might be working with? If the work will be done in a facility with which you are involved, is the project one that is aligned with the mission and vision of that facility?

Is the topic manageable, and is the project feasible? Have you the requisite skills for adequately carrying out this particular project? Will the needed participants and the necessary resources be available? If the project is a thesis or dissertation project, are you likely to complete it within approximately twelve to eighteen months? Remember that a dissertation is one delimited research project, not a life's work.

Consider the audience of greatest interest to you, and keep that audience in mind so that the audience's reception of, and benefit from, your work will inform all phases of your research project.

Consider the possible societal impact of your completed research project.

Can the project—whether it be a dissertation or some other research project—be framed as one phase in a greater plan of study? How might you build upon what you learn in this project? What would be some likely next steps?

Do not let your choice of a topic or project be dictated solely by intellectual considerations. Solicit and consider inputs from many sources—from your body, feelings, emotions, dreams, intuitions, and suggestions from others—as well as possible hints, affirmations, lessons, supports, and obstacles provided by the universe.

Experiential Exercise:
Identifying Your Most Burning Question(s)

In an effective research project, the researcher usually seeks to address one major research question or test one major hypothesis. (Sometimes, a very small number—two or three—of secondary questions or hypotheses also might be addressed.) It is important to be able to let possible research questions surface in your awareness, narrow these to a manageable number, prioritize these, and be able to identify the one most meaningful question you hope to answer in a particular research project.

As a beginning exercise, if you were to design a research project to address the research question that is most important to you, right now, what would that question be? If, at the conclusion of your project, you could have learned one thing, what would that be? If a wish-granting research fairy existed and was able to grant you the answer to one research question, which question would you pose to have answered?

My most burning research question is: _____

_____

It is important to have passion for one's research topic. This might be reframed as having great interest and involvement in the topic. However, as in all areas, too much of this might not be wise. There is what I have come to call a "Goldilocks Region" of involvement in one's research topic—being at a distance from the topic that is "just right," not too far but also not too close to it.

Experiential Exercise: Distance/Closeness of the Topic: Exploring the Goldilocks Region

A useful exercise, in choosing a research area, topic, or question, is to imagine how you might place a great number of subjects, topics, or questions on a continuum. Consider which kinds of areas, topics, or questions do not interest you at all, and place these at one end of this imagined continuum. Then consider which sorts of areas, topics, or questions do hold great interest, excitement, and meaning for you. Place these at the other end of this imagined continuum. Now, think of the ones nearest the high interest extreme. Which of these hold the greatest passion for you? Consider them carefully. Does the passionate interest in certain topics seem great enough to sustain your extended work with those topics? Might you be too passionate and involved in certain topics to allow you to devote your time and energy to a scholarly treatment of those topics, rather than be distracted by having to work in a very emotional, personal way with the issues that might arise? If you seem to be too involved or consumed by a certain area, topic, or question, it may be best to wait until you have reached a certain degree of progress and closure in dealing with such issues before deciding to research this. On this imagined continuum, consider which areas, topics, and questions are in the Goldilocks Region—not too lacking in interest and personal relevance, but not too consuming . . . that is, something that is "just right."

Areas, topics, and questions in my own Goldilocks Region include the following:

Most Suitable Researchers

The view that the researcher's qualities and characteristics are irrelevant to what the researcher might find in his or her studies, and that researchers are essentially interchangeable, is increasingly being questioned. It no longer makes sense to consider the researcher and the researched topic as separate and independent. The interrelationship of the researcher and the researched is especially important in educational, psychological, and social studies. Investigations of the so-called *experimenter effect* have shown that the findings of research studies can be influenced by the attitudes, expectations, intentions, and beliefs of the particular researcher who is conducting or even more remotely supervising the study (Blanck 1993; Rosenthal 1966; Rosenthal 2002b; Rosenthal and Rosnow 1969; Rosenthal and Rubin 1978; Rosnow and Rosenthal 1997). Even in the natural science of physics, which studies inanimate systems, the role of the scientist in the outcome of an experiment has been recognized, in the context of the *observer effect* in quantum and entanglement studies (see Aczel 2003; Gribbin 1995; Radin 2006). Some of these experimenter, observer, and related effects can be mediated in straightforward ways such as the choice of procedures to be used in a study or the manner in which the researcher behaves and interacts with the research participants. Other influences may have more subtle mediators, influences which have been considered in parapsychological studies (Palmer 1993; Palmer 1997; Smith 2003; White 1976a; White 1976b).

It is useful to address these issues in the context of the *preparedness* of the researcher. The Roman philosopher Boethius provided one of the earliest and clearest statements of this principle: "Everything that is known is comprehended not according to its own nature, but according to the ability to know of those who do the knowing" (Boethius 1980, 157). More currently, the personal qualities of the researcher are treated through concepts such as the various *sensitivities* of the knower (Skolimowski 1994), the knower's *adaequatio* (adequateness) with respect to what is to be known (Schumacher 1978, 39–60), and the researcher's *theoretical sensitivity*, in the qualitative research approach of grounded theory (Glaser 1978). In the latter, the researcher's prior familiarity with what is studied, along with observational and interpretative experiences and skills help inform aspects of data collection and theory development. The essence of these and other related treatments is that a researcher can know only those things for which he or she has been adequately prepared. Some of this preparation may take the forms of preexisting dispositions, aptitudes, and temperament (perhaps genetically informed), and other aspects may be developed through appropriate experiences and training.

Just as astronomers' and microscopists' discoveries depend upon their observational skills and their familiarity with their telescopes, microscopes, and other instruments, so too researchers' successes in psychological research depend upon their full and competent use of their major research tools. One of the most important tools—perhaps *the* most important tool—in qualitative inquiry is the researcher himself or herself. The researcher's inherent and acquired preparedness will help determine the areas and topics to be investigated; how projects are framed and designed; the nature of research hypotheses or questions; how research participants are sought, found, and treated; how data are collected, analyzed, interpreted, and reported; and where and how one looks for inspiration and support throughout the research process. The major purpose of the present book—especially its Part 2—is to help researchers become more aware of their own observational and other skills and competencies; expand, extend, and fine-tune these; and thereby increase their preparedness and research adequateness.

Despite recognition of the importance of researcher preparation and skills in the research enterprise, in conventional psychological research, little attention has been paid to the role of the researcher's *own being*. Yet, there is an understanding that we can experience, perceive, and know only that for which our sensitivities have prepared us, and that these sensitivities and dispositions depend upon aspects of our very being.

Therefore, first let each become godlike and each beautiful who cares to see God and Beauty. (Ennead 1.6.9) All knowing comes by likeness. (Ennead 1.8.1) (Plotinus 1966–1988)

We behold that which we are. . . . Only the Real can know Reality. (Underhill 1969, 423, 436)

Knowledge is a function of being. When there is a change in the being of the knower, there is a corresponding change in the nature and amount of knowing. . . . Nor are changes in the knower's physiological or intellectual being the only ones to affect his knowledge. What we know depends also on what, as moral beings, we choose to make ourselves. (Huxley 1970, viii, ix)

Practice may change our theoretical horizon, and this in a twofold way: it may lead into new worlds and secure new powers. Knowledge we could never attain, remaining what we are, may be attainable in consequences of higher powers and a higher life, which we may morally achieve. (William James, cited in Huxley 1970, viii)

The persons quoted above were harbingers of what later was to become the field of transpersonal psychology, and it is noteworthy that the *essential nature and being* of the knower became and continues to be one of the major research and content interests of workers in this field. One of the most explicit presentations of this interest is Abraham Maslow's (1968, 1971) emphasis of 'being values" and various "being qualities."

The role of the researcher-instrument's being in determining what can be known is analogous to the role of the nature of a musical instrument (a piano or cello) in the physical phenomenon of *resonance*. Whether a second instrument resonantly responds to a sounded note from a first instrument depends upon the nature and physical characteristics of the second instrument. Sonic resonance occurs only if the to-be-resonant systems are sufficiently similar.

The implication of the Huxley and James quotes, above, is that the quality of being of a knower can be changed—i.e., the knower can be "transformed"—so that previously unattainable knowings now become possible.

Experiential Exercise: Assessing Your Preparedness

Before beginning a new research project, you can assess your own preparedness to undertake the project—not only in terms of your knowledge about the topic but also in terms of your own personal skills, characteristics, and way of being. Your qualities may fit the planned project to various degrees. This recognized degree of fittingness or nonfittingness could lead you to consider either another project or the possibility of altering your own qualities and ways of being so that they might fit better with what you will be exploring in the planned project.

Consider your own knowledge about the topic you wish to investigate and the research methods you might use. Consider, also, your own background and experiences and the degree to which you already possess the skills that will be useful in conducting the study. If some of those skills are underdeveloped, are there ways that you might develop them further, so that they might better serve you in carrying out the planned study?

Consider Knowledge about topic

Examine your temperament and predispositions, and how those might fit and not fit with the planned project. One way to do this is to consider the relative strengths of your four *functions* of thinking, feeling, intuiting, and sensing; your tendencies toward extraversion or introversion, and your tendencies toward judging or perceiving. The so-called Myers-Briggs Type Indicator ® (Myers 1962; Myers 1980) has been developed to assess these characteristics. Many other standardized assessments of personality and abilities could be used for this purpose. These can be augmented by self-assessments, based on your familiarity with your own strengths and limitations. Knowing these, you might choose to address topics and use methods that will engage your present strengths. Alternatively, you might choose to use a more demanding research project as an opportunity to develop yourself in a more balanced way by attending to and enhancing skills that presently are underdeveloped. In any case, know that in conducting adequate research, you will be using *all* of your functions and capabilities, at least to some degree.

Examine temperament predispositions. ← Four functions

4 functions thinking feeling intuiting sensing

To help you prepare psychologically for a research project, the following exercise can allow you identify what might be called your *adversaries* and *allies* in this endeavor. It will be useful to complete the exercise in two ways—first verbally and deliberately, then nonverbally and spontaneously.

Experiential Exercise: Adversaries and Allies (Deliberate, Verbal Approach)

As you are thinking about beginning a particular research project, indicate your responses to the following four items. Once you have written your responses, store them for safekeeping. It will be helpful to review your responses at various times in the future to see if and how your adversaries and allies are indeed showing up.

Item 1: In connection with this research project, my three greatest fears, resistances, and obstacles to completion are:

_____

Item 2: In connection with this research project, my three greatest strengths, allies, and facilitators of its completion are: _____

Item 3: Additional thoughts, feelings, practices, and activities that can support me in this research project are: _____

_____

Item 4: Things to be on the lookout for or to avoid are:

_____

After you have completed the Adversaries and Allies exercise in a deliberate, verbal manner, put it aside, forget what you wrote, and approach the same task in a more relaxed, effortless, creative, image-based, spontaneous, nonverbal fashion, as follows:

Experiential Exercise: Adversaries and Allies (Spontaneous, Nonverbal Approach)

Begin by closing your eyes, relaxing, and setting an intention to learn more from other aspects of yourself. Invite the wisest parts of yourself to share their wisdom about this research process with you, through the vehicle of imagery. Imagine a blank screen—such as a movie screen—before your mind's eye. Now, allow your three greatest fears, apprehensions, concerns, resistances, and possible obstacles to the completion of your research project to appear on that screen, to dramatize themselves—one by one—as images or other representations. Give these time to develop. Observe and witness these. How do these appear? How do they make you feel? Are there certain bodily accompaniments of each of these? Note all of these things, and suggest to yourself that you will remember these images, thoughts, and feelings well. Then, let those three images fade from the screen; let them disappear, and let the screen become blank again.

Now, let the wisest part of you fill the screen with images or representations of your three greatest allies—strengths and qualities that can serve you well in countering the fears and obstacles, and facilitate your progress and completion of your research project. As in the case of the adversaries, give these allies time to develop, then observe them, witness them, note the thoughts, feelings, and bodily sensations that accompany each of them, and remember all of this.

Now, let those three allies remain on your mental screen, as you invite the previous three adversaries to join them. Let all six images or representations be on your mental screen at the same time, and *allow them to interact freely with each other*. Give these interactions time to develop, then watch, observe, witness, note the feeling accompaniments, and remember all of this.

Now, let all six images/representations fade from the screen. Remain relaxed and attentive as you slowly open your eyes, and record all that you remember about the images/ representations and the accompanying feelings, thoughts, and bodily sensations. Ground and preserve your experiences by drawing and writing them.

Once you have completed this second (spontaneous, non-verbal) exercise, compare what it revealed with what you had written in the first (deliberate, verbal) version, noting any similarities, differences, elaborations, or nuances.

Know that the allies can always be with you and can be invited to assist you in this project and in all other research endeavors.

As a final exercise in assessing your readiness for conducting a particular research project, respond to the following items. Your responses will provide useful indications of what you already know about this project and will help you identify gaps in your knowledge that must be filled before you begin the research. You may use this exercise as a checklist of work already completed and work remaining to be done.

Experiential Exercise: Readiness Assessment

The general topic of this research project is:

My specific research question or hypothesis is:

The significance, value, or usefulness of studying this topic is:

Three articles or books on the topic/question are (put the most important one first):

_____

_____

_____

The methods of investigation I am considering are:

___ surveys   ___ questionnaires   ___ interviews

___ self-reports   ___ in-depth case   ___ several cases

___ experiment   ___ assessments   ___ observations, logs

I will analyze my data and present my results using:

___ group statistics   ___ correlations   ___ meta-analysis

___ thematic content   ___ themes   ___ narratives analysis

___ participant reports ___ heuristic/organic/intuitive approach

For this study, I am considering the following *methodological* innovations:

This research question is important to me because:

How will I *conceptualize*, model, or theorize about my findings?

How might this research project contribute to the advancement of the knowledge base of this subject matter in the scholarly discipline in which I am working?

Does this research overlap or match the interests of my peers, my research supervisors, or other persons that I might interact with during the course of the research?

If "No" to the above question, am I prepared to work fairly independently?

Persons who might help me or serve as resources as I conduct this research project include the following:

Of course, because each of us has particular limitations, no one can be *fully* prepared for all aspects of a research project. We can, however, aim to increase our preparedness in as many ways as possible. An additional way to optimize preparedness is to organize an *integral research team*, composed of several researchers with varied strengths and limitations. As they work together—in the planning, conducting, and reporting of a collaborative research project—the limitations of the various group members might cancel one another and the strengths amplify each other, allowing the team to approach and complete the project with greatly enhanced adequateness.

Most Suitable Research Participants

We no longer call the persons who take part in our studies "*subjects*." The term we use most frequently is research *participants*. In some research approaches, the participants are called "*coresearchers*" (to indicate better their important role in the research project). In survey research, they may be called "*respondents*"; in observational or ethnographic research, they may be called "*informants*."

Participants are selected according to the general aims of a study and according to certain inclusion and exclusion criteria. If the aim

Subjects = participants = coresearchers
ethnographic = informants =
Survey = respondents

Idiographic

of a study is to learn things that might be safely generalized to the population at large, then the participants of one's sample should be selected *randomly* from the population (or with some restrictions on the proportions of various types of participants, if one is creating a *stratified random sample*). This sort of study is called a *nomothetic* *Nomothetic* (literally, *law-making*) study; its goal is the discovery of general laws. Quantitative methods typically are used in such nomothetic studies.

However, there are other studies in which one simply wishes to learn whether certain phenomena or experiences exist, to learn more about how they might have occurred in specific individuals or circumstances, and to describe those phenomena or experiences accurately and fully. This sort of study is called an *idiographic* (literally, *writing* *Idiographic* *one's own* or *one's own writing*) study—one that focuses on particular individuals. There is no wish to generalize what is found to an entire population. Qualitative methods typically are used in idiographic studies. In such studies, *purposive sampling*, rather than random sampling, is used. One deliberately seeks out persons who have had a particular kind of experience. The aim of an idiographic study is to increase the researcher's understanding of a particular experience of interest. The studied experience may occur in very few persons, or in several, many, or all persons. The extent and distribution of the experience usually is not of interest in an idiographic study. If those issues are of interest, the researcher would conduct a nomothetic study instead.

Some researchers, especially those in the so-called natural sciences, do not recognize the value or even the possibility of studies that are not nomothetic in their aim. To them, all research should focus on the discovery of general laws—principles that apply to everyone, not simply to a subset of individuals. For example, a biologist I once knew used to criticize and refuse to accept the findings of some of my own research studies because, he argued, "not everyone can do these things [i.e., the phenomena explored in these studies]."

This calls to mind a well-known statement of philosopher/psychologist William James:

> If I may employ the language of the professional logic-shop, a universal proposition can be made untrue by a particular instance. If you wish to upset the law that all crows are black, you must not seek to show that no crows are; it is enough if you prove one single crow to be white. (James 1956, 319)

Just as it takes only one counterinstance to disprove a general law, it is not necessary to demonstrate that a given experience occurs in all,

purposive sampling

many, or even several persons in order to make a case for the existence and importance of that experience: even a single instance will do.

In purposive sampling, the researcher can approach persons already known to have had the experience being researched, advertise for persons who have had that experience, and ask others to nominate persons that they know to have had the experience. Word-of-mouth participant solicitation and the snowball technique, in which finding one appropriate participant leads to finding still others, can be used effectively.

Generally, and for both ethical and methodological reasons, it is best to conduct research with persons who do not know the researcher well. The ethical aspect is that one should avoid dual relationships: One should not conduct research with persons with whom one has another current professional relationship—with a person who is a client or employee. Also, it may be difficult for someone who is close to the researcher to participate in a study in a truly voluntary manner or to truly feel that she or he can withdraw from the study at any time (both of those requirements are essential aspects of informed consent). The methodological aspect is that someone who knows the researcher well might provide information, during the study, that fits what the participant knows or guesses about the researcher's likely views about the topic, rather than providing accurate, unbiased information about his or her own experience.

relation of researcher

organic inquiry

The above being said, a case can be made for working with persons who are well known to the researcher. Such close persons may be more able to disclose meaningful information about the studied experience, especially if a sensitive topic is involved. Additionally, rapport already will have been established with the participant, and this might facilitate the exchange of the most useful information during the study. Working with close persons is most common in researchers using the *organic inquiry* approach (described in the next chapter).

close persons to researcher

We recommend that individual researchers carefully consider the pros and cons of working with persons with whom they have close relationships, and make their decisions based on the nature of the relationship, the nature of what is being studied, and the particular persons and circumstances involved.

Participants closeness to study

In addition to his or her closeness to the researcher, the participant's closeness to the investigated topic also should be considered. Everything mentioned above, regarding the researcher's "Goldilock's Region" also applies to the participant. Participants should be selected so that their participation in the study will fall within their comfort zones. The energies and attention of a participant who is too embroiled in the topic might interfere with his or her ability to sufficiently reflect on and report on the experience or issue being studied. Having already reached some degree of closure with the topic also will allow the participant to be able to retrospect, reflect on, and describe a greater extent of an experience (especially one that may have unfolded gradually over time) than would be possible for someone who is just beginning or is in the midst of an intense experience.

In soliciting participation, and in interacting with selected participants during the actual study, the integral inquirer pays special attention to the manner of communicating with these persons. Ads, letters, flyers, other solicitation materials, consent forms, and other written materials are prepared carefully, using language that will be understandable and meaningful to a wide range of participants. In personal communications, the researcher can be attentive to clues as to the background and interests of individual participants, so as to be able to speak to them in ways that they are most likely to understand and appreciate. To detect such clues and to be guided by appropriate, and sometimes subtle, feedback from participants, the researcher uses conversational, intentional, and attentional skills more fully and in more nuanced ways than is typical in conventional research. Later sections of this book will help the integral inquirer identify and further develop these skills.

Experiential Exercise: Alternative Ways of Finding and Communicating With Participants

Choose an experience that you would like to explore more deeply, and imagine a research design that would allow you to study that experience carefully.

What is the experience?

Which aspects of the experience do you most wish to learn more about?

How would you go about finding research participants for your study?

How could you design flyers or other communications for potential participants in order to help them know whether they would be appropriate participants for this study?

Which sorts of questions might you use for screening potential participants to determine whether they might be included in, or excluded from, this study?

How would you go about determining the best ways of communicating with and interacting with your participants during the actual study?

In addressing these questions, consider explicit verbal communications as well as more subtle, nonverbal ways of attending to and communicating with your potential and actual participants.

Multipurpose Research Sessions

What happens during a research session is one of the instances in which the integral (i.e., inclusive and integrated) nature of the present research approach is most evident. Usually, research, practical work with clients, and the researcher's own personal and psycho-spiritual growth and development are considered quite distinct and are deliber-ately kept separate in practice. To the integral inquirer, this separative

Not Separate of integral [handwritten annotation]

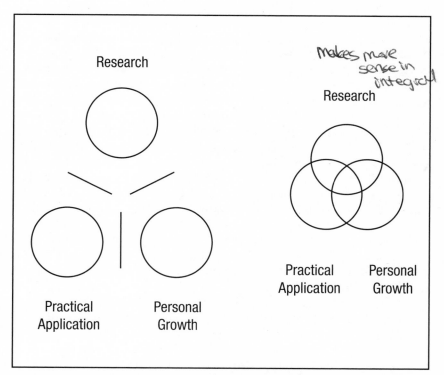

Makes more sense in integral [handwritten annotation]

Figure 2.1. Separative versus integrative approaches to areas of human concerns.

approach does not make sense. Not only does it encourage artificial distinctions, but it also fails to recognize the similarities of many of the processes present in these three areas of human concern. In contrast to a separate approach, integral inquiry highlights and emphasizes the common, overlapping features of these areas.

Similar processes occur naturally in research, in practical work (in therapeutic, counseling, guidance, educational, nursing, and training sessions), in everyday life, and in pursuing one's own psychological development and one's spiritual path.

Engaging in disciplined inquiry

These processes include being informed not only by intellectual concerns but also by feelings and intuitive considerations, being mindful, making careful observations, exercising discernment, noting patterns, attempting to identify the possible sources of things, attempting to do these things without too much attachment, bias, or prejudice—and doing this so that we and others may benefit from what is learned. All of this is engaging in disciplined inquiry. In *research*, we go about this more carefully and more formally. The African-American folklorist and writer, Zora Neale Hurston, put this nicely: "Research is formalized curiosity. It is poking and prying with a purpose" (Hurston 1996, 143).

If one's approach is prepared carefully and is sufficiently inclusive, a research session can serve multiple purposes—simultaneously providing opportunities for knowledge gain for the discipline, clinical and educational benefits for the research participants, and psycho-spiritual growth and the possibility of transformative change for the researcher.

Typically, the goal of research is considered to be the acquisition of new knowledge or information that benefits, primarily, one's professional field of inquiry. In integral inquiry, this goal of information continues to be present, but it is supplemented by additional goals of assimilation, integration, and transformation—for all concerned.

goal of integral inquiry

It is too much to expect a narrowly or artificially addressed topic or assessment to involve oneself, one's research participants, or one's audience (unless the latter is quite specialized) in a personally meaningful way. This, of course, accounts for the frequent dim views of laboratory research, experimentation, and exact but, too often, insufficiently relevant operational definitions and assessment inventories. Judiciously selecting a topic that is very meaningful to one's likely participants—and this usually involves choosing a topic of great relevance, heart, and meaning to the investigator as well—can allow the participants to revisit, examine, and integrate important areas, concerns, and issues of their lives. A research session, in other words, may become an opportunity for practical application—a clinical or educational opportunity. This is especially likely to happen if *qualitative* research methods are used, because these allow for greater self-searching, self-expression, and self-work on the part of the research participants.

Researchers such as Pennebaker (1995) and Wickramasekera (1989) have documented the health and well-being benefits to research participants of disclosing and assimilating meaningful experiences—especially experiences that previously had not been shared with others (as is often the case with profound transpersonal, spiritual, or exceptional experiences). As the investigator works, qualitatively, with these same important issues and topics, she or he may learn something new or resonate to something familiar, which, in turn, can provide occasions for self-transformation. If the research findings are presented to audiences in a sufficiently rich and particularized manner, the audience, too, may experience transformation. Thus, the typical boundaries among research, practical (especially, clinical) applications, and psycho-spiritual growth and development melt away during rich qualitative studies of meaningful topics. The goals of these typically separated areas become naturally interconnected and simultaneously satisfied.

Choosing a personally meaningful and important topic—which is virtually guaranteed, if one is addressing transpersonal and spiritual issues and exceptional human experiences—helps assure that one's findings will have applicability to others (will generalize well) and will be of use to others (will have pragmatic validity). Addressing large and significant issues assures that these apply to many persons. This allows even studies with relatively small sample sizes to be efficient and profitable for all concerned.

The Researcher's Sources of Inspiration and Information

It has been observed that researchers often study their own issues. Topics and areas that are either problematical or of great interest in their personal lives tend to find their ways into their research projects. Researchers vary in their degree of awareness of this process. Some acknowledge this and discuss the connections in their writings. Others deny any such connections. For still others, this process may not apply at all.

Among qualitative researchers, these life-issue–research-issue correspondences are very prominent. This is quite fitting. Because qualitative approaches focus on descriptions of human experiences, it is advantageous for researchers to have had those experiences themselves. This allows researchers to add first person appreciations to the usual third person findings, greatly extending and deepening their understanding of the experiences being studied.

So, one of the major sources of inspiration and information for a research study of a particular experience will be the researcher's own history of identical or similar experiences. These experiences may force themselves upon the researcher's awareness, compelling the researcher to design a study to explore these further—perhaps to learn more about how others have had and dealt with similar experiences. In the absence of this forceful arising, the researcher can reflect on the most meaningful experiences of the past, with the aim of discovering which of these might be most worthy of formal study.

About Relevant Literature Reviews

To supplement personal, experiential knowledge, the researcher can be inspired and informed by a great variety of other sources. The most obvious, of course, is the extant literature in the area of one's professional discipline that deals most directly with the chosen topic. However, the integral inquirer is not content with such a limited approach but will delve not only into such local resources but also widely and deeply into treatments of the topic in a variety of sources: the literatures of the natural sciences, psychology, sociology, anthropology, the social sciences and human sciences generally, philosophy, literature, the arts, and the various spiritual and wisdom and folk traditions. The integral inquirer will not hesitate to explore personal and anecdotal evidence bearing on the topic, and will welcome inputs that may arise from transpersonal sources, including materials from special dreams, unusual states of consciousness, and spiritual practices.

In describing the fruits of these explorations, in one's written literature review, a useful approach is to review first the most essential information from various areas briefly, in order to provide an overview and contextualization of the present work, but then quickly focus on only the most relevant, salient areas for a deeper and more detailed presentation. It also is useful to consider one's initial literature review to be a *provisional* one, covering what the researcher thinks and feels is relevant at the beginning of the study. As the study progresses, and especially after data have been collected and treated, the researcher is likely to realize that additional literatures are relevant to the final interpretation and reporting of the findings. All good research projects yield surprises—information not previously anticipated. After all, this is what discovery is all about. The unexpected, surprising findings will suggest new literatures to be explored in a very focused manner.

This can be added to the material presented in the earlier, provisional literature review or, more honestly, the new information can be presented in the discussion section of the research report.

In planning and presenting literature reviews of what is known about the research topic, there is a temptation to restrict attention to a too-limited time window. This seems to be but another aspect of a pervasive syndrome of overvaluing the latest new thing. Such time-limited literature reviews suggest that knowledge has an expiration date—that findings and thoughts older than five years or so can be discounted as no longer valid or applicable. Although progress undoubtedly has been made in many areas (chiefly in terms of technology), there are many instances in which early thinking and work rival, and sometimes even surpass, more recent efforts. It seems unwise to ignore or disdain important findings merely because they were published some time ago. In some cases, modern workers may not even be aware of the existence of relevant early work. Such ignorance is an insult to the practice of good scholarship.

We could delve more deeply into older works. In the grocery business, it is a common practice to "rotate one's stock"—making older materials more accessible so that they have a chance of being purchased and used, rather than languishing out of reach. We tend to reverse this practice in our scholarly and empirical work—emphasizing the very latest reports, methods, and data, and ignoring older thoughts and findings as though they have passed their expiration date. One consequence of a lack of awareness or valuing of earlier thoughts, findings, and writings is a continuing inadvertent reinvention of the wheel—and with, perhaps, less enduring and less effective materials—by current researchers. How wise is this practice?

It is generally assumed that the growth curve for the accumulation of knowledge is *exponential*—i.e., early increments in knowledge are relatively small, but later become larger and larger (see Figure 2.2). This is undoubtedly true in cases involving technology and in knowledge involving phenomena that depend upon recent technology for their detection and study (studies of the very small, very large, and very fast in physics, astrophysics, biology, and medicine). However, there are two other kinds of growth curves that may characterize knowledge accumulation in other areas. One of these is a *linear* curve, in which the increasing growth of knowledge over time is fairly consistent, neither speeding up nor slowing down in later periods, compared with earlier periods. Another is a *logarithmic* curve, in which knowledge growth is very rapid in its early phases, quickly reaching a high point, and then growing only very slowly thereafter.

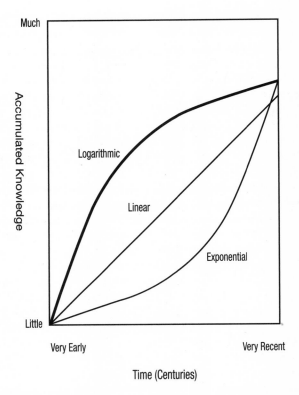

Figure 2.2. Three possible time courses for the accumulation of knowledge.

It may well be that the growth curve for the most important and meaningful knowledge within psychology and philosophy is logarithmic in nature—largely acquired very early and incremented only slightly thereafter.

This is because the subject matter in these disciplines—our own behaviors, thoughts, feelings, and images—were readily available for our observation and conceptualization at very early stages of our development. These processes and observations were parts of everyday life, even during our very earliest days as a species and as individuals. (The same conclusion may also be true for knowledge gains involving naked-eye astronomy and for observations of the natural world of plants and animals—in these cases, the subject matter was generally available and accessible to all at very early dates.) This perspective on knowledge accumulation is consistent with the well-known comment of philosopher Alfred North Whitehead (1929) that "the safest general characterization of the European philosophical tradition is that it consists of a series of footnotes to Plato" (63). I mention these considerations to indicate that we need not neglect or devalue early knowledge claims simply because they are old or even ancient.

An additional value of exploring and citing very early literature is that finding recent ideas in these very early sources can help foster an attitude of *humility*. This helps one recognize, more fully, that one is not as original and clever as one otherwise might think; that certain ideas were present for others, even long ago, and that one is often simply rediscovering what has gone before.

Variety of Evidential Sources

The integral researcher values evidence from a variety of sources. The holistic/integral research skills treated later in this book allow the researcher to access information gained through the use of alternative forms of knowing, many of which typically are ignored or downplayed in conventional research.

In the researcher's review of relevant information, there is a place for knowledge gained through personal experiences of the researcher and of others. A useful way of presenting such informa-tion in a literature review is to create a special section that could be labeled "Personal and Anecdotal Evidence." The researcher's own experiences of the researched topic, along with relevant information and stories of others, could be presented in this section. Including these in a separate section accomplishes two goals simultaneously: It indicates that the researcher is able to discriminate this kind of less formally collected information from other kinds of information, and it also indicates that such information is indeed *evidence*—albeit of a different sort.

Mentioning the nature of evidence reminds me of an interaction I had many years ago with a physicist. He was questioning some of my research findings because of the nature of the evidence. "Suppose one varies certain things at one location and notes orderly changes in a person's verbal or written or drawn responses in another location; would that be doing science?" I asked. "No," he replied. Then I asked, "what if one varies the very same things at one location and notes orderly changes in the physical tracings or outputs of recording instru-ments at that other location; would that be doing science?" "Yes," he replied. To me, this physicist's responses revealed a misunderstanding of the nature of scientific inquiry. To him, science was related to the *physical nature of dependent variables,* rather than to a *process of inquiry.* The integral inquirer recognizes that authentic scientific inquiry can appropriately address a very wide range of assessed phenomena.

Experiential Exercise: Relevant Inspiration, Information, and Personal Experience

Think of an experience that you would like to explore more fully and deeply:

I am interested in the experience of _____

_____

What are some of the kinds of things you most wish to learn about that experience?

Which of your own personal experiences might you remember, attempt to relive, and consider more deeply, in order to learn more about the experience you are interested in?

If you have not had exactly the experience you wish to study, have you had *similar* experiences? What are those experiences, and what might they have in common—with the experience of interest as well as with each other?

Are there other aspects or issues in your personal life that might have a bearing on this kind of experience or on a research project that you might design to study this kind of experience?

Have other persons shared with you information, anecdotes, or stories about their own experiences that were identical or similar to the experience of interest?

What are some other sources of inspiration and information you might consult in order to learn more about this kind of experience?

Consider how you might use the information you provided above in planning, carrying out, and reported the findings of a research project devoted to an exploration of the experience of interest.

Major Types of Research Questions
and Fitting Approaches and Methods

General Considerations

All scholarly, scientific, and disciplined inquiries are devoted to seeking answers to important questions. Some even have remarked that the nature of one's questions is more important than the answers one obtains. In quantitative and qualitative research, there are both commonalities and differences in the ways questions are framed and addressed. In quantitative research, one frames *hypotheses*. These are really guesses about how nature will answer the researcher's questions. In a way, they are tests of the researcher's knowledge and cleverness about how things work. One frames an hypothesis and then goes about designing a study—usually an experiment—whose results will either falsify or confirm that hypothesis. Technically, the results of a study serve to either falsify the hypothesis or fail to falsify the hypothesis. The latter case usually is described as "confirmation of the hypothesis," but this is not quite accurate. Hypotheses involve specific kinds of outcomes of studies; they are narrow and focused in scope. The quantitative research enterprise is *proof-orientated* in that the researcher seeks to *test* hypotheses, to determine which ones are accurate and of value and which are not. In qualitative inquiry, one frames *research questions*, rather than hypotheses. Research questions are more open-ended than hypotheses. They ask about what might be the case, rather than make predictions that a specific outcome or answer might be the case. In this sense, the research question approach is *descriptive* rather than proof-orientated in nature. An example of an hypothesis would be "persons who have had near-death experiences tend to have reduced fears of death." An example of a research question would be "what are the attitudes toward death of persons who have had near-death experiences?" Note that in the first case, one makes a prediction or guess that a certain outcome will be present, whereas in the second case, one simply asks which outcomes might be present.

Although quantitative and qualitative approaches can be distinguished on the basis of their emphases on hypotheses or questions, it is important to recognize their many overlapping features. One of these features is the iterative, back-and-forth nature of the research process. In quantitative hypothesis testing, initial observations (findings) lead to the development of certain conceptualizations (theories). From those theories, predictions are made about new findings. The new findings may be consistent with the predictions, in which case the theory is not disconfirmed or abandoned; or inconsistent with the predictions, in which case that aspect of the theory is disconfirmed and is either abandoned or changed. There is an ongoing dance between theory (understanding) and observations (findings), with each informing the other.

Although there are important differences, the essential nature of the qualitative *grounded theory* approach (Glaser and Strauss 1967; Strauss and Corbin 1990) is very similar to what has just been described. In this approach, there is an ongoing growth of understanding of a topic through the continuing interaction of what is found during interviews or other forms of data collection (the *grounding* of the approach in descriptive, empirical findings) and the developing conceptualization of what those findings might mean (the *theory* aspect of the approach). This dialogical (mutually exchanging and interacting) process also is seen in the so-called *hermeneutic circle* in various forms of hermeneutic inquiry—the back-and-forth movement in which one gains increased understanding of the meaning of a text by studying its individual parts in relation to the whole, and the whole in relation to its parts (Ormiston and Schrift 1990; Packer and Addison 1989). Here, the text need not be a written document, but also could be an experience or some other topic or circumstance that one seeks to interpret.

The movement between the parts and the whole *and* dialogic engagement with data are important components in Rosemarie Anderson's intuitive inquiry approach (see Chapter 1), in which one confronts collected data through one's initial understandings (or *lenses*, analogous to one's beginning conceptualization or theory), but then allows those lenses to be eliminated, incremented, transformed, or refined as required by the nature of the newly collected data.

In hermeneutics and intuitive inquiry the researcher explicitly states and actively utilizes his or her highly personalized understandings in the research process. The individual nature, background, and experiences of the interpreter are of utmost importance in these, and in related, approaches. While a discussion of the nature of interpretation among the many approaches to qualitative research now available goes beyond the purposes of this book, qualitative approaches—such as phenomenological psychology, grounded theory, narrative research, and organic inquiry—tend to prefer interpretation close to the words and expressions in the texts studied. However, even among these methods, in actual studies, many differences are found in interpretive levels—some studies reporting only quoted excerpts from the texts studied, others relying on psychological concepts and theory for interpretation, and every possibility between these two alternatives.

Still another area of overlap of quantitative and qualitative approaches is that neither of these is pure; rather, each contains at least some features of the other. For example, many different qualities (i.e., *kinds* of things) are part of and can be examined in quantitative studies and findings; and the themes that emerge in many qualitative studies can be quantified by noting and reporting their differing *densities* or degrees of presence in participant reports (i.e., *amounts* of things). Quantity and quality each are present, to some degree, in the other, and each can shade into or blend into the other, not unlike the complementary black and white colors of the Chinese *yin-yang* symbol (see Figure 2.3). Perhaps not coincidentally, this symbol also is suggestive of the hermeneutic circle described earlier.

neither is pure

Specific Types of Research Questions

Table 2.1 summarizes four major types of research questions that one can ask about any given experience or research topic, what each type of question can reveal about the studied experience or phenomenon, and which research methods or approaches best serve each type of question. The four types of questions are designed to illuminate respectively the nature of an experience itself; how that experience might be understood, interpreted, or explained; the accompaniments of the experience; and the aftereffects of the experience. These aspects of experience, conceptualization, process, and fruits closely correspond respectively to the four well-known goals of science and of conventional research: to describe, explain, predict, and control aspects of what one is studying.

4 types of ?s

Figure 2.3. The *yin-yang* symbol suggestive of complementarity.

Table 2.1. Four Types of Research Questions and Research Approaches Serving These

Qualitative			Quantitative
Idiographic			Nomothetic
Describe	Explain	Predict	Control
Experience	Conceptualization	Process	Fruits
What is the experience of x? How is x perceived by the participant?	How can we conceptualize x? What are useful explanations / interpretations of x? How have those interpretations changed, historically?	How does x unfold as a process? What are the concomitants of x? What sets the stage for the occurrence of x? What facilitates x? What inhibits x?	What are the outcomes, consequences, fruits of x? How might x itself be a fruit or outcome of another experience of event?
	Qualitative Approaches / Quantitative Approaches		
Phenomenological Experiential Heuristic Narrative Life Stories Case Studies Feminist approaches Organic inquiry Intuitive inquiry Ethnography* Autoethnography*	Theoretical Historical Grounded theory Textual analysis Discourse analysis Hermeneutical	Correlational Causal-comparative Field studies* Ethnography* Autoethnography*	Experimental Quasi-experimental Single-subject Action research*

*These asterisked approaches are largely qualitative in nature. Their placements in this table indicate that they might serve the description of experiences (Column 1) but also are relevant to observations of processes and their unfolding and outcomes (Columns 3 and 4).

The Nature of Experiences

The first question type, and the one typically of most interest to qualitative researchers, addresses the nature of an experience itself, focusing on describing the experience deeply, in terms of its subjective appreciation by the research participant. In asking this type of question, the integral inquirer seeks to elicit from the participant, then to present to the audience of one's research report a very rich, "thick," inclusive description of a particular experience. Ideally, the description will include as many of its facets as possible: its cognitive, feeling, imaginal, and bodily aspects. *Experience has two meanings*

Experience has two meanings. The first is relatively discrete, time-limited, and subjective; it is a momentary appreciation or apprehension, by the experiencer, of *what it is like, internally, during a particular moment or circumstance.* Some philosophers might call these *"qualia"*; these are particular forms of conscious awareness. Clear examples are the experiences of pain, discomfort, anxiety, frustration, unreality, joy, relaxation, wonder, awe, and equanimity. Somewhat more complex examples include experiences such as having compassion for someone; feeling resonance with a client; feeling a profound connection with nature; experiencing deep gratitude; experiencing genuine forgiveness; feeling unconditionally loved; feeling that one is not being understood; feeling "heard" and understood; "coming home" when first encountering a person, place, or situation; a déjà vu experience; and encountering a divine presence during a near-death experience.

Experience also has a second meaning, referring to a more complex, *longer-term set of inner events*. Examples of this more enduring form of experience include what it might be like to be an only child, to be the parent of a child with autism, to be left-handed in a right-handed world, to be an older person returning to college or graduate school, to have gradually changed or transformed one's worldview, to have lived a charmed life, to live with a parent who has an Alzheimer's condition, to have shifted to a simpler and more authentic way of living, to be shy, to be living with intractable pain.

The research approaches or methods listed in the table's first column are especially well suited to address both of these types of experience. At the conclusion of a study using one of these approaches, the researcher is able to present rich and full descriptions of the studied experience in the forms of concise narratives, portraits, or depictions or sets of emerging themes. The researcher will present both common and unique (less common) aspects of the experience, provide indications of the degree of presence or density of the various aspects, and present good examples, in the participants' own words, of those aspects.

The emphasis, here, is on providing rich descriptions of participants' self-perceived, self-reported raw and uninterpreted subjective experiences. Therefore, research approaches that emphasize explanations or interpretations of these experiences, or their accompaniments or outcomes—assessed in an objective, from-the-outside, third person manner—are not as applicable to this goal. An important qualification is needed here. It is quite possible that at least some participants might include their own experiences, perceptions, thoughts, and feelings about accompaniments and outcomes of a certain experience or kind of experience. It seems unwise to exclude such first-person information from the descriptive participant accounts, even though that information might include views of how an experience seems related to other experiences or events. Stated in another way, interpretations, understandings, and explanations of experiences are themselves experiences, albeit of a somewhat different sort; there is no need to exclude such experiences merely because they are more cognitive than others. (Or, stated in still another way, the head is part of the body, and thoughts can be important aspects of experiences!) The researcher can include these kinds of personal views of participants, indicating that these are *self-perceived* accompaniments, outcomes, and interpretations.

Experiential Exercise: Considerations for an Experience-based Question

Consult Table 2.1 in carrying out this exercise.

Imagine that you are about to design a research project with the aim of richly describing a particular experience.

Which experience would you select?

What are your personal connections with that experience?

If you have had an identical experience, spend some time recalling that experience, and provide as rich and complete an account of the nature of that experience as possible.

How would you frame a research question that can provide you with a rich and inclusive description of that experience?

Which research approach would you select as most appropriate for yielding a useful description of that experience?

Which research approaches seem least appropriate to this aim?

The following is offered as an example of an experience-based research study, "Experiencing tears of wonder-joy: Seeing with the heart's eye" (Braud 2001a):

> In this report, the researcher presented experiences of "wonder-joy tears," as described by the researcher himself and by twelve additional research participants. Participants described their felt sense of the experience, along with their own views of the triggers, meanings, interpretations, and life impacts of the experience. Wonder-joy tears are not tears of pain, sadness, or sorrow. Rather, they are accompanied by feelings of wonder, joy, profound gratitude, awe, yearning, poignancy, intensity, love, and compassion. They are an opening up of the heart to the persons or profound circumstances being witnessed. These tears, with their accompanying chills and special feelings, seem to be the body's way of indicating a profound confrontation with the True, the Good, and the Beautiful—an indication of directly seeing with the eye of the heart, soul, and spirit. Additionally, they can indicate moments of profound insights. The researcher discussed the potential guiding and transformational aspects of these experiences.

> The participants were unselected students in a small research group and colleagues selected purposely on the basis of their likelihood of having had such experiences. The raw data consisted of written responses to a semi-structured questionnaire. These responses were treated by qualitative thematic content analysis. First, major themes were identified by the researcher working alone and by each respondent working alone. Next, the themes and findings were discussed and developed further in group meetings. The researcher integrated and summarized the findings, prepared them in tabular formats, returned them to the participants for their verification and approval (*member*

checks), then reorganized the findings for presentation in the article. The qualitative research methods used in this inquiry shared features of phenomenological (Valle, 1998), heuristic (Moustakas 1990), experiential (Barrell, Aanstoos, Richards, and Arons 1987), intuitive (see Chapter 1), and integral (this chapter) research approaches. The methods also relied on additional assumptions and principles of the various transpersonal research methods presented in detail in Braud and Anderson (1998).

Conceptualization of Experiences and History of Their Understandings

The second set of questions addresses attempts to conceptualize, interpret, and explain an experience, and how such attempts have occurred and changed through history. These questions address the realm of theory, and those interested in this approach attempt to discover underlying or overarching principles or mechanisms through which experiences come about or are manifestations. Researchers interested in this approach are not content to simply describe experiences or other occurrences, but seek to learn more about *why* and *how* such experiences occur. The approach might be called *description-plus*. The phenomena to be described must, of course, first be specified and described, but then the researcher goes the extra step of interpreting and seeking to understand why the experience might take the form that it assumes, why it might emerge in certain ways—in other words, what might account for its nature, and perhaps its functions.

The research approaches listed in the second column are most closely aligned with this conceptualization aim. However, approaches listed in other columns might contribute to theoretical understanding, as well, through the relevant additional information they might provide.

Experiential Exercise: Considerations for a Conceptualization-based Question

Consult Table 2.1 in carrying out this exercise.

Imagine that you are about to design a research project in which you intend to conceptualize, explain, interpret, or provide a theoretical account of a particular experience.

Which experience would you select?

What are your personal connections with that experience?

What are your own thoughts about what might underlie that experience?

How would you frame a research question that could help you conceptualize and increase our theoretical understanding of that experience?

Which research approach would you select as most appropriate for yielding a useful conceptualization, interpretation, or explanation of the experience?

Which research approaches seem least appropriate to this aim?

Which sorts of underlying or overarching principles or processes might you investigate?

The following description of a recently completed dissertation project can serve as an example of a conceptual, theory-based research study, "A transpersonal approach to somatic psychodiagnostics of personality: A contribution towards its development, dis-ordering tendencies, and embodied transcendence" (Bento 2006):

> The researcher explored how the body's movement in spatial orientation may play an influential role in the dis-ordering tendencies of personality. The researcher theorized that stimulation of the motor/sensory system in movements through various spatial planes substantially impacts perceptions of self, others, and the world. These perceptions can form the basis of the evolving personality, viewed as a state of consciousness on a continuum of adaptations to self, others, and the world, rather than a set of fixed traits. Research findings were consistent with the researcher's theoretical conceptualization in that fixations in movement in three spatial planes correlated with fixations in personality.

> In conducting the research, a causal-comparative approach was used to determine possible relations between twelve fixated spatial orientations and twelve clinically recognized personality disorders. A total of seventy participants were involved in the research. Each participant had an opportunity to experience all twelve spatial/movement exercises as both a participant and an observer. The researcher

recorded data from both the participant's experience and the observer's experience in order to include both subjective and objective perspectives. At the conclusion of each movement exercise, each participant completed a descriptive survey—answering questions about various cognitive, emotional, and behavioral reactions and changes he or she experienced during the movement explorations, and about possible ways of experiencing self, others, and the world if the participant were to be locked into one of the twelve spatial fixations of movement. Other instruments were used to assess characteristics associated with twelve personality disorders. Meaningful relationships were found between experiences associated with the twelve spatial/ movement exercises and characteristics of the twelve personality disorders.

Unfolding, Facilitating and Inhibiting Factors, and Accompaniments

The third set of questions addresses issues involving the process and dynamics of an experience. How does the experience unfold and manifest itself as a process? What might set the stage for the occurrence of the experience? Which factors tend to foster or to inhibit the experience? What are the accompaniments of the experience? These sorts of questions aim to illuminate what might be called the *atmosphere* of the experience.

Research approaches that address interrelationships are most appropriate for exploring this third set of questions. Interrelationships can be studied *quantitatively* by means of *correlational* and *causal-comparative* studies. Correlational studies use well-established statistical methods to formally determine the directions and degrees of relationships between or among two or more variables. In such an approach, quantifiable aspects of the studied experience (measures of its frequency of occurrence or strength or degree of presence) can be correlated with other variables of interest. For example, is the tendency for an individual to have the studied experience related to standardized measures of the physical and psychological health and well-being of that individual? Do persons who have many experiences of this type tend to exhibit increased tendencies toward openness and acceptance toward a variety of "others" (other people; other cultures; other views; other beliefs; other ways of knowing, being, or doing)?

In a causal-comparative study, group statistical methods are used to determine whether groups already known to differ in some way also might differ in some other ways. For example, do two groups of participants already known to be "high" or "low" in terms of the likelihood or strength of a certain experience, X, also differ in their tendencies to be compassionate toward others? Do members of different identified cultures tend to differ in their likelihood of having experience X?

In the qualitative domain, a researcher or research team might make observations of which sorts of factors are related to an experience of interest, using field study and ethnographic methods. One could observe, in oneself—as a member of a particular culture—which factors tend to be related to an experience of interest, using an auto-ethnographic approach.

Even using some of the more descriptive research approaches (listed in the table's first column and covered above), a researcher can study which factors are *perceived by the participants* as going together, as being importantly interrelated. Through reflection and retrospection, participants may be able to indicate which factors seemed most and least supportive of the emergence of a certain experience. Persons in whom an experience has developed over time can give useful accounts of how that experience dynamically unfolded, and which things seemed to help or hinder its development. Participants can describe which sorts of things went along with their experience of X—i.e., they can provide useful accounts of the experience's accompaniments (concomitants, correlates).

Atmosphere

In short, the atmosphere that preceded or accompanied an experience can be determined through the use of standardized observations or assessments, carried out by the researcher in an objective, third-person manner (as in the approaches listed in the table's third column), but also can be learned through the descriptive, first-person participant reports of their own self-perceived and self-determined views of that atmosphere (as in the approaches listed in the table's first column).

A caveat is in order, regarding the risky nature of reaching causal conclusions on the basis of correlational and causal-comparative studies. The findings from such studies do not justify causal claims or, especially, *directional* causal claims. From the results of such studies, we can know that associations or relationships exist, but we cannot know with any degree of certainty whether one of the elements in the relationship causes the other element. If a consistent relationship is found between factors A and B, it is possible that A "causes" B, but it also is possible that B "causes" A, or that both A and B are "caused" by some still undetected factor C, or that A and B simply happened to co-arise, to simultaneously emerge as parts of some larger, more inclusive process. As a specific example of these issues, suppose a strong statistical relationship is found between moderate intake of red wine and certain indications of improved health. It may be the case that some ingredients of the wine might indeed foster improved health. However, it might be the case that healthier persons have certain temperamental, personality, or acquired characteristics that lead them to drink moderate amounts of red wine. It may be the case that some other factor causes both the tendency toward moderate wine drinking and the tendency toward better health. It may be the case that moderate wine drinking and good health happen to co-arise, as parts of some more general systemic pattern. It is unwise to prejudge which of these alternatives actually is the case. Instead, a series of carefully designed additional studies can be designed to test each of these alternative possibilities. Only when these more thorough examinations have been completed will it be possible to reach a conclusion with increased confidence. A similar warning applies to conclusions based upon participants' reports of self-perceived relationships.

Experiential Exercise: Considerations for Process-based Questions

Consult Table 2.1 in carrying out this exercise.

Imagine that you are about to design a research project to explore a process-related question about a particular experience.

Which experience would you select?

What are your personal connections with that experience?

In your own case, what seems to have set the stage for the emerging of the experience? Did there seem to be triggers or catalysts for the experience?

In your own case, how did the experience seem to unfold through time? How might it have developed over time?

In your own case, did you notice whether certain other things tended to go along with your experience? When you had the experience, what other things might have increased or decreased?

In your own case, what seemed to make the experience more likely? What seemed to make it less likely?

How would you frame a research question that could help you learn how the experience might have unfolded or manifested itself over time?

Which sorts of questions would you ask in order to learn about factors that might either foster or interfere with that experience?

How might you explore the correlates/accompaniments/concomitants of that experience?

Which research approaches seem most appropriate for exploring the questions you framed above?

Which research approaches seem least appropriate to the aims mentioned above?

Two studies are summarized here as examples of research projects that focused on accompaniments.

The first example is a mixed-methods study with a quantitative, correlational component and qualitative thematic analysis component, "Transpersonal and cross-cultural adaptability factors in White Euopean American men: A descriptive and correlational analysis" (Broenen 2006):

The researcher explored correlations between transpersonal and cross-cultural adaptability factors in a study involving 141 White European American men. In the quantitative portion of the study, participants completed two standardized spirituality assessments and a standardized cross-cultural adaptability assessment. Correlational statistics and multiple regression analysis revealed significant relationships among the psychometric scores, particularly between spirituality and cross-cultural adaptability ($r = .66$). Two subscale pairings accounted for most of this relationship: spiritual qualities of inner resources and unifying interconnectedness correlated strongly with the cross-cultural qualities of emotional resilience and flexibility/openness respectively. Participant age correlated moderately with certain of the assessment measures.

In the study's qualitative portion, participants indicated the factors that most helped or hindered their abilities to relate to people who were different from them. Thematic content analysis identified five categories of response items, each of which further subdivided into helper and hinderer themes. Participants who scored higher on the cross-cultural adaptability measure generally listed more helper items and fewer hinderer items. Five helper themes (acceptance, openness, positive self-regard, connectedness, and empathy) frequently emerged in participant responses and bore strong conceptual overlap with the operationalized definitions of both transpersonal and cross-cultural adaptability constructs.

The second example is a qualitative research project, "Triggers, concomitants, and aftereffects of EHEs: An exploratory study (Brown and White 1997):

The researchers examined written narrative accounts of fifty participants who had described details of their exceptional human experiences (EHEs). These were experiences that fit one of the following five main classifications: mystical/unitive, psychic, unusual death-related, encounter, and enhanced (more common exceptional experiences such as peak experiences, flow experiences, and so on). The accounts also included some indication that the experience had been transformative (qualitatively shifted the participant's lifeview or worldview). A qualitative thematic–content-analysis approach was used to identify themes relevant to the triggers, accompaniments, and aftereffects of these experiences. For present purposes, only information relevant to triggers (as stage-setters) and accompaniments will be presented here.

A total of 189 triggers were identified. The EHEs were most frequently triggered during conditions of meditation and prayer, impasse, surrender, exploration, human interactions, spiritual emergency, the death of another, depression, fatigue, crises in personal relationships, and insight into problems. Some unique triggers involved agony, burnout, physical diagnoses, and sleep.

EHE accompaniments were classified as either physical, physiological, psychological, or spiritual. Of the 89 types of *physical* accompaniments extracted from the core accounts, the most frequently mentioned were substance

seen as illusory, body luminosity of another, luminosity
of the environment, silence, white light, streams of light,
colors, touches, and transparent body. Of 97 identified
physiological accompaniments, the most frequent were energy
influx, weeping, weightlessness, hyperacuity, fatigue, body
luminosity, shape-shifting sensations, tingling, and time loss.
Other physiological concomitants included body experiences
as flaming, glowing, levitating, or transparent; inner light;
involuntary movements; loss of pain; feelings of swirling,
melting, flooding, floating, pulling or being pulled; and
perceived dramatic shifts of body temperature. Of the 83
psychological accompaniments identified, the most frequent
were perceptual and cognitive shifts, amazement, boundaries dropping away, conviction, illumination (aha!), wonder,
connectedness, mental clarity, thinking, imaging, and not
thinking. A total of 86 types of *spiritual* accompaniments
were identified, the most frequent of which were ego surrender; overwhelming wonder, awe, and joy; surprise;
sensing or being a being of light; overwhelming love; sense
of a greater Self; rapture and ecstasy; feeling astounded or
dumbfounded; unconditional love. Other frequently reported
spiritual accompaniments included feelings of truth, simplic-
ity, profundity, gratitude, sacredness; feeling "quickened,"
thrilled; knowing to the core; feeling forgiven or uplifted;
and overwhelming bliss, peace, and surrender.

Outcomes or Fruits of Experiences

The fourth set of questions addresses the aftereffects, outcomes, or
fruits of experiences. These kinds of questions can be framed in two
ways: (a) What are the aftereffects of experience X? or (b) How might
experience X itself be an outcome or aftereffect of some other experience or event? To address these types of questions with confidence,
experimental or quasi-experimental approaches are most satisfactory.
These may take the forms of conventional laboratory experiments,
intervention or outcome studies, or randomized clinical trials. Single-
subject studies (of the types used in Skinnerian/experimental analysis
of behavior studies) and action research also might be applied here.

    In causal-comparative and correlational projects, the studied
experiences and events already have spontaneously occurred; it is as
though nature already has conducted the experiment, and the investigator belatedly examines the results. In an experiment, intervention
trial, or outcome study, the investigator actively and deliberately

applies some variable and notes its effects on some other variable. Such an approach may be used straightforwardly in studying familiar and common experiences. Experiences and events of interest can be treated as either independent or dependent variables, and their influence or presence can be quantified.

However, an integral inquirer is likely to be interested in spiritual, transpersonal, exceptional, or nonordinary experiences. Such experiences tend to occur spontaneously and more often in a context of grace rather than one of effort or deliberate induction. Therefore, conventional quantitative experimental and intervention approaches usually are less appropriate and less feasible for studying these types of experiences. Instead, one can attempt to note various outcomes through observational studies and through qualitative studies of the reflections and retrospections of persons who have had such experiences. Participants can describe the possible aftereffects, life impacts, or work impacts of their profound and meaningful experiences. Alternatively, the researcher can explore whether such experiences themselves might have been outcomes or fruits of some other experiences or events—either through observations or through studying participants' self reports. Participants' self-perceived outcomes of experiences or events can be studied using the experience-relevant approaches listed in the first column of the table and already discussed above. In such studies, it is useful to explore both short-term and longer-term aftereffects, because these might be quite different, especially in instances of experiences that might seem negative at the time of their occurrence and shortly thereafter, but might lead to more positive outcomes later on.

Experiential Exercise: Considerations for Outcome-based Questions

Consult Table 2.1 in carrying out this exercise.

Imagine that you are about to design a research project to explore the possible aftereffects, outcomes, or fruits of a particular experience.

Which experience would you select?

What are your personal connections with that experience?

In your own case, what seem to have been the most important aftereffects or outcomes of that experience? In the short term? In the longer term?

How would you frame a research question that could help you learn about the short-and long-term outcomes or after-effects of such an experience?

Which research approaches seem most appropriate for exploring the question you framed above?

Which research approaches seem least appropriate to the aim mentioned above?

As an example of an outcome study, I have summarized experiments conducted in the increasingly popular area of *positive psychology*.

"Positive emotions broaden the scope of attention and thought-action repertoires" (Fredrickson and Branigan 2005, 313–32):

The researchers conducted two experiments, involving 104 research participants, to test the first author's theory that positive emotions broaden the scope of attention, thought, and action tendencies. In each experiment, participants viewed a film that elicited either amusement, contentment, neutrality, anger, or anxiety. In the first experiment, scope of attention was assessed using a global-local visual processing task. In the second experiment, thought-action repertoires were assessed by simply counting the number of responses a participant made to the statement, "I would like to _____," which could vary from zero to twenty. In the first experiment, positive emotions broadened the scope of attention relative to a neutral state. In the second experiment, positive emotions broadened the thought-action repertoires relative to a neutral state, and negative emotions narrowed the thought-action repertoires relative to the neutral state. Analysis of variance and t-tests were used for comparing and contrasting the scores in the various study conditions.

Blends of Question Types and Approaches

The research project examples described above were chosen to illustrate how they addressed one of the four major sets of research questions. Notice, however, that the projects addressed more than one of these sets. Braud (2001a) focused not only on the nature of the wonder-joy tears experience, but also explored the experience's triggers, accompaniments, and outcomes. Bento's (2006) study was described in order to illustrate its conceptual/theoretical features, but the project was conducted in a causal-comparative manner and also made use of deliberate move-ment/spatial interventions (exercises) that had associated outcomes, and the study involved both quantitative and qualitative aspects. Broenen's (2006) study included not only a quantitative correlational component, but also a qualitative component that examined several process aspects of the cross-cultural adaptability and transpersonal experiences of his participants (factors that most helped or hindered their abilities to relate to people different from themselves). Brown and White (1997) treated not only the accompaniments and triggers but also the nature of the exceptional human experiences and their self-perceived aftereffects (outcomes); they also were able to quantify the relative densities of the various qualitative themes that emerged in their study. The Fredrickson and Branigan (2005) study exemplified an intervention or outcome study, but it was strongly informed by a theory about the functions of positive emotions (see Fredrickson 2001). These five studies had at least some integral features in the sense that they examined a variety of aspects of the experiences of interest and they employed a variety of research approaches and methods appropriate to the study of those different aspects.

Similarly, the integral researcher can consider which of the four major types of questions would address aspects of an experience of greatest interest to the researcher. The researcher might focus on deeply exploring only one of the question types—the single area that is most important. The researcher might prioritize the four questions types and choose to explore only the one or two with the greatest priorities. Still another possibility—and the one that would be most inclusive and hold the greatest possibility of full integration—would be for the researcher to address all four types of questions. The question types might be addressed to different degrees, depending on the researcher's interests and on practical considerations and possible limitations. In the latter instance, the researcher would remain alert to the risks of attempting to explore too many aspects at once and thereby being unable to explore each particular aspect with sufficient thoroughness and in adequate depth.

Regarding Methods: Terminology, Choices, Blends, and Caveats

Researchers differ in their use of various research-related terms. Often, the terms *methods* and *methodologies* are used interchangeably. In my own understanding, and for purposes of this chapter, I take *methodology* to mean the formal study of methods and their associated philosophical assumptions and implications. *Methods* are the actual procedures, techniques, and activities that a researcher uses in gaining knowledge, testing knowledge claims, and communicating newly acquired knowledge to others. Methods are the *tools* than a disciplined inquirer uses in her or his work; examples of these are questionnaires, *Methods* interviews, standardized assessments, statistical analyses, qualitative thematic analyses, and so on. To me, the various inquiry forms that are listed at the bottom Table 2.1 (phenomenological inquiry, heuristic research, case studies, intuitive inquiry, grounded theory, experiments, and so on) seem larger than methods. For these, the term *approaches* seems more appropriate. Approaches are larger, more inclusive, and *Approaches* usually involve sets of methods. In teaching my own research courses, I have likened *methods* to *tools* and *toolboxes* and likened *approaches* to overarching *umbrellas*. Approaches involve rich and interacting sets of features (like the individual ribs of an umbrella). They have distinctive philosophical assumptions and stances, ways of involving (or not involving) the researcher, ways of interacting with participants, and ways of collecting, treating, and communicating data and findings. These specific ways and tools (methods) are treated in separate sections, below.

Today, it is popular to explicitly identify ways of situating one's research that are even larger than approaches. These are the *paradigms* within which one chooses to work. These have been given names such as *positivist/postpositivist, constructivist, transformative,* and *pragmatic*. In an earlier work (Braud and Anderson 1998, 240–55), we presented still another paradigm: the *transpersonal* paradigm. These large systems are analogous to meta-umbrellas or, perhaps, *circus tents;* these are overarching worldviews or mindsets, each having its own favored ontology (view of reality), epistemology (ways of knowing), approaches, and methods.

The integral inquirer recognizes the value of mixing, blending, or combining different methods or approaches in a single study or series of studies. An advantage of this practice is that it provides greater coverage of a research topic, with each aspect addressing what other aspects might lack. This is analogous to "feeling the elephant" in a variety of different ways, and feeling many different parts of the elephant, in order to reach a more complete apprehension and understanding of the nature of the elephant. Indeed, this is our chief rationale for presenting the various research skills and practices in Part 2 of this book.

Regarding choosing and mixing methods or aspects of approaches, the most important guiding principle is that one's research questions should lead and determine the choice of methods and approaches.

Begin by identifying the research question that is most important to you, then find the methods or approaches that might best serve this and subsequent questions. Never reverse this process.

3 ways of designing a research project (handwritten margin note)

In my own research courses, I suggest three ways of designing a research project. First, one can simply specify the tools/methods (interviews, questionnaires, standardized assessment instruments, data-treatment procedures) one intends to use in the project and name the study according to those. Second, if one can identify an inquiry approach that fits, in its full form, the aims of the study, one can select that approach (heuristic research, intuitive inquiry, narrative research, experimental approach), honor all of its aspects, and name the study according to that approach. Third, one can mix methods or aspects of approaches, selecting those that best serve one's aims; in this case one could indicate that the use of certain methods or aspects of one approach are *informed by* aspects of another approach. (This is like emphasizing certain ribs of the informing-approach umbrella.) In the latter case, care is needed to assure that the things mixed are compatible and that one does not distort a method or aspect by using it in an inappropriate manner or context. Useful treatments of methods, approaches, paradigms, and mixed-methods can be found in Mertens (2009) and in Creswell and Plano Clark (2006). It is important never to become enslaved to one's methods, and never to emphasize one's methods more than the content of what one wishes to study—i.e., always exercise mindfulness and discernment and avoid *methodolatry*.

> I suppose it is tempting, if the only tool you have is a hammer, to treat everything as if it were a nail. (Maslow 1966, 15–16)

> Seekers clinging to method . . . are like silkworms spitting out thread binding themselves. (Cleary 1999, 10)

While in graduate school, I learned of a research professor who had his students destroy the physical apparatus they had used in their research projects, once the studies had been completed. He did this to help the students resist the temptation of designing follow-up studies to fit what had gone before, simply because that apparatus was readily available. A similar temptation exists regarding familiar research methods or approaches. Also, just as one can build a new apparatus to serve a research plan, it sometimes is necessary to invent new research methods to serve research interests for which existing

methods do not fit or fit poorly. Integral inquiry encourages innovations of methods and of all other aspects of the research endeavor.

Modes of Knowing

The integral inquirer recognizes and honors the many alternative
modes of knowing in all aspects of research. These include not only
the familiar intellectual forms of knowing, treating, and expressing
information, but also feeling-based, body-based, imagery-based, and
intuitional modes that usually are less appreciated in disciplined
inquiry. These additional modes of knowing, framed as holistic skills,
are treated in great detail in Part 2 of this book.

    Alternative modes of knowing have been addressed through
theory and research in areas dealing with multiple forms of intelligence (Gardner 1983; Gardner 1993; Gardner 1999); emotional intelligence (Goleman 1994); social intelligence (Goleman 2006); spiritual
intelligence (Vaughan 2002); "feminine" ways of knowing, being, and
doing (ways of learning about and interacting with others and with
the world that are characterized by feeling, receptivity, subjectivity,
multiplicity, nurturing, cooperation, intuition, relatedness, and connectedness [Belenky, Clinchy, Goldberger and Tarule 1997; Shepherd
1993]); and functioning in a variety of conditions of consciousness
(*normal or ordinary, altered, nonordinary,* and *pure*; see Forman 1997;
Forman 1999; Grof 1972; Tart 1975). Other ways of knowing include
tacit knowing (silent, inarticulate, implicit knowing with strong personal,
individual features; see Polanyi 1958; Polanyi 1966), and *mimesis* (in
which, as a member of the audience of a performance, one comes
to know through imitation, personal identification, and sympathetic
resonance with a performer; see Havelock 1963; Simon 1978). Related
to mimesis is participation in *ritual*, which can itself provide forms of
knowing not otherwise possible (Deslauriers 1992).

    An example of tacit knowing is a young child's knowledge of
trajectories of moving objects. Young children are able to predict the
paths of thrown balls with great accuracy, enabling them to catch these
almost unerringly. Yet, they are not able to express, verbally, *how* they
know so much about trajectories. It has taken scientists centuries to
formally express some of this trajectory knowledge, by way of equations that now allow placements of projectiles, even into deep space,
with amazing precision. Another instance of tacit knowing is one's
ability to recognize faces, albeit without being able to say just how
one does this. These are only a few of the many instances in which

we know more than we can say. One of the most dramatic forms of tacit knowing occurs in mystical and unitive experiences, which are noted for being *ineffable* (indescribable, inexpressible; see Braud 2002d). These examples should not obscure the fact that a very great number of our common, familiar experiences and action skills are ineffable, in both their subjective quality and how they are accomplished.

An additional form of knowing that has received relatively little attention in the context of research and disciplined inquiry is *direct knowing*. Such knowing can occur through sympathetic resonance, empathic identification, parapsychological processes (such as telepathy, clairvoyance, and precognition), and certain forms of intuition. These processes are covered in detail in Part 2 of this book. Perhaps the most extreme, and also the most controversial, form of direct knowing is knowing through being, through becoming, or through identifying with what is to be known. One description of this form of knowing is the process of *samyama* in the Yogic tradition of Patanjali, in which one identifies with what is to be known through the practice of deep concentration, meditation, and absorption in an object or focus of intention and attention. The Indian philosopher Sri Aurobindo has used the terms *intuition* and *knowledge by identity* for this form of direct knowing (see Braud 2010 for treatments of these forms of knowing within Indian philosophy and psychology).

The use of a great variety of ways of knowing, in all aspects of research, is well-aligned with the principle of *radical empiricism* advocated by philosopher-psychologist William James (1976). This is an epistemological stance in which one includes *only* what is based in experience, but includes *everything* that is based in experience. James also espoused a *radical ontology*—although he never used this term—in which the real is considered to be anything that we find ourselves obliged to take into account in any way (James 1911). (Reminder: *Epistemology* has to do with ways of knowing, and *ontology* has to do with the study of being and existence.)

Epistemology ↗   Ontology

Experiential Exercise: Forms of Intelligence and Knowing

The ten forms of intelligence indicated in Figure 2.4 are relevant to ways of knowing because the different intelligences involve different kinds of information, and they access, process, and express information in different ways. Consider the skills that are implied by the names of each of these multiple intelligences. Each of us possesses all of these forms of intelligence, but they are present and used in different degrees.

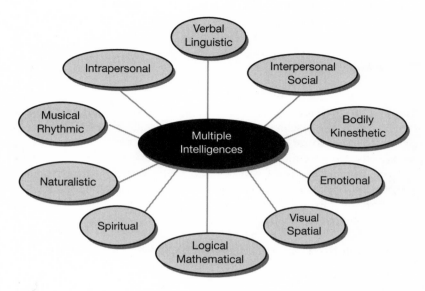

Figure 2.4. Ten different forms of intelligence

How aware are you of the operation of each of these ways (ways of knowing about yourself and others and ways of functioning in the world)?

Which of these are very familiar, well-practiced, and well-developed in you?

Which of these do you have greater difficulty accessing or using effectively?

How might you go about discovering more about your less developed intelligences and be better able to access and use them more easily?

Similarly, consider the other forms of knowing mentioned in the previous section—feeling-based, imagery-based, intuitional, knowings in altered states of consciousness, tacit, mimesis-based, and direct. How many of these can you identify in yourself? How might you become better acquainted with these and perhaps make greater use of these in your life?

Many of these skills, and related skills and forms of knowing, will be treated in detail in Part 2 of this book.

Modes of Data Collection

Collecting data (handwritten margin note)

In a previous section, I highlighted differences between approaches and methods, and related *methods* to the various techniques, procedures, and tools used by the researcher. Integral inquiry recognizes and advocates the use of a wide range of methods for the data collection phase of a study. These data collection tools allow the researcher to access information from a variety of sources and help provide a more inclusive description of the topic, phenomenon, or experience being studied.

For the information acquisition stage of a study, original data can be collected using the following methods and skills:

> standardized assessment instruments (psychological, physiological, biomedical, behavioral, parapsychological)
> questionnaires
> interviews
> surveys
> observations of others
> self-reports (or self-observations and self-reflections)
> reports offered by others
> textual material; public and archival data
> asking participants to contribute nonverbal materials such as artwork or photos
> transpersonal sources (accessing unconscious material, dreams, intuition, imagery, feelings, bodily sources, parapsychological knowings, direct knowing)
> treating research participants appropriately and compassionately
> exercising mindfulness, discernment, and appreciation of differences

The integral inquirer not only will collect data from a variety of sources, but also will make use of multiple modes of knowing (treated above) in accessing and treating the information from each source, and also will consider collecting relevant information not only from the formal research participants, but also from others who know the participants and might be able and willing to provide additional information about them and about the accompaniments and outcomes of their experiences, from these other persons' "external" points of view. These others could be persons who know the participants very well (family members, loved ones) and persons who know the participants less well (fellow workers, acquaintances). This approach of soliciting information from a variety of informants is a variation of the so-called *360-degree feedback* procedures used for evaluating performance in various organizational contexts.

Experiential Exercise:
Most Fitting Data Collection Methods

Imagine that you are designing a study for exploring a particular experience of great interest to you.

Review the methods of data collection mentioned in the previous exercise.

Which of those methods would be most fitting for your project?

Which methods seem least fitting?

The examples that follow provide merely a small sampling of the variety of ways in which researchers have collected data for their research studies. Countless projects have collected data using standardized assessment instruments. Because these uses are so common, specific examples need not be given. However, it is useful to mention three excellent reviews of standardized assessments that address many of the transpersonal and spiritual experiences and constructs of interest to integral inquirers: MacDonald, Friedman, and Kuentzel (1999), MacDonald, Kuentzel, and Freidman (1999), and MacDonald, LeClair, Holland, Alter, and Friedman (1995).

The following can serve as examples of some less frequently employed approaches to data collection:

In part of her study of nonverbal dreamwork, Nancy Fagen (1995) collected nonverbal representations of dreams that had been incubated with the intention of having the dreams themselves comment in their own nonverbal way on her study and on her participants' experiences during the study.

Genie Palmer (1999) attended to happenings in her environment and included descriptions of the occurrences and synchronicities that she experienced, as researcher, during all phases of her study of disclosure and integration of exceptional human experiences.

In her study of true joy in union with the Divine in mystical Christianity, Susan Carlock (2003) analyzed written texts of selected Christian mystics of earlier centuries.

In a study of the use of spiritual guidance and expressive arts in integrating the aftereffects of near-death experiences, Ryan Rominger (2004) used the expressive art created by his participants during small group sessions for identifying pictorial themes of their experiences and their aftereffects.

In the somatic psychodiagnostic study summarized earlier, William Bento (2006) had his participants engaged in various movement exercises and collected first-person information from participants about their experiences and perceptions while engaging in these movements; he also included third-person information from outside observers of the participants' movements and actions during the exercises.

In his study of a Long Dance ceremony, with an entheogen component, Jaysen Clark (2007) collected and analyzed the intentions of participants in the Long Dance, which they had indicated on cloth intention banners; he included photos of these banners in his research report.

In part of her research on anomalous experiences associated with death, Alcione Wright (2010) is proposing to make observations of deathbed experiences.

Before beginning their projects, many researchers frame (and sometime ritualize) specific intentions regarding the types of participants that they hope will show up for their studies. Uses of intention and ritual are treated in detail in Part 2 of this book.

Modes of Data Treatment and Interpretation

Just as the intuitive inquirer uses a variety of sources in collecting data, he or she also uses a variety of personal skills and ways of working with data in the second major phase of a study. In this phase, the researcher attempts to organize, analyze, treat, integrate, summarize, understand, and interpret the data and findings as fully as possible.

For the data treatment and interpretation stage of a study, the researcher can work with data and findings in the following ways:

> scoring assessments, making judgments about qualitative responses
>
> organizing the data
>
> carrying out statistical analyses (including meta-analysis) of quantitative data
>
> carrying out thematic analyses and interpretations of qualitative data
>
> preparation of concise narratives, portraits, depictions of participant experiences or stories
>
> using the researcher's self-reflections
>
> using holistic skills and resources (pattern recognition, deduction, induction, analysis, synthesis, mindfulness, discernment, appreciation of differences, intuition, gestalt apprehension, dreams, imagery, emotion, movement, creative expression, symbols, metaphors, archetypal elaboration)
>
> relating findings to research questions and to extant literatures

In each of the data-treatment steps, the researcher can work with the data analytically and linearly, as well as synthetically and in a gestalt (overall pattern apprehension) manner. The researcher can examine, treat, and interpret data and findings during various conditions of consciousness—in alert waking consciousness, in conditions of relaxed awareness, during active imagination and guided imagery, following meditation, during and after the use of a *focusing technique* (see Gendlin 1978) to reveal otherwise ignored information via subtle feelings, during and after movement exercises, during dreamlike or twilight conditions of awareness, and during and following release of effort in which one ceases active conscious processing and allows incubation and unconscious processing to occur and augment one's understandings. The foregoing are various ways of deploying attention. Many of these practices are treated in more detail in Part 2 of this book.

Experiential Exercise: Most and Least Familiar or Favored Data Treatment Modes

Review the various ways of treating and interpreting data that are mentioned in the previous exercise. Once you have done this, address the following questions:

> With which of these do you feel you have adequate familiarity and preparation to use them properly in a research project?
>
> For which of these might you require additional information or training?
>
> Which resources might you seek out in order to increase your competence in using these procedures and techniques?
>
> Which of these best fit your own interests and preferences?

Here is a small sampling of innovative ways in which researchers treated their data in the second major phase of their research studies:

> Before working with her collected qualitative data in conventional analytical ways, Dorothy Ettling (1994) entered a meditative state during which she attended to her own emotions and intuitions while listening to recorded participant interviews. She listened to the tapes several times, attending each time to a different aspect of the material—its emotional, intuitive, rational, or specific content. She allowed metaphors and other forms of creative expression to arise in her, to convey meanings not readily expressed in more linear, rational forms.
>
> Along with more conventional ways of working with his data, Alzak Amlani (1995) attended to his emotional and intuitive reactions, as well as to his visual, auditory, and proprioceptive imagery, while listening to taped participant interviews during a quiet, meditative state. He elaborated the resulting images by exploring their metaphorical, symbolic, and archetypal aspects and developed cross-cultural, mythic personifications of his research participants.

In her study of dance as a spiritual practice, Jan Fisher (1996) sought to reproduce in herself, as researcher, the same *being movement* experience she was studying in her research participants by engaging in being movement, herself, many times during this phase and other phases of her research project.

In her study of cultural isolation, assimilation, and integration among Filipino immigrant women in their journeys to wholeness, Sophie Arao-Nguyen (1996) had her participants use words as well as nonverbal imagery on identity shields in telling their stories during group meetings. She used these shields in all three major research stages. She also used her own bodily knowing, creative expressions, intuition, as well as rituals and dreamwork in working with her data.

In determining whether the experiences of participants in an entheogenic-enhanced Long Dance ceremony had transpersonal features, Jaysen Clark (2007) created various matrices through which he compared the features of the Long Dance with features extracted from several treatments of the nature and characteristics of transpersonal experiences, which he found in the published literature.

In his study of transgenerational post-Holocaust trauma, Mark Yoslow (2007) constructed a shadow box that included physical and imagistic representations of his studied experience. In this and other research phases, this shadow box helped inform his understanding of the experiences he was investigating.

Modes of Expressing and Communicating Findings ~~Findings~~

The ways chosen to express and report one's findings in this third major research phase depend upon the researcher's own preferences and upon the nature of the audience that the researcher most hopes to reach.

In the reporting and communicating stage of a study, the researcher can use the following means of expressing findings:

statistical outcomes, tables, and graphs, in quantitative research projects

narratives, themes, metaphors, similes, and symbols in qualitative projects

nonverbal creative expressions
audio-visual accompaniments (including CDs, DVDs)
active links to additional Internet and website information
suggestions to readers to prepare themselves to appreciate
    the findings in certain ways (including suggestions for
    altering consciousness)
presentations via articles, book chapters, and books
presentations via lectures, workshops, trainings
action outcomes (follow up activities, meetings, groups,
    projects, organizations)

A variety of presentation formats can be used in written and orally-delivered reports of findings in order to address the preferences of both researcher and audience. Narrative text, tabular presentations, and visual graphs and diagrams speak in different voices and languages to persons with different preferred ways of providing and receiving information. Because of space constraints in conventional journal articles, redundancies in ways of presenting information are discouraged. However, the integral inquirer recognizes that conveying the same information in different ways can be useful in allowing more persons to comfortably receive and appreciate the offered information.

Different types of audiences (intended recipients of information) have different preferences and habits of communication. Research reports can be tailored to fit those preferences. For example, persons in medical or clinical fields tend to value quantitative findings from outcome studies, intervention studies, and randomized clinical trials. If one wishes such persons to attend to one's study and findings, framing them quantitatively, and using statistical, tabular, and graphical presentations, could be especially effective. Other persons tend to be more interested in and impressed by rich stories and personal anecdotes. In these cases, qualitative framings and concise narrative presentations would be well appreciated.

In reporting results of qualitative studies, one can report the essential findings in narrative form, presenting these as concise stories, vignettes, or depictions and portraits (as recommended in heuristic research). Alternatively, one can identify themes, and present these either tabularly or narratively, along with a small number of excellent examples of each theme, preferably in the participants' own words. The themes can be quasi-quantified—providing indications of how common or rare they are, by including counts of how many participants reported each theme. These counts provide indications of the relative densities (and, thus, perhaps of the relative importance) of the various themes. It may be useful to describe both the themes that one expected to find (anticipated themes) and those that one did not necessarily expect to find (emergent themes) in one's study.

In reporting their findings, researchers often restrict these communications to other professionals, and even to professionals who happen to be working in a narrow field of specialization. Integral inquirers hope to disseminate their work more widely, by preparing reports in ways that will make them more accessible to professionals in a variety of areas as well as to the general public. So, in addition to more technical articles and books, researchers can prepare popular and semipopular articles and books, describing their studies and findings in more general terms. They can share their findings and thoughts not only through presentations at professional conferences and meetings, but also through exhibits, public lectures, workshop presentations, media presentations, and so on.

One frequently encounters assertions that the best way to "advance the field" of one's professional area of inquiry is to publish *informational* articles targeted to one's peers. This may be true in more technical areas. However, in areas of interest to the integral inquirer— such as philosophy, psychology, spirituality, and the social and human sciences—there are additional ways of advancing the field. One of these is to speak to the many persons in the general public who have strong interests in topics in these areas, increasing both their knowledge and their support. Still another approach is to plan, conduct, and report studies in ways that might facilitate *transformational* changes in the researcher, the research participants, and in those who receive the research findings. Changes in the very being of these persons may, in ways that we do not fully understand, contribute importantly to personal, social, cultural, and planetary changes.

Experiential Exercise: Possibilities for Presenting One's Findings

Imagine that you are designing a study for exploring a particular experience of great interest to you.

Imagine that you have completed your study and wish to communicate your findings to a particular audience for a particular purpose.

What is that audience and purpose?

Review the various ways of presenting and communicating findings listed in the previous exercise.

Which of these might you use in presenting your findings to your chosen audience?

Which of these presentation modes seem least fitting for this particular audience?

The following are a few examples of alternative ways of presenting and communicating one's research findings.

Sophie Arao-Nguyen (1996), in the study already mentioned, used the identity shields as one way of expressing her findings. Her study also included various action-related follow-up features: individual and group action plans, workshops, and retreats.

In a study of the experience of the loss of fertility during the childbearing years, Wendy Rogers (1996) used stones on which the essential qualities of the experience had been painted as part of a reader-interactive creative synthesis component of her results presentation. The stones provided concrete, weighty, tactile representations of aspects of the studied experience.

As part of his research project exploring the experiences of researchers who had conducted organic inquiry projects, Michael Hewett (2001) presented aspects of his findings in the form of a one-act play and video.

Several researchers have included instructions in their research reports that are designed to help readers appreciate their findings more fully by entering certain states of consciousness before reading their results sections. Researchers are beginning to include CDs, DVDs, and active links to websites along with their research reports, so that readers of these reports can gain additional information and sometimes partici- pate interactively with aspects of the reported studies. As described in Chapter 1, researchers are increasingly using *embodied writing* in presenting their findings to others.

Challenges For This Approach

The wide-ranging, inclusive nature of integral inquiry presents two major challenges to those who would use this research approach. First, because of the wide range of methods and aspects that can be considered and adopted for each research stage, this approach can be a demanding one for the researcher if it is carried out fully and adequately. It requires either increased expertise on the part of a single researcher or the cooperation of members of a research team who might contribute individual talents to the research endeavor. Another demanding aspect is that because the researcher will be working intensively in a whole-person way with a topic of great personal interest, the researcher actually becomes engaged in two projects at once—an outer exploration (the ostensible research project itself) and an inner exploration (in which the researcher will encounter his or her own personal issues and transformative possibilities). It is important to attend to these according to their momentary demands. If these go out of phase, it will be necessary to delay or modify work at one level so that adequate time and energy can be devoted to the other level that is calling out for attention. A second challenge is the risk of spreading one's efforts too thinly—attempting to include too many components in a research design and thereby being unable to address each component sufficiently fully.

Addressing these two concerns would involve a careful consideration of the researcher's degree of preparation and a determination of whether the researcher possesses the requisite skills or can readily acquire them. It also would be necessary to consider each potential research component carefully, and include only those that are most essential for a rich exploration of a chosen topic, experience, or research question.

Another way of addressing the "spreading thin" challenge is to design one's project as a research *program* with serial/sequential aspects—with its components spread out over time—rather than attempting to include all aspects/components simultaneously in a single study.

Implications for Substantive Content of the Human Disciplines

This chapter has addressed the many ways in which the process of disciplined *inquiry* might be expanded so as to yield a more complete account of what is being studied. An implication of the practices and principles described in this chapter is that the *substantive content* of the human disciplines themselves might similarly be expanded to include hitherto neglected topics, subject matter, and resources.

Investigators have established various areas of study and often have defined the boundaries of these areas rather narrowly. These areas—i.e., the familiar scholarly disciplines—have been divided even further into what might be called subdisciplines. For example, psychology has been separated from other areas concerned with the study of human functioning and human experiences. Psychology itself has been subdivided into a number of schools or forces (behaviorist/cognitive, psychoanalytic/depth psychological, humanistic/existential, transpersonal), and then narrowed even further into specialized interest areas (consider, for example, the fifty-six divisions of the American Psychological Association and the ten divisions and thirteen sections of the British Psychological Society). The rationales for narrowing areas and the resultant outcomes of such narrowings are sometimes useful and beneficial, sometimes not.

Just as integral inquiry recognizes the value of including a wide range of methods, practices, and principles, psychology itself might be similarly broadened to include a wider range of emphases. Such a broadened form of psychology—an *inclusive and integrated psychology*—would allow itself to be informed by the methods, findings, theories, implications, and applications of all of the forces mentioned above and also would welcome inputs from related areas of study such as integral psychology, positive psychology, parapsychology and psychical research, the great spiritual and wisdom traditions, the humanities, and the arts. As will become evident to the reader, such inclusiveness and integration already can be found in the approaches and skills treated in this chapter and in this book as a whole. This might serve as a model for similarly expanding the substantive content of scholarly disciplines themselves.

CHAPTER 3

Organic Inquiry

Research in Partnership with Spirit

Jennifer Clements

> Faith lets us move forward. Doubt lets us change course. Lacking either, progress is uncertain.
>
> —J. B. Clements (pers. comm.)

Organic inquiry is an emerging approach to qualitative research that attracts people and topics related to psycho-spiritual growth. The psyche of the researcher becomes the subjective instrument of the research, working in partnership with liminal and spiritual influences. A three-step process of preparation, inspiration, and integration guides both the data collection and the analysis.

Called "organic inquiry" because it's a living and therefore mutable process, the approach invites transformative change, which includes not only information, but also a transformation that provides changes to both mind and heart. It offers a process for cultivating these changes, not only to researcher and participants, but more importantly, to readers of the research. Stories present the findings using both feeling and thinking styles in order to offer the reader an opportunity for transformative interpretation.

In the spring of 1993, Dorothy Ettling (1994), Lisa Shields (1995), Nora Taylor (1996), Dianne Jenett (1999), and I—searching for avenues of research where the sacred feminine might be included—began to develop the ideas that would become organic inquiry. We wanted a way of working where the positive values of cooperation and inter-dependency were appreciated, where diversity would make us equals rather than causing separation, and where spiritual experience would not be forced into the shadow of rational thought (Clements, Ettling, Jenett, and Shields 1998: Clements, Ettling, Jenett, and Shields 1999).

Since that time, organic inquiry has grown within the context of student work at the Institute of Transpersonal Psychology. It has offshoots in other schools, but the methods presented here will be ones largely developed through student work at ITP.

Perhaps the most important and noteworthy aspect of organic inquiry is its emphasis on transformation as well as information. The approach incorporates the idea that research can include spirit, body, and feeling as well as mind (Braud and Anderson 1998). Guided by transpersonal psychology's many models of human development, organic inquiry uses the context of a particular topic to offer *trans-formative change*, defined as a resulting restructuring of worldview that provides some degree of movement along a lifetime path toward transpersonal development. Organic inquiry invites transformative changes of both mind and heart.

Transformative changes of heart—the training of ego to tolerate and support collaboration with liminal and spiritual sources—require a temporary suspension of critical thinking in order to access non-egoic input. Afterwards, ego steps forward to integrate the new material into the study. In this approach, the restructuring of worldview (both inner and outer) may be recognized through increased connection to self and Spirit, as well as a desire to be of service.

When she began her study of beauty, Maja Rode (2000) was "not fully aligned with transformation as the goal of research" (278) believing it would indicate a nonacceptance of her current self and a contradiction of her chosen spiritual path. Over the course of her research, her opinion changed as she saw that transformation need not be fueled by judgment about one's current self, but might instead be seen as a natural movement toward wholeness.

Exercise: Transformative Change

Using the relaxation methods described in previous chapters, move into a state of curious awareness.

Review your life, identifying the highs and lows, moments that were life-changing—whether they occurred in a crowd of others or alone, were violent or peaceful, joyful or tragic. Make a list.

Examine the list. How did these moments change your life? Did they result in changes of mind and changes of heart?

Keep this list to use in later exercises.

The organic orientation includes the assumption of the mystical tradition that divine/human interaction is available to one who is open (Van Dusen 1996; Van Dusen 1999). This chapter uses the terms *liminal* and *liminal realm* to describe a state beyond ego that may be visited by the individual psyche to gather useful experience, a state where the ego is barely perceptible (Hall 1987; Hopcke 1991; Turner 1987; van Gennep 1960). The word *liminal* comes from the Latin *limen*, meaning threshold. We may learn to cross the threshold beyond ego, gather experience, and to return "so that the deeper ground of the archetypal field can be seen, experienced, and allowed to flower" (Hopcke 1991, 118). Crossing the threshold takes the psyche to a less structured and less familiar state, where experience may be witnessed, but not created or controlled by ego.

The terms *Spirit* and *spiritual* describe the influences and sources beyond ego that have a seemingly beneficial impact, often accompanied by feelings of awe and a sense of direct intent on the part of the spiritual source. Spirit is assumed beyond any universal definition, but available within the context of the particular personality, beliefs, and experience of the researcher and the setting of the research method. The term *liminal* is used to indicate a more neutral influence beyond ego.

Exercise: Liminal and Spiritual Experiences

In a state of curious awareness, review the list of experiences made in the previous exercise.

Are any of them liminal or spiritual?

How do liminal ones feel different from spiritual ones?

Does this discussion bring to mind additional life-changing experiences to add to the list—dreams, visions, inner conversations, unusual coincidences?

Consider how the added experiences may have provided changes of mind or heart.

A major challenge in the discussion of organic inquiry within the context of traditional research is that it cannot be fully understood by the intellect. Can one fully analyze any more-than-intellectual concept like, say, falling in love? As with many transpersonal topics, full appreciation requires a personal experiential encounter. Confusion and judgment are common responses to experiences we haven't had, because there's no basis for understanding.

In a nutshell, then, organic inquiry is an emerging approach to qualitative research, which is especially meaningful for people and topics related to psycho-spiritual growth. One's own psyche becomes the instrument as one works subjectively in partnership with liminal and spiritual sources, as well as with participants who are able to relate their stories of the experience being studied. Analysis, which involves the cognitive integration of liminal encounters with the data, may result in transformative changes to the researcher's understanding and experience of the topic. Stories as evocative vehicles of feeling as well as thinking, present a diverse and intimate view of the topic in order to engage the individual reader in a parallel process of trans-formative interpretation.

An Organic Image

Stories and metaphors invite the participation of feeling and intuition, which can facilitate an experience of the flavor of organic inquiry. This particular use of a metaphorical description emerged early in our dis-covery of the approach. The term *organic* evolved from the notion of growth within the context of nature, a process that both includes and transcends human understanding. We came to see the characteristics and growth of an organic study in terms of the image of the growth of a tree. The five characteristics of organic inquiry—*sacred, personal, chthonic, related,* and *transformative*—are cumulative rather than suc-cessive. They happen simultaneously rather than in any given order.

Sacred: preparing the soil. Before a seed is planted, the earth is prepared. Similarly, participation in the organic approach calls for spad-ing up old habits and expectations to cultivate a sacred perspective.

Personal: planting the seed. Planting the seed represents the initial experience of the topic by the researcher. The best topic will have pas-sionate meaning because it has been the occasion for the researcher's own psycho-spiritual growth.

Chthonic: the roots emerge. Just as the developing roots of a tree are invisible and beyond intention, an organic inquiry has an under-ground life of its own because of its subjective and spiritual sources. Like a living tree, the process is allowed to evolve and change.

Related: growing the tree. Participants' stories are the branches that join and inform the trunk story of the research.

Transformative: harvesting the fruit. The fruits of organic inquiry are the transformative changes it offers, changes of mind and heart, particularly for its readers.

Prerequisites

This approach is not for everyone. Attitudes about the topic, process, researcher, participant, and reader may be incompatible with many researchers and many topics.

While many qualitative inquiries may benefit from an appreciation of this orientation, the ways of being and knowing used in this approach are especially appropriate to topics of a psycho-spiritual nature.

The approach requires a researcher to have a developed understanding of her or his psyche—both its strengths and its weaknesses—since that psyche is the instrument of the study. Because of the subjective and spiritual nature of this approach, discernment is important in order to avoid clouding an understanding of the data. Researchers need to know the differences—in their responses and in the data—between subjective and objective, spiritual and material, self and other. They need healthy egos in order to step beyond them, developed feeling and intuitive senses to appreciate liminal experiences, and strong intellects to assess the validity of the organic process as it progresses. Characteristics that would disrupt the integrity of this process include inflexibility, inauthenticity, hubris, and spiritual materialism.

Caryl Gopfert (1999) who studied betrayal among students of Zen Buddhism discussed the pros and cons of this self-as-instrument approach, writing that her personal experience of the topic seemed a requirement in order for her participants to be willing to reveal their own stories. She wrote that it also provided a deeper and more empathic understanding of their experiences. She could sense what they felt because she had felt it herself.

The selection criteria for participants include finding individuals who have had meaningful experience with the topic of study, who have an open-minded understanding of it, and who have both willingness and ability to articulate their experience.

The ideal reader will be willing and able to engage with the material both intellectually and emotionally, allowing it to effect transformative change.

Additional Influences

As mentioned above, feminist research played a substantial role in the origins of organic inquiry. It suggested the importance of balancing objectivity with subjectivity, in process as well as content (Behar 1996; Belenky, Clinchy, Goldberger, and Tarule 1997; Brown and Gilligan 1992; Gilligan 1982; Miller 1986; Nielsen 1990; Reinharz 1992; Shepherd 1993). The organic approach also reflects the self-as-instrument and the implied transpersonal emphasis of the heuristic research of Clark Moustakas (1990) and Clark Moustakas and Bruce Douglass (1985). Other approaches that have been influential include intuitive inquiry developed by Rosemarie Anderson (1998, 2000), integral inquiry by William Braud (1998c), and cooperative inquiry by John Heron (1996) and John Heron (2000).

The emphasis on working in partnership with liminal and spiritual sources beyond ego grew from the influence of transpersonal psychology. The approach invites and incorporates archetypal experiences, both transcendent and immanent, spontaneous and intentional, liminal and spiritual—experiences that are beyond ego. The sacred and transformative orientation of organic inquiry has grown out of the theories of analytic psychologist Carl Jung (1966, 1969, 1971, 1973) and anthropologists Arnold van Gennep (1960) and Victor Turner (1987). Other influences include narrative theorists Edward Bruner (1986), Steven Crites (1986), Michael White with David Epston (1990), and Rhea A. White (1997, 1998). The writings of transpersonal theorist Hillevi Ruumet (1997, 2006) and mystics Emanuel Swedenborg (1963) and Wilson Van Dusen (1996, 1999) have also been important.

It is important to acknowledge researchers who are studying concepts related to transformative change. These are authors such as Jack Mezirow and colleagues (2000), who are investigating how worldview may become restructured by critical reflectivity, which offers what he has named "perspective transformation."

Because of organic inquiry's strong emphasis on *stories*, this approach of course has important commonalities with various narrative approaches to psychology and research. Descriptions of such narrative approaches can be found in Bruner (1987, 1990), Lieblich, Tuval-Mashiach, and Zilber (1998), Mishler (2000), Sarbin (1986), and Josselson (2004).

A list of studies conducted between 1994 and 2003 that have contributed to the growth of organic inquiry, mostly done at the Institute of Transpersonal Psychology, may be found in Braud (2004). Additional informing dissertation projects have been conducted after 2003 by Kueppers (2004), Magnussen (2004), Kaplan (2005), Martire (2006), and Caldwell (2008). A longer version of the theories and procedures of organic inquiry is available from the ITP library (Clements, 2002).

A Closer Look

Organic inquiry offers a semi-systematic approach to including trans-egoic influence within a context of disciplined inquiry. The goal of the work is to offer transformative change for individual readers, encouraged by the study's report of similar changes in the researcher and the participants. Readers are invited to engage with the study, using mind as well as heart and allowing it to relate to and impact their own experience of the topic.

The researcher may not hope to invite transformative change through will alone. Because of its spiritual and liminal sources, the process of an organic study may resist the constancy expected in traditional research. By choosing the approach, the researcher commits to an archetype of transformation that may be actively facilitated, but may not be controlled. Trans-egoic sources—like dreams, synchronicity, or creative expression that originate beyond ego— may be invited, but likely not directed.

Exercise: Unpredictability of Liminal/Spiritual Experience

Consider the liminal and spiritual experiences on your list.

Did you feel you made them happen or did they come to you uninvited?

Did you feel in control at the time you were having them? Did they sometimes surprise you?

During the inquiry, a researcher repeatedly follows a three-step process—*preparation, inspiration* (stepping to the liminal realm beyond ego to gather data), and *integration* (cognitive examination of data with ego engaged). The psyche of the researcher becomes the willing setting for a working partnership between the researcher's understanding and experiences of liminal wisdom.

The transformative goal of organic inquiry is offered to the reader by way of the stories of the participants, as well as through the story of how the researcher has changed as a result of the study.

These stories invite the individual reader to participate in a similar process of informative and transformative growth. Stories are valuable adjuncts to conceptual formulations and descriptions because they evoke not only thoughts, but feelings as well. Stories serve as vehicles to deliver us to the liminal realm where transformation is possible, and they also form the cognitive container for ego's changing identity as it experiences new liminal material. The priority of the details of our life stories change as we reinterpret them based on new experience (Crites 1986; Hopcke 1989).

To illustrate this concept, here's a story. Several years ago, I was teaching a class on organic inquiry at ITP. I began, as these classes often did, with a meditation encouraging students to consider a connection beyond ego—a *muse of the research*—for the project they would be doing that quarter. In the silence, I invited my familiar spiritual connection to emerge. I sat, curious, until an image took form. In my mind's eye, I saw instead a *kachina*, one of the tall dancing gods of the Hopi and Zuñi Indians. Then I saw our group encircled by an outer ring of kachinas, one for each of us. They stepped and swayed forward and back, feathers in hand. I felt their eagerness to be with us. They came without emotion; however I felt an emotional reaction, which overflowed into silent tears. I felt the awe that can accompany this sort of transpersonal experience. When I opened my eyes, I considered the meaning of what I had seen and intuitively understood it. Intuition, as used in this chapter, unlike logical thinking, knows what it knows instantly and without question. It is not necessarily the only truth, but it is immediate and feels certain. In this moment, I intuitively understood that the presence of the kachinas was a confirmation of my hope that the students might make their own personal connections beyond ego. At the end of the meditation, I told the class what I had seen, and we discussed its meaning.

This story is an example of the form that liminal/spiritual experience may take. The controlling mind steps aside, inviting liminal experience to come to consciousness. Afterwards, the experience may be intellectually integrated into ego-awareness by considering its meaning and making it part of our conscious experience.

Exercise: Research Muse

If you are currently investigating a research topic or working on a project, review that project in your mind and move to a state of relaxation.

Invite some aspect of the project to serve as your muse.

After the experience, write about it, even if you feel no muse was present. Liminal experience is unpredictable and often has a timing and language of its own.

Making a Case for Liminal Process

Liminality has been the object of investigation as subliminal self (Myers 1903) and transliminality (Sanders, Thalbourne, and Delin 2000; Thalbourne, Bartemucci, Delin, Fox, and Nofi 1997). It also resembles concepts of increased openness (Costa and McRae 1985) and increased thinness or permeability of boundaries (Hartmann 1991).

A frequent topic of transpersonal research, liminal activity has less often been part of its methods. Experiences such as meditation, dreams, genius, exceptional sports experiences, psychic abilities, and creativity have been studied and state-specific experiences have been considered (Tart 1972), but liminal experiences have not always been embraced as research procedures. Opening the door to liminal influence, however, requires a researcher to adopt a different attitude toward the topic, the methods, and the purpose of a study. Egoic control is relinquished during the time the psyche is a visitor in this realm. Afterwards, when the threshold has been recrossed, the controlling ego may be invited to examine and integrate what was experienced.

Experiences beyond ego are inherently difficult to research. They leave no evidence other than memory. Skepticism is warranted regarding the details of this type of encounter. Occasionally, I have an experience, and later when the associated feeling has subsided, I doubt its validity. My ego dismisses it as unreliable and ultimately useless. Carl Jung (1973) addressed this disbelief in his memoir, where he described his own spiritual companion.

> Philemon and other figures of my fantasies brought home to me the crucial insight that there are things in the psyche which I do not produce, but which produce themselves and have their own life. Philemon represented a force, which was not myself. In my fantasies I held conversations with him, and he said things, which I had not consciously thought. For I observed clearly that it was he who spoke, not I. (183)

William Braud (1998a) addressed the issue of varying realities:

> To the physical scientist, the *real* is what is external and measurable, what can be accessed by the senses or physical instruments and verified by the senses or physical instruments of others. To human beings, inner events—that are unobservable from the outside—can be as real or more real than outer events. (236)

To a transpersonal scientist, then, what is real includes not only that which is physical and that which exists as inner experience, but also, that which may originate in nonegoic states of consciousness.

Theoretical Antecedents of the Three-step Organic Procedure

Anthropologist Arnold van Gennep (1960) determined that a "complete scheme of rites of passage theoretically includes preliminal rites (rites of separation), liminal rites (rites of transition), and postliminal rites (rites of incorporation)" (11). A rite of initiation includes all three stages. Victor Turner (1987) focused on the second stage of the model, the "betwixt and between" (3) period of liminal initiatory experience. In this stage, one abandons identity, status, property, and expectations in order to connect with the infinite in a profound reflection that affects changes "as a seal impresses wax" (11). These descriptions suggest the potential for intentional liminal experience whereby we may leave our everyday level of operation and establish connection with something greater.

Carl Jung's concept of the transcendent function is a model of personal and collective transformation that "arises from the union of conscious and unconscious contents" (Jung 1969, 69). To arrive at the transcendent function, we find an access to the unconscious material. In a process Carl Jung called "active imagination," we pay attention to whatever fantasies and associations present themselves within the context of a prevailing mood. From this, he wrote, will come a symbolic or concrete expression of the content of the mood. He insisted that only after the inner material has been experienced should we allow the conscious mind to engage with it. It is in this meeting, this bringing together of opposites (the unconscious experience and the conscious interpretation) that the transcendent function is produced, "a living, third thing" (90).

Carl Jung has described a procedure whereby we may choose to intentionally visit the liminal realm not only to gather experience, but to return with it to the world of the ego in order to integrate it and thereby effect "a change in personality" (Jung 1966, 219).

The field of transpersonal psychology offers a variety of models showing human evolution from infancy through adulthood (and beyond), including levels of spiritual development (Ruumet 1997; Ruumet 2006; Wade 1996; Washburn 1995; Wilber 1995). The work of Hillevi Ruumet represents an elegant model of spiritual growth, which accompanies a necessary and parallel psychological development.

The model includes two series of tasks. During the first, we develop a strong ego, and during the second, ego learns to realize its transpersonal potential. To move beyond the first series, to the second, requires a transition. The ego that we have been ardently perfecting during the first series of tasks gives way to a recognition that it is part of something greater, a process that is often neither expected nor welcome. To address the second series of tasks, we make a series of returns to earlier levels. Each new level of spiritual growth requires returning to work with unfinished psychological issues of the earlier ego-developing levels. Spiritual work is not done except in partnership with psychological development.

Organic Three-step Procedure:
Preparation, Inspiration, Integration

Arnold van Gennep defined liminal experience; Carl Jung suggested a means of employing it; and Hillevi Ruumet explained the lifetime developmental process of learning how to get to it with some regularity. These three demonstrate, from varying perspectives, that the mystical experience of immediate and intentional connection between egoic and liminal realms is real and available, not for all, but for many.

Underlying all of the methods in an organic inquiry, from choosing the topic to presenting the final form of the research, lies a fundamental model, a three-step procedure, which offers the possibility for experiencing transformative change. This process, simply stated, is one in which an individual moves from the realm of ego-control to a liminal encounter, gathers experience, and returns to integrate it into the ongoing inquiry.

Step One—Preparation

The three-step visit to liminal experience and back can be either an intentional or a spontaneous experience. The intentional version will probably occur in the context of a preplanned procedure within the research design. Robin Seeley (2000), who studied women's experiences of finding their life vocation, designed her participant selection to include a vision fast when she intentionally invited spiritual assistance.

Before the researcher intentionally departs for the liminal realm, there are tasks to be accomplished in the world of ego. Some of these tasks may be deliberately accomplished, and others may happen beyond intent. This will vary from researcher to researcher and also from one experience to the next.

The first task is to recognize a question or intent. The second involves encouraging the ego to adopt a state of curious ignorance. For some, whose egos have a strong attachment to being in charge, this is a challenge. For others, it's easier. Denise Hutter (1999) reflected on her natural ability to accomplish this task: "At times I felt that this study had a life of its own and was directing me every step of the way" (28).

Third, the ego adopts an attitude of respect for the values of reverence, cooperation, and mutuality. One becomes the willing instrument of the study. The final step of preparation is opening to liminal experience.

No two individuals reach spiritual or liminal experience in the same way. Carl Jung (1971) defined four functions or orientations to life experience: thinking, feeling, intuition, and sensation. These four may also be used to describe ways of moving into and out of liminal experience.

Two of the functions, thinking and feeling, are ways of choosing. Thinking makes logical choices whereas feeling chooses based on subjective value and worth. The remaining two functions, intuition and sensation, are ways of perceiving. Sensation gathers experience by way of the physical world, though inner response colors the perception. Intuition knows without being aware of how it knows. Carl Jung called it "a kind of instinctive apprehension" (453).

Traditional scientific procedures and concepts make use of all four of these functions, though they usually give credit to only two, thinking and sensation (Shepherd 1993). The scientist who gathers data through measurement—how long, how far, or how much—is using sensation. The thinking scientist uses logic to sort and develop concepts and models for theoretical systems. Less understood and accepted in research procedures is the intuitive genius of an Albert Einstein who acknowledged that his discoveries arrived more through intuition than logic (discussed by the mathematician, Hadamard, as cited in Vaughan 1979). Rarely is credit given to the role of the feeling function in science. In fact some scientists assert that science is free of the feelings that ordinarily inform values in all human activities (Shepherd 1993, 51).

Jung's theory suggests that each of us by nature prefers one or two functions to the others. In the interest of balance, organic inquiry encourages a conscious investigation of the potentials of all functions, even a researcher's lesser developed ones. Following is a discussion of the roles of the four functions in preparation. In reality, however, the four rarely operate separately.

Preparation Through Thinking

Both meditation (focused attention) and contemplation (attention focused on a particular text or topic) are traditional pathways to spiritual experience. William Braud described another way of using thinking to move into a liminal experience in "An Experience of Timelessness" (1995a). While reading an article about time-related phenomena, he decided to test the author's suggestion that the context of time is inescapable. Using focused attention, he used thinking to move beyond space and time to an experience beyond ego. Describing the experience, he wrote, "I feel I deliberately started constructing a time-absent experience as an intellectual exercise. . . . I controlled the beginning of the exercise. But soon, the experience grew to something unexpected and uncontrollable" (65). Thinking served as the vehicle and then gave way, allowing his psyche to cross the threshold.

Dianne Jenett (1999), in her study of the Indian ritual of *Pongala*, wrote that she used her thinking mind to act "as if" there was a goddess informing her work, and that this served as an invitation to what became a long and successful partnership with her.

Preparation Through Feeling

The primary use of the feeling function as a way to spiritual or liminal experiences is through stories. Stories can be used to gather, understand, interpret, and explain the data and findings of a study. They are both method and results. They are the soil, the seed, the plants, the roots, and the fruit all at once. Stories inherently communicate on the level of evaluative judgment more effectively and efficiently than the conceptual process of the thinking mind. Mystics have traditionally used poetry, painting, music, and stories rather than intellectual descriptions to communicate spiritual inspiration.

Carl Jung's theory of archetypes suggests that at the root of effective stories lie "patterns of psychic perception and understanding common to all human beings" (Hopcke 1989, 13). Archetypes of transformation communicate through stories as they "function autono-mously, almost as forces of nature, organizing human experience for the individual" (16).

Exercise: Thinking vs Feeling

Thinking and feeling are ways of choosing—one is logical and linear, the other is based on value, on likes and dislikes.

In a state of relaxed and curious awareness, consider your own personality—your way of making choices. Consider how you make major decisions and also how you make everyday ones.

Are you more logical or more feeling? Which style is a strength, and which is more difficult for you to accomplish?

Preparation Through Sensation

Sensation can be used to intentionally spark spiritual or liminal expe-riences through a formal procedure like holotropic breathwork (Grof and Bennett 1992). Less formally, many use creative techniques or movement. Rituals of sharpening pencils, lighting candles, automatic writing, and beginning work at a particular time or date—all invite participation of influences beyond the rational realm. Water often invites altered states. Repetitive practice, whether athletic, musical, or meditative, may stimulate liminal experience.

Preparation Through Intuition

Intuition delivers the big picture, as opposed to sensation's fondness for details. Intuitive information may be visionary. It may be an insight or an understanding. The use of intuition is less a matter of taking action and more about clearing the way. When using intuition, after the early steps of preparation, one shows up and waits for illumina-tion, which often feels immediate and certain. An often-successful approach to intuitive liminal or spiritual experience was illustrated above by Carl Jung's conversations with his inner Philemon (1973). Spontaneous synchronicities (seemingly coincidental events that carry unconscious intuitive meaning) have played a role in many organic studies, like malfunctioning equipment or the right person showing up at the right time. While usually spontaneous, dreams can also be intentionally invited to serve as avenues of intuitive connection to liminal experience. David Sowerby (2001), in his study of intuitives, successfully used dream incubation in the analysis of his data.

Exercise: Sensation vs Intuition

Sensation and intuition are ways of perceiving, of absorbing information—one involves the details of touching and listening and seeing—the other is global and immediate.

Consider how you perceive. Are you more sensate or intuitive? Which is your strength and which is less comfortable and natural for you?

Sangeetha Menon (2002), a researcher of consciousness who investigates the essentially subjective nature of experience, describes her approach as "equal amounts of . . . spiritual practice, . . . meditative reflection, and . . . discussion" (69). She uses meditation, study, prayers, dialogue with her spiritual teacher, painting, poetry, web design, and photography to prepare her mind for her research.

Linda Loos (1997) described using a thinking approach to inviting intuition in her analysis, writing that she would absorb "vast amounts of information from various sources, play with it in a variety of configurations, and wait for the *mandala of meaning* to jump out at me in a rush of inspiration" (86).

In her study of rites of passage, Denise Hutter (1999) used all four functions, using her strongest, feeling, as a point of entry. She explained that she learns experientially and that feeling informs her body, which triggers an intuitive experience that pulls her into a deeper level of inner work. Given time and the creative response of her unconscious, her understanding would move from confusion to integration where critical thinking could then participate. Knowing her own psyche allowed her to design her study to use her stronger functions to encourage her weaker ones.

Step Two—Inspiration

In this second step of the organic three-step process, the researcher steps over the threshold into the liminal realm in search of inspiration. We are out of ego's territory. We may not determine the outcome of the experience. Victor Turner (1987) suggested that while there, an individual is in a paradoxical realm of "pure possibility" (7), which can result in a profound inner change. Carl Jung (1969) described it is as a place that is liminal to the controlling ego, but not to the aware psyche. The ego must endure being largely powerless, but the psyche may willfully explore.

Linda Loos (1997) described the unpredictable nature of liminal experience. She often had to tolerate not knowing where she was headed with an idea, or finding meaning that was opposite her expectations. Trying to force meaning from a liminal source would result in her being more and more stuck, "like a cow foundering in quicksand" (441). Likewise, Lisa Shields (1995) found herself sitting at her computer for long periods, unable to write, taken over by the archetype of the witch who called her "a lazy-good-for-nothing"(252).

Conversely, Philipa Caldwell (2008) made lists of research-related sensate tasks, but if she was unable to accomplish a task, it was assigned to a "list for the universe" and often, thereafter, the solution arrived easily and on its own.

Sandra Magnussen (2004), who studied the effect of Tibetan Buddhist guru yoga practice on psychotherapy practice, invited the participation of her teachers and their lineage, "reciting mantras and asking for clarity and guidance throughout the process of this study" (87).

"The experience itself," wrote Wilson Van Dusen (1999) "can vary from small incidents to life-changing visions in which a person loses all contact with this world for a time" (3). Both liminal and spiritual experiences are often difficult to later put into words. He describes receiving a divinely inspired poem.

> I *felt* something about to emerge. In the midst of this experience, key phrases may come to me. I don't really sense the central theme and organization until it is all set down. Then the poem's theme and organization come as something of a surprise. It feels as though the poem has been given to me. (25)

Familiarity and Confirming Signals

Every intuitive encounter seems to make the next one more available. David Sowerby (2001), in his survey of how professional intuitives recognize and interpret their inspired information, found that their success depended on developing *familiarity* through a trial and error personal relationship with their own source of inspiration. The personal relationship between an individual and a spiritual source develops like a friendship. This could take the form of the earlier mentioned muse of the research. Ginger Martire (2006) befriended her angry feelings during PMS in her study of menstrual consciousness, transforming the monthly experience into an opportunity to be in partnership with her *menstrual muse.* This practice became an integral part of her research design.

Several years ago, I explored the notion of spiritual partnership (Clements 1999). Interviewing thirteen people from a variety of professions who related to Spirit in a variety of ways, I found that some heard words, and others saw visions. Some were informed by direct intuition, while some others relied on synchronicity. Angels, shamanic spirits, God, a deceased relative, and the goddess were all described as helpful and immediate spiritual partners.

The people I spoke with reported involuntary *confirming signals* that accompanied their connections to Spirit. A writer said he wept uncontrollably when in conversation with the Divine. A filmmaker felt hairs rise on her body to inform her when she was on the right track. A minister experienced a physical trembling of her body. A researcher in India felt significant certainty in moments of spiritually derived truth. Synchronicities also confirmed her interpretations. Confirming signals for others included strong feelings of joy, contentment, love, and wholeness.

Many of these are reactions that one neither could nor would make up. Different in nature for every individual, these signals were ways to discern which thoughts were inspired by Spirit, and which might be ego's work. They were proof, not to others, but to the one who experienced them. An organic researcher may develop this type of vocabulary of confirmation over time.

Robin Seeley (2000) described her experience of confirmation. "I feel my body tingle, then a rush of energy courses through me . . ." (9). Caryl Gopfert (1999) described confirmation coming as "a flash of insight, [or] expansive heart feeling or moment of deep empathy, or even through the repetition, vividness, or lingering impression of a word, phrase, or theme. It came sometimes through a felt sense in the body and a resulting insight" (159).

Exercise: Confirming Signals

Return to your list of life-changing moments.

Were there times you experienced confirming signals of the importance or the truth of what was happening—like tears, hairs rising, tingling, an expansive heart feeling, or an insight? Sometimes these signals will occur in the function that is least developed—an insight for a sensate person, a burst of feeling for a thinker.

Write about these experiences.

Step Three—Integration

The final part in the three-step procedure, after preparation and inspiration, sees the researcher returning to the rational world with newly collected experience. The ego's role during the previous step of inspiration was to stand just outside the door as protector, supporter, and witness. In this step, the ego respectfully engages with the material, examines its meaning, and is simultaneously changed by it.

Jungian analyst James Hall (1987) has suggested that it is the nature of the psyche to move along a path of ongoing transformation. The ego learns to move in a bigger arena both in the inner realms of the individual and collective psyche and also in the outer world. The transformation of the individual involves moving toward intimacy with all humanity as well as a greater harmony with the unconscious.

Using Stories for Integration

The organic approach uses stories during the preparation stage in order to induce liminal or spiritual encounters. Stories may also serve as the setting for the integration of material that was gathered during the stage of inspiration.

Our life is a story, and as we experience growth and transformation, our story changes—including our past, our present, and our future. As we change, we view the past differently; we live the present in a new way; and the potential for the future is expanded. When linear and logical expectations are interrupted by liminal experience, one's story is likely to change to accommodate this disruption. Experiences of the past can take on an alternative meaning (Bruner 1986; Crites 1986; Murray 1986; White 1997).

Exercise: Story

Choose an incident from your list of transformative moments.

Write the story of that experience.

Consider how you would have written it after it first happened? Has the story changed?

Keep this story to use in future exercises.

Integration Toward Self, Spirit, and Service

In organic studies, the integration of transformative change has been seen to show up in three ways. One may become more self-aware. One may develop a greater facility in connecting to the changes of heart and mind available from the liminal and spiritual realm. Finally, one may come to feel a greater desire to be of service in the world.

The first of these three indicators is increased self-awareness—a coming to know one's own personality in order to make best use of abilities, experiences, and resources. This is the training of ego, the changes of heart, in order to support the ego's collaboration with spiritual guidance. Stories offer a way for this to happen.

Stories of adults have an innately temporal quality. This orientation toward progression makes stories the ideal setting for psychospiritual growth (Bruner 1986). "Story as a model has a remarkable dual aspect—it is both linear and instantaneous" (153). This instantaneous yet linear quality allows us to easily identify with the aspects of a story that offer the potential for personal development.

Kevin Murray (1986) suggested just how stories may change us when he wrote "more than one possible account can be construed from the events of a person's life, according to the perspective of the biographer" (277). Not only does every person have a different story, every individual has an infinite number of stories, depending on the context of the moment when the story is being told.

Previous events may take on new meaning and change our story. A new discovery or even a recalled memory within a new context can radically rewrite previous experience. Stephen Crites (1986) wrote: "the self is a kind of aesthetic construct" (162). We choose, consciously or unconsciously, which events to accumulate into our ongoing self-narrative and which to dismiss. "I recollect the past out of my interest in the future" (163).

Like clothes from a closet, we attire ourselves in memories from the past, which are carefully chosen to support our image of where we are headed. We are lured by the future to reconstruct memories of the past. Each new story is utterly convincing and a persuasive substitute for the former one.

Philipa Caldwell (2008) explored the transformative effects of stories on women touched by cancer or chronic illness. Her participants reported that hearing the stories helped to integrate their own experiences. They felt emotional healing. The stories of others helped to rewrite their own.

In her description of the integration of exceptional human experiences, Rhea White (1997) has described a process by which transformative change may result in the second form of transformative change—increased connection to Spirit. Each of us lives with a narrative of who we are at the moment within our given circumstances. That story rarely reflects a reality greater than the one defined by our ego. "The self these stories are about is almost always the ego-self. Mention is rarely made of moments of contact with the All-Self" (108). However, when we spontaneously experience an event that cannot be contained by the ego's understanding, we have the option of rewriting our story to include it. "It is narrative that enables us not to identify solely with either self, but to experience ourselves as a consciousness that moves back and forth and in between, not dissociated from either" (101). "The All-Self also seemingly collaborates in the process by presenting images, ideas, and concepts in sometimes seemingly miraculous ways" (103).

Rhea White also wrote that association with Spirit begins a potentially long-term process that can transform our worldview. "This process becomes not only personally but socially meaningful" (97). We connect to an ever-widening circle of similarly inclined people.

Wilson Van Dusen (1996) has suggested the form that a transforming individual's desire to be of service might take. He described what he calls *love of the life*, a concept developed from the writings of Emanuel Swedenborg (1963), that describes the unique abilities each human has. It is the work that we love doing and that makes us most useful. "The love of the life contains the whole design of the person" (Van Dusen 1996, 90). "People who have enjoyed mystical experiences want to aid the design of creation. . . . They seek to be useful in life, to contribute something to the All" (Van Dusen 1999, 22).

Linda Spencer (1995) noticed that she cared more about people after completing her research. Caryl Gopfert (1999) realized she was ready to be a Zen teacher. Rose Pinard (2000) found out that she wanted a career working with the diversity issues of organizational change.

"We work on ourselves, then," wrote Ram Dass and Paul Gorman (1985), "in order to help others. And we help others as a vehicle for working on ourselves" (227). One helps not only because there is a need, but also because it is an offering to Spirit, an act of gratitude and reverence, and a natural result of our own ongoing transformation.

Exercise: Self, Spirit, and Service

Consider the story you just wrote.

How did that event change you? Did it change the way you see yourself? Did it affect your connection to spirituality? Did it make you want to be helpful to others?

Write about it.

Application—Researcher's Story

The first step in an organic study, once the topic is chosen, involves writing the story of the researcher's personal experience of it. The topic is likely to have a profound personal significance, and this is the place to examine and record that. Vulnerability is an important part of successfully writing this story. However, the shadow of vulnerability—solipsism—should be avoided. Organic inquiry, with its invitation to explore the depths of our psyche can be a temptation to indulge in self-satisfying, but unnecessary revelation. The researcher's story is written before any data are collected, so it may serve as a record of that preliminary experience before it has been affected by others' stories.

Exercise: Generous writing

Review the story you wrote earlier of one of your life-changing moments.

Write it again in a way that offers a reader the benefit of your learning, so that it is a story that serves the reader rather than your own need to be understood.

Application—Data Collection

In interviews associated with organic studies, researchers ask participants to describe their own specific and detailed experiences of the topic. Some ask participants to consider a list of questions or complete a survey or self-examination on the topic before the interview. Diane Schwedner ((2003), studying women's shoes as vehicles for psycho-spiritual growth, did this. Similar to Rhea White's (1998) Exceptional Human Experience spiritual autobiography, Diane Schwedner requested that her participants write an Exceptional Shoe-Story Experience, examining the roles shoes had served in their personal growth.

Most researchers have lists of subsidiary questions, which they hold to the side until hearing the full story, knowing that many of these questions will be answered in the course of the storytelling. Before the interview, the researcher intentionally moves into a frame of mind where Spirit may participate as well as ego. We intend that the interview will itself be a liminal or spiritual experience so that transformative change may occur. A variety of procedures may be used to invite liminal or spiritual experience—including ritual, creating an altar, lighting a candle, meditation, silence, poetry, or prayer.

The ego needs to relinquish control over the interview, but not to collapse. An interview invites intimacy, but not merging with the participant. In an organic inquiry protocol, questions are held lightly. The relational quality of the interview is more important than asking every question of every participant. One invites the participant to exceed one's expectations rather than to meet them. During the interview, the researcher maintains a double focus attending not only to what the participant is saying, but also to her or his own inner response. Response notes, recorded after the interview, will be used in the analysis. After her interviews, Caryl Gopfert (1999) took notes on the mood and affect of her participants as well as her own perceptions, insights, intuitions, and bodily feelings.

Data may also be gathered in a group setting. Some studies include this as an opportunity for participants to respond to each other's individual interviews, while others gather their initial data in the group meeting. Some researchers have found that a group format amplifies the meaning of their data (Seeley 2000).

Application—Analysis

The analysis of an organic inquiry will include liminal and subjective methods that the researcher hopes will result in findings that encourage transformative change as they invite individual readers to engage with the data. An organic analysis has three parts: the *participants' stories*, the *group story*, and the report of *transformative change*.

Participants' Stories

The intended outcome of the first part of the analysis is a pure rendering of the experience of the individual participants with little presence of the researcher.

Examining the interview data, in order to write these stories is another opportunity to use the three-step procedure of preparation, inspiration, and integration. We approach the liminal or spiritual realm to gain an inspired understanding of the participant's story in order to edit it into a version that will, in turn, inspire the reader directly. In the interests of a balanced inquiry, the data may be examined four separate times. With each listening or reading, the researcher prepares and crosses the threshold to observe feeling, intuition, sensation, or thinking, whichever of the four is being examined, to choose which words vividly recreate the experience of the participant. One of Rumi's poems taught Annick Safken (1997) to wait for a window to open in order to understand her participants' experience, to sit in a silence that was both literal and metaphorical.

Michael Hewett (2001) searched for *hot spots* in his interviews, where he and/or the participant felt emotional resonance. Jane Sholem (1999) wrote poetry to understand the participants' experience. Lisa Shields (1995) asked each participant to bring a favorite fairy tale, which served as a context for examining that participant's experience of beauty and body image. Caryl Gopfert (1999) used her skill in ikebana to make a flower arrangement following every interview as a way of exploring its unconscious meaning. Dea Cioflica (2000) used collages in a similar way.

When the examination is complete, the edited story may be constructed. Using an intentional creative process, the researcher becomes a novelist, using the clarity of research in the service of appealing to the imagination of the reader. The researcher likely uses sensate details and feeling descriptors more than thoughtful reflections or intuitive insights, which will be emphasized in the more logical and conceptual group story that follows.

The variety of approaches to harvesting stories from participants' experience is reflected in the names used for them in studies. Denise Hutter (1999) called her stories *heart portraits*. Marilyn Veltrop (1999) created *narrative poems*. Sophie Giles's (2000) were *portraits*, where those of Lisa Shields (1995), Dianne Jenett (1999), and Maja Rode (2000) were *dialogues*. Annick Safken (1997) provided *vignettes*. Caryl Gopfert (1999) wrote *short stories*.

Group Story

Typically, an organic study will include more than ten participants, so a reader may have a variety of experiences of the topic with which to identify. After the participants' individual stories are written, the collective meaning of them is studied. How do the stories' similarities and differences result in a larger meaning? What new insights emerge that will theoretically inform the topic of the research?

The group story has two parts. First, it is an edited experiential report of any analysis that has already occurred as a part of the data collection from interviews, from a group meeting with the participants, or from subsequent contact with the participants. Second, it is a theoretical synthesis of the researcher's understanding of the data.

Philipa Caldwell (2008), after asking each participant to create a metaphor from her own story, combined the metaphors into a "federation of images in the spirit of an American quilt" (3) as part of her group story. The images were presented as distinct but in relationship with each other.

Meaning derived from thinking (using Jung's typology) grows from a logical distillation, while meaning derived from intuition seems to appear out of the blue, having a sense of wholeness to it and an inherent structure that does not come from a linear thought process. As noted above, science sometimes places a higher level of trust in rationally derived meaning than in conclusions arrived at intuitively. Organic researchers may rely on a personal vocabulary of confirming signals, as mentioned above, to validate intuitive meaning.

Transformative Change

Where the group story is likely an example of changes of mind, transformative change deals also with changes of heart in which one's guiding egoic identity and worldview may change. These changes may occur either spontaneously or intentionally, in an instant or over a long period of time. The researcher examines them in terms of developing concepts of self, Spirit, and service.

Caryl Gopfert (1999) described how her participants' experiences of betrayal made her relive her own. Over time, this changed her feelings about what had happened to her. She began to see the value of her teacher beyond his mistakes. She felt compassion for her teacher and by way of that her own desire to take up her future as a teacher of Zen—changes to self and a new desire to be of service.

Transformative change in the participants may be found in several settings: as part of their original stories, during the interview as a result of having had their stories heard by the researcher, because of the impact of a group meeting, or as a result of reading the edited versions of their and others' stories.

The researcher is likely to be changed by the study more than the participants due to greater personal involvement. After analysis of the data collected from participants and without referring to the initial story or other notes, the researcher writes a new account of her or his experience of the topic, including the process of the research. A comparison between the researcher's new story and the original one will be the first indicator of the researcher's transformative change. After comparing the before and after stories, the researcher may return to journal entries, response notes, and comparisons with the participants' stories in order to find and report on the trail of transformative change that led from the researcher's before story to the story written later.

Sophie Giles (2000) analysis of her own transformative change in her study of dreams of divorced women was the seed for this method. After completing her analysis, she returned to her original story and was surprised to see how much her new understanding of the events had changed her story. "I no longer felt that I had to justify ending the marriage. It was as if I had lost ego attachment to telling my story a certain way" (233). In her research design, she had set the intention to be attentive to how she was changing as a result of the study.

Julie Gauthier (2003), who studied the hero's journey at midlife, noted that in addition to her changes, she also saw the ways in which she had not changed: she "saw with fresh eyes the parts of me that are still the same in spite of my own long journey" (239).

Reports of transformative change, by *early readers*, often three in number, specifically solicited by the researcher, is the final part of a study's assessment of transformative change. Evaluated using the self, Spirit, and service indicators of transformative change, early readers' spontaneous reflections offer some indication to the researcher of the transformative potential of the study for the reader. They also serve as an additional stimulus to the reader in terms of how the material might be transformative. Depending on whom the researcher chose, these readers may represent a range of responses, from a feeling response to an informed opinion. Both are valuable.

Exercise: Story Analysis

Examine the story you have been writing of one of your life-changing moments.

Look at it in terms of thinking vs feeling and sensation vs intuition. Which are natural strengths and common means of expression for you?

Rewrite the story including all four—thoughtful revelations, feeling descriptions, sensate details, and intuitive insights.

Presentation to the Reader

Because organic inquiry has the goal of offering transformative change to the individual reader, the researcher presents the results of the research including stories that are aimed at catching the attention and encouraging the participation of the reader.

This process suggests a third use for stories in organic inquiry. Earlier uses included a way to induce liminal and spiritual experience and a way to integrate this experience into our own identity. In this third possibility, the researcher intentionally constructs stories to invite the reader to participate both liminally and cognitively. The first use of stories offers *induction*, the second offers *integration*, and this third use offers an *invitation*.

Stories suggest an *interplay* whereby the reader experiences the parallel between her or his own story and the one on the page. The reader steps from thinking to intuitive knowing, from logic to insight. The carrying of two simultaneous and parallel experiences has produced a third and new experience with new meaning. A process of surrender and synthesis takes place. The ego surrenders its ability to logically comprehend the parallel interplay, and a synthesis of old with new offers creative insight. It suggests new ways to reassemble the facts of the reader's life into new stories that offer new outcomes. The integration that previously took place for the researcher may now happen for the reader. One story speaks to another, and a new story emerges.

In presenting the study, the researcher first intentionally invites readers to participate. Second, the researcher offers transformative material, which includes the stories of the participants and the story of the research, in a form that will invite crossing the threshold into the territory beyond ego. Third, the researcher offers her or his own story of integrating the material as a model for a similar process by the reader.

Exercise: Interplay

Choose a short favorite story, perhaps a fairy tale or fable.

Read the story, observing the interplay between your life
and the story you are reading.

Does having read the story in this way change your own
story?

Write about the change.

Transformative Validity

Qualitative inquiry examines the validity of a study based on its textual authority rather than its numerical accuracy (Denzin and Lincoln
2003). It also strives for consensus and coherence (Braud 1998a). Besides
textual authority and patterns of consensus and coherence (which do
apply to the validity of the more traditional part of an organic analysis,
which is part of the group story), the organic approach suggests and
encourages transformative change for the individual reader. Every
reader is on a unique path of development, so the valid transformative outcome for one reader will necessarily be distinct from that of
another. Consensus is unlikely.

This type of validity is personal and not necessarily generalizable
or replicable. Validity is measured by asking the question, "Is this
useful to me?" A study has *transformative validity* when it succeeds in
affecting the individual reader through identification with and change
of her or his prevailing story, as witnessed in the arenas of self, Spirit,
and service. The responses of early readers, described above, can give
some indication of a study's potential transformative validity.

Accurate and detailed reporting of an inquiry's procedures on all
four levels of experience—thinking, feeling, sensation, and intuition—
offers a balanced assessment. The researcher looks at the participants'
stories, the group story, and the transformative change—three views
of the same data, as well as changes to both heart and mind, trying to
avoid a one-sided evaluation. A high level of consciousness is helpful,
as well as careful reporting and self-examination—consistently examining the value of one's own subjective evaluation, the influence of Spirit,
and the intent of the original data. Internal validity can sometimes be
assessed using confirming signals like chills, a feeling of certainty, or tears.

Limitations and Future Challenges

Organic inquiry is inherently inexact due to procedures that involve
working subjectively and in partnership with Spirit. When we feel

we have been inspired by material beyond ego, what truly is the source of this material, and can we assume it is accurate? What does the term *accurate* really mean under these circumstances? Each study is accurate only to its own intentions. Investigations in the fields of psychiatry, psychology, mystical studies, and parapsychology suggest useful indicators of accuracy, however our present understanding of these indicators remains limited. The source of inspiration and the manifestation of that source vary from one researcher to the next, making this type of research difficult or impossible to duplicate. The setting is unavoidably subjective. Is one merely making up the liminal/spiritual response to one's inquiry? Aside from the use of confirming signals, in itself a subjective evaluation, we have no measures of accuracy. As mentioned before, consensual validation is unreliable.

Because the researcher is the instrument of the study, distortions are unavoidable. A self-important researcher, a deluded researcher, an angry researcher, a confused researcher, or a sentimental researcher—each will have harmful and limiting effects on the outcome of the study. Even a balanced researcher, if such a person exists, hopeful for results that satisfy expectations, may edit or interpret the data in unintentionally distorted ways. The researchers can only hope to be sufficiently self-aware to be able to acknowledge biases and assumptions, so that he or she may become informative filters rather than unseen confounding factors

The researcher who chooses organic inquiry will probably be one who has experienced many of Hillevi Ruumet's (1997, 2006) stages of psycho-spiritual growth. In addition to self-awareness, the prerequisites for adopting this approach include previous personal spiritual experience, an interest in exploring it, and a willingness to be yanked around in the process. "Doing organic inquiry is demanding and challenging. It is not for the faint of heart or faint of mind, nor is it an appropriate approach for those who are not willing to experience transformative change" (Braud 2002a, 10).

A final potentially limiting factor to the successful outcome of an organically framed study is the willingness of the reader to engage with the study in a sufficiently intensive way to allow for the possibility of transformative change. A reader's appreciation of an organic inquiry requires an experiential and personal engagement. Ideal readers are willing to take the time and make the effort to expand their perception to include not only intellect, but also sensory, feeling, and intuitive ways of knowing in order to experience an interplay with the inner stories that define their identities. Some readers will find the organic approach meaningful because of its spiritual, Jungian, feminist, and subjective orientations, whereas others will find those qualities alienating. Many of the limitations of organic inquiry are endemic and unavoidable. Others suggest the future of the approach.

Organic theory and procedures are based almost entirely on Western transpersonal concepts. Except for the research of Dianne Jenett (1999), who used organic inquiry to study women's ritual in Kerala, India, little cross-cultural organic research has been done. How do liminally-based research concepts play out in non-Western cultures? So far as I know, organic methods have not been used in any quantitative research projects. The approach might be useful in data collection, analysis, and presentation.

Aspects of the approach that invite further study include the nature of liminal/spiritual experience and its availability, the concept of interplay in the effectiveness of stories as agents of transformative change, the reliability of confirming signals such as tears or chills as indicators of liminal/spiritual contact, the impact of personality styles on the design and process of organically framed research, a discrimination between changes of heart and changes of mind, a validation of self, Spirit, and service as effective and adequate measures of transformative change, and an examination of the concept of transformative validity.

Of greatest interest to me would be inquiry into the usefulness of our experience that the Divine willingly and intentionally participates in our research endeavors. Liminal experience is the foundation of organic inquiry. When liminal becomes spiritual, and one feels the awe or presence that accompanies that sort of encounter, something more is happening. An exploration of this phenomenon would be fruitful.

Introduction to Part 2

Transpersonal Research Skills and the Preparedness of the Researcher

The Japanese Zen Master Sogaku Harada (1871–1961), after extensive personal training in his tradition, eventually moved to Komazawa University, where he taught Buddhism for twelve years. Growing increasingly dissatisfied with this work, due to its narrow focus on academic and theoretical aspects of Buddhism, which left him little time to help students have the direct experiences so important in the Zen tradition, he left his university post to become abbot of Hosshin-ji Monastery. There, he lived and trained students, in an experiential and more satisfying manner for the remaining forty years of his life.

Some of the views of ancient spiritual and wisdom traditions (Hinduism, Taoism, Buddhism) have remarkable parallels with the view of the nature of the world that has been emerging in modern physics. The former were arrived at experientially, through personal spiritual practices that are highly valued in those traditions. The latter arose primarily through empirical findings and rational thought. Although the resultant views of these two approaches share similarities, the life experiences of practitioners of the two approaches tend to be quite different: profound personal and transformative changes in the former case, and increased academic and theoretical understandings in the latter case.

We mention the above considerations as two of many possible illustrations of the limitations of exclusively abstract, theoretical, academic, and objective approaches, when these are unaccompanied by concrete, experiential, practical, and "subjective" components.

Our purpose, in Part 2, is to highlight a greater range of personal skills and practices that can help balance those usually presented in treatments of research. Conventional research skills include maintaining an objective uninvolved stance, practicing keen observation, engaging in critical thinking, utilizing a problem-solving ability, knowing how to find and evaluate relevant information, and having the ability to effectively analyze data and to clearly communicate one's findings to one's professional peers. The skills presented in Part 2, which can be called *transpersonal, complementary, holistic,* or *integral* skills, allow a researcher to bring more personal qualities and potentials to bear in any investigation, thereby addressing the researched topic more fully and gaining a greater understanding than otherwise would be possible. These skills can allow researchers and students to expand their personal awareness in ways usually thought of as more relevant to personal and spiritual growth than to the conduct of research. The skills enhance the *preparedness* or *adequateness* of the researcher and allow expanded forms of study planning, data collection, data analysis and interpretation, and communication of research findings.

This enhancement of the researcher's preparedness and sensitivities is extremely important because of the researcher's crucial role in any research project. The researcher's own qualities inform all aspects of a research study. These qualities help determine the subjects and topics to be investigated; how projects are framed; the nature of research hypotheses or questions; how research participants are treated; how data are collected, analyzed, and reported; and where and how one looks for inspiration and support throughout the research process. Researcher characteristics are especially important in *qualitative* research, in which the researcher is the major instrument in the research project, and in which all materials are collected, processed, and interpreted through the filters that are the researcher's personal qualities.

Certainly, researchers already use these complementary research skills informally and to various degrees in the planning and carrying out of research studies. However, they tend not to use these skills formally and systematically, nor are there efforts to deliberately train themselves to develop these skills and sensitivities more fully. Even when researchers use the skills (in the *context of discovery* in which research actually is practiced), rarely do they mention these in their research reports (in the *context of justification* in which one formally communicates one's work to colleagues). By identifying, practicing, and perfecting these skills, a researcher can more effectively confront the whole of what is studied with the whole of his or her being. Explicitly mentioning the use of these skills in one's research reports can encourage other investigators to become more aware of these and to benefit from their more extensive use.

It is likely that the researcher already has used the complementary skills described in Part 2 in aspects of life other than research—in optimizing everyday functioning, in various professional applications (clinical, counseling, education, wellness applications, physical training), and perhaps in fostering self-awareness for purposes of psycho-spiritual self-development. These same skills can be further fine-tuned and made more effective and efficient by means of deliberate practice. The descriptions, background information, and experiential exercises offered in Part 2 can allow any researcher to enhance each of these skills and use them more effectively in each of the major phases of any research project. After becoming more familiar with these skills, the researcher will be able to teach these to the participants in a research project so that they, too, might more fully and more accurately describe their experiences and carry out various interventions or treatments more effectively. The researcher also can encourage readers of their research reports to use these same skills to more fully receive, understand, and apply the communicated results of research projects.

For many years, we have been successfully teaching these complementary skills in a course called "Integral Research Skills," which is the first in a sequence of research courses offered in our graduate psychology program. Learning how these skills—already familiar to students in their own lived experience, but not in the context of research—can be translated for use in the service of research provides a very accessible introduction to research. The skills initially were called *integral research skills* because when used together they can help provide a complete and integrated (integral) appreciation of the topic being studied.

We provide, below, a quick overview of the skills themselves, along with brief descriptions of how each skill can be practiced and used:

> *working with intention*: awareness of, and deliberate framing of, intentions for all phases of a research project; facilitates the realization of study aims
>
> *quieting and slowing*: sets stage for use of other skills, relaxes and quiets, reduces distractions and noise" at many levels, reduces structures and constraints, allows change, allows fuller observations and appreciation of more subtle aspects of what is studied
>
> *working with attention*: practice in deploying, focusing, and shifting attention; deautomatizing attention; attending to different forms and channels of information; changing

focal plane or magnification of attention; developing witnessing consciousness

auditory skills: practice in devoting more complete attention to external and internal sounds and to sound memories and sound imagination

visual skills, imagery, visualization, imagination: practice in devoting more complete attention to outer and inner sights and images; use of memory images, visualization, spontaneous and guided imagery; active imagination; empowered imagination

kinesthetic skills: practice in knowing, remembering, and expressing knowing and being through gross and subtle movements

proprioceptive skills: practice in identifying and attending to subtle visceral and muscular sensations; working with felt senses, feelings, affective knowing

direct knowing, intuition, empathic identification: identifying with the object of knowing; knowing through presence, empathy, sympathy, compassion, love, being, becoming, participation; sympathetic resonance; empathic identification; parapsychological processes

accessing unconscious processes and materials: reducing egoic control; tacit knowing; liminal and transitional conditions; incubation; attention to vehicles that carry previously unconscious information; identifying unconscious tendencies

play and the creative arts: fosters curiosity, creativity, and insight; encourages beginner's mind; provides novelty, new combinations; encourages excitement, enthusiasm, exploration

We should mention why these skills may qualify as *transpersonal* skills. First, many of the skills have provided the basis for practices that are of importance in spiritual and wisdom traditions that have transpersonal relevance. Most notable in this connection are the skills of working with intention and attention, quieting and slowing, visualization, and forms of direct knowing. Second, a practice may be considered transpersonally relevant if it is carried out with a transpersonal intention or if it has transpersonal accompaniments or outcomes—i.e., if it is associated with or fosters increased self-awareness, an expanded sense of identity, and expanded ways of knowing, doing, and being in the world, beyond the usual egoic modes of functioning. All of these complementary skills can yield these expanded outcomes by facilitating the actualization of many of the practitioners' inherent, latent potentials.

Suggestions for Using the Skills

Both students and already accomplished researchers can identify and practice these skills through the use of the experiential exercises presented in Part 2 and in variations that a course instructor might provide. The exercises then indicate how students and researchers might use the skills, in themselves—as researchers—in the three major phases of any quantitative or qualitative research project (planning and collecting data, working with data, presenting data). They also are encouraged to introduce the skills more fully into their professional work and into their lives, in the service of their personal growth and development.

In addition to working with these skills, themselves, as researchers, students are encouraged to consider ways in which they might request the research participants in their future studies to use similar skills—for purposes of remembering, reliving, and communicating past or present experiences to the researcher, in ways that might be more complete, detailed, and accurate than what might be possible without the use of such techniques. Also, students are asked to consider how they might ask the audiences/readers of their research reports to use similar skills, in order to more fully receive the findings that are being presented to them.

In order to develop the skills more fully and perfect them, we recommend that they be practiced on an ongoing basis, rather than confining their use only to certain weeks of a course. Like any other skills, these can be progressively improved through diligent practice.

We encourage instructors, students, and already accomplished researchers to creatively develop their own variations on the experiential exercises presented in Part 2. We also encourage everyone to consider other personal practices, with which they already are familiar, and imagine ways in which these distinctive skills might be applied in the service of research.

CHAPTER 4

Intention, Quietude and Slowing, Attention, and Mindfulness

Working With Intention

A good intention clothes itself with power.

—Ralph Waldo Emerson

In phenomenology and phenomenological psychology, *intentionality* usually has the meaning that mental acts, experiences, and consciousness are always *about* or *of* something; they *stretch out to* or *point to* something other than themselves. The term suggests a relationship between the perceiver and what is perceived, between the knower and what is known. In this book, however, we are using the common term *intention* and using this in its ordinary sense of an aim, purpose, or goal-directed volitional activity. Perhaps intention could best be understood as *attention focused on some goal*.

About Intention and Its Uses

In psychology—and, as we will demonstrate, in research—attention and intention are extremely important concepts. In fact, these may well be the two most important principles or processes in all of psychology. We are goal-directed organisms, and attention and intention guide us in realizing our goals. A moment's thought easily reveals how intention, in the sense of goal-direction, is intimately involved in most of our actions, thoughts, images, feelings, and emotions.

In daily life, as well as in psychological research, intentions may be considered as intentions per se, or they may take the form of *wishes* or *expectations of desired outcomes*. The following listings indicate a wide range of contexts that demonstrate the great power of intentions in bringing about desired physical, physiological, and psychological outcomes.

In our everyday lives, the power of intention is revealed in

familiar goal-directed volitional actions and mentation

wedding and partnership vows

the vision and mission statements of organizations

the essential natures of memory, imagery, and planning

suggestion and expectation effects, in self or others

self-fulfilling prophesies, wherein one's expectation of an outcome actually contributes to the manifestation of that outcome

the placebo effect, in which physicians' and patients' beliefs about the healing capabilities of agents or procedures can endow these with healing powers

parapsychological phenomena—such as telepathy, clairvoyance, precognition, and psychokinesis, in which focused intentions can influence what can be known or accomplished, even at a distance and beyond the reach of the conventional senses and motor systems

distant, spiritual, or mental healing, in which intentions for specific bodily changes and for the increased well-being of others can actually foster such outcomes

prayer, in which intended benefits may occur

dream incubation, in which intended knowledge or solutions may come to pass

realizing and manifesting thoughts or outcomes via "affirmations" and "co-creation" of desired realities

afterlife experiences, in—for example—the Tibetan Buddhist tradition

Similarly, in a clinical and educational setting, in professional contexts, and in research projects, the power of intention has been revealed in

the Pygmalion effect, in which preexisting teacher expectations can strongly influence their views of, and even the actual performances of, their students

expectancy effects and experimenter effects in laboratory studies, in which experimental outcomes can be influenced by the beliefs, biases, and expectations of researchers and their helpers, even through quite subtle and indirect means

biofeedback and psychophysiological self-regulation, in which the body's reactions and condition conform to intended changes

homeostatic and self-regulatory activities, in which intended resting conditions are achieved

doctrinal compliance, in which dreams and experiences of clients tend to match the theoretical views and expectations of their therapists

hypnosis, in which suggestibility greatly increases and in which imagined changes and outcomes readily occur

fostering the well-being of others, in all services and service professions

In all of the above instances, the process in question operates in the service of an individual's intentions. In some cases, intention may work indirectly, by helping to focus attention and actions, increase motivation, or modulate and guide other psychological processes. However, in all of the instances, intention also plays a more direct goal-directing function, actively contributing to the realization or manifestation of a particular desired outcome.

In my own life, I (W. B.) experience the power of intention constantly—in guiding my plans, actions, memories, and areas of work and play. I also have witnessed the great power of intention in my various research projects. Research participants' intentions to change their physiological activities and conditions and alter their immune system functioning were effective in doing these things in various biofeedback, self-regulation, and psychoimmunology studies. In various parapsychological investigations, research participants were able to effectively guide and focus their accurate awareness of spatially or temporally remote target events (in studies of telepathy, clairvoyance, and precognition) by suitably directing their intentions (Braud 2002b). In other studies, in research areas that explore direct mind-matter interactions and direct mental interactions with living systems (DMILS), research participants were able to affect the activities of a variety of physical and biological systems, directly and at a distance, through the appropriate deployment of intention (Braud 2003a). In these projects, successful outcomes seemed related to the degree to which the research participants were able to fill themselves with full, firm, and effective intentions while at the same time avoiding too-effortful striving.

It is clear that an investigator, through her or his selections, preferences, biases, expectations, and other qualities, can influence each and every phase of a research endeavor. Recent research has indicated that similar influences can be exerted by the very intentions of an investigator. Because this is the case, it is wise for researchers to be aware of their intentions and their power in influencing study outcomes. This chapter section offers information and advice that students and other researchers can use in optimizing the efficacy of intention-setting in all aspects of research.

Experiential Exercises

IMPORTANT: Before beginning any of the experiential exercises in Part 2 of this book, first prepare yourself by carrying out the Basic Instructions for All Experiential Exercises that can be found in Chapter 1. Once you have prepared yourself, by means of that exercise, carry out the following exercise that provides an example of how intentions might be framed, set, and held for research purposes. Later, you can use similar procedures for framing intentions for the various stages of any research project.

Generalized Research Intentions

Step 1. Complete the Basic Preparatory Instructions for All Experiential Exercises described in Chapter 1.

Step 2. When you are ready, focus your attention on the research project you are about to undertake.

Step 3. Now, frame some general intentions about your aims and the goals you hope to accomplish through your research project. In framing/setting your intentions, use words, images, and feelings that seem most appropriate and fitting for your temperament and style, and that match well your intended goals.

Step 4. Your generalized research intentions framing might resemble the following:

I set and hold the intentions that throughout the creation, development, and carrying out of this research project on [name the research topic] inspirations, thoughts, images, feelings, findings, and interpretations will arise naturally and effortlessly and that I will access, understand, integrate, communicate, and apply these in ways that will be useful for our understanding of this subject matter, for advancing this field of study, and for the increased well-being of everyone involved in this study and for society and for the planet as a whole.

Step 5. As you frame and hold your intentions, confidently imagine that everything you are intending already has come to pass, and fill yourself with gratitude that these goals have been accomplished. Let the intentions leave you, like butterflies carrying them—as aims, expectations, and wishes—into the world at large.

Step 6. When you have released these intentions, gently bring yourself to this present time and place, gently open your eyes, take a deep inhalation, and as you exhale, let yourself begin to engage with the materials at hand, knowing that the intentions you set will be fulfilled—for your own benefit and for the benefit of others.

Step 7. If it seems appropriate, you might ground the exercise and your experiences during the exercise by writing some quick notes or by drawing or by movements that might help you concretize and remember the experience. Then, confidently and with gratitude, move on to the next phases of your work.

Step 8: Hold these intentions in your heart, and remember them and reinforce them often, during the course of your research project.

Next, we identify the three major stages of any research project and indicate specific intentions that can be set for each of these stages.

Using the Intention Skill in the Three Major Research Stages

All empirical research projects involve three major stages or phases. The first stage is one of preparing for and collecting data. In the second stage, one treats, analyzes, and interprets the data. In the third stage, one reports one's findings to particular audiences. The researcher can set intentions for each of these three stages. It is important to set these intentions in ways that optimize the likelihood of making valid observations and discovering the truth of what one is studying—without introducing biases, distortions, and confounds (artifacts) into one's work and findings. Stated otherwise, *it is important to seek nature's actual answers to the questions we ask, rather than seek the answers that we might prefer or those that might confirm our personal expectations and desires.* A challenge, in setting intentions, is to frame them in ways that support valid discoveries, rather than possibly inaccurate confirmations of our preferences. We can accomplish this by carefully considering the wording of our intentions.

Because we are unlikely to be aware of many of the possible side effects and aftereffects of intended outcomes, it is wise to frame our intentions—both in research and in our daily lives—in *qualified* or *conditional* ways. For example, we can add to an intention thoughts and words such as the following: ". . . provided there are no undesirable or harmful accompaniments or outcomes associated with the realization of this intention" or ". . . in ways that are for the greatest good for all."

The researcher can frame and hold intentions for the following aspects of the three major research stages.

For the *planning and data collection* stage:

> selecting a topic that is meaningful for the researcher, the research participants, and the advancement of this area of study
>
> becoming aware of information relevant to the chosen topic—through effective literature reviewing and contacts with others
>
> finding the most appropriate research participants—i.e., persons whose reports will accurately and fully illuminate the topic being studying
>
> collecting data in ways that are as free from personal biases as possible

For the *data treatment and interpreting* stage:

> examining and summarizing data in ways that are true to what they suggest and as free from personal biases and expectations as possible

using the most appropriate quantitative and qualitative
    methods in analyzing and treating the data
becoming aware of meaningful patterns in the data
becoming aware of both obvious and subtle interrelation-
    ships in the data
treating the data fully and completely
developing meaningful and accurate interpretations of the
    data

For the *data reporting* stage:

reporting findings and conclusions clearly and accurately
communicating findings using language and presentation
    modes that will be well understood and appreciated by
    the desired audience(s)
reporting the study and its results in ways that will suggest
    useful implications and possible practical applications
    of this work

We leave it as an exercise for the student or researcher to create his or
her own specific intentions for all three stages of particular research
projects. It is useful to be attentive to how the intentions are working
and how they are interacting with the various aspects of the research
process. A research journal can be used to track the efficacy of one's
research intentions.

This intention skill, as well as all of the other skills described in
this book, can be used in two ways in any research project. The most
important way is for the researcher, herself or himself, to use the skill
as a way of preparing for and carrying out each aspect of a project.
Throughout this book, we emphasize this personal use the skills, by
the investigator. A second, and optional, way of using the skills is to
instruct one's research participants to identify and use the skills in certain parts of the research project, if this seems useful and appropriate.

Additional Considerations

Although we have described the skill of working with intention in
isolation, in actual practice it will be mixed or blended with other
research skills, which will be presented later. Intention will almost
always be combined with the skill of efficient attention deployment
and the skill of visualization.

Should the researcher wish to do so, the act of setting intentions can be dramatized or ritualized by developing a specific, concrete procedure for framing the intentions. This could take the form of a structured physical procedure or ceremony, which the researcher can conduct in privacy. The intentions could be concretized—by, for example, writing them on special slips of paper—as a way of paying them increased attention and honoring them more thoroughly. The increased density of attention devoted to intentions by dramatizing or ritualizing them may grant the intentions greater efficacy. Ritual itself can be considered a specific form of intention.

One may question why intentions have efficacy at all: What might account for their effectiveness? At the very least, intentions may do their work indirectly—by frequently calling to mind one's aims and goals. The greater the *awareness* of one's goals, the easier it will be to know when one is on track in approaching these goals or when one has been distracted and is off track. With this knowledge, one can self-correct one's approach and actions, so as to increase the likelihood or speed of reaching one's goals. Another function of intentions is—again, through the reminders that they provide—that of increasing one's *motivation* to reach the goal and increasing the incentive value of the goal. Increased motivation and incentive can, in turn, foster greater and more effective goal-directed actions.

In addition to the above, intentions can act much more directly—in actually helping to bring about goal events in some teleological (goal-influenced) manner. Exactly how this comes about remains mysterious. Yet, there is convincing empirical evidence that our intentions can indeed act directly upon the physical world in order to help bring about desired events and outcomes (Braud 1994a: Braud, 2003a; Radin 1997). Apparently—and under special circumstances—intentions can shift the probabilities of occurrence of intended events, especially in conditions characterized by increased indeterminacy, randomness, or free variability. The process seems similar to the quantum physical process of "collapse of the state vector" by an observation or measurement—in which a diffuse, probabilistic wave-like process that is everywhere and everywhen becomes concretized and localized in a discrete, particle-like form that exists in a specific place and time. The process through which goal events might be actualized through intention also has been described, albeit in differing terms, in many of the major spiritual and wisdom traditions.

In framing intentions, I (W. B.) have found it important to emphasize the desired *outcome* (goal) rather than the *means* (process) of actualizing that goal. If we focus on a particular *means* of accomplishing something or of hoping how something will occur, we might pick an inappropriate process—one that is not the most effective way of realizing the goal. We may not be sufficiently wise to know the best means to an end. However, if we frame the intention in terms of the goal itself, *other means* might become available to actualize that goal.

A related thought: In everyday life, often our goals themselves might not really be the most needed ones or the most effective ones for our greater well-being and psycho-spiritual development. What *seems* to be an important and necessary goal or intended outcome at a certain moment may turn out not to really be in our best, eventual interest. A lack of wisdom and lack of appropriateness that could apply to some means (processes) also can apply to some ends (goals, outcomes) themselves.

So, rather than focusing on particular outcomes or goals—in daily life, as well as in research—sometimes it may be wiser to focus on (frame an intention for) whatever might be best for our own increased understanding, well-being, and development and that of others and of the world at large. We often know so little about what might really lead to what.

All of this is to suggest that we be mindful of possible unanticipated side effects and aftereffects of our intentions—and of *all* of our thoughts, feelings, images, and actions—and be discerning in their use.

Supplementary Resources

There are several areas related to intention in addition to those treated above. One of these is the concept of *intentionality*, which is treated extensively in phenomenology and in psychological and transpersonal phenomenological research. Interested readers can explore this concept in Moran (2000) and in Valle (1998). Intentions, in the form of *expectations* of researchers and of research participants, can play important roles in determining the outcomes of experiments, even when the latter are carefully controlled. Readers may explore the power of intention in these experimental contexts in literature relevant to issues of *researcher biases, experimenter effects,* and *demand characteristics.* Useful treatments of these areas can be found in the following sources, as well as in earlier works by these same authors: Orne (2002), Rosenthal (2002), Rosnow (2002), and Whitehouse, Orne, and Dinges (2002).

Quieting and Slowing the Bodymind

Delight is the secret. And the secret is this: to grow quiet and listen; to stop thinking, stop moving, almost to stop breathing; to create an inner stillness in which, like mice in a deserted house, capacities and awarenesses too wayward and too fugitive for everyday use may delicately emerge. (McGlashan 1967, 156)

Try to be mindful and let things take their natural course. Then your mind will become still in any surroundings, like a clear forest pool. All kinds of wonderful, rare animals will come to drink at the pool, and you will see clearly the nature of all things. You will see many strange and wonderful things come and go, but you will be still. (Chah 1985, frontispiece)

About Quietude and Slowing and Their Uses

We can use various quieting techniques to set the stage for the more effective use of the other research skills treated in this book. These quieting techniques help free the researcher from distractions. They also help make subtle details and other forms of knowing accessible. Quieting and slowing techniques work at various levels—some working chiefly to quiet and slow down certain bodily processes, reducing muscular and autonomic distractions or "noise," others working to quell cognitive noise ("monkey mind"). Having a quiet body and mind can help the researcher better appreciate aspects of what is studied (by slowing things down and allowing closer or different forms of observation).

Many meditation procedures and yogic practices, such as special postures (*asanas*) and breathing practices (*pranayama*), implicitly make use of quieting and slowing techniques. In a sense, quieting and slowing our body's activities allow them to recede to the background of attention, thereby allowing subtle perceptions to rise to the foreground. Noticing the essential or characteristic features of data is very important in both qualitative and quantitative data analysis and interpretation.

Quieting and slowing include muscular relaxation, autogenic exercises, hypnosis, biofeedback, guided imagery, meditation, contemplation, and entering the Silence. In addition to reducing noise or distractions, quieting techniques can free the bodymind from strong structures or patterns, induced by either external or internal sources. Freed from such structuring and constraining forces, the bodymind may be more labile, and this increased free variability can result in more efficient shifts, changes, and new creative possibilities. Quieting techniques help us empty ourselves of the old and familiar so that we may be filled with new and unfamiliar forms of knowing, being, and doing.

The following Table 4.1 provides a quick indication of various sources of "noise" or distractions as well as corresponding techniques that can be useful in reducing these. In this table, the term *noise* does not mean noise in the sense of loud, meaningless sounds only. *Noise*, here, means any irrelevant activities, distractions, or interferences—of whatever nature.

Table 4.1. Sources of "Noise" or Distractions and Techniques for Reducing These

Sources of Noise, Disturbances, Distractions of the Bodymind	Techniques for Reducing Noise and Quieting the Bodymind
Sensory noise/distractions	Quiet environment, closing eyes, sensory restriction or sensory deprivation, hypnosis
Muscular noise/distractions	Progressive muscular relaxation
Autonomic and emotional noise/distractions	Autogenic training, breathing exercises, and spiritual heart exercises
Left-hemispheric noise/distractions (excessive intellectual analysis)	Emphasizing right hemispheric activities (increased nonverbal activities)
Cognitive noise/distractions	Meditation and contemplative techniques
Effortful striving	Acceptance; surrender; letting go; releasing effort
Interference from other information	Trial-and-error practice with feedback; mindfulness and discernment

In the table, the various techniques in the right-most column are ways of quieting or dampening the excitations that are listed in corresponding sections (rows) of the left-most column. We can quiet ourselves at all of these levels by using a variety of techniques. Note that some of the techniques might work primarily at certain levels but might influence other levels as well. In other words, the various noise/distraction levels are highly interrelated, as are the various noise-reducing, distraction-reducing, quieting techniques.

In everyday life, we have used these various techniques for relaxing and quieting the bodymind in order to rest, rejuvenate, combat stress, foster creativity, explore new ideas, and inspire our writings. In research projects, I (W. B.) have used quieting techniques when participating in my own experiments and other studies. Research participants in my studies frequently have used these techniques as ways of setting the stage for, and fostering, their own psychoimmunological, health-enhancing functioning and for accessing and demonstrating their own psychic functioning in various parapsychological experiments.

Some research projects also seem to require a slower and more relaxed pace than I (R. A.) typically am accustomed to, especially in my professional life. However frustrating it may be to my work schedule, if I want a satisfying and successful outcome, I try to adjust my pace to the project rather than force the project to adjust to mine. Since most people seem to have characteristic work rhythms and pace, regardless of the project at hand, learning to fine-tune one's pace to the project seems both prudent and useful. Of course, discovering and integrating a quieter, natural rhythm and pace into one's life can also benefit overall well-being, health, and peace of mind.

Experiential Exercises

The Basic Preparatory Instructions for All Experiential Exercises that you worked with earlier contain several quieting components. In this chapter section, we will present additional bodily and mental exercises that will allow you to relax and quiet yourself much more thoroughly and deeply. These detailed exercises are designed to help you relax your muscles (progressive relaxation exercise), relax and quiet your internal systems and emotions (autogenic training exercise), and let your mental functioning become more peaceful and quiet (meditation exercises).

Unfortunately, physical and mental activities do not always want to quiet and slow down—or they seem to do so reluctantly. Accustomed to the fast pace of modern life and the mental and emotional chatter that usually accompany a hurried life style, you may find the experiential exercises in this section difficult or rebel against them. If at any time, you find that the exercises make you feel disoriented or dizzy, modify them. For example, instead of spending thirty minutes to complete an exercise, try doing it two or three times for shorter periods of time. At the end of the first experiential exercise, additional suggestions are also offered that may suit you better. As with all the research skills presented in this book, quieting and slowing down become easier with practice. Additional slowing experiential exercises can be found in the Embodied Writing section of Chapter 7.

The best way to treat these exercises is to make audio tape recordings of these instructions in your own voice, speaking slowly and leaving adequate pauses and times for the experiences to occur. Later, with your eyes closed to avoid distractions, you can follow your own prerecorded instructions.

Slowing Down Exercise

Note: In preparation for this exercise, you will select a mandala, painting, photo, or other image as a focus of concentration. Any image will do as long as it has a fair bit of visual detail. When you begin, place the image in front of you.

When you are ready to begin, focus your gaze on the mandala, painting, photo, or image in front of you. Choose a point on the image at which to begin. As slowly as you can, move your eye around the image. You can move around the image in any direction or pattern, but do so very slowly. Continue this slowed-down concentration for at least ten minutes. If you notice that you want to speed up, simply return to slowing down.

After about ten minutes, close your eyes and focus inwardly for a few minutes.

Maintaining your slowed-down concentration, gently bring a life situation or a research topic to awareness. Recall a particular moment or past activity in which you were directly engaged in the life situation or the research topic. Pick one instance and relive it through all your senses *as though in slow motion*. Notice what you feel and sense about it for roughly five minutes.

When you feel complete, return gradually to everyday awareness.

For about ten minutes, write down any impressions or insights you had about the life situation or your research topic, or express them in symbols or images using art supplies.

Repeat this exercise from time to time to update your familiarity with your topic.

Alternative Concentration

Most people are highly focused when engaged in activities they love. Activities like fly-fishing, cooking, gardening, and acts of affection are good examples of enjoyable activities that lend themselves to a slowed-down pace. If focusing on an image did not help you to quiet and slow down, choose an activity you love and engage in it at a slowed-down pace. Do the exercise as above, substituting this alternative activity for the slowed-down concentration on the image.

Progressive Muscular Relaxation Exercise

This is an exercise for physical relaxation. Relaxation is the elimination of all muscular tension. Make yourself as comfortable as you can. When you relax, do not think about these instructions. Just follow them passively and automatically. When tensing any part of your body, leave all other muscles completely relaxed. *Be careful not to overdo the tension in any muscle group.*

Begin by curling your toes downward into a tense position. Tense up more and more and notice the discomfort. Hold this tension for a moment . . . then let go . . . relax. Relax your toes completely and feel the difference. Instead of curling your toes, arch them up toward your face and feel the tension and discomfort all along your shins. Hold this tension for a while . . . then relax. Feel the relief in your legs. Next, curl your toes again and tense up your entire legs and calves, making sure the rest of your body is completely relaxed. Hold this tension . . . then relax. Enjoy the feeling of relief that accompanies the removal of muscular tension. Relax all tension, release all pressures, place your body in a state of deep relaxation, going deeper and deeper every time.

Now, tense your stomach muscles as tightly as you can. Hold this tension . . . relax . . . relax. Let go completely. Relax. Now arch your back and feel the tension all along your spine. Hold the tension . . . relax. Settle down comfortably again. Allow your body to sink pleasantly onto the surface that is supporting it. Let go of all of the tension in every muscle of your body. Now focus attention on your arms and fists. Relax the rest of your body completely. Tense your fists and bend your arms at your elbows, flexing your biceps. Hold this as tightly as you can . . . then relax. Let your arms flop to your sides. Relax completely. Now, take in a deep breath, fill your lungs, feel the tension all over your chest. Hold this breath . . . then exhale. Feel the relief as you exhale. Relax. Make sure that all of the body parts that you have concentrated on are completely relaxed. If there is any tension, relax those muscles completely.

Now, press your head back as far as it will go. Feel the tension in the muscles of your neck. Hold that tension . . . then relax. Relax your neck. Relax your head. Bend your head forward now . . . touch your chest with your chin. Hold that tension . . . relax. Relax completely. Now, tightly squinch up all the muscles of your face and around your eyes, making a face. Hold this tension . . . relax. Remove all strain and tension. Relax your neck . . . your throat . . . your mouth . . . relax even your tongue . . . relax your scalp . . . smooth out the muscles of your forehead and your scalp . . . relax your eyes and all of your facial muscles. Relax . . . relax. Relax every muscle of your body. Focus on that area that is most relaxed and imagine that same pleasant positive, relaxing feeling to spread, engulfing your entire body in one comfortable, warm, pleasant feeling of relaxation.

Relax totally and completely. Scan your body again for the slightest bit of muscular tension. If you find tension anywhere, relax it. Replace it with relaxation . . . until your entire body is limp and loose and relaxed, like an old rag doll would appear to be. And you are that relaxed. Your relaxation will continue and will deepen through the remainder of this exercise. Now take a deep breath . . . and exhale . . . and as you exhale, you relax more and more. With each breath, you're becoming more deeply relaxed. To relax even more deeply, count mentally from ten to one, and with each count, feel yourself going deeper and deeper into a profound relaxed state . . . an ideal state. (Count from ten to one, slowly.) Relax. Maintain this relaxed state for as long as you wish.

When you wish to return to your regular state of consciousness, take several deep breaths, mentally count from one to ten, then return to your usual state of being—feeling fine and functioning normally and efficiently.

The exercise just presented involves *alternate tension and relaxation*. This is a good way to begin learning relaxation. Once this has been practiced several times and mastered, the tension components can be eliminated, and one can practice *relaxation alone*, calling attention to major parts of the body—from toes to head—and deeply relaxing each part in turn.

Autogenic Training Exercise

This autogenic (self-created) training exercise is designed to help you relax and quiet your autonomic nervous system—the system that regulates your emotions and your unconscious bodily functions. The intended effects will occur naturally and automatically as you repeat to yourself the phrases you're about to hear. Don't exert any effort whatsoever; don't try to make these changes occur. Just passively attend to the parts of your body as they are mentioned, and the effects will automatically occur. Don't try to make anything happen, because it will happen on its own as you mentally repeat these phrases:

I feel quite quiet. I am beginning to feel quite relaxed. My feet feel heavy and relaxed. My ankles, my knees, and my hips feel heavy, relaxed, and comfortable. My solar plexus, the whole central portion of my body, feels relaxed and quiet. My hands, my arms, and my shoulders feel heavy, relaxed, and comfortable. My neck, my jaw, and my forehead feel relaxed. They feel comfortable and smooth. My whole body feels quiet, heavy, comfortable, and relaxed. I feel quite relaxed.

My arms and hands are heavy and warm. I feel quite quiet. My whole body is relaxed and my hands are warm . . . relaxed and warm. My hands are warm. Warmth is flowing into my hands. They are warm . . . warm. All of my extremities are heavy. All of my extremities, especially my hands, are warm.

My heartbeat is calm and regular. My heartbeat is regular and calm. My entire circulatory system is functioning flawlessly, smoothly, regularly.

It breathes me. My breathing is calm and regular. My breathing is very peaceful and regular. It's taking care of itself. It's as though something is breathing me. In . . . and out. Calmly. Regularly.

My solar plexus, the central area of my body, is warm.

My forehead is cool. My forehead and the area around my forehead are cool.

I am very peaceful, quiet, and relaxed. My extremities are heavy. My extremities, especially my hands, are warm. My heartbeat and respiration are calm and regular. My solar plexus, the central portion of my body, is warm. My forehead is cool.

Maintain this relaxed and quiet state for as long as you wish.

When you wish to return to your regular state of consciousness, take several deep breaths, mentally count from one to ten and with each count, let yourself return to your usual state of being—feeling fine and functioning normally and efficiently.

Although the autogenic training exercise just described can be used alone, it can be made even more effective if it is preceded by progressive muscular relaxation.

IMPORTANT: After practicing any of these exercises, return slowly to your ordinary state of consciousness. Do this by opening your eyes, taking several deep breaths, stretching all of your muscles, and perhaps shaking your arms a bit. *Be certain you have returned to an alert state before going about your everyday activities.*

The next exercises involve ways of quieting one's mind. Mental quietude can be accomplished through the use of concentration and meditation exercises. These exercises also involve the skill of *effectively deploying attention.* The attentional skill will be covered more fully in the next section of this chapter.

There are countless forms of concentration and meditation that could be used to reduce cognitive noise, to quiet our constant mental chatter and calm our mind's restless activity. We will present only two such mental-quieting exercises—one involving attention to breathing and one involving attention to a repeated mental sound. The mental sound exercise can be found in the auditory skill section of Chapter 5.

As with the two previous exercises, it will be good to audiotape record these mind-quieting exercises in your own voice, speaking slowly and with pauses (indicated by the . . . in the text), and later play the tape and follow your own prerecorded instructions.

Attaining Mental Quietude Through
Attention to Breathing: Four Variations

Variation 1

Begin by finding a quiet place and time when you will not be disturbed. Close your eyes, and relax yourself as thoroughly as possible. When ready, attend fully to your breath . . . to your exhalations . . . your inhalations. Breathe using your diaphragm, your abdominal muscles, rather than you upper chest muscles. Exhale deeply . . . let all of the stale air flow out of your lungs. Inhale deeply . . . fill your lungs completely with fresh air. Breathe deeply and regularly. Pay attention to the felt movements of your abdomen . . . as you breathe naturally, regularly, and fully . . . attend only to your breathing. Simply observe your breathing . . . do not attempt to alter it . . . simply notice it, witness it. If other thoughts stray into your mind, gently push them aside and return your attention to your breathing. Acknowledge the thought, but quickly and peacefully dismiss it and return to your breathing. Direct your full awareness to the movements and feelings of your breathing.

Variation 2

Relax yourself, then focus attention on your breathing as you did before. This time, however, imagine that you can see the air flowing in and out through your nose . . . imagine it as a clear mist. Watch and feel the air move in and out through your nostrils . . . as you breathe deeply and regularly . . . smoothly and effortlessly.

Variation 3

Relax . . . and focus on your breathing as you did before. Continue to relax. This time, breathe smoothly and effortlessly as you count your breaths mentally, in this simple manner: one, as you breathe out . . . two, as you breathe in. Repeat your counting . . . over and over. Focus your awareness only on your breathing . . . and your counting. One . . . two . . . one . . . two. . . .

Variation 4

Relax . . . and focus your attention on your breathing. This time, focus complete awareness upon the transition or changing point between breathing out and breathing in . . . and between breathing in and breathing out. Continue to relax . . . continue to breathe deeply, regularly, smoothly, effortlessly . . . as you now attend only to the transition point between breaths . . . the changing point between exhalations and inhalations.

You've briefly experienced several methods of focusing on your breathing. Practice each method for longer periods of time and choose the one that feels best for you. Practice it often. This focus of attention upon your breathing will help quiet your mind. In addition, you are learning a skill, learning how to consciously direct your full awareness and concentration. This skill will improve, generalize to other aspects of your life, and help increase your efficiency.

REMEMBER: After carrying out any of the experiential exercises described in this book, be certain you have returned to an alert state before going about your everyday activities.

Using the Quieting and Slowing Skill
in the Three Major Research Stages

Here are some specific examples of how the quieting skill might be used, personally, by the researcher in the three major stages of any research project. These uses are written here in a first-person format.

In the *preparatory and data collection* stage of my research project, I will use quieting and slowing to

> help me to set intentions more appropriately and embed them more strongly in my daily habits and rhythms
>
> help me change my mental attitude, emotional state, or rhythm in ways congruent with my research topic
>
> help me remind myself of the importance of this research project and why I am conducting it
>
> have a fresh mind, body, and emotions as I clarify my topic, purposes, and the audiences I wish to reach through this project
>
> help me "break set" and be less confined and constrained by old habits as I think about creative ways to conduct this study
>
> help me enter states of bodymind in which I am most able to meet, establish rapport with, and be open to my research participants and to what they will report to me
>
> adjust my bodymind so that I am more sensitive and aware, using all of my senses during my data collection—to maximize what I will learn from my research participants

In the *data treatment and interpreting* stage of my research project, I will use quieting and slowing to

> help me empty myself of preconceptions, biases, and expectations in analyzing and interpreting my data
>
> help me become more aware of my biases, as they surface during this stage of my research project
>
> help me adjust my rhythm so I will notice what is important in the data more easily
>
> increase the likelihood that I will be able to access a bodily felt sense of what is most and least important as I work with my data
>
> help me remember and relive what my participants reported to me during the data collection stage as congruently as possible with their sensibilities, attitudes, and rhythms

maintain a condition of freshness and of "beginner's mind"
that can help me be more sensitive to finding what is
most important in my data

set the stage for better use of my intuition in sensing meaningful patterns in my data

care for myself during this process—taking necessary breaks
to avoid fatigue

In the *reporting/communicating* stage of my research project, I will use
quieting and slowing to

help decrease any anxiety I might have about writing my
research report

help me have a fresh and open mind as I consider the best
presentation modes, organization, and language to use
in reporting my findings

help me imagine likely audience reactions to what I am
presenting and use this as guiding feedback in my actual
report writing

use a style and cadence in report writing and other presentations of findings that invite my audience to genuinely
hear what I am communicating

We recommend that the student or researcher think about specific
ways that she or he can practice the quieting and slowing skill and
apply it in each of the three major research stages. An optional exercise would be to consider how the researcher might instruct research
participants to use this same skill.

Additional Considerations

In connection with this quieting and slowing skill, we often used the
term *bodymind*. We did this to emphasize the intimate interrelationship
among physical, physiological, and psychological processes, and to
play down the usually suggested dichotomy between body and mind.

The relaxation, quieting, and slowing techniques described in this
chapter section have been richly applied in psychology. For example,
the relaxation procedures initially explored by Edmund Jacobson (1938)
later were used extensively in areas of behavior therapy, especially in
the form of "systematic desensitization," used for reducing various
fears, anxieties, and phobias. A useful review of this early work can be
found in Franks (1969). Relaxation and quieting techniques have been

used extensively in both research and practical applications in areas of hypnosis, biofeedback, and psychophysiological self-regulation. Physical relaxation and mental quietude also are common accompaniments and aftereffects of various forms of contemplation and meditation. A useful treatment of the very extensive research literature on meditation can be found in Murphy, Donovan, and Taylor (1997).

In considering the role of concentration and of certain forms of concentrative meditation in clearing and quieting the mind, the following analogy might be useful. Just as regular, large ocean waves can subsume and organize a set of smaller, more random and less organized ripples, so too can attention, when consistently applied to one object (one's breath or a repeated inner movement or sound) replace the mind's random stirrings with one larger, more consistent, simple, and repetitious pattern. If that pattern presents itself over and over again, one adapts or habituates to it—and it, too, can seem to vanish from one's awareness, leaving one's mind relatively "empty," quiet, and peaceful.

As mentioned in this skill's introductory section, a condition of bodymind relaxation and quietude is one that has many useful accompaniments and aftereffects. This tranquil, unstructured, unconstrained condition can allow a kind of freshness and beginner's mind that can foster creativity, through the breaking of prior sets and habits, and can permit other forms of perception and knowing to emerge and be applied to one's research project.

Additional useful treatments of processes very relevant to the nature and power of the quieting and slowing skills addressed in this section can be found in the following sources: Benson (1975), Braud (2002b), Goleman (1988), Hunter and Csikszentmihalyi, (2000), Judy (1991), Keating (1991), LeShan (1974), Naranjo and Ornstein (1971), Pennington (1980), and Schultz and Luthe (1969).

Efficiently Deploying and Focusing Attention

My experience is what I agree to attend to. Only those items which I notice shape my mind—without selective interest, experience is an utter chaos. Interest alone gives accent and emphasis, light and shade. . . . (James 1950, 402)

About Attention and its Uses

Once the bodymind has been prepared—through quieting or other appropriate procedures—one can practice techniques of deploying and focusing attention. The control and modulation of one's own attentional processes can play a very important role in research. Ways of working with attention include "de-automatizing" attention from its usual automatized (robot-like) or habitual mode, shifting attention from outward to inward foci, slowing down or speeding up attention, focusing attention on particular aspects to be investigated, making the focus of attention smaller or larger (changing the focal plane or magnification of one's attention), and observing what is occurring in different channels of one's bodymind. One can practice attending to different channels of information and practice shifting from channel to channel in order to increase one's overall appreciation and apprehension of any object of inquiry. These channels—several of which will be treated in detail in the following chapters—include vision, audition, proprioception, kinesthesia, thoughts, images, feelings, emotions, memories, anticipations, intuitions, and direct knowing. One can learn to discern what is available in each channel and to discriminate the nature and sources of all of this content. One can practice deep and careful (in both meanings of the word *careful*—"filled with caution" and "filled with caring") listening to others and to nature, and deep and careful seeing of others and nature. One can release controlling one's attention and allow it to float freely and hover evenly (Speeth, 1982), in the manner of *witnessing consciousness*. One can allow new understandings to surface, in the context of a group field, as in Bohmian dialogue practices (Bohm 1996). *Focusing* techniques, developed by Eugene Gendlin (1978) and his co-workers, may be useful in bringing attention to bodily conditions and accessing the body's knowledge and messages.

One can observe not only the object of inquiry, but also what happens in its vicinity or context. Noticing various environmental events (curious things that just happen, relevant readings or other useful resources that present themselves) can provide expanded understanding of what is being studied. Environmental events (synchronicities, serendipitous occurrences) can even provide forms of confirmation or affirmation that one is on the right track, and they may also indicate negations or warnings that one is proceeding in a way that is not useful or wise. Such observations and lessons are part of what has been called the "context of discovery"; although crucial in any form of research, these real-life influences are rarely mentioned in formal research reports.

All of the above are ways of paying attention, of realtime observing. They are skills of observing, noticing, and mindfulness that can be enhanced through practice. Along with developing the skills themselves, it is important to note carefully, remember, record, and document one's observations so that these can be worked with and reported later.

Spiritual and wisdom traditions recognize special forms of attention beyond those to which most of us are accustomed. These may be called forms of spiritual attention; contemplation; reflection; seeing with an inner eye; seeing with one's heart, soul, or spirit; listening to inner guidance or to the still, small voice within. These special forms of attention are treated by Needleman (1991), Amis (1995), and Tart (1986, 1994, 2001), and in the *Philokalia* (Palmer, Sherrard, and Ware 1979–1995), *The Way of the Pilgrim* (French 1965) and the Patanjali Yoga Sutras (Prabhavananda and Isherwood 1969; Taimni 1981). Some have suggested still another form of attention or awareness that is content-less or objectless (see Forman 1997; Forman 1999; Valle and Mohs 1998; Merrell-Wolff 1973). Special kinds of attentiveness and awareness have been treated in the literature on mystical experiences (Braud 2002d; Deikman 1980a; Deikman 1980b; James 1980; Progoff 1957).

Mindfulness can be understood as a special form of full and deep attentiveness. It also manifests as being present in time, having the capacity to identify and disidentify appropriately, having self-awareness, and having skills of self-observation.

Identifying, recognizing, and practicing these various forms of attention, and learning to appropriately focus and deploy one's attention, are skills that are essential to useful and productive research.

In my own life, I (W. B.) have tried to further develop my own attentional skills in order to be more sensitive to what might be helpful and harmful in my environment and in increasing my discernment of the most useful and productive people, places, and ideas to approach and which to avoid. It is true that energy follows attention. However, I also have learned how to let my attention follow my energies in determining which activities to engage in at which times. Watching where my attention is going at any given moment also gives me clues about my current motivations and needs.

In my own research work, I practice being optimally attentive to which subject areas, topics, and questions might be most usefully explored in research projects. I also attempt to focus my attention strongly on the most salient aspects of what I am reading or learning from discussions and presentations of others. I am attentive to my bodily reactions and feelings with respect to what I am exploring and uncovering in my research preparations, procedures, and findings. In carrying out my research projects, I deliberately shift my attention, back and forth, from specific study details and specific findings to the larger picture or greater context in which the present project is but

a small part. My own studies in areas of psychoimmunology, physiological self-regulation, and parapsychology (Braud 1978; Braud 1981;
Braud 1992; Braud 1995b) rely importantly on certain uses of attention
by my research participants. I'll describe some of this in more detail
in the later chapter section on *direct knowing*.

Experiential Exercises

For this skill, the experiential exercise involves practicing shifting one's
attention outwardly and inwardly in various ways while acquiring
information in the form of a *research interview*, so that your intake of
information becomes deeper and more complete. Once the bodymind
has been prepared—through quieting or other appropriate procedures—
you are ready to practice techniques of *deploying and focusing attention*.

Note: For purposes of this exercise, the interview could take
a variety of forms. It might be a "live" interview that you conduct
with someone about any topic of interest. In this case, simply have
someone discuss some topic while you keep your own comments
and prompting to a minimum. It might be an audio- or video-taped
interview that you conducted and recorded earlier for later listening
and viewing. You might watch a television broadcast and treat this
as a surrogate interview. If you do this, an actual news interview or
something similar would be best—i.e., someone talking about a topic for
some reasonable length of time. You might even consider interviewing
yourself, via a mirror, as you discuss some topic of interest. You might
videotape yourself, as you discuss something of great interest with the
camera. In lieu of any of the previous procedures, you might *imagine*
an interview. Be playful and creative in choosing and setting up the
interview. Some students have been especially creative and playful,
and have used this as an opportunity to "interview" a pet animal or
even some relatively interesting and complex aspect of a particular
environment, through careful observation and attentional shifts.

Practice in Directing and Shifting Attention

Step 1. Prepare yourself by following the Basic Preparatory Instructions for All Experiential Exercises. Begin, as
usual, by setting a firm yet gentle intention that you will
perform the exercise in a useful manner, that you will learn
useful things in carrying it out, that the exercise will be
enjoyable, and that there might be future benefits to others
of your present work with this exercise. Quiet your body-

mind in a way that is appropriate for you. Relax . . . slow down . . . witness your breathing . . . notice how your body is being supported by the surface beneath you. Suggest to yourself that you will remain relaxed yet quite alert, sensitive, and attentive during the rest of the exercise. Set an intention that you will be able to shift your attention appropriately and effortlessly, in order to notice important things, during the exercise.

Step 2. Once you have prepared yourself, begin attending to an interview (see the note above).

Step 3. As the interview is in progress, practice shifting your attention to various channels. Notice what happens as you deliberately shift your attention, during the course of the interview, to emphasize respectively, the words the person is using, the changing tone of voice of the interviewee, and the body language and changes in body language of the interviewee. Deliberately shift your attention to how you are receiving and responding to the information being presented—notice how your body responds to various things the interviewee says, notice any feelings or emotions that arise within you as you listen to the interviewee, notice any movements that occur in you, notice any images that might arise. Notice associations and memories that might arise. Witness yourself witnessing the interview. Imagine viewing and appreciating the interview from a perspective other than yours or the interviewee's—what is the entire interview like from that other perspective? Notice what is happening in the environment, around the interviewee and around you. Shift your perspective, your attention, from the figure of the interviewee speaking to the background from which this figure stands out.

Step 4. Shift your attention to these various foci or objects and hold attention at each suggested place long enough to note what is happening. Then move attention to another channel or locus. Once you have sampled many of these places for deploying your attention, complete the exercise, and maintain a relaxed, alert, attentive state while you journal for five or ten minutes, describing what happened during the exercise, and writing these observations to preserve them and to ground the exercise. Remember: You do not have to limit your "journaling" to written words. You can include nonverbal expressions such as drawings, paintings, symbols, collages, and movements, as well.

Step 5: Review what you have drawn and written for what you have learned about this attention-focusing and attention-shifting skill, as well as the new things you have learned about the process of interviewing and the content of interviews—and new things you might have learned about yourself.

Step 6. Repeat this exercise from time to time to update your familiarity with this skill and its uses.

Using the Attention Skill in the Three Major Research Stages

Here are some specific examples of facets to which a researcher can direct attention during each of the three major stages of research.

In the *preparatory and data collection* stage of a research project, the researcher can direct and focus attention on the following aspects of the study:

if and how the project has importance and holds meaning for the researcher; attending to bodily reactions and "felt senses" via Eugene Gendlin's "focusing" procedure (Gendlin 1978) can help in this assessment

ways in which the study might serve to advance our understanding of the subject matter and topic, and contribute to the growth of the discipline

what are the most salient findings and theories, as found in the reviewed literature?

the research approach and design that might best serve the hypotheses or questions of the study

the most important procedural steps to build into the study

the best ways to find the most appropriate research participants

identifying the researcher's preconceptions and possible biases

identifying the study's demand characteristics (aspects of the study's procedures, environment, and general context that might influence the participants' experiences and

what they might think about the study) and considering
how those might influence the study's results
identifying the conditions that will help participants be as
comfortable as possible during the study
how will the researcher communicate the aims of the study
to the participants in ways that will be clear and effective?
observing the participants carefully to assure that they
truly are comfortable during the study, and making any
necessary changes to assure such comfort
have the participants understood what is being asked of
them, and decide whether they are providing useful
responses to the researcher's questions?
attending to many channels of communication in the participants, and shifting from one channel to another. As
mentioned in the experiential exercise, attending not only
to speech or written *content*, but also to the participants'
voice qualities, bodily changes, and so on
attending to the researcher's own internal reactions upon
receiving information from the participants (bodily reactions, feelings, associations)
attending to what is happening in the immediate outer
environment at the time of the study; could those environmental events have relevance to what is being studied?
recognizing whether the study is going according to protocol
and whether any procedural changes might be advised
knowing when sufficient material has been collected and
it is time to stop

In the *data treatment and interpreting* stage of a research project, the
researcher can direct and focus attention on the following aspects of
the study:

identifying/recognizing what is most salient in one's data
identifying meaningful patterns in one's data
using one's own bodily and affective reactions as useful
indicators of something about the qualities of different
aspects of one's data
when reviewing a participant's account of an experience
that is being studied, shifting one's point of view to
that of the participant, which may permit insights into
the nature and meaning of the experience that otherwise
might not be possible

being more confident about the true *source* of what one
reports: is this information really present in the collected data or is it coming from the researcher's own
preferences, expectations, wishes? (This is another way
of saying that it is important to practice *discernment* in
reviewing one's findings.)

noting not only consistencies in one's data, but *exceptions*,
as well

recognition of ways in which one's findings support or do
not support one's hypotheses

knowing when sufficient analysis or data treatment has
occurred, and it is time to stop

In the *reporting/communicating* stage of a research project, the researcher
can direct and focus attention on the following aspects of the study:

the best ways of organizing one's materials in reporting them

one's care and clarity in writing in order to avoid vague,
unclear, or ambiguous statements

the completeness and professional nature of the report

care about not overgeneralizing one's findings or conclusions

remembering to indicate possible limitations of one's study
and one's findings

considering how my intended audience(s) might respond
to each aspect of what is being written

the researcher's own needs and self-care

knowing when the reporting is sufficient and it is time to
stop

The reader is invited to fine-tune and expand upon the above listings
of ways of using attention in specific research projects.

Additional Considerations

It is possible to make a strong case that *intention* and *attention* are
two of the most important—if not *the* most important—processes in
psychology and in human functioning. Evidence for the great power
and importance of attention is provided by the following aphorisms
about intention:

Where and how we place attention determines what we
experience.

Interacting adaptively with the external world depends on learning how to effectively deploy attention.

Attention focused inwardly—on or within the body—can allow the body's healing processes to occur effectively and efficiently. For example, pain signals call attention to areas in which healing processes are needed. We can generalize this to emotional and cognitive conditions that "call out" for attention and healing, as well.

Once we have quieted ourselves (by slowing down, relaxation, etc.), we can make use of our condition of decreased distractions (reduced noise) in order to begin to access more fully the subtle events (internal and external) that previously might have been masked by such interferences. The two epigraphs by McGlashan and Achaan Chah at the beginning of the chapter section on *quieting* offer poetical statements of this process.

A fullness and freshness of attention brings with it many gifts—efficient thinking and action; ability to be more fully present with and for others; feelings of empathy and compassion.

Attending to something fully—while trying to minimize preconceptions, histories, associations, memories, anticipations, and so on—brings a feeling of beginner's mind, with its gifts of freshness, invitation and welcoming, curiosity, and delight.

The learned skills of relaxation, biofeedback, self-regulation, and self-healing have strong attentional components—what we can attend to well, we can bring under voluntary control.

Meditation is really working with attention—training it to be concentrated and focused or diffuse and open.

When we attend to someone or something, we open up an amazingly effective two-way communication channel that can be used for acquiring knowledge about, and for influencing the object of that attention.

Attending well to something is, of course, essential to use-ful perceptions, understanding, learning, and the laying down of memories.

There is a form of knowing in which we can directly know what we "become"—i.e., what we merge with through a fullness of attention. This could be called "direct knowing, knowing through identification, knowing through being, or knowing through becoming (the object of one's knowledge)."

The meditative and spiritual practice of *mindfulness* is another name for the efficient deployment of attention.

In various spiritual and wisdom traditions, there is a form of attention called *attention of the heart*. This is a form of knowing involving the eye of the heart or the eye of the spirit. The heart can know what the senses and mind alone cannot know. As Blaise Pascal (1941 p 95) pointed out: "*Le coeur a ses raisons que la raison ne connaît pas*" (The heart has its reasons, which reason does not know).

The focusing process, as developed by Eugene Gendlin (1978), emphasizes a particular way of working with atten-tion to recognize subtle bodily and feeling messages that otherwise might be ignored; the process can foster physical and psychological well-being.

To not pay attention is to ignore, and to ignore results in ignor-ance.

The transpersonal quality of *appreciation of differences* requires attention to the unique qualities that distinguish individuals and cultures from one another and from ourselves.

We have been addressing ways of paying attention to various foci. A complementary aspect is *receiving the atten-tion of others*. When we pay attention to others, we can be fully present to them, treat and honor them as unique individuals, and listen to their distinctive experiences and stories. In this way, we are *respecting* and *regarding* them in special ways. Having attention paid or devoted to one is just as beneficial to the receiver of that attention as it is beneficial to the giver of such attention. In this connection, the concepts of *research*, *respect*, and *regard* are interrelated. These all have to do with honoring their object with careful, repeated, and full attention.

CHAPTER 5

Visual, Auditory, Visceral, and Movement-related Senses

Perception is cumulative, generally simultaneous, and necessarily selective. Rarely does one part of the sensory system act alone. Nearly all sensory signals go first to a relay station in the thalamus, a central structure in the brain, for integration with other sensory input and then to primary sensory areas of the cortex and "higher centers" for interpretation and response. For example, dimensional interpretation of a visual image is cued by information from touch, smell, taste, sound, movement, and visceral activity. In the big view, all senses are one.

—Andrea Olsen (2002, 57)

In the West, in everyday life, we usually recognize the five specialized sense perceptions of sight, touch, smell, taste, and sound. However, neurologists and psychologists identify several other sense perceptions within the human body, including a sense of balance called "equilibrioception," derived from sensations from fluids in the inner ear, a sense of orientation of our limbs and movements in space called "proprioception," and a sense of overall sense of movement called "kinesthesia." A complex of sensations also arises from the many organs *within* the body, which is referred to as the visceral sense in this chapter. In addition, the psychologies of Eastern spiritual and religious traditions, especially Buddhism, consider sense perceptions a state of being, that is, a way of sensing the world in expanded ways via the senses. Sense perceptions are used conventionally but are also considered perceptual windows for apprehending the world more profoundly. Chögyam Trungpa (1999) states a Tibetan Buddhist view:

. . . your sense faculties give you access to possibilities of deeper perception. Beyond ordinary perception, there is super-sound, super-smell, and super-feeling existing in your state of being. These can be experienced only by training yourself in the depth of meditation practice, which clarifies any confusion or cloudiness and brings out the precision, sharpness, and wisdom of perception—the newness of your world. (23)

Obviously, scientific research always involves collecting and analyzing data derived from the perceptual senses. What is desired are externally-verifiable data, that is, data that can be observed by another person or measured by a machine. However, in transpersonal research and in related human science disciplines, it also can be useful to include subtle sense perceptions that expand beyond the ways in which the senses are used throughout a research project—from articulating a research topic, designing a study, collecting data, analyzing and interpreting data, and preparing a research report. Conventional and expanded data can complement and deepen understanding of research topics. This chapter explores both the conventional and expanded uses of the senses so that beginning and seasoned researchers may make choices appropriate to their topics, goals, audiences for which the research is intended, and the researchers' views concerning data and insights from sources outside what is ordinarily considered objective and externally verifiable.

In recent years, Western science—especially in areas of sensory physiology, physiological psychology, neuroscience, cognitive neuroscience, and neuropsychology—has begun to explore the amazing complexity of the human perceptual and imaging systems. Advances in technology may in time substantiate aspects of the Eastern "science of the mind" derived from hundreds of years of introspective, meditative analysis. The coming together of Western science and Eastern wisdom traditions is exemplified by recent conferences at leading universities in which the Dalai Lama and Western consciousness researchers met to exchange findings and ideas. Outcomes of some of these conferences are summarized in books by Harrington and Zajonc (2008), Hayward and Varela (2001), and Houshmand, Livingston, and Wallace (1999). The current coming together of Western science and Eastern wisdom traditions is in itself an advancing "science" of discovery, synthesizing centuries of human understanding that brings insight to the capacities—some yet to be discovered—within human experience.

Specifically relevant to this chapter, our human ability to walk across the room is not only a finely coordinated set of physical sensations, neural impulses, and physical movements, but is also determined by our ability to image ourselves walking. We can imagine ourselves walking because of thousands of similar experiences since childhood that have built upon one another in complexity and nuance. Given the role of higher-cortical forms of imagery in perception, implicating all the senses, the perceptual senses are more simultaneous or continuous with one another rather than discrete. An extreme form of sensory functioning called "synesthesia" involves the simultaneous activation of several senses, such as experiencing colors, shapes, or textures when one hears particular sounds (Marks 2000). A more everyday example of the perceptual confluence of the senses might involve listening to a song that evokes feelings and memories and in turn evokes responses within the body that give the song added meaning and nuance. Moreover, when we recall something from the past, we are not watching a silent movie from a bygone era. Memories are often full of "sound and fury." Some form of imagery seems implicit in nearly all interpretation and understanding. Therefore, we begin this chapter with the visual sense, because most people use visual metaphors for describing imagery, even if the image contains texture, smell, taste, and/or sound.

In this chapter, we limit our discussion to the auditory, visual, visceral, and movement-related senses in order to give glimpses of the ways in which the perceptual senses may be used in both conventional and expanded ways. Note that according to sensory physiology and even in Tibetan Buddhist thought all perceptual senses are rooted in or involve the sense of touch in some way (Denma Locho Rinpoche, pers. comm.)—visual sensations touching retinal cells, and olfactory sensations touching olfactory receptors, and so on.

The experiential exercises in each section of this chapter invite readers to explore and practice each of these four senses for themselves. Although we will not directly discuss the tactile, gustatory, and olfactory senses in this chapter, many of the experiential exercises throughout this book involve these senses as sources of data and insight relevant to all phases of research.

Vision Skills: Imagery, Visualization, Imagination

Ibn al-'Arabi refers to this faculty of the empowered imagination by the word himmah. Himmah refers to that transfiguration of the mystic's imagination that allows him to do two important things: (1) it allows him to convert the imaginative faculty into an "organ" that perceives subtle realities or spiritual dimensions that otherwise lie hidden to physical sense organs and (2) it allows him to endow the creations of his own imagination with objective, extramental existence through a process involving both concentration and mental projection. (Hollenback 1996, 252)

Of course, the researcher uses familiar vision skills for interacting with the outer world in all phases of research—for reading and summarizing relevant literature, writing and diagramming plans for a study, preparing and using various standardized assessment instruments, watching the research participants during the data collection stage, attending to the data during the analysis and interpretation stage, and preparing a written research report. Such outer focusing of vision-related skills can be complemented by internally focused visual skills. These inner vision-related skills take the forms of images, visualization, and imagination.

Visualization, Imagery, Imagination and Their Uses

Images—not only visual imagery, but imagery in any and all of the various modes or channels—can carry information and knowledge just as, or sometimes better than, words can. Attending to spontaneously arising imagery can inform the researcher. *Memory images* can provide additional information about the object of inquiry. Used in this manner, imagery can serve as a vehicle for "time-displaced," rather than realtime, observations. The researcher can use memory images to more vividly relive experiences that are similar or identical to what is to be studied in a particular research project.

The researcher can use *visual imagery* for anticipating and planning all of the necessary steps of a research project—finding research participants, considering all necessary procedural steps, thinking visually about how the data might be treated and reported, and so on. Imagery—in the form of imagining what might be—also can be used to bring new, creative possibilities to mind. This skill can be used in the process of "imaginative variation" in some forms of phenomenological research (see, for example, Moustakas 1994).

Imagery also may be used in a more active, deliberate mode as a vehicle of attention and intention, in order to help bring about desired goals—as we saw in the previous chapter. The term *visualization* is often used for the employment of imagery in such a deliberate, active mode. As in the case of imagery, visualization may occur within any of the sense modalities and need not be limited to the visual mode. Certain psychological conditions may facilitate the incidence, vividness, and power of imagery. Some of these special conditions include deep relaxation, spontaneous dreams, incubated dreams, hypnagogic states (Mavromatis 1987), hypnosis, and the use of ambiguous backgrounds onto which imagery might be projected. In many spiritual and wisdom traditions, methods are suggested for working with images and for empowering them for particular purposes (Corbin 1972; Corbin 1981; Hollenback 1996). Such uses are particularly prominent in forms of Tibetan Buddhism, in certain Kabbalistic methods, in imaginal work in Sufi traditions (Ibn 'Arabi), and in the Jungian practice of active imagination (Hannah 1981). Imagery also finds a place in more mundane contexts, such as behavior therapy, mental practice of sport and athletic skills, memory facilitation, and so on.

Consider for yourself the many ways in which imagery and active imagination affect your life. Which colors and patterns are harmonious to you, annoy you, stimulate you, incite your creativity? What do you actually remember about a human face, your own face, or your dreams? Have you ever "seen" an idea or visualized the solution to a problem? Can you imagine into different futures or possibilities as though dreaming forward in time? Can you imagine, for example, planning, carrying out, and reporting the results of a particular research project? Can you see the research report? Can you read its title, notice how it feels in your hand, or scan its findings?

In my own life, I (W. B.) use visual imagery and visualization extensively. I use these processes especially for representing intended outcomes and goals when I set, frame, and hold intentions, and also use them for aiding my memory (by visualizing places or settings in which I first experienced the to-be-remembered information). In my research projects, participants in my studies often use visualization and imagery skills in representing desired outcomes in biofeedback, physiological self-regulation, and psychoimmunology studies, and as vehicles for accessing parapsychologically acquired information and for representing goal events in studies of direct (distant) mental influence.

As one example of the power of visual processes in research, I once was struggling for months in attempting to understand a particular scholarly and research issue involving the role of interconnectedness, altruism, and selfishness. On one occasion, I practiced the "handmade midrash" technique developed by Jo Milgram (1992; see exercise in the Play section of Chapter 7) while filling myself with the issue I wished to solve and holding an intention for a solution. As I organized the hand-torn paper segments into a visual collage, the answer to my previously resistant issue suddenly became crystal clear. The visual (and manual) process had revealed what months of more intellectual, verbal thought-based work had not been able to accomplish.

Experiential Exercises

We include two experiential exercises that will allow you to practice visualization and imaginal skills in connection with research projects you are considering.

HINT: You can read these instructions beforehand, then do the exercise. Alternatively, you might make an audio tape recording of these instructions to yourself in your own voice, leaving adequate pauses and times for the experiences to occur, then play the created instruction tape, as you follow the instructions with your eyes closed.

Experiential Exercise:
Revisioning a Relevant Prior Experience

As usual, it will be helpful to begin this exercise by using the Basic Preparatory Instructions for All Experiential Exercises described in Chapter 1.

Find a place and time that will allow you be undisturbed while you carry out the exercise. Close your eyes and become comfortable and at ease. Think about a particular experience you would like to explore in a research project. It is best to choose a positive experience—one that you will enjoy revisiting. Relax your bodymind, and allow all external and internal distractions to fall away. Witness your breathing for a few moments. Center your awareness fully in the present moment. Give yourself a suggestion that your visual experiences during this exercise will be especially clear, vivid, and informative.

Now, in your imagination, recall a particular—and particularly rich—experience that is closely related to what you will be studying in your research project. Ideally, this is an experience identical or similar to the ones you will be studying—an experience you yourself have had. Fill yourself with that experience. Mentally, relive that experience. Remember and reconstruct it so fully and clearly that it is as though you are having that experience right now. Take some time to allow your reexperiencing to become as full, rich, and complete as possible.

Now, what does your visual sense reveal about the experience? What are your visual surroundings at the time of this experience? What are its colors, shapes, textures? What is happening in your visual imagery—before your mind's eye? What shapes, colors, brightnesses, darknesses, shapes, forms, and textures arise before your mind's eye? Observe them, witness them, as they effortlessly and clearly appear. Remember them well. What do your visual images and sensations reveal about the experience and about its circumstances, accompaniments, and outcomes? What are the visual contents that arise—the people, objects, forms, backgrounds, fields? Are they static? Do they move, change, transform?

Enjoy this revisioning experience for a few moments—as though it were a movie unfolding vividly before you.

Remember what you experienced, and when you are ready, open your eyes and draw and write an account of your experience. This will help ground the experience, and help you recall the lessons it provides.

Experiential Exercise: Three Visual Gifts

Prepare yourself, as you did in the previous exercise. Again, relax and let distractions melt away. As you relax more and more, give yourself a firm yet gentle suggestion that this exercise will provide you with rich and informative experiences in your visual imagination. With your eyes closed, and your bodymind comfortable, relaxed, and free, allow yourself to become eagerly expectant about what will spontaneously and clearly arise during the rest of the exercise.

When you are ready, imagine that you are relaxing comfortably and peacefully in your favorite place in nature. It is as though you actually are present in your favorite natural place. Notice the surface that is supporting you in this place . . . the sounds around you . . . the fragrances . . . the temperature . . . is there a breeze? . . . Let yourself enjoy being here, in your imagination for a moment.

Now, somewhat magically, three very attractively wrapped gift boxes appear on the ground before you. The boxes seem to be glowing and pulsating with a curious, inviting energy. One box is blue, one is yellow, and one is green. Intrigued by what the boxes might contain, you approach the first box—the blue box—and eagerly undo its blue ribbons and its blue wrappings. When you lift the blue lid from the box, a strange and very pleasant blue mist issues forth from the box. You watch, delighted, as the mist forms itself into an interesting and informative scene in the quiet air before you. As in a waking dream, the mist is forming itself into a visual dramatization of an important lesson about your research topic. Depending on the stage of your work, the scene, shapes, and images that form in the pleasant blue mist can reveal something useful and important about your topic, research questions, design, participants, results, or provide an effective visual answer to any question you have about your work. Watch that visual answer unfold . . . and learn from it. Watch, enjoy, and learn from the visual scene that unfolds before your grateful mind's eye. Observe carefully the shapes, colors, and scenes that form and swirl and change and transform before your mind's eye. The visual information may inform you directly and obviously, or it may suggest more subtle knowings. After a few moments, the mist gathers itself into a stream and is drawn back into the blue box. You cover the box with its blue lid . . . thankful for the experience.

Now, repeat this exercise with the other two boxes. From the second yellow box, there emerges a pleasant yellow mist. What forms does it assume? What informative scenes related to your research project does it reveal for you? Witness the visual images that spontaneously emerge . . . learn from them . . . remember them. . . . After a while, the yellow mist gathers itself into a flowing stream and is drawn back into the yellow box. You cover the box with its yellow lid . . . thankful for this second experience, which adds to what you observed and learned from the blue mist.

Now, repeat the exercise with the third, green, box. What do you observe in its green mist? What do the visual images into which it forms itself allow you to become aware of, regarding your research project? Witness the visual display . . . learn from it . . . remember the lessons it provides. After a few moments, the green mist gathers itself into a glowing, translucent stream, and flows back into its green box, which you cover with its green lid.

When you are ready, open your eyes, and draw and write what you observed and learned from the three colored, visual imagery displays. This will help ground the experience, and help you recall and profit from it later.

Using Vision-related Skills in the Three Major Research Stages

Here are some specific examples of facets to which a researcher can apply visual, visualization, and imaginal skills during each of the three major stages of research.

In the *preparatory and data collection* stage of a research project, the researcher can use vision-related skills in the following ways:

Visual memory images can be used to help the researcher recall and imaginally relive experiences that are relevant to the study. By remembering as much as possible about one's own experiences, one is better able to study the similar experiences of others more fully and deeply.

Visually imagining each step of the research procedure— both from the researcher's point of view and from the participant's point of view—can allow the researcher to plan the study more carefully and avoid missing any necessary procedural steps.

The researcher can ask research participants to use their own visual imagery to aid them in recalling and reliving aspects of the experiences that they will be reporting during the study.

The researcher can ask participants to bring to the study various photographs and other visual materials that could help them recall the experiences they will be discussing.

The researcher can attend to the visual appearances of any data collection forms and standardized assessment instruments used in the study to assure that they are clear, inviting, professionally prepared, and aesthetically pleasing.

Of course, the researcher will use visual skills to be very aware and observant of the participants' actions and visual cues during research interviews, and in carefully reading transcripts of those interviews.

Video recording could be used, to capture visual, nonverbal aspects of interviews, provided this is appropriate and comfortable for the participants.

Researchers can suggest that their participants can use visual expressions (photographs, drawings, paintings, collages) to help them better express their experiences or feelings related to the topic being researched.

In the *data treatment and interpreting* stage of a research project, the researcher can use vision-related skills for the following aspects of the study:

Researchers can use visual memory images to help recall the participants, their reports, and other circumstance of the study, while they are working with the data collected in that earlier research stage.

The researcher can use visual mind-mapping (Buzan 1991) to help organize and make sense of collected data and patterns that might exist in those data.

The participants' reports and other collected materials may elicit visual images that could increase the researcher's understanding of the data.

Visual images and visual associations that spontaneously arise during data treatment can provide clues as to the meanings of various findings.

Dream imagery could be relevant to and aid the researcher's understanding of what was learned in a research study.

The researcher can use visual creative expressions (drawing, painting, collage work) to help provide greater understanding of what the research findings might reveal.

In the *reporting/communicating* stage of a research project, the researcher can use vision-related skills for the following aspects of the study:

> The researcher can use visual memory images in recalling what the participants provided, as she or he writes about what was learned from them.
>
> Care can be taken to assure that the research report is visually clear, inviting, attractive, and professionally prepared.
>
> In addition to the usual linear text, the researcher can consider visually enhancing the research report through the use of tables and figures, and even artwork and photos.
>
> The researcher can visualize possible audience reactions to various aspects of the report, as these are written, and let this serve the function of guiding feedback in the preparation of a final research report.
>
> Guided imagery can be used to prepare, relax, and care for oneself in this research stage and in all research stages.

We invite the reader to fine-tune and expand upon the above listings of ways of using vision-related skills in specific research projects.

Additional Considerations

The familiar saying, "a picture is worth a thousand words," is quite true. Pictures, and visual perceptions (of both inner and outer objects) are able to provide rich, complete, integrated, and instantaneous appreciations that are very difficult, and sometimes impossible, for linear sequences of words to provide. Visual and visualized images have a special holistic, gestalt quality that verbal, analytical prose does not possess. Consider, for example, the ease and speed with which one can visually identify someone's face as opposed to the difficulty of describing that face using words. Because of the power of imagery—whether prompted by outer or inner sources—including visual and visualized components in each stage of one's research project can be quite productive and rewarding for the researcher, the research participants, and those who receive the final research report.

Visualization and visual imagination can be used as carriers or vehicles for other psychological processes. Intentions can be framed, set, and held using visual imagery of the intended outcomes. Memory can be aided through the use of visual imagery in which the to-be-remembered contents are "placed," mentally, in various "locations"—in the so-called "method of loci" as used by the Greek lyric poet Simonides of Ceos (see Yates 1974) in the fifth century BCE. Visualization has been used, often and successfully, in helping person's reduce fears and anxieties through the therapeutic method of "systematic desensitization," in which previously fear-arousing situations are vividly imagined and visualized during conditions of deep relaxation in order to extinguish the previous fear responses. Athletes have used visual imagery to mentally practice their athletic skills in addition to their usual physical practices. Images can serve as vehicles for accessing parapsychologically acquired information—as in, for example, precognitive dreams—and also for exerting direct mental influences upon a variety of physical and biological systems (see Braud 2001b; Braud and Schlitz 1989). An extremely practical application of visualization is in the use of imagery to enhance one's physical, psychological, and spiritual health and well-being (Sheikh 1986; Sheikh 2001; Sheikh 2003).

The Auditory Sense:
Listening to and Creating Sound in Research

The bristly bundle of "stereocilia" at the top of the cell quivered to the high-pitched tones of violins, swayed to the rumblings of kettle drums, and bowed and recoiled like tiny trees in a hurricane, to the blasts of rock-and roll. (Goldberg 1995, 35)

We are surrounded by sound and vibration. Some of them are within our perceptual range and others are not. Our domestic cats and dogs respond to sounds we do not hear. Vibrations in the atmosphere, such as radio, cell phone, and broadband waves, pass through our bones and tissues much of the time. Sitting in a medieval cathedral listening to an organ playing, we hear the tones with our ears and via the chambers of our pelvis that resonate with the lower frequencies. Atoms vibrate throughout the universe. While sleeping, our auditory sensors are still on alert; otherwise, we would not awake up to the sound of a slamming door or an alarm clock. We hear these sounds because the sensory receptors of our inner ear convert the frequencies in our environment to mechanical and wavelike motions and finally neurochemical signals that travel to our brain stem, thalamus, limbic system, and cortex for interpretation.

What we hear is both internal and external, and objective and subjective as well. While reading a letter or email from a loved one, we often hear the sender's voice as we read. Sometimes we hear songs playing as though inside our head for hours or even days after a concert. An angry conversation may leave an auditory impression that is hard to diffuse except over time. Sacred drumming and music in spiritual traditions worldwide can elevate people to reverie and ecstatic states. In some spiritual traditions, especially in the East, great musicians are revered as mystics who teach through the sounds they create. Similarly, in many religious traditions, while reading and studying scripture are valued, listening to scripture read aloud is considered essential for genuine understanding. For example, in Buddhism, a *lung* is the recitation of the words of the Buddha recited or chanted by a teacher who received the spoken words in a lineage of recitation going back to someone who heard the Buddha speak them. Listening to a lung is thought to impart realizations greater than commentaries or teachings about the original text. Similarly, the Qur'ān is widely read, but understanding the Qur'ān is a matter of truly listening. Gerald Bruns (1992) tells us that

> Qur'ānic exegesis . . . is quintessentially an exegesis of the ear, since the eye alone cannot know what it is reading. This does not mean that the Qur'ān is not for study and that one should not search the text and meditate upon its smallest detail; but each detail is accessible only through listening . . . one cannot, strictly speaking, hold the Qur'ān in one's hands (away from oneself) . . . rather, as a recitation the Qur'ān surrounds us with itself, fills the space we inhabit, takes it over and ourselves in the bargain. The whole movement of reading as an appropriation or internalizing of a text is reversed. Here there is no grasping and unpacking and laying the text bare. On the contrary, reading is participation. (126)

In this brief introduction to the auditory sense, it is important to understand that hearing and listening, like all the perceptual senses, is a sophisticated resource for insight. Of course, we need to record, analyze, and interpret literal sound. However, hearing and listening can also render a great deal of complexity of meaning and depth to many research projects if researchers integrate the use of the auditory senses in nuanced ways. The experiential exercises below provide a few ways that you might begin to explore the sensitivity of the human auditory system and prepare yourself to integrate conventional and expanded ways of hearing and listening to your research project.

Experiential Exercise:
Attention to Inner Sound and Silence

Take a deep breath . . . and as you exhale, relax deeply. Become as comfortable as possible. Dismiss all thoughts, feelings, and images from your mind . . . let your mind be still as best you can.

Focus, now, on an inner sound. Choose a word, very short phrase, or feeling that is simple, pleasant, and meaningful to you. Many people choose the word *one*, or *love*, or *peace*. You might try the word *calm*, or *quiet*, or *relaxed*, or *peaceful*. Simply repeat the word or phrase mentally, again and again, in a slow natural rhythm. Push all thoughts from your mind and attend only to your centering word. If anything distracts you, gently dismiss the distraction and return your attention to the word. Focus your full awareness upon your sound, as you repeat it mentally, again and again. Do this for a while. . . .

After you have focused on your word for a while, stop attending to the word and allow your mind to become blank, still, and silent. Focus on the enveloping silence surrounding you. You might wish to imagine a circular fence around you to help keep out thoughts that like stray sheep may creep in to disrupt your silence. When a thought-stray appears, be patient . . . like a shepherd . . . and guide the stray away. No matter how many times the stray returns, gently guide it to the edge of awareness.

Invite silence, both inner and outer, to nourish you and bring rest, quietude, and balance to your life. Rest in silence, the absence of sound.

Enjoy the nourishing silence for as long as you wish . . . then stop this exercise when the time seems right.

Experiential Exercise:
Listening to and Expressing Auditory Impressions

Session 1

Let your bodymind quiet and your awareness expand. Gently remind yourself of your research topic. Bring to your awareness a particular instance in which you experienced the phenomenon you wish to study (or one very similar to it). Allow your awareness to remember the instance in all its sensory dimensions.

As your senses expand, attend particularly to the sounds accompanying the experience. Initially, they will probably be only external sounds. Listen slowly, picking up nuances if you can. Then, begin to listen to and imagine whatever inner sounds you may hear. Are there sounds within your body? Are tunes or melodies or lyrics prompted by this auditory emersion? Are there sounds, lyrics, or voices that seem to come from your past or from far away? Notice what you hear. When you feel complete, return to ordinary awareness and take notes or journal or draw pictures to record your impressions.

Session 2

Let your bodymind quiet and your awareness expand. When your bodymind quiets and your awareness expands, gently remind yourself of your research topic. Bring to your awareness a particular instance in which you experienced the phenomenon you wish to study (or one very similar to it). Allow your awareness to remember the instance in all its sensory dimensions.

Without thinking much about it and without much ado, get up, walk around, and pick up simple objects in your environment to make sounds that somehow evoke an auditory expression of a recollected experience. You may wish to use chopsticks as drum sticks, spoons as a percussive instrument, or a closet door as "swisher." Maybe you'd like to sing, chant, whistle, call, or even scream. Notice what you do and hear yourself sound. When you feel complete, return to ordinary awareness and take notes or journal or draw pictures to record your impressions.

Experiential Exercise: Listening to Outer Sounds

Note: Practice this experiential exercise in a relatively quiet place so that you can attend to the quiet sounds around you and sounds at a distance. (This exercise was informed by a conversation with Zen Buddhist teacher Sonja Margulies.)

Let your bodymind quiet and your awareness expand. When your bodymind quiets and your awareness expands, begin to attend to sounds that you usually do not notice because they do not signal threats or they seem peripheral to whatever you are doing. Notice what you hear when your mind is free of mental chatter. You might suddenly notice the birds singing near your house, distant highway traffic, or children playing in your neighborhood. If you are doing this exercise at night, you might even hear the low-pulsing, buzzing sound of electricity in your house.

Notice that attention to ambient sounds helps you quiet your mind because it distances you from your thoughts. If thoughts appear, gently move them to the edge of awareness and continue to listen to the external sounds available in your environment. Enjoy the extension of your awareness outward into your environment through sound and the "absence" of self.

Enjoy this state of awareness as long as you wish . . . then stop when the time seems right.

Experiential Exercise: Listening for Nuance

When your bodymind quiets and your awareness expands, gently remind yourself of your research topic. Bring to awareness an experience of talking to another person about the experience you wish to study or one very similar to it. Recall the experience in your imagination as best you can. If you have a recording of an interview of someone describing an experience you wish to study, listen to it now. You might even record your own memory of an experience related to what you wish to study and then listen to it.

Listen to the overtones, nuances, pauses in the person's voice that you may have missed the first time, using your new appreciation for subtlety of sound (that includes silence). If you have the luxury of having a recording of an interview, listen to it again and again until you feel you have truly heard all the overtones, nuances, and pauses in the speech pattern. Listen beyond the point in which you are utterly bored with the content of what they are saying because the nuance of sound is usually beyond what interests the conceptual mind. Take notes or draw insights you have based on listening again . . . and again.

Next time you conduct an interview, use these skills during the interview to hear more. Next time you are analyzing or interpreting data, imagine the sounds of your interviewee speaking in order to let the sound of the timbre and sound of the other's voice inform your analysis and interpretation.

Using the Auditory Sense in the Three Major Research Stages

Here are some specific examples of facets to which you, as a researcher, can apply aspects of sound, hearing, and listening skills during each of the three major stages of research. Suggestions about the use of the visual sense (mentioned in the previous section) may also apply to the auditory sense as well. For example, video recordings record sound.

In the *preparatory and data collection* stage of a research project, you might use the auditory sense in the following ways:

Auditory memory can help a researcher relive her own experiences related to the topic studied. You might try to recall the experience by focusing on the sounds you can recall. These recollections may help you to ask research participants relevant questions in an interview because you are more familiar with the possible "soundtrack" of similar experiences.

Research participants often neglect to report the background soundtrack associated with recalled experiences. However, if you ask them to focus on the sounds that occurred, they often can recall them readily and in detail.

Ask participants to bring to an interview personal sound recordings, musical recordings, or musical instruments that may prompt or support their recollection of past experiences or otherwise support their research participation.

Ask participants to sing a song, hum a tune, or tap a rhythm that seems congruent with recollected experiences or with how they are feeling while participating in the study. Follow up with questions about how participants understand the relevance of that song, tune, or rhythm to their experience.

Bring musical instruments, drums, or sound-making objects to a study so that participants can use them to evoke the tempo or feelings associated with the past or during their participation in the study.

In the *data treatment and interpreting* stage of a research report, you might use the following the auditory sense to support analysis and interpretation:

If you video or audio recorded an interview, listen to the recording with your eyes closed. Focus on the nuances in the participant's voice, sounds in the environment, and sounds associated with the participant's behavior. Also listen to the nuances in your own voice and other sounds you, as the researcher, made during the interview as indications or reminders of your initial reactions.

While analyzing and interpreting data, your reactions are signals about what is important in the data. For example, while listening to a participant's recorded voice, note the sounds they make that attract, irritate, or are neutral to you. Take note, too, of the sounds in your environment that attract, irritate, or are neutral to you, especially while engaging in challenging aspects of the analysis.

Use sound to help you organize or notice patterns in your data. If an interview reminds you of a song or tune, take note of the song or tune as potential insight about the data.

Just as visual images may help you identify common features among participants' reports, the emotional or feeling tone is often better represented by sound, especially music or song lyrics. If you are having difficulty understanding the emotions or feelings of participants or sense that underlying emotions and feelings were not directly expressed in the participants' words, sing a song, hum a tune, or tap a rhythm that expresses the emotional or feeling tone of data to you. You may even wish to sing, hum, or tap in response to various parts of a large data set to help you identify common features or recognize patterns that you may otherwise miss.

> Often researchers play music while analyzing data. If you do, notice what musical selections you make while analyzing different sections of a data set. Your selections may give you clues about the data that might otherwise go unnoticed.

In the *reporting/communicating* stage of a research project, you might use the auditory sense in the following ways:

> When writing a research report, recalling the sound of participants' voices may help you relay their experiences more accurately, especially if you are trying to relay the participants' emotions and feelings.
> If possible, with permission from participants, include a digital recording of the participants' voices in the document or provide an Internet link to these recordings.
> As you write, use rhythms and your writer's voice to evoke in the readers an emotional and feeling tone that reflects your current understanding of the topic studied.
> Most people laugh, cry, holler, and grimace while they read, at least occasionally. Ask readers to take note of the spontaneous sounds they emit while reading. You might also ask them to respond to specific findings with their own voice by singing or making sounds aloud or on a musical instrument.

We invite all readers to fine-tune and expand upon these suggestions by creating auditory-sense skills that suit their research goals and individual personalities.

The Visceral Sense:
Sensations Originating From Within the Body

> Your body is not a machine, rather a wonderfully intricate interaction with everything around you, which is why it "knows" so much just in being. . . . You can sense your living body directly under your thoughts and memories and under your familiar feelings. (Gendlin 2007, 1)

In this chapter, the term *visceral sense* is used to describe the many senses originating from organs within the human body. There are many sense receptors spread throughout the organs of the body, including those that monitor blood chemistry, heartbeat, blood pressure, and digestion. Along with these visceral processes, skeletal muscular tension changes are also implicated. The body's recognition of these sensations are ongoing processes within the autonomic or visceral nervous system that constantly monitors and controls the vital organs. Ordinarily, we do not pay much conscious attention to these complex sensations within our bodies unless something goes wrong. If we get dehydrated, if our heart beat becomes unusually rapid, or if our blood-sugar level is low, we tend to notice these.

An important part of the autonomic nervous system is the enteric nervous system within the lining of the digestive tract. This complex network of nerves lines the entire digestive tract, from mouth to anus, and is part of the peripheral nervous system. What is unique about the enteric nervous system is that it can register impulses, remember, and feel in ways that are independent of the brain and spinal cord. Michael Gershon (1998) refers to the sensations arising in the enteric nervous system as "the second brain." For Andrea Olsen (2002), the enteric nervous system is the "brain in the gut," constantly "processing sensory information and maintaining homeostasis, with little or no interaction with the brain and spinal cord" (52). Most of the time, we are not consciously aware of these sensations. Nonetheless, most of us are likely to remember times in which we had a gut feeling about a situation that we could not help but notice. We got a creepy sensation in our belly when we met someone or entered a room. A particular street at night seemed dangerous, and we walked another way to our destination. Of course, sometimes we interpret these feelings incorrectly and yet, at other times, we are uncannily correct. Whether we are right or wrong, quite likely, our enteric nervous system is signaling us to be attentive and careful, even if our rational mind has no idea why. In a sense, our primitive, mammalian body is working on our behalf. These sorts of subtle inner reactions may be what underlie certain forms of intuition.

Recent evidence suggests that the heart itself, as well as the gut, possesses brain-like anatomical structures and functions. For information about the "heart brain" the interested reader can consult this website: www.heartmath.org/research/research-our-heart-brain.html. Since the enteric nervous system is functioning constantly, we can learn to attend to its sensations and use them as sources of information and insight in our everyday lives and apply them to research as well. However, modern, industrialized cultures rarely emphasize these sources of information or insight in our educational systems or in the rearing of children. So many of us are unaccustomed to sensing into our bodies, even to notice the onset of a headache or flu until the tension becomes so great that we cannot ignore it. The good news is that we can learn to pay attention to the sensations within our bodies and especially those arising from the neural network in the digestive tract. Unfortunately, the bad news is that learning how to notice and accurately interpret these inner sensations can take a lot of time and practice. Especially, if we are going to use these sensations as sources of information about others and in research, we need to discriminate these sensations from our own desires and projections. Often, our strong, inner reactions have more to do with our own personal histories and what we might want from another or a situation than it has to do with the other person or situation. Only repeated practice of witnessing our own habitual forms of reactivity will allow us to finely discriminate between the viscera-related information that belongs to us and those that belong to someone or something outside of ourselves. Even with experience, we can still be wrong, so caution is advised. The two experiential exercises in this section invite you to begin this exploration.

Experiential Exercise: Inner Sensing

Note: For this exercise, you will need to select three photos, symbols, or objects that have personal significance for you. If you are studying a particular research topic, you might pick objects that remind you of that topic in a significant or symbolic way. Place them in front of you so you can see and move them easily.

Let your bodymind quiet and your awareness expand. When you are ready, with your eyes closed, begin to witness the subtle sensory impulses that originate inside your body. You will feel sensations arising from the organs of your body, especially within your digestive tract. Witnessing the impulses inside your body is a form of inner body scanning. The impulses are probably soft and gentle unless you are experiencing pain or tension. However, even when relaxed, most people will find some tension or discomfort somewhere in their bodies. Relax stressed parts of your body one by one until you are at ease as much as possible. If you fall asleep, you probably need to sleep and do this exercise another time.

Once you feel relaxed and are not distracted by pain or tension, turn your awareness to the subtle sensations and feelings arising from within your body, being especially aware of sensations in your digestive tract, commonly known as your belly or gut. Observe without judgment. Take particular notice of how your body feels before you open your eyes.

When you are ready, gently open your eyes. Gaze lightly at one of the objects you have chosen and placed in front of you. Notice the changes that occur within your body for a few minutes.

When you are ready, gently move your gaze to the second object. Again, notice the changes within your body for several minutes.

When you are ready, gently move your gaze to the third object. Again, notice the changes within your body for several minutes.

When you feel complete, return to quiet meditation and gradually to everyday awareness.

For about ten minutes, write down any impressions or insights you had about each of the three objects or express them in symbols or images using your art supplies.

If you wish to refine your capacity for Inner Sensing, you may wish to practice this exercise many times with different objects and situations until you become familiar with your habitual ways of responding. Some of the exercises in the embodied writing section of Chapter 7 also explore the visceral sense, and you might wish to use them as well.

Experiential Exercise:
Exploring the Felt Sense Through Focusing

Note: Over the last three decades Eugene Gendlin (2007) and colleagues have explored, refined, and researched a technique known as focusing (see www.focusing.org), which explores the felt sense within the body. This experiential exercise is adapted from the Six Steps of Focusing in Gendlin (1996).

Let your bodymind quiet and your awareness expand. When you are ready, begin to witness the sensations and feelings inside your body especially those arising from your chest and gut. Sense within your body. Do not try to change what you sense or how you feel. Maintain a little distance between your witnessing awareness and the feeling states that arise. Just notice them.

From among the sensations and feelings that arise, select sensations or feelings that reflect a challenging personal situation and use those sensations or feelings as the focus for the rest of this exercise. Still maintaining a little distance between yourself and the sensations and feelings, observe the entirety of how you feel about the problem or situation. Your sensations and feelings about the problem or situation are likely to feel vague and unclear. Just notice them.

Pick a word or image to describe the vague feelings you feel. In Focusing, the word, phrase, or image is called "a handle" because it gives the focuser an identifying reference for the vagueness. The handle may be a word like *yucky*, *dull*, *sad*, *scary*, or *sharp*. Find just the right word, phrase, or image that fits your internal feeling state.

Go back and forth between your feeling state and the handle. Change the handle until it fits your feeling sense just right.

"Now, ask: what is it, about this whole problem, that makes this quality (which you have just name or pictured)" (Gendlin 1996, 2) the way it is? What inside me feels this way? What's underneath this problem or situation? When you ask these questions, a felt sense may occur as a slight shift or release in your body. If no felt shift occurs, do the exercise another time or by focusing on another problem or situation.

Stay with the felt sense for a while, gently receiving and releasing into it. Several felt senses may arise. If so, stay with each them as they arise.

When you feel complete, return to quiet meditation and gradually to everyday awareness.

Using the Visceral Sense in the Three Major Research Stages

Here are some specific examples of ways that you, as a researcher, can apply your understanding and awareness of internal bodily sensations in each of the three major stages of research. Review earlier suggestions about the use of vision-related skills and auditory-related skills, as they might apply to the use of viscera-related skills as well.

In the *preparatory and data collection* stage of a research project, you might use the visceral sense in the following ways:

> By recalling a personal experience closely related to your research topic and exploring accompanying responses within your own body, you are likely to be more familiar with the internal bodily responses that may accompany such experiences and, therefore, ask relevant questions of research participants. Especially in fields such as health and wellness, knowledge of inner bodily responses may be essential to understanding a research topic.

> As research supervisors, we often suggest that researchers document their personal responses to a research project in a log or journal as they go along. If you become adept at viscera-related skills, you might wish to include some of your internal responses in that log or journal. Although you may choose not to report these responses in a scientific report, having a log or journal that records your personal process at the time of the response will allow you to check on the accuracy of your memory of your earlier thoughts and responses as well as use some of your records as data in ways appropriate to your particular study.

> If internal physical responses are important to understanding a particular research topic, you might ask research participants to explore their inner sensations during their participation in a study. For example, if your participants tell you they get a headache every time they talk about a particular topic, you might ask them to gently explore the accompanying internal responses that preceded the onset of the headache.

In the *data treatment and interpreting* stage of a research report, you might use the visceral sense in the following ways to support analysis and interpretation:

> While analyzing and interpreting data, your responses to data are signals about what is important. While listening to an interview or watching a video recording of a research participant's responses, notice your internal

response as a source of potential insight about the data. Your own visceral responses provide clues as to possible interpretations. You might wish to simply observe your inner responses or adapt the focusing technique above to data analysis and interpretation.

If you notice similar visceral reactions to certain types of participant responses, your reactions may signal important features of the data that might not be apparent in the participants' words or actions, as recorded. If you are especially skillful at observing your own internal responses to others and discriminating them from your own desires and projections, you may be resonating with the unarticulated, visceral responses of research participants. You might also check the accuracy of your visceral responses to participants' data in subsequent interviews with participants.

In the *reporting/communicating* stage of a research project, you might use the visceral sense in the following ways:

Use your memory of your own visceral responses while conducting interviews and analyzing and interpreting data in order to render clarity and authenticity to your written report.

If internal bodily states are relevant to your topic of study, explore ways to include details of these participant responses in your report. Since scientific reports often summarize common features across many participants, it may be useful to include long excerpts from verbatim transcripts or access to excerpts or digital recording via Internet links.

We invite all readers to fine-tune and expand upon these suggestions by creating viscerally-related skills that suit their research goals and individual personalities.

The Movement Sense:
Sensing, Perceiving, and Expressing Movement

Mind and movement are two parts of a single cycle, and movement is the superior expression. (Maria Montessori)

> Wash the dishes relaxingly, as though each bowl is an object of contemplation. Consider each bowl as sacred. Follow your breath to prevent your mind from straying. Do not try to hurry to get the job over with. Consider washing the dishes the most important thing in life. Washing the dishes is meditation. If you cannot wash the dishes in mindfulness, neither can you meditate while sitting in silence. (Hanh 1975, 85)

Have you ever watched a celebrated pianist play or sopranos sing? Perhaps you noticed that that their entire bodies are moving, undulating, keeping rhythm. Likewise, conductors often become famous for their conducting style. Choral and symphony conductors are not just monitoring the tempo and signaling the baritones or percussion section when to chime in, but seem to play the music in their bodies; every part of the body in motion. The same applies to fine potters at the wheel—not just their hands but their entire bodies attend to the spin speed and molding fluidity of the clay between their fingers. Similarly, have you ever watched a great chemist at the bench or writer at the keyboard? They are not motionless; even their concentration is formed of muscles held in tension. Equally so, conducting research implicates movement too. Ideally, research praxis might be considered movement in action like so many creative processes. The entire body might be involved in all stages of research in one way or another.

Neurologist Oliver Sacks (1987) has proposed that *kinesthesia*, our sense of movement, is our sixth sense, involving a continuous yet usually unconscious flow of movement. Similarly, psychologist Howard Gardner (1983, 1999) has introduced a form of intelligence known as "kinesthetic thinking" that denotes the skilled use of the body, especially in highly practiced activities such as driving one's car well, dancing, gymnastics, or cooking. Even the resolution of mechanical problems is often accomplished by manipulating machine parts with one's hands without thinking through the problem beforehand. Based on numerous other experiences, one's hands seem to know what to do next. If any of us needed to think through the motions involved in driving a car and had to watch and direct our hands and feet consciously, we would not be able to watch the traffic, too. Neurologists call our sense of awareness of motions in space "*proprioception.*" Spread throughout the body in joints, ligaments, tendons, muscles, and the inner ears are proprioceptors that register and transmit sensory information about movement, balance, and bodily position. If we are fatigued or under the influence of alcohol or certain other drugs, our proprioceptive sense is impaired and we are more likely to fall or make a mistake in judgment. Proprioception informs all movement, and skillful, fluid movement is impossible without it.

In spiritual traditions worldwide, transpersonal psychology, and applied fields of dance and massage, we can also bring the practice of mindfulness to movement. In cultivating mindfulness in our activities, we become more relaxed and peaceful but potentially more insightful as well. Elsa Gindler (1995), a foremost teacher of movement in Berlin during the 1920s and 1930s, made the following statement about the advantages of movement to creative activities:

> . . . we see over and over again that people who accomplish the most are fresher than those who do nothing. And if we observe successful people we can often see that they display a wonderful flexibility in reacting, in constantly changing from activity to rest. . . . One must first come to know—through observing oneself—just what one does with breathing while brushing one's teeth, while putting on one's socks, or while eating. So we begin by attempting to waken in our students an understanding of what happens in these daily performances. Then we have them try to make any movement without interfering with breathing. This requires so much work that one could probably stay with it forever. (9)

The experiential exercises in this section will help you explore these possibilities and potentially apply them to your research activities. There are many kinds of movement and movement mindfulness practices. You may be well practiced in one yourself, such as fly fishing, sky diving, or competitive sports-car driving.

Experiential Exercise: Walking Mindfully

Note. This experiential exercise will help you become more aware of the tactile sensations and muscles in your body by focusing on your feet as you walk. Most of the time, we move without particular mindfulness of what we are doing and how we are moving. Walking mindfully is a well-known Zen Buddhist practice that places attention in physical motions. Once you learn to walk mindfully, you can gradually apply what you have learned about mindfulness to other actions—such as washing dishes, conversing with others, data collection and analysis, interviewing or observing a research participant, and so on.

When you are ready to begin, stand up and stretch your body gently. Begin with your limbs, then your head and neck, shoulders, torso, and abdomen. Notice what parts of your body resist gentle movement and stretching. Notice the parts of your body that feel tender, numb, or painful. Notice the parts of your body that feel relaxed and at ease. You might want to shake your body as though to "shake loose."

When you are ready, slowly take a few steps forward. Walk in your usual manner but slow down. Put your awareness in your feet and witness the sensations in your feet. If you are able to put your awareness in your feet as they touch the ground, you will probably slow down even more.

Notice how you place each foot on the ground. What part of your foot touches the ground first, next, and so on? Where is the pressure? How does the pressure of your foot on the ground change as you move forward? Does your foot roll forward or is it nearly flat on the ground? Is the pressure of one foot on the ground different than the other? Are your feet straight ahead, directed inward, or directed outward? Is one foot more inward or outward than the other? Are your feet relaxed or tense? Sore? Numb? Stiff? Achy? Happy? Does one foot feel different than the other? Spend about ten minutes walking with your awareness focused on your feet.

Experiential Exercise: Exploring Authentic Movement

Note: For this exercise, you will need to dress in comfortable clothes that allow you to move freely. Prepare an exercise space in which you have privacy and plenty of space to move freely and without bumping into things that may harm you or cause you to fall. Weather permitting, this exercise can be done outside in a private and open space.

This experiential exercise is an adaptation of a style of spontaneous movement called "Authentic Movement"

(Adler 2002; Pallaro 1999; Stromstead 1998; Whitehouse 1958). Authentic Movement was developed by Mary Starks Whitehouse as a form of dance therapy in the 1940s and 1950s. Since then, Authentic Movement has been used as a wellness and personal-growth practice. Whitehead (1958) describes Authentic Movement:

> In allowing the body to move in its way, not in a way that would look nice, or that one thinks it should, in waiting patiently for the inner pulse, in letting the reactions come up exactly as they occur on any given evening . . . new capacities appear, new modes of behavior are possible, and the awareness gained in the specialized situation goes over into a new sense of one's self driving the car, or stooping with the vacuum cleaner, or shaking hands with a friend. (250)

Session 1

Once you feel ready to begin, bring to mind a personal problem or situation that you wish to resolve. Recall something specific and vivid.

Focus your attention on your body. Feel its subtle movements even as you are sitting quietly in the exercise. Your chest lifts and falls, and your abdomen moves in and out with each breath, in a way specific to the moment. Many tiny muscles in your face support your expression and subtly change without conscious notice. Begin to witness the small and large movements of your body. There is no need to interpret your body's movements, just notice them.

With your attention on your identified problem or situation, lift your hands and arms and begin to gesture spontaneously as from *the inside of your body outward to the world*. Do not direct your gestures with conscious thought or intention. Move your hands and arms, allowing the subtle musculature of your "animal body" to move you. Gesture spontaneously from the inside out. Note the size, rhythm, direction, and emotional significance of your gestures. While gesturing, notice your movements so you can reflect later on what your gestures communicate about your identified problem or situation. Spend several minutes gesturing.

Again, without conscious thought, spontaneously begin to move your entire body about the room or outdoor space. Move your entire body as though moving from the inside out. Open your eyes slightly so you can move freely without bumping into objects or falling. Allow the large and small muscles of your animal body to move you. Again, do not direct your movements willfully. Move spontaneously from the inside out. Notice the size, rhythm, direction, and emotional significance of your movements. As you move about the space, notice your movements. Note your movements so you can reflect later on what your movements communicate about your identified problem or situation? Spend at least ten minutes moving in this way.

When you feel complete, slow down your movements and gently sit down and relax. Allow your breath to relax until you feel quiet and rested within. Return gradually to everyday awareness.

For about ten minutes, write down any impressions or insights you have had about your research while moving or express them in symbols or images using your art supplies.

Session 2

If you have a research topic in mind, you can repeat the experiential exercise exactly as above *except* substitute an experience of or related to your research topic for an identified personal problem or situation.

Repeat this exercise from time to time to update your familiarity with your topic.

Additional Option for Sessions 1 and 2

An optional aspect of this exercise involves asking a trusted friend to witness your movement as is commonly done in Authentic Movement practice developed by Janet Adler (2002). If you want someone to witness your movement, invite them into the space before you begin and ask them to sit comfortably where they can observe but not interfere with your movements. Ask them to read this exercise before beginning so that they know what is happening and what is expected of them. After you complete your movements, the witness writes or draws his or her own experience of your movements. After both you and the witness have written or drawn notes, you may wish to converse. You, the mover, speaks first. Once the mover has shared her or his experience of your moving, the witness describes what she or he witnessed.

Using the Movement Sense in the Three Major Research Stages

Here are some specific examples ways that you as a researcher can apply movement in each of the three major stages of research. Review earlier suggestions about the use of the visual, auditory, and visceral senses as they might apply to the use of the movement sense as well.

In the *preparatory and data collection* stage of a research project, you might use the movement sense in the following ways:

Explore the research topic via gestures, movements, and dance in order to deepen your own understanding of the topic. Use that basis to generate your research question precisely and for framing interview questions.

Invite research participants to gesture, move, or even dance in response to their relayed experiences. Later, you might ask them to reflect on the meaning of their movements.

Invite witnesses to watch and reflect upon the gestures and movements of research participants. Thereafter, you can use the witnesses' responses as complementary data.

For topics directly related to physical movement, be sure to include movement *as* data and make a visual recording that can be used later for analysis and interpretation.

In the *data treatment and interpreting* stage of a research report, you might use the movement sense in the following ways to support analysis and interpretation:

Respond to data supplied by research participants with your own gestures and movements. Thereafter, reflect on the meaning of your gestures and movements. If you notice patterns in your own movements, they may signal important features of your data.

Try moving gently and mindfully in response to participant data in the style of Authentic Movement above and notice what your body signals as important. Then, use your movements as information relevant to analysis and interpretation.

In the *reporting/communicating* stage of a research project, you might use the movement sense in the following ways:

When writing a research report, remember that all human activities, including mental activity, is essentially a form of movement or activity. Therefore, you might wish to invite readers to reflect on the fluidity, change, and movements taking place in any experience or topic studied. Put another way, what is the dynamic of change or transformation taking place in the researcher, research participants, or readers that might escape statistical analyses or words?

Invite readers to gesture, move, and dance to your research reports so that they can experience and witness your research findings through the outward movements of their own bodies.

After your research report is written, move in response to the completion of your research project as a gesture of closure for yourself.

We invite all readers to fine-tune and expand upon these suggestions by creating movement-related skills that suit their research goals and individual personalities.

CHAPTER 6

Unconscious Processes, Direct Knowing, and Empathic Identification

Accessing Usually Unconscious Processes and Materials

The unconscious is nothing other than that which we have been unable to formulate into clear concepts. These concepts are not hiding away in some unconscious or subconscious recesses of our minds, but are those parts of our consciousness, the significance of which we have not fully understood.

—Adler 1935, 3

Man's task is to become conscious of the contents that press upward from the unconscious.

—Carl Jung

Every extension of knowledge arises from making conscious the unconscious.

—Friedrich Nietzsche

Ways of Accessing Usually Unconscious Processes and their Uses

Unconscious processes occur beneath the surface of our awareness and beyond our usual egoic control. Examples include tacit (silent) knowing (see Polanyi 1958; Polanyi 1966) and the work that our bodymind does as it incubates dreams and as it presents new solutions and creative insights. After immersing oneself in information, conscious knowledge, and discursive thought about some topic—letting go, releasing effort, surrendering, and letting things incubate can later yield new ways of understanding, new solutions, inspirations, illuminations, insights, and epiphanies. Increased attention to subtle internal bodily conditions, reactions, feelings, and imagery also can provide access to materials and processes that otherwise might remain unconscious and inaccessible.

There are many ways of accessing materials and processes that formerly were tacit, silent, unconscious, previously outside of our usual conscious awareness. One way is to pay more attention to what our bodies might reveal about aspects that are unknown to the rest of ourselves. Another way—as Freud (1955, 1914) pointed out—is to learn from our unintentional slips of the tongue and unintended but revealing changes in our behaviors, perceptions, and memories. Other "revealers of the unconscious" include bodily illnesses, dreams, and images and feelings that come upon us unbidden. Active imagination is still another of these royal roads to the unconscious, as are forms of guided imagery, creative expression, automatic writing, automatic speaking, and "incubation"—in which things remain active beneath the surface of awareness, only to bubble up into our consciousness at some later time. Some of the sensory and motor automatisms (muscle testing, using a hand-held pendulum, and so on) provide still other ways of accessing our unconscious, as does the process of focusing (developed by Eugene Gendlin 1978). In this chapter section, we explore some of the ways in which previously unconscious materials might be identified, accessed, and used.

It is important to note that some of the approaches mentioned above are controversial for some psychologists. The controversies involve not the procedures or methods themselves, because these can be easily described and replicated and often are quite effective. Rather, the controversies involve *interpretations* of the nature of the processes assumed to underlie some of the methods—that is, exactly what is going on when one uses some of these methods and *how* the methods are able to yield their often impressive results. As in all aspects of research, it is important to distinguish procedures and findings from the alternative interpretations and conceptualizations of what might lie behind those procedures and findings.

In my own life, I (W. B.) have used various forms of dream incubation, guided imagery, and paying greater attention to my reactions and conditions (bodily reactions, behaviors, memories, perceptions) as ways of accessing previously unconscious materials and information—for purposes of problem solving, decision-making, or simply for augmentation of available information about various topics. I have used similar procedures in various research projects for preparing both myself (as researcher) and my research participants.

Experiential Exercises

In the experiential exercises of this chapter section, we will invite our unconscious processes to share some of their gifts with us. We will do this, first, by incubating dreams that might comment in their own ways upon particular aspects of a research project.

Dream Incubation:
Asking One's "Dream Maker" for Research Advice

The exercise involves asking dream advice about a research project. Such a procedure could be used in any and all stages of a research project. For now, we will focus on its use in the planning stage.

Before asking for the dream advice, saturate yourself with information related to the matter at hand. Think about the matter throughout the day. Bring as many relevant aspects as possible to your mind. Ask yourself repeatedly for a useful answer to your question. Imagine your dream maker presenting a useful answer to you in the form of a dream or series of dreams. Imagine yourself clearly receiving this dream advice, remembering it well, and being able to understand and apply it. These are all preparations and pre-intentions for you to set.

The question could be about selecting a particular project, fine-tuning and framing particular research questions or hypotheses, choosing the best research method, making a research-related decision that you are finding difficult, seeking the answer to some aspect of the project that is puzzling you, determining the best way to go about finding appropriate research participants—anything at all that you might be finding challenging about your project.

Just before going to sleep, relax, clear your mind of other things, and focus on the question you would like to put to your dream maker. Present the question as clearly, specifically, and concisely as possible. Ask, explicitly, for a dream or dreams that will supply useful advice about your question—perhaps a new and successful way of looking at or understanding things. Once you have specified the question clearly, give yourself a firm suggestion, and permission to have a dream or series of dreams that will help you answer your question. Imagine yourself remembering this dream in the morning and being pleased with the outcome. Smile. Then, let go of the process. Surrender. Turn the matter over to your unconscious processes . . . and fall asleep thinking, "I will receive a useful dream about my question." Be confident that this will happen. Sleep well!

As soon as you awaken, record as many details of your dream as possible—not only using words, but using drawings or movements as well. Study your dreams, carefully, to find any relevant advice they might have offered about your research.

As an optional procedure, you might ritualize the process in some way. For example, just before retiring, you might drink half of a glass of water. As you do this, fill yourself with the intention that you will have a very relevant and informative dream, and that, when you drink the rest of the glass of water, the next morning, you will recall and understand the dream and its advice very well. When you awaken the next morning, complete the process by drinking the other half of the glass of water and, when doing so, allow yourself to remember and understand your dreams. In the morning, draw and write quick accounts of your dreams—this will help you to note the advice and will allow you to study it more deeply later.

Another way to ritualize the process is to write your question before going to bed—in a short note addressed, "Dear Dream Maker, I would like you to supply an answer to the following question. . . ." You might also tape record your question, just before going to sleep; then, in the morning, tape record your answering dreams. Don't forget to include drawings, movements, or other ways of expressing both questions and answers.

You might try this process for one or for several consecutive nights. Sometimes the answers are given all at once and clearly. Sometimes, they may be given gradually and more subtly. If nothing special seems to happen, repeat the process several times, over several nights. Even when you do receive useful dream advice, repeating the exercise may sometimes fine-tune, extend, and supplement that advice. Confidence and patience are important.

Enjoy the exercise. May it be both rewarding and productive for you.

In addition to dream incubation, several additional means are available for accessing previously unconscious information. For these, we provide only brief descriptions. We recommend that readers consult the indicated resources for further details about these techniques.

The previous dream incubation exercise involved a naturally occurring nocturnal dream. It also is possible to use deliberately induced dreams and dream-like conditions as opportunities for accessing information that otherwise might remain unconscious. Several procedures exist for inducing *waking dreams* (see Watkins 1977) and certain *twilight conditions of consciousness*, which share some of the features of nocturnal dreams. Two of these twilight conditions are the *hypnagogic* (sleep-entering; see Mavromatis 1987) and *hypnopompic* (sleep-leaving) states. We enter these states naturally every time we fall asleep and awaken. However, we usually remain in these states only very briefly and often don't recall was happens during these brief visits. It is possible to induce a hypnagogic state more deliberately, to extend its duration, and to more readily access information made available in this state.

Encouraging Hypnogogia

One way to use a hypnagogic state for accessing previously unconscious material is simply to pay greater attention to your mental content, especially your imagery, whenever you are drifting into sleep. You can use specific intentions for fostering greater awareness and memory for what happens during the hypnagogic state.

A simple method for extending the duration of a naturally occurring hypnagogic state is to place your forearm in a bent, upright, yet very carefully and effortlessly balanced position as you prepare to fall asleep. When you enter the hypnagogic state, the associated decrease in muscle tension will cause the arm to fall. This can help increase the level of activation or arousal experienced during the state, and this can help you remain more alert and aware than usual. If you repeatedly place the arm upright again, once it falls, it is possible to hover in the hypnagogic twilight state longer than usual, and access and remember better the information that now becomes available during this state.

Additional ways of accessing previously unconscious material and information include processes of *active imagination, increased attention to subtle bodily conditions and reactions, automatisms,* and *creative expression.* We address each of these briefly below and invite the reader to consult the recommended resources for further information about the details of these procedures.

Active imagination is a way of consciously working with arising unconscious material. The approach is most often associated with Carl Jung and his followers; however, similar methods can be found in many earlier esoteric, spiritual, and wisdom traditions. In practice, one sets the stage for the emergence of previously unconscious images and then participates actively with these—interacting consciously with these once they have emerged. The emerging content has an autonomous character, and one can dialogue with it and learn from this interaction. The emerging material can have rich symbolic aspects and often is personified during the course of these interactions. The process is similar to that of a *lucid dream* (in which it is possible to deliberately interact with dream characters and influence the course of the dream; see LaBerge and Gackenbach 2000), in that one remains alert and active during the interactions. The use of guided imagery and the procedure of dialoging with some inner guide (a personification of inner wisdom) can be considered variations of the active imagination approach. Useful treatments of active imagination can be found in Hannah (1981) and Johnson (1986).

Increased attention to subtle bodily conditions and reactions involves just what is mentioned—paying much closer attention to one's bodily condition (including symptoms of comfort, discomfort, and illness) and bodily reactions, and attending more fully to unintentional slips of the tongue and unintended but revealing changes in behaviors, perceptions, and memories. Eugene Gendlin's (1978) method of *focusing* can be used to access the meanings of subtle bodily conditions and feelings.

Automatisms are instances in which our bodies make automatic movements and actions without our usual deliberate, voluntary instructions. Typically, we are not aware that we are responsible for these movements and sometimes not even aware of the movements themselves. Usually, the movements are subtle. Examples of these include muscle testing (in which muscle tension or strength may vary when we are exposed to certain materials or asked certain questions about our bodies) and the use of a handheld pendulum (which sometimes can move in different patterns to reveal answers in response to questions). The pendulum moves in response to very subtle hand or finger movements (known as *ideomotor reactions*), which are amplified and displayed by the pendulum. The hand and finger movements are influenced by the pendulum holder's expectations, attitudes, and unconscious knowledge about the answers to the questions being asked. Another instance that could be included in this class would be the feelings we experience as we hope for one outcome rather than another—while engaging in some random decisional process (such as a coin flip) or the feelings of pleasure or disappointment that we might experience in reacting to the outcome that has occurred. Although we might think consciously that we have no preference regarding the decision, our feelings can reveal a preference that has been present all along, but which had remained unconscious until the random decisional process is occurring and threatening to exclude the unconscious, preferred choice. Automatic writing (see Muhl 1963) and automatic speaking are extreme, dramatic instances of automatisms.

Creative expressions, in a great variety of modes, often allow us access to previously unconscious information. These expressions take the form of drawing, painting, working with clay, and engaging in spontaneous movements. These nonverbal procedures can be quite revealing of unconscious motives, preferences, and information, and what is revealed in these ways can supplement our usual word-based functioning. Of course, creative expression also can make use of words, as in poetry writing and fiction writing. These two modes of writing can allow information not ordinarily available to come into our awareness. For more detailed treatments of creative expression, see the Creative Arts section of Chapter 7.

All of the techniques mentioned above can be used to serve various aspects of our research endeavors. As we practice any of these skills and methods as research supports, it is important that we set intentions that research-relevant information will arise as we engage in these practices.

Accessing Usually Unconscious Materials
for the Three Major Research Stages

We organize this section somewhat differently than previous sections. We suggest that the various techniques mentioned above for accessing previously unconscious material, might be used for all three major research stages in order to gain additional helpful information about each stage and to help the researcher make decisions about aspects of each stage. Thus, the procedures for accessing information that might otherwise remain unconscious can be used for the *preparatory and data collection, data treatment and interpreting,* and *reporting and communicating* stages of any research project in the service of the following aims:

> to be more fully informed about the project's subject matter, topic, and approach
>
> to better contextualize the study, both personally and in terms of the field as a whole, and to better understand the project's importance and meaning
>
> to be led to, and understand well, the published literature that is most relevant to the study at hand
>
> to effectively consider the audience(s) one most hopes to reach via this study, and for which purposes
>
> to design the study in the best way possible
>
> to find the most appropriate research participants
>
> to determine the best ways of interacting with participants
>
> to determine the best ways of collecting data
>
> to learn as much as possible while working with the collected data—to find previously hidden patterns in the data
>
> to interpret and conceptualize the data accurately and well
>
> to report the study and its findings thoroughly and clearly
>
> to maximize the intended audience's reception, understanding, appreciation, and use of the communicated findings
>
> to address well the implications and possible practical applications of the study's findings
>
> to plan, conduct, and share the study's results in ways that are maximally beneficial for the researcher, the research participants, the intended audience, the field, society, culture, the environment, and the planet at large

We invite the reader to fine-tune and expand upon the above listings of ways of using these accessing skills in particular research projects and to consider specific ways that the skills might be used for realizing each of these objectives.

Additional Considerations

Chthonic has to do with the underworld—processes that occur in the depths, usually hidden from our view, beneath the surface of our awareness. Chthonic processes happen without our conscious awareness or our usual egoic control. From a surface view, nothing special seems to be happening, yet—unseen and seemingly apart from our usual ways of doing things—important changes are indeed occurring, similar to the growth of plant roots deep within the soil. Related to the chthonic are conditions of auspicious bewilderment, uncertainty, apparent disorder (chaos), and the liminal or transitional conditions in which we are betwixt and between, having given up an older way or identity but not yet having acquired a new way or identity. Letting go of one's attachment to outcomes or to particular products or goals can favor the harvesting of gifts from the chthonic realm. Chthonic conditions favor creativity so that prior confining structures or organizations of thought may dissolve during such states, allowing new structures and organizations to emerge. Chaotic and chthonic conditions help empty us of the old and familiar ways of knowing, being, and doing, so that there is room for acquiring new and less familiar knowledge and ways of being and doing.

The previously treated skills of slowing and quieting, intention setting, and directing attention away from outer concerns and toward inner experiences are useful in setting the stage for the emergence of chthonic, unconscious processes, materials, and information. Those skills help reduce usual impediments to the operation and surfacing of unconscious processes and information, and they also help us more readily access and remember the previously unconscious material once it emerges.

We think it is important not to reify the unconscious as through it were some location or entity within the bodymind. It seems more appropriate to treat the unconscious as a process, a mode of functioning that we usually cannot or do not describe in words. Simply put, the unconscious is that which is currently "untalkaboutable." Once attention is directed to such material, we are able to represent it specifically and concretely by means of feelings, images, thoughts, and then by words.

We also think it is unwise to reify what is responsible for the various automatisms and sources of inner guidance mentioned above. It seems that, although they give the appearance of being autonomous beings or entities, these are other aspects of ourselves—other modes of our own knowing, doing, and being—that become active and more available under special conditions.

Supplementary Resources

For additional information about the various processes mentioned in the above section on ways of accessing previously unconscious materials and processes, we recommend the following supplementary resources:

For general treatments of the unconscious: Ellenberger (1970) and Whyte (1978). For treatments of chthonic, liminal, anti-structure, and chaotic conditions and their relevance to psychological processes: Braud (1985), Clements (Chapter 3 of this book), Combs (1996), Hansen (2001), McMahon (1998), and Schwartz-Salant and Stein (1991). For information about creative problem solving in dreams: Dalton (1952) and Krippner and Hughes (1970). For additional treatments of incubation, creativity, and inspiration: Hart (2000b), Koestler (1976), and Moustakas (1990). For an increased understanding of how depth-psychological and Jungian-based treatments of the unconscious might be applied in research: Coppin and Nelson (2004), Romanyshyn (2007), and Todres (2007). For consideration of African and Egyptian contributions to our understanding of the unconscious: Bynum (1999).

Direct Knowing

We know a thing only by uniting with it; by assimilating it; by an interpenetration of it and ourselves. . . . Wisdom is the fruit of communion; ignorance the inevitable portion of those who "keep themselves to themselves," and stand apart, judging, analyzing the things which they have never truly known. (Underhill 1915, 4)

The truth, insofar as it can be stated in words, must always be a set of instructions on how to awaken the non-dual mode of knowing, therein to experience reality directly. (Wilber 1979, 58)

The simplest description of intuition is the direct knowledge of Reality, a knowledge in which the knower is not separate from either the process of knowing or the object which is known. . . . It is the consciousness of the subject . . . meeting up with the consciousness in the object. . . . In using intuition one has to become involved in what one knows, but without getting lost in it. . . . Intuition underlies virtually all forms of knowing, whether instinctive, aesthetic, imaginative or intellectual. (Salmon 2001)

About Direct Knowing and its Uses

In *direct knowing*, one becomes directly aware of something—-i.e., without the usual intermediaries of words or sensory transmission of information from the object of knowing to the knower. Note that this latter phrase is simply a communication aid; in certain states of consciousness, the distinction between knower and known vanishes; indeed, this is the major lesson of direct knowing. Variations of direct knowing include intuition (in one of its meanings), psychic functioning, participatory knowing, and knowing by being or becoming or identity. Direct knowing also is closely related to processes of empathy, sympathy, identification, resonance, vicarious experience, emotional contagion, and "group mind." It also is related to the processes of insight and inspiration and, perhaps, even to what is known in the spiritual domain as "revelation."

In direct knowing, one identifies with the object of knowing— and, especially, with the experiences of other persons—and therefore knows in a first-person manner. This form of knowing de-emphasizes a hard subject/object distinction or boundary. The process is closely related to experiences of presence, compassion, and love. In each of these cases, there appears to occur a kind of merging or identification of the knower with the object of inquiry, attention, or affection.

In research, direct knowing can allow one to apprehend and appreciate what one is studying more deeply than otherwise would be possible. Through its role in sympathetic resonance, direct knowing also may serve as a way of validating the accuracy or truth of various knowledge claims. Empathic identification with the participants in our research projects can help us in learning from them and understanding their experiences. This kind of attitude toward, and relationship with, our research participants can be fostered by qualities of trust, openness, respect, caring, and loving-kindness (the Buddhist practice of *metta*).

The direct knowing process importantly overlaps the processes of intention and attention, covered in earlier sections of this book. Indeed, *all* of the skills described in this book are implicated in direct knowing, either as ways of setting the stage for direct knowing's emergence or as ways of accessing the information that direct knowing provides. Slowing and quieting techniques can help set the stage by reducing some of the sources of noise or distraction (described in detail in the skill section on quieting) that ordinarily might interfere with the operation of direct knowing and with the subtle information that it can provide. Intention can be used to direct the process, to indicate what is to be the focus of direct awareness. Attention can be directed toward the object of inquiry and also toward the inner vehicles of thoughts, feelings, and images through which direct knowing can be accessed. The various sensory and quasi-sensory modes of vision and audition (in both their outer and inner, imagery, forms), proprioception, and kinesthesia serve as the vehicles through which the directly known can emerge into consciousness. The skills of working with previously unconscious material also are relevant, because initially the direct knowing process is unconscious and only becomes conscious later through the appropriate deployment of attention.

I (W. B.) have accessed direct knowing in my everyday life by attending to and honoring my various hunches, intuitions, and parapsychological experiences and noting instances in which these did and did not convey accurate information. Direct knowing—expressed behaviorally—often has led me to be in the right place at the right time in order to avoid dangers or to satisfy various needs and intentions. In research, I have used direct knowing in finding useful research projects and relevant literature, in finding appropriate research participants, and in interacting with these participants in optimal ways and learning more fully about their experiences.

Experiential Exercises

It is possible that direct knowing is a component, albeit a typically unrecognized one, of many or even all of our everyday interactions with others and with the environment. We can use this naturally occurring process as a research skill by attending to it more fully, deliberately setting the stage for its less impeded operation, and increasing our awareness of the ways in which the knowledge gained in this way might emerge into consciousness.

This simplified exercise in direct knowing is designed to provide a flavor of the skill, and how it might be practiced, albeit more fully and more carefully in the context of research. For this exercise, you will need the assistance of another person. *That person will relive some important experience, and you will seek to gain direct knowledge of that experience, beyond what ordinarily might be possible through the use of words and sensory cues.* Read the following exercise completely first so that you understand its various steps fully before you actually do the exercise.

Experiential Exercise: Practicing Direct Knowing

Assure that someone will work with you in doing this exercise. Find a time and place where the two of you can work together in a way that will be comfortable and undisturbed. You can do the exercise when the other person is nearby—indeed, this is how the skill ordinarily is practiced (as it occurs naturally, in everyday interactions, and as it might occur in an actual research interview setting or in an educational, training, counseling, or therapeutic setting). However, it also is possible to do the same exercise with someone who is located in another room or even at a much greater distance.

Inform your helper that, when you say the word *now*, that person is to relive some important experience that she or he had earlier, and that the person would like you to know about and understand as fully as possible. *The helper is to relive a particular, specific experience*—as fully and completely as possible. Ask the helper to fill herself or himself with the experience—in all of its features: The helper should reexperience the full experience, as though it were happening right now, including as many bodily, mental, emotional, imagistic, relational, and spiritual aspects as possible. It would be best, of course, to have the helper choose a *positive* experience to relive or reexperience, and also that the experience be one that the helper is willing, and even eager, to share with you.

Ask also that when you later say "now," and the helper relives the experience, that the helper hold an intention that you will become richly aware of the experience. That is, the helper should wish and want you to also become aware of, and share in, the rich experience that she or he is reliving.

It is, of course, important that the helper not tell you in advance which experience she or he will be reliving. Your helper should not say anything while reliving the experience. The point of this particular exercise is for you to come to share that experience directly, without preknowledge and without the help of the usual word-based and outer sensory cues.

Begin the exercise, as usual, by letting yourself and your helper become as comfortable as possible. Let inner and outer distractions fall away. Let yourself, and your helper, become relaxed and centered. Use attention to your breathing and other familiar means for relaxing and quieting yourself. Ask your helper to do the same. Let go of all bodily tensions, and rest and relax.

When you feel comfortable and relaxed, let your mind become open to knowing and sharing in the important experience that your helper is about to relive. Give yourself a firm yet gentle instruction to allow yourself to become quite fully aware of the experience that your helper will soon relive. Let yourself be empty, otherwise, so that you will be open and receptive to your helper's experience.

When you are ready, say the word *now*. As your helper relives the meaningful experience, allow yourself to share that experience. Allow your awareness to expand to include the awareness of your helper and your helper's experience. Allow yourself to relive your helper's experience as though it were your own. It *is* your own. Let yourself become as fully aware as possible of the important experience that your helper now is reliving. Let all of the qualities of that experience come into you, fill you, be fully present in you. Attend to how the information arises, directly and effortlessly, within you. Scan the various aspects of yourself—your images, thoughts, bodily sensations and feelings, emotions, memories, your entire imagination and your entire self—so that you can attend to and remember anything that is closely related to your helper's experience. *Spend a few moments becoming directly and fully aware of the experience that your helper is reliving* . . . and remember this accurate information clearly and well.

It probably is a good idea to keep your eyes closed during this experience—to allow yourself to focus your attention inwardly, and to avoid external distractions. You might ask your helper to keep eyes closed as well.

When you are ready, gently open your eyes and draw, write, and express in other ways (movements) as much as possible of what you just learned about your helper's experience. Your helper might continue reliving the experience as you make your written or drawn record.

After you have finished your record, ask your helper to describe his or her relived experience in as much detail as possible, and notice how much of that experience you have been able to share.

Approach the exercise confidently and enthusiastically. We think both of you will have interesting and useful experiences. Enjoy the exercise!

The above exercise is, of course, simply a way of illustrating the direct knowing skill under artificially arranged conditions. The skill would be used much more naturally and spontaneously in an actual research setting. In such a case, it could be guided more efficiently through the use of specific knowledge-serving intentions, set previously by the researcher.

The direct-knowing skill differs from many of the other skills treated in this book in that it is not one that simply can be turned on and off at will. One can set the stage for direct knowing, and one can become more attentive to it and receptive of its gifts. In this, it is somewhat like sleep. We cannot actively will ourselves to sleep. Instead, we invite sleep by reclining, relaxing, freeing ourselves from distracting thoughts, reducing the light level around us, and framing an intention for sleep. Once those favorable conditions are present, sleep comes. So, too, we can invite and encourage direct knowing by arranging conditions favorable to its appearance. We provide below a brief description of how this might be done.

Experiential Exercise:
Encouraging Direct Knowing in a Research Context

Prepare yourself, as usual, by following the Basic Preparatory Instructions for All Experiential Exercises described in Chapter 1. Practice what you learned previously about each of the other skills as you use them in the service of direct knowing.

Set an intention that is appropriate for the given stage of research. For example, for the planning and data collection stage, set an intention for efficient, accurate, and useful direct knowing regarding all of the aspects of this stage—knowledge that will help you in effective planning, making useful decisions, finding and interacting with participants, fully appreciating their experiences, and so on. (See the next section for additional suggestions for using the skill in each research stage.)

Use what you have learned about the slowing and quieting skills in order to relax and free yourself from outer and inner distractions.

Use what you have learned about the attention skills in order to focus attention chiefly on two things:

Focus as fully as possible on what you wish to know directly. For example, in gaining direct knowledge about a participant's experience, attend as fully as possible to that participant; imagine becoming that participant; frame an intention to share that participant's experience; imagine what it is like to be that participant and to be having the experience that the participant is reporting.

Focus as fully as possible on your own inner experiences—on your subtle bodily reactions and condition, on your images, thoughts, and feelings. These will be the vehicles or carriers through which you will become aware of your direct knowing. In other words, shift your attention to your own inner experience, once you feel you have identified as much as possible with whatever you wish to know about directly.

Use what you have learned about the other skills (visual, auditory, proprioceptive, kinesthetic, working with unconscious materials) in order to become more aware of the information that these modes are presenting to you.

Frame an intention that you will remain aware of the most important aspects of the focus of your attention and of your direct knowing, and that you will remember this information well and be able to record it in writing, drawings, and movements later, and be able to report it effectively later on.

Enjoy the experience, and be grateful for the new knowledge and insights you receive in this way.

Using the Direct Knowing Skill in the Three Major Research Stages

Here are some specific examples of facets to which a researcher can apply the direct knowing skill during each of the three major stages of research.

In the *preparatory and data collection* stage of a research project, the researcher can use all of the research skills described previously in order to focus direct knowing on the following aspects of this stage:

knowledge about what is most important about this topic and study

knowledge about the best ways to find and interact with research participants

direct knowledge of the experience being reported by one's participant

In the *data treatment and interpreting* stage of a research project, the researcher can use all of the research skills described previously in order to focus direct knowing on the following aspects of this stage:

knowledge of what is most important in one's data—i.e., its most essential features

knowledge of the most accurate and complete interpretation and conceptualization of the data

In the *reporting/communicating* stage of a research project, the researcher can use all of the research skills described previously in order to focus direct knowing on the following aspects of this stage:

knowing the most effective way of communicating to one's chosen audience

appreciating likely audience reactions to various aspects of one's research report, and using this as guiding feedback in tailoring the report

In addition to the above, the researcher can pay attention to various hunches and intuitions that occur during any and all phases of a research project; these may be manifestations of direct knowing. The researcher also can pay greater attention to the contents of dreams, because these, too, can be carriers of direct knowing. Finally, the researcher can be attentive to shifts (especially unusual ones) in behaviors, perceptions, and memories, because these also can be the bodymind's way of helping to bring direct knowing content into consciousness.

We invite the reader to fine-tune and expand upon the above listings of ways of using direct knowing in research projects.

Additional Considerations

In addition to the forms described above, direct knowing features prominently two areas of research and disciplined inquiry: parapsychological studies and studies of knowing by being/becoming/identity (in several wisdom traditions, especially systems of yoga). In the former, direct knowing can take the forms of telepathy, clairvoyance, and precognition. In the latter, direct knowing can occur during the practice of *samyama* (in the yoga tradition), which involves a deep and full concentration and absorption of attention upon some object of inquiry. Additional details can be found in Braud (2002b), Braud (2008), and Braud (2010).

Empathic Identification

> Feynman revolutionized quantum physics by asking himself questions such as "If I were an electron, what would I do?" (Root-Bernstein and Root-Bernstein 1999, 196)

For the acclaimed geneticist Barbara McClintock, knowing a thing requires empathizing with it. How could she empathize with corn chromosomes? Yet she did. While examining a type of corn fungus under a microscope, her perspective changed from an act of looking at the chromosomes to becoming one with them as though she were them:

> I found that the more I worked with them the bigger and bigger [they] got, and when I was really working with them I wasn't outside, I was down there. I was part of the system. I was right down there with them, and everything got big. I even was able to see the internal parts of the chromosomes—actually, everything was there. It surprised me because I actually felt as if I were right down there and these were my friends. (McClintock, quoted in Keller 1983, 117)

Often, empathic identification seems extraordinary—something only great artists and scientists do. Yet, what could be more ordinary than a mother so identifying with her baby that she senses her child is sick or in danger when the child is out of sight, a cook knowing what spice to add without tasting the dessert, or a ballerina imitating a swan with uncanny semblance? What each is doing is skillful, of course—and yet something more. That something more might be called "empathic identification" with another person, object, or animal. Often they sense and feel the world of the other accurately and respond congruently with that knowing. The world of the other yields to their understanding. In Chapter 1 on intuitive inquiry, empathic identification is portrayed as one of several modes in which our human intuitive sensibilities find expression.

In a chapter on empathizing in *Sparks of Genius: The Thirteen Thinking Tools of the World's Most Creative People,* Robert and Michele Root-Bernstein (1999) describe one example after another of eminent writers, actors, dancers, musicians, hunters, and scientists who attest to their becoming at one with an object of knowing. Writers and actors become the character they portray, albeit temporarily. Musicians feel that their instrument is playing them as much as they are playing it. Successful hunters anticipate the intentions and actions of their prey. Physical scientists imagine what a photon or atom might do under specific circumstances.

In a uniquely insightful discussion, therapist and researcher Tobin Hart describes what he calls deep empathy in the context of psychotherapy:

> Most of us notice that when we pay attention and simply open ourselves to the person in front of us, we come closer

to understanding their experience. . . . But when such an opening does occur, there are sometimes moments when understanding of the other deepens beyond what I can easily explain. I seem to experience the other's feelings directly in my own body or recognize patterns, histories, or meaning that do not appear to come from interpreting the words and gestures that we exchange. . . .

Beyond the exceptional depth that this knowing seemed to provide to the therapy, I came to rely on these connections as a kind of. sustenance. At that time in my life, these were the moment when I felt most human, most intimate with the world, and probably stayed working as a therapist for many years because this practice brought heart and wisdom to the surface. (2000a, 253)

In contrast to empathic identification as a research skill, emotional empathy is a complex emotion (or motivation) with prosocial implications, which has been the focus of considerable recent research in humanistic and positive psychology (David 1996; Penner, Fritzsche, Craiger, and Freifeld 1995; Smith 2009; and Volling, Kolak, and Kennedy 2009). In an influential review, Batson (1998) defines emotional empathy as "an other-oriented emotional response elicited by and congruent with the perceived welfare of someone else" (286). Often, perceiving that another is in need leads to altruistic or helping responses toward the other, whether or not the other feels needful of help. Certainly, empathic identification may also include feelings of emotional empathy and lead to altruistic actions. However, *accuracy* is a defining characteristic of empathic identification as a research skill. Without empathic accuracy, insight relevant to that object of knowing is unlikely.

This section on empathic identification concludes with a word of caution: The challenge of empathic identification, both in everyday life and research, is the possibility of becoming overwhelmed by the emotions and felt impressions of others or situations. In research, the researcher may begin to feel as though he is living the qualities of the research topic too personally. Especially as one is learning or practicing empathic identification, one can feel rather like a "psychic sponge," soaking up into oneself the emotions and feelings of others and situations without modulation. When the research topic itself examines challenging experiences—such as trauma, abuse, violence, and disease—feeling overwhelmed by the experiences of others is also more likely. Suffice it to say that appropriate emotional boundaries can be learned over time. However, even experienced trauma workers will tell you that well-honed boundaries can break down, especially when one is tired or sick. Therefore, give yourself permission to leave a situation, conclude an interaction, or reschedule an interview if you feel uniquely vulnerable. Take responsibility for taking care of yourself. Note that the empathic identification exercise below includes instructions for monitoring your own comfort level during the exercise.

Experiential Exercise: Empathizing With Other

Do this exercise on a day when you have a certain degree of freedom to determine most of your activities and move about freely. If you have responsibilities for small children or other responsibilities that occupy you most of the time, spread out this exercise over several days when you are freer to move about at will.

Remember that empathizing with distressed or difficult circumstances can feel stressful to you. Therefore, only empathize when it feels safe and comfortable for you, that is, when you are not emotionally challenged in any way. If at any time you feel anxious during this exercise, stop immediately.

At the start of the day, set an intention to empathize with the objects, small animals, or people around you for three fifteen-minute intervals during that day. You may either choose the three intervals at the beginning of the day or let the intervals spontaneously occur as though the "other" were choosing you over the course of the day.

Choose only one object, small animal, or person at a time as the object of your attention. When the time for empathizing begins, imagine what it is to be that person, plant, pet, or object as best you can. Try to imagine how the other feels and moves, sees the world, hears sound, etc. Try to get inside the other, experiencing the world from her, his, or its side. If you spend the entire fifteen minutes empathically identifying with your cat or sports car, that's fine. The quality of your experience for empathizing is what matters most.

Allow yourself to be surprised about how easy this exercise is to do. Witness your insights so you can recall them later.

During the last fifteen-minute interval, shift your attention to a specific aspect of your research topic.

At the end of each interval, make some spontaneous notes about your experience.

In the *preparatory and data collection* stage of a research project, you might use empathic identification in the following ways:

As you are exploring your own understanding of the topic, you might try to select environments and situations often associated with your topic and then attempt to understand the significance of environments or contexts from their contextual point of view.

If certain objects or symbols are related to your topic in the theoretical or empirical literature, you might wish to invite them to "relate" their own stories before data collection. Imagine what the objects or symbols might have to say about the experience you are studying. Use the insights you gain to help you write interview questions.

Invite research participants to bring an object or symbol that signifies the topic to them in some way. During the interview, ask participants to imagine what stories the objects or symbols have to say about the topic.

While collecting data or interviewing research participants, keep notes on empathic impressions you might have about how the other person is experiencing from their point of view but not saying aloud. If and when appropriate, ask your research participants if your insights resonate with their own experiences. Record their responses.

In the *data treatment and interpreting* stage of a research report, you might use empathic identification to support analysis and interpretation in the following ways:

While analyzing and interpreting data, notice spontaneous empathic impressions you might have about the participant's point of view. At a later time, review your empathic impressions for that participant to see if any patterns emerge in your observations of your own impressions. As data collection continues for other participants, review your empathic impressions to see if common patterns emerge across participants.

If you are being stuck at a particular point in data analysis and interpretation, shift your attention and imagine what features of the data your participants might think and feel important and how they might interpret them.

As a thought experiment, imagine what the data might have to say if data could talk, feel, and move. You might wish to do this occasionally during data analysis and interpretation to keep your imagination lively and to maintain focused attention on what the data are revealing rather than what might only be important to you as the researcher. In this way, you might enhance your opportunities to be surprised by your own findings.

CHAPTER 7

Play, Creative Arts,
and Embodied Writing

"My name is Alice, but"—

"It's a stupid name enough!" Humpty Dumpty interrupted impatiently.

"What does it mean?"

"Must a name mean something?" Alice asked doubtfully.

"Of course it must," Humpty Dumpty said with a short laugh:

My name means the shape I am—and a good handsome shape it is, too.

With a name like yours, you might be any shape, almost."

—*Through the Looking Glass* (Carroll 1962, 186)

Play

Infants often begin to play within the first half-hour of birth. In actions of simple curiosity, a baby explores that external world in eye and muscle movements and in progressively complex movements, such as sucking, grasping, and shaking of objects. As is commonly observed, spontaneous play wanes as time progresses through childhood and adolescence. By late childhood and adolescence, play is typically channeled into games and sports and the mastery of new skills. By young adulthood, play activities are usually scheduled into complex adult activities, including periods for relaxation and entertainment. Of the few "Alices in Wonderland" who escape conventionality and still play as adults, some are thought fools or odd, and others are genuine geniuses who may change our world for the better.

According to numerous great writers, scientists, and musicians, play is an essential component of creativity and insight; therefore, in the flow between play and other activities, such people are likely to abet the new (Michalko 2001; Root-Bernstein and Root-Bernstein 1999). Though others thought Alexander Fleming had an unusually messy chemistry bench, his playful experiments painting tiny images with bacteria helped Fleming isolate the first antibiotic known to us as the *Penicillin nototum*. From noticing a wobbling plate thrown across a cafeteria, the jokester and physicist Richard Feynman found inspiration for working out the equations for wobbles and then, for fun, moved on to quantum electrodynamics. For scientists such as Fleming and Feynman, play abounds and sometimes discovery joins their play.

Play specialist O. Fred Donaldson (1993) agrees. Play is a natural life force, ever joyful. Known for his healing work with children and animals, especially wolves and dolphins, Donaldson avers that to "play is to be irrationally crazy, to engage in a meta-pattern of belonging that connects life forms across special and cultural barriers" (xv). He invites young children to be his teachers, connecting to their world as follows:

> I continue my apprenticeship with many children, including Christian, a four-year-old with cerebral palsy, with whom I play each week. Each day we play together is a new day in which we unfold with each other and explore new possibilities of motion and touch. He lies on his back, resting on a mat in the classroom. I whistle softly and call his name. He turns his head and smiles in recognition. I move slowly to his side, saying his name. He giggles and extends his body in excitement. I touch his hand, yet am careful not to encroach upon him. I whistle. He squirms and smiles. I put my hand within the range of his arm and move in concert with his motions. I roll him over on top of me and he laughs out loud. (141)

In psychology, Jean Piaget (1929, 1972) describes the nature of children's play and development with amazing clarity. Interestingly enough, compared to research as conducted today, Piaget's initial theories were based on observations of his own growing children and only later confirmed in observations of other children and by others (Piaget and Inhelder 1969). In Piaget's own words

> Play begins, then, with the first dissociation between assimilation and accommodation. After learning to grasp, swing,

throw, etc., which involve both an effort of accommodation
to new situations, and an effort of repetition, reproduction,
and generalization, which are the elements of assimilation,
the child sooner or later (often even during the learning
period) grasps for the pleasure of grasping, swings for the
sake of swinging, etc. In a word, he repeats his behavior
not in any further effort to learn or to investigate, but for
the mere joy of mastering it and of showing off to himself
his own power of subduing reality. (1962, 162)

The newly learned activity is now subordinate to the child's developing ego. No longer needing to learn the motions of grasping and
swinging, the child grasps and swings because it feels good—and play
begins. In play, the force of accommodation to reality is less pressing
than that of assimilation. Temporarily, "assimilation is dissociated from
accommodation" (162). In children, of course, play may continue for
long periods of time for sheer delight—no other motive need apply.
For adults, play is more an option or flow between assimilation and
accommodation and may in some ways be related to the flow experience described initially by Mihaly Csikszentmihalyi (1990). In Piaget's
terms, adult thought inevitably requires some "equilibrium" (162)
between accommodation to reality and assimilation of reality to the
ego. Perhaps returning to the sheer delight of play requires returning
to our childhood "no-sense" acts of engaging and belonging to the
world as O. Fred Donaldson (1993) suggests.

In philosophy, Hans-Georg Gadamer (1976, 1998b) describes
understanding and play similarly. In a field of philosophy known as
hermeneutics, Gadamer is concerned with the fundamental involvement of objective and subjective awareness in the act of knowing. That
is, understanding is an interpretive (or hermeneutical) act, intrinsi-
cally intersubjective, that takes place through an interplay between
a person's objective and subjective awareness. In understanding,
nothing is truly objective or subjective. Play per se involves a curious "loss of self" (Gadamer 1976, 51) and "simply 'happens' to the
player independently of his or her intentions" (88). "Play fulfills its
purpose only if the player loses himself in play" (Gadamer 1998b,
102). Like Piaget, Gadamer sees play as a temporary suspension of
the demands of reality.

Using Gadamer's notions of play as an explanatory construct,
Jennifer Schulz (2006) has recently developed a practice for creative
writing called "Pointing" that has intriguing possibilities for collaborative research. In an article addressed to phenomenological researchers, Schulz invites workshop participants, either creative writers or

qualitative researchers, "to suspend the classroom selves" and "the structure of play takes over" (223). In Pointing, participants—while listening to texts written by others—are asked to respond by pointing to words and phrases that resonate with them personally, and to freewrite or generate poems for the words they have written down. In a series of such activities, the participants find a new voice in their writing that feels both satisfying and original to them and others in the group in a way quite similar to the unique voice found by writers and researchers using embodied writing (Anderson 2001; Anderson 2002a; Anderson 2002b) described later in this chapter.

Play Experiential Exercises

Begin all experiential exercises with the Basic Instructions for All Experiential Exercises.

Learning to Play Again: Play Exercise #1

Note. For this exercise, you will need to find a child less than seven-years-old who is willing to play with you for at least a half hour. You can also do this exercise by playing with a puppy or kitten if a child is not available.

This exercise follows the advice given by play specialist O. Fred Donaldson (1993) discussed above.

Try to enter in the child's world. Be gentle. Give the child "space" to initiate activity. Forget about being an authority. Adapt a beginner's mind. Let the child lead you, perhaps imitating his or her motions. As appropriate, verbally or nonverbally, ask the child to teach you how to play. Of course, do not engage or encourage any activity that would harm the child or yourself in any way.

Continue playing for about a half hour, allowing the child to teach you how to play. If you get exhausted, stop. Adults playing with children can get tired very quickly. When done, thank the child. Often a hug will do just fine.

When you get home, make a few notes about what you learned about play or about yourself during this exercise.

Finally, consider the following questions relevant to your research topic:

1. How might you approach your research topic more playfully? Put another way, how can you free yourself from expected outcomes for your study? Brainstorm possibilities and write them down.

2. How might playful research strategies, especially data collection, invite more creative and exploratory responses from research participants? Brainstorm possibilities and write them down.

3. How might play inform data analysis, that is, free you from what you already think you know about the topic? Brainstorm possibilities and write them down.

4. How might a playful approach inform your presentation of findings? Brainstorm possibilities and write them down.

Colored Paper Tear or "Handmade Midrash": Play Exercise #2

Note. For this exercise, you will need two or three sheets of at least five different colors of colored paper, a few old magazines, a glue stick, and a large piece of white paper. When you are ready to begin, sit down with the colored sheets of paper, old magazines, glue stick, and white paper close at hand. This exercise was inspired by the exercises in Handmade Midrash *by Jo Milgram (1992).*

Once you have quieted your mind, bring your research topic to awareness. Recall a particular moment or past activity in which you were directly engaged in the phenomenon you wish to study. Perhaps the experience you wish to study is one you have had yourself. Perhaps you have observed others and can recall and relive their experience as though it were your own. Pick one instance and relive it through your five senses.

Once you are alert to the past experience, open your eyes and begin to express your lived experience of the phenomenon in an image, using the materials before you. Do not think. Do not ponder. No scissors allowed. Pretend you are back in kindergarten. Pick up the colored paper and/or magazines and begin to tear and rip them until you discover shapes that you like. Assemble the colored shapes in a manner that suits you. When you are satisfied with the arrangement of shapes, glue them to the white sheet of paper to create an image. While doing this exercise, tell your inner critic to take a nap. Just enjoy, delight, and play!

When you feel complete, return gradually to everyday awareness and take an appreciative look at the image you have created. Take note of any obvious relationships to your research topic.

Write down any insights or sketch any images or symbols you had about the topic while doing this exercise.

Repeat this exercise from time to time to update your familiarity with your topic.

"Pointing" Data Analysis and Interpretation: Play Exercise #3

Note. For this exercise, you will need to locate a short description of a topic you would like to study. This description may be taken from a research account, a short story, or a newspaper. You may also use an original interview transcript from your own study. Ideally, this exercise is best done in a group of five to fifteen people. You will need at least one partner to complete this exercise.

This exercise is adapted from a research practice called Pointing, developed by Jennifer Schulz (2006) for the purposes of creative writing and collaborative qualitative research.

Read the description aloud in the group. The description can be read by the instructor or someone else not involved in the exercise. You may also tape or digitally record the description beforehand and play it for the group.

As you listen to the description, point to words and phrases that resonant with you, as though they jump out at you as you listen. Jot these words and phrases down.

As a group, say aloud the words and phrases that resonated with you. Briefly discuss what you learned about the
experience by rehearing the description through the words
and phrases noted by others.

Write a fifteen-minute spontaneous, freewrite about a situation in your own life that is similar or related to the one
portrayed in the description. Freewriting involves writing
without stopping or editing, simply letting the words go
wherever they want to go.

Read your freewrites aloud to one another. As you listen
to the freewrites of others, point to words and phrases in
their writings that resonate with you and jot them down.

Write a short poem using the words and phrases you have
just jotted own. Incorporate as many of the words and
phrases as you can without changing them.

Read your poems aloud to one another. Briefly, as a group,
discuss what you learned from the exercise about the topic.

On your own, write down any personal insights you had
about the topic and how you might use Pointing or your
own adaptation of it in qualitative data analysis and interpretation. Also, ask yourself whether any aspects of the
exercise surprise or frustrate you.

Creative Arts

Be in harmony . . .
If you are out of balance,
take inspiration from manifestations of your true nature.
(Leloup 2002, 27)

Before thought and mental chatter begin, from time to time, all of
us experience a nonreflective place from which intuition, inspiration,
and creativity arise naturally. Sometimes spontaneously, sometimes
by setting the conditions carefully and waiting, new symbols, images,
ideas, or thoughts arise in our awareness. Typically, we feel surprise
and delight. Such creative expressions are ordinary events, occurring
whenever they happen in whatever context, whether while cooking,

making love, or analyzing research data. In *Dharma Art*, Chögyam Trungpa (1996) describes this nonrelective, egoless place from the perspective of Tibetan Buddhism:

> The absolute truth of egolessness does not need any [of our ordinary] comforts. A sense of empty-heartedness takes place where we lose our reference point. If you do not have any reference point at all, you have nothing to work with, nothing to compare with, nothing to fight, nothing to try to subtract or add into your system at all. You find yourself absolutely nowhere, just empty heart, big hole in the brain. Your nervous system doesn't connect with anything, and there's no logic particularly, just empty heart. . . . Instead, you are suspended in space, in a big hole of some kind. That sense of suspension is the ground, according to the non-reference point view of how to perceive absolute symbolism. That experience of suspension is the canvas or the blackboard where you paint your pictures, your symbolism. . . . I'm not saying that you flip into that state of mind, and you are stuck with that particular experience for the rest of your life, necessarily. But we do have such a state of mind; such an experience occurs all the time. (40–41)

Today, we might describe such experiences as cerebral, right-brained processes that encourage imagery, gestalts, and patterns as opposed to cerebral, left-brain processes that encourage linear thinking, logic, reason, and analysis (Taylor 2008), as described in depth in Chapter 1 on intuitive inquiry. In recent years, creative processes have been integrated into personal growth and healing modalities, including psychotherapy and counseling (Kalff 1980; Mellick 1996; Rogers 1993; Romanyshyn 2002) and health (Sheikh 1983; Sheikh 2003). Carl Jung's (1959, 1972, 1973) seminal writings on dreams, symbols, and active imagination have played a major role in prompting the integration of the creative arts, personal growth, and healing modalities. Jung (1973) himself engaged in what he calls unconscious materials via various processes, including dialogue with dreams and inner figures, painting of mandalas, and sculpting with rock in his garden. Since then, Jungians and others, especially Jill Mellick (1996) and Natalie Rogers (1993), have expanded the "media" for active imagination to other expressive forms, such as sandplay (Kalff 1980; Lowenfeld 1979; Lowenfeld 1991) dance and authentic movement (Adler 2002; Chodorow 1991; Pallaro 1999), psychodrama (Moreno 1993), drama, clay, poetry, collage, photo montage, automatic writing, calligraphy, visions, and music. In the business and corporate industry, the creative arts have been used to spark innovation, especially technological innovation (Microsoft Research and Duggan 2008; Ogle 2007)

Creative arts and performative processes have also been applied to research praxis in various ways throughout the health and social sciences since the late 1980s. Among the first application of creative arts methods was Collier and Collier's (1986) exploration of photography, film, and video to understand human behavior and culture. Visual methods in social science research have been particularly well explored (Banks 2001; Bauer and Gaskell 2000; Emmison and Smith 2000; Leavy 2008; Rose 2001; Stanczak 2007; Sullivan 2004; and van Leeuwen and Jewitt 2001). More recently, Hervey (2000) has introduced dance and movement methods, and Denzin (2001b), Gergen and Jones (2008), and Jones (2006), among others, have advanced the performative representation of human experience in research praxis. Braud and Anderson (1998), Eisner (1998), Knowles and Cole (2007), Leavy (2008), McNiff (1998, 2003), Romanyshyn (2007), and Todres (2007) have introduced a wide range of creative, expressive, and imaginal processes into qualitative approaches to research. Summarizing the broad intention of these methodological innovations, art-based researcher Shawn McNiff (1998, 2003) distinguishes art-based research "by its use of the arts as objects of inquiry as well as modes of investigation" (McNiff 1998, 15). Artistic knowing complements and enhances what we can know by reason alone.

Creative Arts Experiential Exercises

Most of the experiential exercises in this book involve the creative arts in one way or another. Therefore, the exercises immediately below explore creative and expressive arts processes *not* presented elsewhere in this book. Experiential Exercises #1, #2, and #3 are original takeoffs of my (R. A.'s) own on collage making, sandplay, and psychodrama respectively as potential resources for research praxis. As with all the experiential exercises in this book and worthy of repeating here, these creative arts exercises can used be in research to (a) inform a researcher's personal growth and transformation; (b) support and balance more conventional research approaches; (c) access cerebral right-brain functioning as a mode of investigation per se; and/or (d) develop into complementary or primary modes of data collection, analysis, interpretation, and presentation of findings. Begin all experiential exercises with the Basic Instructions for All Experiential Exercises.

Expressing Insights via Collage:
Creative Arts Exercise #1

Note. Before beginning this experiential exercise, collect old magazines, printed images, and copies of photographs that you can use as the basis of a collage. You will also need scissors, a glue stick, and a large piece of white paper, such as butcher block paper, on which to arrange and glue your collage images. Place all these materials in front of you before you begin.

When your awareness feels relaxed and alert, ask yourself a question about your research topic that helps clarify your understanding of the topic or the research methods and procedures you are using. Once you have your question clearly in mind, write it down.

Holding the question lightly in awareness, look through the images and choose those that have an immediate appeal. Do not analyze the images or why they may be important. Choose as many images as you wish so long as they can reasonably be arranged on or attached to the large piece of white paper in some way.

When you feel you have finished choosing images, begin to arrange and move the images around on the white paper. Continue this process until you feel satisfied with the arranged images that form your collage.

Once you feel satisfied with your assembled collage and feel complete, look at it with appreciation without interpreting it for several minutes, simply noticing the whole of the collage image and the relationships (or their lack) between the individual images as you have arranged them. Do not interpret; just notice.

Either by yourself or with a partner, invite the collage to inform you about the question you have asked by engaging in a verbal and nonverbal exchange with the patterns and relationships represented by your collage. If you have a partner, share your impressions of your collage and invite your partner to take notes about what you say and to ask questions that deepen your understanding. Do not invite your partner to interpret your collage.

Once you (and your partner) feel complete with the previous step, write down or sketch your own thoughts and feelings about what you have learned.

Creative Expression and Sandplay: Creative Arts Exercise #2

In preparation for this experiential exercise, gather together a number of objects related in some way to your research topic and place them near you so can reach them easily. Typically, sandplay uses a tray filled with sand set on a small table. Your "sandtray" is a clean and cleared out area on the floor immediately in front of you. Give yourself at least an hour for this experiential exercise.

This exercise is inspired by techniques associated with sandplay therapy in which a child or adult creates an imaginary representation of their life world on a tray of sand in the presence of a therapist. Originally, sandplay therapy was developed by Margaret Lowenfeld (1979, 1991) and Dora Kalff (1980) and has become a well-established mode of psychotherapy, especially in working with children. This experiential exercise emphasizes creative expression through sandplay.

When your awareness feels relaxed and alert, consider your research topic. Let your topic surface into awareness. Allow your sense of the topic to come alive by thinking of a concrete personal example of the experience you wish to study. Recreate that experience in your imagination using all your senses.

Once the experience seems vivid and alive, invite your imagination to pick and arrange the assembled objects to inform you in some way about your topic. If you need to get more objects from around your house or work space, do so. Continue arranging and rearranging the assembled objects until you feel a sense of completion.

Once you feel satisfied with your assembled objects and feel complete, look at them with appreciation without interpreting them for several minutes, simply noticing the whole of the assemblage and the relationships (or their lack) between the various objects as you have arranged them. You might even imagine that an unknown part of yourself is informing you about your topic as though you are learning something for the very first time.

Once you have noticed the wholeness and relationships between your assembled objects, invite them to inform you about or to update your current understanding of your research topic. Engage in a verbal and nonverbal exchange with the patterns and relationships that you notice among the objects. Take notes or sketch what you notice.

Once you feel complete, write down or sketch any additional thoughts and feelings you have about what you have learned about your topic and yourself in relationship to your topic.

Writing Your Discussion via Psychodrama: Creative Arts Exercise

Note: In preparation for this experiential exercise, familiarize yourself with the established norms for the discussion section or chapter of a scientific research report. In brief, typically, a discussion of research findings examines and critiques the study's unique findings in relationship to prior research and theory on the topic, explores how the findings advance the current understanding of the topic and the study's limitations, and makes suggestions for future research.

This exercise is inspired by a mode of group psychotherapy called "psychodrama." Originally developed by Jacob Moreno (1993), psychodrama now has many therapeutic, personal growth, and business applications. In psychodrama, each person portrays the "players" in a particular situation, such as the members of the focus person's family of origin. For example, if a small group were enacting a psychodrama of your family of origin, you would name and describe the significant players and give a brief description of a typical situation in your family. Others in the group would portray the significant players in your family of origin, enacting the family dynamics as best they can.

In this exercise, you will imagine a short skit in which the various voices of a discussion ask and answer questions about your research findings—each in its own style. You might give the players in your imaginary psychodrama distinct personalities, opinions, styles of expression, and names. This exercise is particularly appropriate after data analysis is complete but can be done beforehand by imagining possible findings ahead of time.

When your awareness feels relaxed and alert, in your mind, review what you intuit or know about your research findings. Consider the implications of your findings as they relate to your literature review of relevant studies and theories. What are the likely criticisms of your study from the points of view of other researchers and theorists? How would you critique your study yourself? How might you answer their questions and critiques? How might they respond to you?

When you have reviewed the possibilities, imagine that each point of view, critique, or response has a distinct personality. Give the personality a name and a voice. Imagine what each personality looks like and the sounds of their voices. Be imaginative and playful. Have fun.

Once you have a distinct personality and voice for all of the significant characters in your discussion of findings, imagine them conversing and interacting with one another. Write down what they say to each other and how they say it.

After you have enacted this psychodrama-informed discussion, imagine in what ways this exercise informs your understanding of your topic and how you might wish to incorporate your insights from this exercise to enliven the writing of a discussion section or chapter. Write your thoughts down.

Embodied Writing

Designed to further both personal transformation and research praxis, embodied writing (Anderson 2001; Anderson 2002a; Anderson 2002b) portrays the lived experience of the body by conveying in words the finely textured experience of the human body. Human experience is relayed *from the inside out*. Entwining human sensibilities with the sensibilities of the world, embodied writing is itself an act of embodiment that nourishes an enlivened sense of presence in and of the world. In an attempt to describe human experiences—and especially profound human experiences—as they truly are lived, embodied writing tries to give the body voice in ways typically not honored, especially in research praxis.

Epistemologically aligned with philosophic phenomenology and phenomenological research methods, embodied writing seeks to portray experience from the point of view of the lived body—*leib* rather than *körper* in Edmund Husserl's (1989) sense. The researcher collects, analyzes, and presents research findings, fully intending to invite readers to encounter the narrative accounts for themselves and from within their own bodies through a form of sympathetic resonance. (See the Transpersonal Forms of Validity section of Chapter 8 for a discussion of sympathetic resonance and its applications.) Ultimately, as a communication tool for empirical research and writing in general, the value of embodied writing depends on its capacity to engender a quality of resonance between the written text and the senses of readers that permits them to resonate closely with the phenomena described from within their own bodily senses. The readers' perceptual, visceral, sensorimotor, kinesthetic, and imaginal senses are invited to come alive to the words and images as though the experience were their own, akin to the way we might read fine poetry or fiction.

Though obvious now, over time what has surprised me (R. A.) the most was the capacity of embodied writing to call forth the writer's unique voice or way of writing. Writers gain voice, a particular voice. Far from making everyone sound alike by employing a specific style of writing, embodied writing seems to call forth the unique qualities of a writer. While the distinctive features of embodied writing are evident in the two examples that follow below, each writer sounds different than the others. In the act of writing, slowing down and looking for resonance within one's own body seems to reveal the tangibly unique—and sometimes ineffable—qualities of the writer's experience and way of being in the world.

Seven Distinctive Features of Embodied Writing

Excerpted below from Anderson (2001), the seven features of embodied writing are inherently related and flow easily one to another. Researchers are invited to include features appropriate to their research topics and intended audience as well as features that serve their abilities as writers. An individual writer or researcher might employ or emphasize some or most of these features to render an account, but not necessarily all of them all the time.

1. *True-to-life, vivid depictions intended to invite sympathetic resonance in the readers or audience.* The most distinctive feature of embodied writing is its intent to invite sympathetic resonance in others. The finely nuanced quality of the writing invites readers or listeners to palpably feel the writer's experience or something much akin to it. In a sense, the experience itself becomes palpably present and therefore present to others.

2. *Inclusive of internal and external data as essential to relaying the experience.* Embodied writing includes *both* internal (imaginal, perceptual, kinesthetic, and visceral data usually known only by the experiencer) and external sources (sometimes observable to others, but not always, such as sensorimotor reactions and context) of information. Embodied writing values both internal and external sources without privileging one over the other.

3. *Written specifically from the inside out.* Embodied writing drops the external witnessing perspective customary for conventional, objective science. The body speaks for itself through the vehicle of words. Like any medium of expression, words often elude the immediate fullness of experience. Yet, to the extent possible, embodied writing positions the writers' voice inside the body as it lives, letting the body's perceptual matrix guide the words, impulse by impulse, sensation by sensation.

4. *Richly concrete and specific, descriptive of all sensory modalities, and often slowed down to capture nuance.* Embodied writing invites a lively sense of living here and now by attending rigorously to minor external and internal details as they arise in experience in a manner similar to phenomenological research accounts. Embodied writing accounts are often slowed down, in the temporal sense in order, to relive and record nuance with minimal narrative context.

5. *Attuned to the living body* (leib *rather than* körper *in Husserl's (1989) sense).* Living in a body is to live fully attuned to the sensual matrix of the world. As Maurice Merleau-Ponty (1962, 1968) points out so well, the body lives inhabiting the world and the world inhabiting the body. Embodiment involves not only our physical senses here and now but our sense of being alive in the flesh moment to moment.

6. *Narratives embedded in experience, often first-person narratives.* If the writer is speaking of his or her own experience, the first person is used for referential accuracy and vitality of expression.

7. *Poetic images, literary style, and cadence serve embodied depictions and not the other way around.* Embodied writing values vivid accounts of lived experience over literary artfulness. A good phrase or artful

expression is extraneous to a sentence unless it supports an embodied description. Embodied writers often use acoustical cadence, such as *andante* as in walking or *allegro* as in lively movement, to mirror the sensory or emotional tone of the experiences described.

Examples of Embodied Writing

In the first example of embodied writing below, Martina Juko Holiday (pers. comm.) describes her experience of directing her fellow students in a scene from *Taxi Driver,* a play by Paul Schrader. Notice how vividly she portrays the sounds, smells, and tactile sensations, combining embodied writing features in a lively narrative.

> The air all around me is alive with actors' voices and the smell of cigarettes. My red boots flash through the crowd, "Goin' up, guys," my gentle tone breaks up laughing conversations outside the theatre. I softly tap a shoulder in a leather jacket, touch a suntanned elbow, "Goin' up, next scene is up in one minute." I nod at our teacher blurring by to take his chair. "Good job, Holiday." His voice is so low—do I finally have the hang of stage managing his class? I stand up straighter. The air, still alive, quiets when he sits.
>
> The lights go down when I nod to Aaron in the booth. There is still enough illumination to read the card with the name of the work and the actors presenting it, but I do not look down at it. I take in the crowd when I turn to announce the scene. I see my friends and fellow swimmers in the Sea of Hollywood looking back at me. There is a collective holding of our breaths, we have left our hometowns to chase our dreams and create a home amongst each other at the Beverly Hills Playhouse. A butterfly dances in my stomach, but a steady voice comes out of my mouth. "This is *Taxi Driver.*"

The next example by Bryan Rich (2000) is a particularly unique example of embodied writing because the description is very slowed down, capturing kinesthetic, perceptual, and visceral nuances in blowing the *shofar,* shaped from a ram's horn to herald the New Year at Rosh Hashanah. Since few readers are likely to have had the experience of blowing the *shofar,* Bryan's portrayal represents a robust test of embodied writing to evoke sympathetic resonance.

[M]y eyes widen with anticipation. I've done this so many times, and still that quiet fear whispers its electricity. The hairs on my forearm become alert and my chest tingles, as they do every time I approach this threshold. I feel my blood move a little faster. My ears prick up and hearing becomes razor keen even as it's suddenly silent inside my head. A small prayer, the primeval curve of the ram's horn shapes my hand and I touch the small opening to my lips—the familiar feeling, there's no way I can fit it quite right except that it fits perfectly, hard against soft, like the first joint of my index finger fits together, or like a kiss.

I have to inhale from deep, and as I inhale time slows down through an endless moment until there is nothing left but now. I begin to blow slowly, and slowly, without forcing, pressure swells from my belly up through my chest. I can feel my heart claiming more space in my chest. . . . My whole body is expanding. It soars, riding the wave of the sound—but not off the ground. . . . Now [the wave] flows inward at the same time, finding and caressing the familiar opening in the inner depths of my belly center. . . . My heart is losing its boundaries as it spreads further in all directions. The spring overflows from the hidden place inside the precisely innermost point in the center of my body and carries me into it. This is the open secret. It's the gently overwhelming place too small to be found by my knowing mind, caressed in my body center and bigger than the sky. (1–2)

Using Embodied Writing in Research

Anderson (2002a, 2002b) details additional examples of embodied writing as well as descriptions and examples of using embodied writing accounts in qualitative research. Summarizing briefly, embodied writing provides research reports a lively, embodied presence as well as having specific applications to research praxis and report writing. Since embodied writing privileges the liveliness of lived experience, other aspects of human experience including external observation and mental discourse are downplayed; therefore, depending on what is needed for a particular research topic, researchers will need to make choices about when to use embodied writing or blend it with other procedures.

In Introductions and Literature Reviews, embodied writing can be used to relay the researcher's personal relationship to the topic or introduce various sections with personal accounts (Carlson 2009; Dufrechou 2002; Dufrechou 2004; Hill 2003; Kuhn 2001; Riordan 2002; and Walker 2003). In a study on bringing the wilderness experience home to everyday life, Laura Riordan (2002) precedes the sections of her conventional literature review with brief embodied writings, rendered in italics, that portray her own experiences in the wilderness, thereby giving her literature review an embodied integrity and relaying to readers her personal relationship to the research topic. Below she portrays her own ascent of Mt. Shasta:

> It is 4:00 a.m. on a cold Labor Day. The cold is not due to the time of year, but rather because we awoke at 10,000 feet, and the waning summer heat has not penetrated this dark and rocky environment. Stars, small blinking red satellites, and intense quiet surround the mountain. Our seven bodies, wrapped in down jackets and sleeping bags, gather for a hot breakfast. We dress in silence, lacing up our rented plastic mountaineering boots in preparation for the final ascent to the 14,300-foot summit of Mt. Shasta. I scramble to attach the clamp-on harnesses to the slippery soles of my already uncomfortable boots. The rest of my body joins my feet in their plea against my will to return to the tent and surrender to the mountain. But I share the same goal as the rest, to get to the top. This climb awards us the experience of climbing on snow and ice, as well as a 360-degree view. What we cannot foresee is how much this experience will change us. Our chilly predawn wake-up call is just a prelude to a universal peak experience. (11–12)

Embodied writing has also been used extensively for qualitative data collection. For example, both Jay Dufrechou (2002, 2004) and Laura Riordan (2002) made extensive use of the Internet to recruit research participants and solicit embodied writings from them. Prospective participants were given a description of embodied writing and some examples, and asked to write embodied descriptions of their encounters with nature. Furthermore, in order to enrich these descriptions with rich sensory and emotional detail essential to embodied writing, Jay engaged in ongoing online dialogues with forty research participants to help them develop their embodied descriptions. Via an online questionnaire distributed through outdoor adventure/education electronic list services, Laura Riordan (2002) recruited sixteen exemplar participants known for their contributions to the field of outdoor and adventure education, either in practice or in research. As Laura's study focused on the integration of wilderness transformation into everyday life, her online questionnaire asked research participants four questions about their wilderness experiences and the integration of those experiences, and also requested them to use embodied writing in answering the questions. In order to solicit embodied descriptions from research participants, embodied writing can also be used to guide a researcher's interview style or support the development of interview questions that invite embodied response, as portrayed in Embodied Writing, Experiential Exercise #5: Interviewing Another Using Embodied Writing Skills.

For the purposes of data analysis and interpretation, embodied writing invites an embodied perspective to data analysis regardless of the specific research method used. For example, in an intuitive inquiry study of mystical poetry and imagination, Dorit Netzer (2008) asked participants to describe the images they formed in responses to hearing mystical poems using embodied writing, and she responded to the participants' data with embodied writing of her own during data analysis. In a heuristic study on peak and mystical experiences in the practice of aikido, Brian Heery (2003) indicates that engaging embodied writing in data analysis and interpretation helped him more deeply explore his own experience with three aikido masters, allowing him to more fully embody the experiences of others for himself. Similarly, in a phenomenological and heuristic study of sacred weeping (Anderson, 1996b), my own deeply somatic experiences of sacred weeping, occurring several years prior to studying that of others, allowed me to understand the accounts of others as though from the inside, even when their experiences were unlike my own.

Perhaps most important, however, embodied writing lends research reports an embodied character that invites readers to experience qualitative data for themselves via sympathetic resonance (Anderson, 1998 2001, 2002a, 2002b), a form of transformative validity known as resonance validity described in Chapter 8. Typically, researchers provide samples of embodied writings from research participants, quoting them directly (Carlson 2009; Dufrechou 2002; Dufrechou 2004; Heery 2003; Kuhn 2001; Netzer 2008; Phelon 2001; Riordan 2002), providing numerous quotes from research participants' embodied writing accounts. Research interpretations follow the presentation of the research participants' own embodied voice, to allow readers an opportunity to experience the participants' writings prior to reading the researcher's interpretation.

Embodied Writing Experiential Exercises

General Instructions

The embodied writing experiential exercises below are organized as a sequence of steps to help you learn embodied writing as a transformative research skill. In each experiential exercise, you will explore and learn new aspects of embodied writing. Each exercise builds upon the previous one. Through these exercises, you will develop a style uniquely your own over time. Begin all experiential exercises with the Basic Instructions for All Experiential Exercises.

To learn embodied writing, having a writing partner or small group with whom you can share your embodied writing accounts and receive feedback is extremely helpful. The section entitled "Forming an Embodied Writing Group" at the end of this section provides guidance on how to form such a group and how to give feedback to one another.

Recollecting Sensory Details, Embodied Writing Exercise #1

Part I

When your awareness feels relaxed and alert, invite your imagination to recall a few life experiences that are *particularly vivid*. Allow yourself to be surprised at what comes to mind. If several experiences appear to awareness, choose one experience that seems quite vivid and easy to recall in detail. Generally, for this first experiential exercise, it is best to pick an experience that took place within a short period of time, such as a few minutes or a half-hour, and contains many sensory impressions. Experiences such as holding a newborn baby, jogging on a beautiful spring morning, receiving good news, or a surprise visit from an old friend would be examples of good choices for this first experiential exercise. If you currently have a research topic you wish to pursue, select an experience of your own that represents that topic in some way.

Once you have chosen the experience, relive it in your imagination by recalling the sensory details of the experience. Using your senses of taste, smell, touch (tactile and pressure sensations), hearing, and vision, relive the experience vividly. Then, expanding beyond the conventional five senses, what muscular and visceral sensations do you recall? What movements did you make? Were there any overall body senses? Witness these recollections so that you can remember them later when you write your embodied writing account.

After you have relived the experience in your imagination, notice whether one sensory modality is more prominent than all the others. For example, if you were listening to birds singing in the morning, sound might be predominant. If you were walking slowly, perhaps the movements of the muscles in your legs and feet captured your attention. Use this focus as a starting point for your embodied writing account. If there seems to be more than one primary sensory modality, choose one.

Return to quiet reflection for a few minutes to help settle and integrate your experience.

Record some notes or images about your experience during this exercise to help you write your account later.

Part II

Reread the Seven Distinctive Features of Embodied Writing, above, before you begin to write.

Using your notes and drawings, write an embodied writing account of approximately three hundred words. Be especially mindful to write *from the inside out* and to evoke *sympathetic resonance in future readers*. Write without concern for perfect spelling, grammar, and syntax. However, after you finish writing, run spell check.

If you have an embodied writing partner or group, share your account with them and respond to each other's embodied writing accounts in terms of how you resonated to them while you read or listened to them read aloud. In this way, the writer will know whether she communicated what she wanted to say and can use your feedback to refine future embodied writing and develop her own unique style.

Now, in Slow Motion,
Embodied Writing Exercise #2

This experiential exercise is *exactly the same as* Experiential Exercise #1 except that you are reliving the experience as though *in slow motion*. See changes in italics below for Part I, Step 5 and Part II.

Part 1.

After you have relived the experience in your imagination, notice whether one sensory modality was more prominent than all the others. For example, if you were listening to a bird singing, sound might be predominant. If you were walking slowly, perhaps the muscles in your legs and feet capturing your attention. *Now, slow down the experience as much as you can and relive in slow motion. Use this sloweddown remembrance as a starting point for your embodied writing account. In slow motion, you are more likely to remember minute detail. If you have difficulty slowing down the pace of your remembrance, you might practice the Slowing Down Exercise in Chapter 4 again.*

Part 2

Using your notes and drawings, write an embodied writing account of approximately three hundred words. Be especially mindful to write *as though in slow motion, relaying minor sensory details*. Write without concern for perfect spelling, grammar, and syntax. However, after you finish writing, run spell check.

Longest Personal History,
Embodied Writing Exercise #3

When your awareness feels relaxed and alert, choose an object in your house with which you have the *longest personal history*. If the object is large, sit down close to it for this session. If it can be easily moved, place the object in front of you or where you can easily see and touch it. If you wish to use this exercise to explore a particular research topic, choose an object that reminds you of the topic in a significant way.

Make yourself comfortable. Again, calm and still your mind. Attend to your breath. As thoughts, sounds, and distractions draw your attention, calmly return to your breath again and again. Still your body and mind for a few minutes in your usual manner before moving to the next.

Open your eyes and gaze for a few minutes at your chosen object. Invite the object to reveal its textures and qualities to you. Then, using your body's five senses of touch, smell, taste, vision, and hearing, explore the object with your hands, eyes, nose, tongue, ears, etc. Explore the object in this way for several minutes. Allow your body to feel the object viscerally. Observe your body's response. If memories are evoked, feel them in your body. Explore until your heart feels full. Do *not* make this experiential exercise mentally complicated and start chatting away in your mind with well-rehearsed messages. Stay with your sensory experiences of the object you have chosen and witness them so you can recall them later.

When you are ready, place the object down gently and respectfully. Remain in reflective awareness as you write your three-hundred–word embodied writing account. If possible, do *not* name the object in your writing. Rather, write about its texture and other qualities as you experienced them with your senses.

If you have an embodied writing partner or group, share your account with them and respond to each other's embodied writing accounts in terms of how you resonated to them while you read or listened to them read aloud.

Embodied Writing, Experiential Exercise #4, Interviewing Another Using Embodied Writing Skills

Part 1

Network with your friends, fellow students, or colleagues and locate someone who has had a vivid experience of the topic you wish to study, and ask them if he or she would be willing to participate in an informal interview about that experience. Following your instructor's instructions and the research ethics requirements of your academic institution, schedule a time for the interview that is convenient for your interviewee in a quiet and appropriate setting for an interview.

If appropriate, you might ask your interviewee to bring an object to the interview that reminds or symbolizes the experience in some way, such as a photo, trophy, article of clothing, or implement associated with the experience.

Having scheduled your interview, find time to center yourself in relaxed awareness. Once your awareness is relaxed and alert, use the embodied writing skills learned in the previous experiential exercises in this section to generate interview questions that help him or her recall vivid details about their experience. Think of your questions as prompts that support embodied recall. Generate at least five questions.

Return to quiet meditation for a few minutes to help settle and integrate your experience. When you return of ordinary awareness, read your potential interview questions for clarity. Revise and organize them in a reasonable sequence for an informal interview exploring the interviewee's experience.

Part 2

Following your instructor's instructions and the research ethics requirements of your academic institution, conduct the interview. If it is appropriate to record the interview, you might wish to do so. Listening to the interview again and again is likely to deepen your understanding of how to use embodied writing skills in an interview context to collect data.

During the interview, take notes about your impressions even if you are able to record the interview. If you are not able to record all your impressions during the interview, take time after the interview to record them.

When the interview is complete, ask the interviewee what else you might have asked that would have helped him recall sensory details.

A few days after the interview, review your notes and listen to the interview recording at least twice. Critique your interview questions and style from the point of view of embodied writing. Did your interviewee provide embodied descriptions that are as vivid in detail as your own embodied writing accounts? If not, why not? What else might you have done or asked to prompt more embodied responses? What will you do next time?

Applying Embodied Writing Skills to Data Analysis and Interpretation, Embodied Writing Exercise # 5

When your awareness feels relaxed and alert, listen several times to the recording of your interview conducted in the previous experiential exercise. If you have the opportunity to transcribe the interview, read it through slowly several times as well.

While remaining in relaxed awareness, listen to or read the interview and notice how your own body responds to the various interview descriptions. Your body has an intelligence of its own, and your embodied responses to interviews may inform you about the data if you are aware and note them. You may respond to some parts of the account more than others and, of course, in different ways. With some portions of the interview, you may experience *sympathetic resonance* to some of the descriptions. With other portions, you may feel neutrality or dissonance. While you are listening or reading, do not judge your response. Simply notice and take notes. If you intend to analyze the interview formally, you may wish to take detailed notes about your bodily responses to the interview data line by line or paragraph by paragraph as appropriate.

When you return to ordinary awareness, read your notes carefully several times. Consider your embodied responses to the interview as additional information about your emotional and somatic responses to the interview data. Integrate these responses with cognitive and other responses as you analyze and interpret the interview. Bodily responses may signal important aspects of the interview data that you can miss with a more cognitive approach to data analysis and interpretation.

Forming an Embodied Writing Group

If you wish to start an embodied writing group or align with an embodied writing partner, you might begin with these simple norms, expanding upon them as suits your purposes:

1. Meet as a group weekly to create momentum and group cohesiveness.

2. Establish norms of confidentiality to protect private information and generate trust among group members.

3. Work in dyads or small groups of five or six people who are willing to share their prepared embodied writing accounts weekly.

4. Read each embodied writing account aloud. Either the writer or another group member may read.

5. Invite group members to give each writer feedback on what resonates for them *within their own bodies*. This feedback allows the writer to know whether or not their writing communicates their intent.

6. Do not dwell on content, grammar, writing style, spelling, punctuation, etc., no matter how interesting or informative.

7. Give feedback clearly and kindly. Accept feedback graciously.

8. Expect the unexpected.

CHAPTER 8

An Expanded View of Validity

On the Nature of Validity

In its etymological origins, *validity* has meanings of strength, worth, value, and price. Conventional definitions of validity focus on the ability of findings, conclusions, or arguments to compel serious attention or acceptance. Judgments of whether statements, arguments, evidence, or conclusions are sufficiently compelling or true typically are based upon intellectual criteria. However, other meanings of *validity* typically are not considered in conventional treatments of validity. Such additional meanings have to do with what is authoritative, brave, bold, courageous, helpful, encouraging, and appropriate to the end in view for a range of audiences who might be served by the findings. The approaches and skills described in this book, which emphasize the personal characteristics and inner experiences of everyone involved in a research endeavor, are closely aligned with these additional root meanings of *valid* and *validity*.

In a chapter of our earlier text, *Transpersonal Research Methods for the Social Sciences* (Braud and Anderson 1998), we described ways in which the usual intellectual approaches to, and indicators of, validity could be complemented by bodily, emotional, feeling, aesthetic, and intuitional indicators that convey other forms of value about scientific and scholarly findings. Such additions allow the construct of validity to become more inclusive and more relevant for our understanding of human experiences that can be both profound and subtle. The final section of this chapter proposes three transformational forms of validity that specify ways in which our notions of validity might be expanded to provide a more inclusive appreciation of the richness of human experience in the human sciences and humanities.

In the preface of his seminal work, *Introduction to the Human Sciences*, German philosopher Wilhelm Dilthey (1989) presented his view:

> All science is experiential; but all experience must be related
> back to and derives its validity from the conditions and

context of consciousness in which it arises, i.e., the total-
ity of our nature. We designate as "epistemological" this
standpoint which consistently recognises the impossibility
of going behind these conditions. To attempt this would be
like seeing without eyes or directing the gaze of knowledge
behind one's own eye. Modern science can acknowledge no
other than this epistemological standpoint. It became further
evident to me, however, that it is from just this standpoint
that the independence of the human sciences . . . can be
grounded. From this standpoint our conception of the
whole of nature proves to be a mere shadow cast by a hidden reality; by contrast only in the facts of consciousness
given in inner experience do we possess reality as it is. The
analysis of these facts is the central task of the human sciences. Thus . . . knowledge of the principles of the *human
world* falls within that world itself, and the human sciences
form an independent system. (50)

The approaches and researcher preparedness skills described in this
book are well aligned with this view of Dilthey and of the many
advocates of a human science who followed him: that it is important
to use and emphasize our own inner experiences and our personal,
subjective, and intuitional skills in order to more fully appreciate the
nature of consciousness itself and the nature of the types of complex,
rich, and meaningful experiences that are of great interest to the human
sciences and humanities. In this view, validity would depend upon
how carefully and appropriately the full panoply of one's skills and
ways of knowing are applied to a given object of study.

We already have treated features of these more inclusive and
extensive forms of validity in various ways in the chapters of Part 1
of this book. Here, we wish to augment what has been offered before
by describing more explicitly some of the forms that validity assumes
in the intuitive, integral, and organic inquiry approaches treated in
those chapters. Before doing this, we provide concise summaries of
the more familiar reliability, validity, and trustworthiness indicators
that frequently have been emphasized in connection with the more
established forms of quantitative and qualitative research.

Established Forms of Validity

Our intention, for this section, is not to provide a detailed treatment
of established types of validity, but rather to briefly describe these so

that we can indicate how these well-recognized forms can be supplemented by other forms of validity that recently have been developed in areas of qualitative research and transpersonal psychology.

Before considering validity issues, it is necessary to address the topic of *reliability*. This is because validity presupposes reliability. Procedures or measures that yield valid outcomes always are reliable; however, reliable outcomes are not necessarily valid.

Measures or procedures are said to be reliable if they yield *consistent* or *repeatable* outcomes. The major forms of reliability were developed in the area of tests and assessments, but these can be generalized and applied, with necessary adjustments, to other aspects of research. Researchers usually recognize four major forms of reliability. Although these forms usually are described in terms of assessment scores and correlations, we have generalized these, in Table 8.1, so that they can apply to outcomes of procedures and studies as well. We also have expanded the usual treatment of *stability* to include *contextual* in addition to the usually described *temporal* stability.

Through the years, researchers have described many different forms of validity, sometimes offering different names for a given form and sometimes organizing the forms in different ways. What follows is a description of the most commonly suggested validity forms.

The most established forms of validity originated in the context of quantitative research. Indeed, these forms were developed in the even narrower area of experimental and quasi-experimental research designs that employed standardized assessment instruments. In this context, two major sets of validity types were developed—one set applying to the overall research design, study, and experiment and one set applying to the specific measurement instruments used in the study.

In the context of *an overall research project*, researchers commonly recognize four major forms of validity—statistical conclusion validity, internal validity, external validity, and construct validity. We list these and describe their most relevant characteristics and subtypes in Table 8.2.

Although the validities mentioned above were established in the context of experiments, these also can apply to other kinds of studies (causal, comparative, and correlational) and even, if suitably reframed, to qualitative studies.

In addition to the foregoing, four validity types have been recognized in the context of the *specific measurement instruments* (assessments, tests) used in a study. These include face validity, content-related validity, criterion-related validity, and construct-related validity. These could be termed forms of *measurement, psychometric,* or *instrumental* validity. Below, we list and briefly describe these four validity types and their subtypes in Table 8.3.

Table 8.1. Forms of Reliability That May Be Applied to Measures, Procedures, and Studies

Reliability Type	Description
Interrater, interobserver, interinvestigator reliability	degree of consistency of outcomes when more than one rater, observer, or investigator measures or describes some characteristic or repeats the same procedure or study
Stability reliability	a measure of consistency of outcomes over time or contexts
Temporal stability	degree to which a given assessment, procedure, or study yields the same outcome at various times; usually described in terms of test-retest consistency; usually indicated by significant positive correlations
Contextual stability	degree to which a given assessment, procedure, or study yields the same outcome in various contexts (samples, settings); high contextual stability would be indicated by high replicability rates in various contexts; could be assessed by means of meta-analysis of study outcomes
Equivalency reliability	degree to which parallel or alternate forms of a given assessment yield the same outcome; in its generalized form, the degree to which very similar procedures or studies yield the same outcome
Internal consistency reliability	degree to which components or elements within an assessment—designed to tap the same construct—yield the same outcome; usually indicated by high positive correlations of assessment items with each other and with total score (measured by split-half reliability, average interitem correlation, average item-total correlation, and Cronbach's alpha); in its generalized form, the degree to which similar procedural or study *components* yield the same outcome

Table 8.2. Forms of Validity Applied to a Research Design, Study, or Experiment

Validity Type	Description
Statistical conclusion validity	Drawing appropriate conclusions based upon appropriate statistical analysis and inferences; drawing an accurate conclusion about whether and to what degree study variables actually covary. Researchers have identified seven major kinds of threats to this form of validity: low statistical power, violated assumptions of statistical tests, fishing and the error rate problem, poor reliability of measures, poor reliability of treatment implementation, random irrelevancies in the study setting, random heterogeneity of respondents.
Internal validity	Refers to the accuracy or legitimacy of conclusions drawn from a design: Are obtained changes or correlations really attributable to the presumed causal variables or relationships, or are they due to possible confounds or artifacts? Researchers have identified thirteen *threats* to internal validity: history, maturation, testing, instrumentation, statistical regression, differential participant selection, differential attrition, interactions with selection, ambiguity about direction of causal influence, diffusion or imitation of treatments, compensatory equalization of treatments, compensatory rivalry by control participants, resentful demoralization of control participants.
External validity	Refers to the generalizability of a study's findings to situations outside of the study's immediate setting. Researchers have suggested twelve types of *threats* to external validity: selection-treatment interaction, setting-treatment interaction, history-treatment interaction,

continued on next page

Table 8.2. *(Continued)*

Validity Type	Description
	measurement time-treatment interaction, lack of explicit treatment description, multiple-treatment interference, the Hawthorne effect, novelty and disruption effects, experimenter effects, pretest sensitization, posttest sensitization, different outcome measures.
Population validity	May the study's results be legitimately generalized to persons not included in the study?
Ecological validity	Will the study's findings generalize to different settings or environmental conditions?
Temporal validity	Will results obtained at a given time generalize to other time periods?
Treatment variation validity	Can treatments vary slightly and still yield similar results?
Outcome validity	Will study outcome for a certain variable also occur to different but related variables or measures?
Construct validity	Refers to the degree to which a study is free from confounds or artifacts, and the degree to which there is a good fit between operations and conceptual definitions. Researchers have identified ten types of *threats* to construct validity: inadequate preoperational explication of constructs, mono-operation bias, mono-method bias, hypothesis-guessing within experimental conditions, evaluation apprehension, experimenter expectancies, confounding constructs and levels of constructs, interactions of different treatments, interaction of testing and treatment, restricted generalization across constructs. See construct validity treatment in the later *measurement validity* section for more information.

Table 8.3. Forms of Psychometric or Instrumental Validity: Validity Applied to Measures or Assessments

Validity Type	Description
Face validity	Does the test/assessment seem valid to the person taking it? Do its questions or scales appear, on the surface, relevant to the topic being measured?
Content-related validity	Are all items on the instrument relevant to the characteristic or feature presumably being measured? Have all aspects of the domain of interest been adequately sampled? Has anything of importance been missed? Relevance and representativeness of content are appraised by persons knowledgeable about the characteristic being measured.
Criterion-related validity	Are scores on the measuring instrument appropriately related to some independent, external indicator of the characteristic being assessed? Such a relationship typically is determined by a correlation coefficient.
Concurrent	Here, data from the assessment instrument and the target criterion are collected at approximately the same time; useful for *diagnosis* of some existing condition.
Predictive	Here, the assessment instrument is administered some time before the future target criterion data become available; useful for *prediction* of future outcomes and for *selection* purposes.
Postdictive	Here, the target criterion already has occurred at the time the assessment instrument is administered.
Construct-related validity	Refers to the degree to which an assessment instrument adequately measures the theoretical construct, hypothetical process, or latent trait that it is supposed to measure.

Table 8.3. *(Continued)*

Validity Type	Description
Factorial	Statistical factor analysis can be used to determine the nature and number of patterns or factors measured by the assessment instrument, the relevance of the factors to the theoretical construct supposedly being measured, and how the instrument's items relate to the various factors.
Known groups	The degree to which scoring patterns on an assessment instrument differ in expected ways for groups of respondents already known to differ in the characteristic being measured.
Convergent	The degree to which the assessment instrument's results *agree* with other measures of *the same* construct.
Discriminant	The degree to which the assessment instrument's results *disagree* with measures of *different* constructs.
Multitrait-multimethod matrix	Measures both convergent and discriminant validity at the same time by concurrently assessing two or more traits and assessing each trait by two or more methods; results are presented in the form of a matrix that can be examined for expected agreements and disagreements (positive and negative correlations) among the measures.
Nomological network	Confidence in the construct validity of an assessment is enhanced when a nomological net has been developed to support the assessment. The nomological network consists of a set of relevant concepts (constructs), a set of observable manifestations (operationalizations) for at least some of these concepts/constructs, and the expected and observed linkages and interrelationships among and between the elements of these two sets. Such a scheme allows a determination of how obtained data patterns match theoretical expectations for those patterns.

All of these mentioned validities interact and overlap to various degrees. Of the many types of validities, it may be argued that face validity is the least important and that construct validity is the most important. Indeed, it has been suggested that there really is only one major form of validity, construct validity, and that the other validities are a variety of ways of establishing or determining construct validity. All of the validities, and especially construct validity, are ways of addressing the major research issues of whether and to which degree a given research hypothesis or research question truly is confirmed or answered, whether an assessment truly measures what it is presumed to measure, and whether what appears to have happened in a research project truly has occurred.

In addition to those treated above, researchers have identified three less familiar forms of validity. *Differential validity* is said to occur if the validity of a measure or procedure varies for different groups, different types of participants, or for different predicted criteria. *Replicative validity* occurs when outcomes can be repeatedly demonstrated across a variety of conditions. In exploring its *incremental validity*, one asks whether the use of a new instrument or method increases one's ability to explain or predict a certain criterion or, aspect of interest significantly better than already available instruments or methods—i.e., whether it provides additionally useful, nonredundant information? Hierarchical stepwise multiple regression analysis typically is used to determine whether additional variance is explained by the introduction of the new variable, above and beyond what can be explained by already existing variables. Incremental validity is most useful in applied areas such as decision making and prediction/selection.

Overview of Qualitative Forms of Validity

Lincoln and Guba (1985) have provided one of the most satisfying treatments of the qualitative equivalents of validity and related constructs in the context of what they termed the *trustworthiness* of an inquiry. Trustworthiness refers to the qualities of research project that increase the likelihood that the audience of a report of that project will pay attention to the project's findings, take them seriously, and find them worthwhile and useful. Lincoln and Guba suggest four major features of any research project that contribute to its trustworthiness: *truth value* (confidence of the truth of the findings for the particular participants and setting involved in the study), *applicability* (of the findings for persons and situations other than those involved in the study), *consistency* (whether the findings are repeatable), and *neutrality* (that the findings are contributed by the research participants and the inquiry conditions, rather than from various biases of the investigator). In the context of quantitative research, those four features appear in the guises of *internal validity, external validity, reliability,* and *objectivity* respectively.

Lincoln and Guba (1985), and many others after them, have argued that the concepts of internal validity, external validity, reliability, and objectivity, *as these are defined and measured in quantitative research,* are not appropriate for qualitative inquiries that use different approaches and have different aims, and that there is a need to reconceptualize these in more suitable ways. For qualitative research purposes, Lincoln and Guba reframed these four features as *credibility, transferability, dependability,* and *confirmability* respectively, and they suggested several techniques that can be used by qualitative inquirers in order to enhance each of these four features. We summarize and briefly describe these features and techniques in Table 8.4.

There have been other suggestions about forms of validity in qualitative research. For example, J. Maxwell (1992) proposed five major forms of validity: *descriptive* (the factual accuracy of the gathered data), *interpretative* (accurately representing the participants' own meanings and interpretations of what is being studied), *theoretical* (the accuracy of more abstract theoretical constructions and meanings that researchers apply to the findings), *generalizability* (the extent to which a researcher can generalize a conclusion within the study's context as well as to other contexts), and *evaluative* (the degree to which the researcher can legitimately apply an evaluative framework and judgments about the study).

Some have criticized Lincoln and Guba's (1985) four major trustworthiness criteria for being too much like the four well-established criteria for study quality that emerged in quantitative, positivistic contexts. However, we consider Lincoln and Guba's scheme to be one that captures well the most essential ways of determining the accuracy and truth value of qualitative research projects.

As an overarching consideration, we offer what may be the most straightforward and direct ways to determine the validity or trustworthiness of the results of a qualitative study. These could be called *investigator validation* and *participant validation.* In investigator validation, the researcher herself or himself, as the main instrument of a qualitative inquiry, bears the chief responsibility for judging the validity of the study's findings. The following two quotes—the first by a psychologist, the second by a physicist—nicely convey the sense of investigator validation:

Table 8.4. Features for Establishing the Trustworthiness of Qualitative Investigations and Techniques for Enhancing Each of These Features

Major Feature	Technique for Feature Enhancement
Credibility (the equivalent of internal validity for establishing the truth value of findings of an inquiry)	prolonged engagement (spending sufficient time with one's participants to learn as much about them as possible; also becoming sufficiently familiar with the contexts in which the participants live and have the experiences being studied; provides scope to one's study)
	persistent observation (providing sufficient opportunity to learn what is most relevant and salient to the topic being studied; avoiding premature closure; provides depth to one's study)
	triangulation (determining the consistency of evidence derived from different sources, methods, investigators, and/or theories, and whether these forms of information converge on the same findings and conclusions)
	peer debriefing (exposing one's hypotheses, questions, analyses, findings, and conclusions to a disinterested but well-informed peer who can play a devil's advocate role, helping the researcher become aware of alternative or previously unconsidered aspects of a study; the peer should not be someone in an authority relationship with the researcher; this supports an accurate *etic* [outsider] view)
	negative case analysis (testing one's conclusions by actively searching for instances that don't fit and modifying one's conclusions by considering those exceptions; being alert to factors that may be sufficient but not necessary for some outcome)

continued on next page

Table 8.4. (*Continued*)

Major Feature	Technique for Feature Enhancement
	referential adequacy (saving original recordings or other data so that these might be reexamined to check on conclusions; part of one's data might be archived and not included in the original analysis, but used as a second data set to confirm conclusions from the first, originally analyzed set)
	member checks (determining whether the persons from whom the data originally were collected agree on the accuracy of the study's data descriptions, interpretations, and conclusions; this supports an accurate *emic* [insider] view)
Transferability (the equivalent of external validity for establishing the applicability of findings of an inquiry)	thick and relevant description (the investigator attempts to provide careful, detailed, rich, thorough descriptions not only of the aspect being studied but also of the context—time, place, culture—in which that aspect was situated); such descriptions are to be obtained from a sufficient number and range of appropriately (purposively) sampled participants; a potential applier judges transferability based on the degree of similarity between the study's context and the context to which one wishes to apply the findings
Dependability (the equivalent of reliability for establishing the consistency of findings of an inquiry)	dependability audit and audit trail (in an analogy with an accounting audit, one carefully examines documents related to all aspects of the research *process* to determine whether and how the research protocol was followed)
Confirmability (the equivalent of objectivity for establishing the neutrality of findings of an inquiry)	confirmability audit and audit trail (in an analogy with an accounting audit, one carefully examines documents related to all aspects of the research *product* to determine whether and how the findings, interpretations, conclusions, and recommendations were coherent and appropriately supported by the data; akin to confirming a bottom line)

The question of validity is one of meaning: Does the ultimate depiction of the experience derived from one's own
rigorous, exhaustive self-searching and from the explications
of others present comprehensively, vividly, and accurately
the meanings and essences of the experience? This judgment is made by the primary researcher, who is the only
person in the investigation who has undergone the heuristic
inquiry from the beginning [through its various phases].
(Moustakas 1990, 32)

The process that I want to call scientific is a process that
involves the continual apprehension of meaning, the constant
appraisal of significance, accompanied by a running act of
checking to be sure that I am doing what I want to do,
and of judging correctness or incorrectness. This checking
and judging and accepting that together constitute understanding are done by me and can be done for me by no
one else. They are as private as my toothache, and without
them science is dead. (Bridgman 1950, 50)

It is important to supplement investigator validation with a second
form—*participant validation*. This form necessitates recognizing, emphasizing, and fully honoring the views of the research participants
themselves in establishing the validity or truth value of a study. In
some of the more recently developed forms of qualitative research—
participatory, cooperative, and action forms of inquiry—the research
participants equally share responsibility with the researcher for what is
planned, carried out, and concluded in all stages of a research project.
Therefore, their judgments about study quality and truth value are
as important as those of the primary researcher. This essential role
of research participants in helping to establish the accuracy of findings was codified in the form of *member checks*, even in early forms
of qualitative research.

Additional Validity Types

Mixed methods legitimation. In the above sections, we have treated
quantitative and qualitative forms of validity or trustworthiness separately. When quantitative and qualitative components are combined in
a mixed-method research design, new issues arise regarding the most
appropriate ways of handling those two components in the interest
of optimizing the truth value of the overall study. Onwuegbuzie and

Johnson (2006) have provided a thorough treatment of these new issues. In doing so, they suggested nine ways of optimizing the truth value or inference quality of mixed-methods designs. We summarize their nine suggested *legitimation types* for mixed-methods research below, in our own words:

> sample-integration legitimation: degree to which overall inferences to a larger population are appropriate to the natures of the different types of participant samples in the quantitative and qualitative components of a mixed design
>
> inside-outside legitimation: degree to which both participant (*emic*, insider) and researcher (*etic*, outsider) views are accurately represented and appropriately balanced
>
> weakness-minimization legitimation: selecting design components so that the weaknesses of some are complemented and well balanced by the strengths of others
>
> sequential legitimation: degree to which study results are free from influences of the sequencing order, per se, of study components
>
> conversion legitimation: maximizing the advantages and minimizing the risks of quantifying (counting) qualitative data or creating narrative summaries of quantitative data
>
> paradigmatic-mixing legitimation: blending of approaches that may have different ontological, epistemological, or methodological assumptions in ways that explicitly recognize these differences and appropriately honor them
>
> commensurability legitimation: departing from the frequent position that different approaches or paradigms are incommensurable and, instead, shifting from one view to another, integrating these, and developing a third view that includes yet transcends either
>
> multiple validities legitimation: properly addressing and satisfying the legitimation criteria of each individual research design component
>
> political legitimation: addressing issues of power and possible tensions among research participants in the planning, conducting, and applying aspects of a research project and honoring a pluralism of perspectives throughout a study

Method validity and approach validity. Validity typically has been addressed in two contexts: standardized measures/assessment instruments and a particular research study as a whole. To these two contexts, we suggest two additional contexts in which validity concerns are applicable. The first of these could be called "method validity," which would address validity issues related to the selection and proper use of particular research methods (tool, practices, procedures). Is the chosen method one that truly promises to yield useful information about the particular topic or process being studied? The second additional validity form could be called "approach validity," which would address validity concerns related to the selection and proper use of a more general research approach (a particular, larger form of inquiry). Is there a good match between the selected research approach and the types of knowledge gains and practical applications that one hopes to achieve in the study?

For further details about the forms of validity treated in the above sections, the interested reader may consult Anastasi and Urbina (1997), Bracht and Glass (1968), Campbell and Stanley (1963), Cook and Campbell (1979), Cronbach and Meehl (1955), Hunsley and Meyer (2003), Lincoln and Guba (1985), Maxwell (1992), Onwuegbuzie and Johnson (2006), Winter (2000), as well as the various research methods texts mentioned in the preface.

Transformational Forms of Validity

Efficacy validity. In conventional research, research findings are thought to demonstrate validity for the many good reasons already cited in this chapter. However, we often find that readers of scientific reports value research findings the most when the findings provide added value to their lives in terms of meaningfulness and insight. Often studies inspire us to think in new ways, asking questions of life that we never asked before. Much of valuable research, especially groundbreaking research, is more about the creative jumps, insights, and speculations than about the empirical or scholarly construction of theory step by step. Therefore, research and scholarly works that inspire, delight, and prod us to insight and action are often as valuable to our disciplinary efforts as the more technical inquirers that may follow.

Originally introduced in intuitive inquiry (Anderson 2004b; Esbjörn-Hargens and Anderson 2005), efficacy validity supports the notion that a reader of research and scholarly reports may change as a result of reading and encountering findings. Therefore, a study is high in efficacy validity if it answers affirmatively to such questions as:

> Was the researcher transformed in the course of conducting the study? Is the reader transformed in some way as she or he reads or applies research findings to life situations?
>
> Did the researcher and research participants gain in compassion and depth of understanding about themselves and the topic in the course of the study?
>
> In reading the report, do readers gain in compassion and depth of understanding about themselves, the topic, or the world?
>
> Is the research report written with such clarity and authenticity that readers feel that they know the researcher's motives for the study and, therefore, can better evaluate the study's relevance to their lives?
>
> Does the study provide a new vision for the future that helps readers ask new questions about their lives and the world?
>
> Are readers inspired by the findings and the vision provided by the study?
>
> Are readers moved toward action and service in the world?

Transformative validity. Related to efficacy validity (and especially the first question immediately above) is *transformative validity* discussed in Chapter 3 on Organic Inquiry. Transformative validity has to do specifically with the extent to which a reader's prevailing life story changes as a consequence of having read research participants' and the researcher's stories as relayed in scientific reports or more popular presentations of research findings to the public.

As a concluding remark on this section, rather than propose additional forms of validity beyond these, we suggest that researchers and scholars indicate to the public which kinds of feedback from them would provide them with the most valid indicators of the value of a particular study. That is, we propose a more in situ approach to validity rather than to rely solely on standardized procedures. Of course, consumers of our findings might find other sources of value or its lack in a study than what we might have imagined, but at least a dialogue would have begun. Without such a dialogue with the consumers of research and scholarly findings, it is difficult to know what is of value, authoritative, or useful to others outside of our disciplinary concerns.

Resonance Panels

Sympathetic Resonance, Resonance Validity, and Resonance Panels as Validity Indicators

Rosemarie Anderson (1998, 73–75, 93) introduced the concept of *sympathetic resonance* and the use of *resonance panels* as an indicator of validity in her chapter on intuitive inquiry in our earlier book (Braud and Anderson 1998). In developing the concept and exploring its applications, colleagues and students found them helpful so William Braud (1998a, 224–30) elaborated in detail on them in the same book. Later, Anderson (2004b) and Esbjörn-Hargens and Anderson (2005) introduced the term *resonance validity* to describe the ways in which sympathetic resonance can be used to evaluate validity within intuitive inquiry and qualitative research in general.

Although the concept can be described in acoustical terms, I (R. A.) trace the origins of this concept to my training in a lineage of Western Sufism established in the West in the early part of the twentieth century by Pir-O-Murshid Hazrat Inayat Khan from Northern India. More than thirty years have passed since that training, so I cannot pinpoint the exact teaching. However, during that period, I learned to witness my internal physical responses during meditation. Thereafter, I began to witness my internal responses to people, events, and environments in everyday life and use my responses to help me evaluate situations and make decisions.

Sympathetic resonance is a psychological principle akin to well-known resonance principles in the physical realm. The essential feature is that if two structures or systems are very similar in nature, an activation or disturbance of one will be faithfully mimicked or mirrored in the other. This can happen very sensitively and selectively. For example, a musical instrument, such as a piano, will vibrate with and itself emit a certain tone when that tone is produced in a similar instrument (a similar piano). Whether or not such mimicking or resonance occurs, and the strength of its occurrence, can be used as an indicator of the similarity of the two instruments. This resonance/similarity idea, when extended into the psychological realm, can be used as an indicator of the *validity* of an investigator's findings. If what is discovered about an experience of one person (or group of persons) also applies to another person (or group of persons), as revealed by the latter's resonance with or mirroring of those findings, then this similar response affirms the findings' validity. Psychologically, resonance is revealed by responses such as "yes, that feels or rings true for me as well," "yes, that is how I have experienced it," or "yes, that is the nature of my own experience." Resonance can have intellectual, emotional, bodily, or intuitive aspects. The degree and extent of such resonance (or nonresonance or even antiresonance) reactions can indicate the degree of accuracy, fullness, or generality of certain findings.

A resonance panel provides a systematic, formal procedure for assessing sympathetic resonance. Carefully selected individuals, who were not involved in the original research study, are presented with the findings that were generated in that study, to determine their degree of resonance (agreement) with those findings. The procedure is similar to what is known in qualitative research as a *member check*. The important difference is that member checks are accomplished by the actual original participants of a research study (who indicate whether or not they agree with the researcher's description and interpretation of their own experiences), whereas a resonance panel involves additional individuals who had not participated in the study that yielded the original findings.

Selecting Resonance Panel Members

A qualitative research study typically involves the exploration of a particular experience in a group of research participants. Therefore, in establishing a resonance panel, one will first choose members who have had that same experience, in order to determine whether these "new" persons who have had an identical experience will resonate to the descriptions and conclusions regarding that experience, as gained through the original study. If the researcher cannot find additional persons who have had that identical experience, another choice would be persons who have had experiences *similar to* the experience that originally was studied. The researcher might also use *proximity* as a selection criterion—choosing persons who are close to the original participants in some way. For example, resonance panel members might be chosen from among family members, friends, or neighbors of the original participants, from some group or organization to which the original participants might belong, or from those who live or work in settings identical or similar to those of the original participants. In alignment with what is known as a *360-degree assessment procedure* in business and workplace studies, one could choose as panel members persons who know the original participants very well, moderately well, or only slightly—thereby sampling various degrees of closeness of relationship. A final criterion for resonance panel selection is *impact*: The researcher may include persons who might have been or might be impacted by the experiences of the original participants. For example, if one is studying forgiveness, panel members could include not only forgivers but the forgiven as well. If one is studying the disclosure of exceptional experiences or of secrets, then one could include not only those who disclose, but also those who are the recipients of such disclosures. In more generalized terms, the panel could include persons who might *have reacted* or might *react in future* to the experiences or circumstances being studied. Regardless of specific selection criteria, the researcher should decide, given the aims of the study, whether she or he favors homogeneity or heterogeneity of the various resonance panel members. Of course, the researcher will explain the resonance panel procedures in detail to potential panel members and have them sign informed consent forms prior to their participation.

Modes of Participation

Although the term *panel* may suggest a group meeting, it is not necessary that the members of a resonance panel be convened at the same time or same location. The panel could participate as a group of persons who gather together to comment upon the researcher's original findings, and this group format could be the most efficient mode of participation. However, a resonance panel also could be structured as a set of individuals who assess a study's original findings at different times and in different locations. Each mode—group or individual—has its own advantages and disadvantages. The group mode, which would function similar to a focus group, would be more efficient and could benefit from a group dynamic in which thoughts and feelings in some members could trigger those of other members, permitting coverage of study aspects that otherwise might be ignored. The danger of the group mode is that the opinions of the more energetic, dominant, or aggressive members might overpower or even distort the views of the less forceful members.

The individual mode could allow easier scheduling and could allow panel members to express themselves more fully and perhaps more independently and more authentically than would be possible in a group setting. In any case, the resonance panel participants would be prepared ahead of their individual or group meeting by being given detailed accounts (written or in some other format) of the study findings that they would later be asked to react to. Sending the appropriate preparatory materials to panel members about two weeks ahead of their actual panel activity is advisable—allowing the members sufficient time to become familiar with the materials.

Presentational Modes

The materials presented to the resonance panel could take a variety of forms. The members could be asked to respond to concise individual summaries of the research participants' experiences. These could be narrative vignettes or presentations similar to the individual depictions or composite depictions that are prepared in heuristic research. Alternatively, panel members might be asked to respond to themes that had been identified in the original study by means of qualitative thematic content analysis. Video or audio recordings—appropriately selected and edited—could be used to present the most important of the original study's findings. Whatever is presented to the panel already would have been checked for accuracy by means of member checks by the original study participants.

Modes of Responding

The researcher has various options for assessing resonance of the panel members. The resonators could be asked to use Likert-type scales to indicate their reactions to various aspects of the original study's findings. They could indicate whether they agree or disagree strongly, moderately, or slightly with each major aspect of the original study's findings, or whether they feel neutral about a given aspect. Such agreements or disagreements could be based on ideas, feelings, emotions, bodily reactions, or intuitions. It would be helpful for the resonators to indicate what is serving as the basis for their reaction. They could be asked to respond either to the individual parts of the original study's findings or to the study's findings considered as a whole. In addition to such quantitative assessments, panel members should be allowed to offer qualitative comments about their degree of resonance (or nonresonance) to the findings, and they also should be encouraged to comment about what seemed especially relevant in the study findings and about things that they feel were left out. Should the requisite equipment be available, a researcher might make use of devices that permit panel members to indicate their degree of momentary agreement or disagreement with aspects of findings by turning a handheld knob in certain ways and have these motor responses tracked and recorded technologically, as is done in certain focus group studies. An even more sophisticated resonance assessment would be to record the resonator's physiological reactions (autonomic activity, as reflected in electrodermal activity) during presentations of various study findings. The latter two suggestions (for possible motoric and physiological indicators) are made simply for researchers with quantitative or technological leanings and who might wish to explore resonance in novel ways.

Analysis and Treatment of Resonance Panel Findings

The aim of the analysis and presentation of resonance results is, of course, to indicate if and how the various resonators responded to various aspects of the original study's descriptive findings. These resonance results can be summarized and presented either quantitatively or qualitatively or in both forms, and they can be presented in both overall and individual formats. The researcher could indicate degrees of resonance to various study findings—either quantitatively (by summarizing Likert-scale outcomes) or qualitatively (by indicating whether all, most, many, some, few, or no members resonated to which original study findings). In other words, the researcher would report both agreements and disagreements among the resonance results of the various panel members. Just as the original findings of any qualitative project are likely to be very individual and variable, so too would be the resonance results. Different panel members would be expected to feel differently about different aspects of the original findings. The researcher would report indications of both central tendencies and variability of resonance results.

By identifying and reporting patterns of resonance, antiresonance, and neutrality, the research will be able to suggest which aspects of an original study's findings might be generally applicable or accurate, which might be partially applicable or accurate, and which might apply to or be accurate or valid for certain types of individuals but not for others. As has been suggested elsewhere (Anderson 1998, 74–75), by noting the patterns of reactions in various subgroups, a researcher could create a type of political, social, or cultural *mapping* of the whole or of parts of research findings. The researcher could construct a modified sociogram with concentric circles indicating which research findings are immediately apprehended, recognized, and reacted to with consonance, dissonance, or neutrality and which types of persons or groups respond in these various ways.

However the resonance results are assessed, the researcher should address and honor the inputs from each of the resonance panel members. The researcher can qualify or further elaborate on the original study's findings in light of the resonance panel data. As was described for *lenses* in the intuitive inquiry chapter of this book (Chapter 1), based on resonance panel results, conclusions about specific original study findings might be modified in minor or major ways or not changed at all. The qualitative comments of certain resonance panel members might even suggest new findings about the experience being studied, just as new lenses might emerge during Cycle 4 of the intuitive inquiry process.

CHAPTER 9

A Transformative Vision
for Research and Scholarship

My deep sigh rises above as a cry of the earth and an answer comes
from within as a message.

—Pir-O-Murshid Inayat Khan (Khan 1960, 72)

In alignment with the values both explicit and implicit in
the methods, skills, and experiential exercises in previous
chapters, in this final chapter, we propose a transformative
vision for research and scholarship that supports positive
individual, communal, and worldwide transformation. We
live in challenging times. Only human beings working collectively can resolve our climate, economic, environmental,
social, and political woes because we are the source of
the problems. If academic disciplines and communities of
scholars continue our separatist disciplines that tend to
aggrandize disciplinary pursuits and related industries, the
woeful tale of the exhaustion of the environment and the
encouragement of general mayhem is likely to continue
globally. Another possibility might be that academic inquiry
will become increasingly sidelined from the global discourse
that resolves real problems, a dismissal which seems to us
to be already occurring in some public sectors. We hope
that the human sciences and humanities will rise to the
challenges of our time, exploring new and transformative
strategies to meet concrete problems in the world, both
local and global in character. We need a new science and
new humanities infused (or reinfused) with their original
vision to enrich the greater whole, a global community
that includes the more-than-human world. (Abram 1996)

303

To enact a transformative vision of research, the scholarly community needs to make several changes about how we think about our academic pursuits—and in particular, academic psychology. First, we propose that we begin to honor all the world's wisdom psychologies, not only psychology as it has historically developed in academic and professional circles in the West but inclusive of the wisdom psychologies embedded in the religious, spiritual, and indigenous traditions, practices, and rituals around the globe. Hundreds, if not thousands, of these wisdom psychologies exist worldwide; each in its own way with the potential to enrich our collective understanding. We would be remiss to ignore a single one. Who are we to know—or not know— if the wisdom of one small group in a remote corner of the world does not provide the elixir that resolves a local or global problem? Without enriching our lives with the insights of these major and minority religious, spiritual, and indigenous traditions, we will never know what we may have lost. Much of this plethora of wisdom still exists worldwide and needs to preserved and understood by others, and especially by researchers and scholars for whom these wisdom traditions bear witness on topics relevant to our respective disciplines. In terms of international politics, gone is the era in which one dominant political agenda can determine the global discourse that resolves our common problems, even at its own peril.

Second, we propose that the scholarly and discourse communities of the world contribute collectively to the reinvention of ourselves as a global community that includes the more-than-human world and affirms our interdependence on one another and the natural world. The more-than-human world includes all the creatures and natural forces of the globe we call "Earth" and those of interstellar space as well. We do not know in what "mix" we survive, and humility is in order. The more-than-human world also includes spiritual forces that infuse conventional reality with meaning and verve; these, too, have and create life as is well understood in various ways in traditions around the world.

Third, we propose that all people worldwide become perfectly themselves in their own time and place. No people or group need imitate another. Now is the time to understand that our diversity and otherness is an asset and not a liability to global conviviality and peace. As a species, ultimately, we cannot survive without our diversity—whether we are talking about the diversity of bacteria, seeds, plants, insects, animals, mammals, or human cultures. Only in our diversity, *might* we survive.

Enlarging Our View of Research and Scholarship

Implicit in this transformative vision of research and scholarship is the understanding that transformation can be individual, communal, and global, thereby expanding beyond the usual focus on individual personal growth and transformation in humanistic and transpersonal psychology. The vision includes the many ways that human experience supports *end goals* such as health and well-being, peace and harmony, compassion and kindness, and integrity and truthfulness—including the possible reconceptualization of many ordinary, neglected, anomalous, or pathologized experiences in transformational terms. To support these end goals, we encourage a language of mutuality that incorporates within itself a language of self and other, a language of "we" that includes "me" and "you." In this view, we are already present in the needs others present. Such an encompassing view is encapsulated in the African philosophy and way of life known as *Ubuntu* (see Louw n.d.a.; Louw n.d.a.), exemplified in the Zulu maxim *ubuntu ngumuntu ngabantu* (a person is a person through other people) (Schutte 2001). The essence of this tradition can also be conveyed in the expression, "I am because we are; we are because I am."

This transformative vision for research and scholarship recognizes the mutual, reciprocal interaction of individual, collective, and global aspects. Evidence and theory from areas as diverse as esoteric wisdom traditions, quantum physics, and parapsychology suggest that a view of individuals as separate and isolated from each other is incorrect and misleading. Instead, the actual world appears to have features of deep interconnectedness and nonlocality. What we know and how we act are not separate from what the collective knows and how it acts. What one learns about one can be applied to the other; what benefits one, benefits the other. Indeed, "other," here, is simply a figure of speech. With this in mind, one does not really leave the study of one's immediate community or the global community when one studies individual inner experience, and this can be useful, especially if motivated by a concern for its relevance to the collective, and to end goals and values. This view is consistent with the recognition that there are "[those] who have given their life in service to humanity by discovering that global consciousness comes from the exploration of the inner self" (Targ and Hurtak 2006, xxiv).

In addition to enlarging one's view of research to honor both individual and global aspects, one also might bear in mind the suggestions of Ernest Boyer. Boyer (1990) has suggested a view of scholarship that includes four domains or dimensions. He identified and described the four scholarships of *discovery* (conducting, and leading students in, original empirical research; an emphasis on new findings), *integration* (theoretical and interdisciplinary work; emphasis on new conceptualizations and understandings; writing), *teaching* (dissemination of knowledge, in all of its forms—teaching, mentoring, modeling, being [embodiment and intention]), and *application* (offering professional services to others; community-based practices; addressing groups and one-on-one). These four modes also can be used to characterize *different forms of research* and *different ways of advancing the fields* not only in transpersonal psychology but in other academic disciplines as well.

Strategies for a Transformative Vision for Research and Scholarship

Collaboration with Scientists and Scholars Across Disciplines

It seems likely that the greater the range of one's knowledge and experiences of the world at large, the greater will be the possibility of enlarging and transforming one's appreciation and understanding of self, others, and the world—i.e., the more likely will be the transformation of one's selfview, lifeview, and worldview. We suggest four possibilities for expanding one's knowledge and experiences through research and scholarship. The first possibility is to do this *within oneself*—to increase, as much as possible, the range and depth of one's personal experience of aspects of oneself, of others, and of the world. This would involve not only exposing oneself to wide-ranging content but also making use of as many of one's forms of intelligence and ways of knowing as possible. These latter expansions can be aided through the use and training of the skills treated in Part 2 of this book. Given the limitations of what is possible for an individual to know and experience, a second possibility is to become part of and work in collaboration with *a team of inquirers* who have similar interests and aims.

A third possibility is to *foster the expansion of one's specific discipline,* so that it becomes more inclusive and integrated in both its methods and its substantive content (as already was described in the final section of Chapter 2). For example, if one is working within the field of psychology, one can seek to have one's understanding informed by the thoughts and findings of as many of its subareas as possible. From inquirers with behavioral and cognitive preferences, one can learn much about our functions and abilities and the constraints on these, and learn the usefulness of objective, standardized, and usually quantitatively determined principles and practices—especially in areas of sensory and perceptual functioning, learning, memory, motivation, and thinking. From inquirers with preferences for psychoanalytical and depth psychological approaches, we can learn about ways of becoming aware of previously "unconscious" processes and content, about the nature of unconscious motivations, and about the role of early experiences in influencing our later ways of functioning. From those of a humanistic and existential persuasion, we can gain richer understandings in areas such as choice, responsibility, human potentials and growth, self, self-actualization, health, love, hope, creativity, our intrinsic nature, being, becoming, individuality, authenticity, and meaning, and also learn the value of qualitative inquiry approaches in exploring such topics. From inquirers with a preference for a transpersonal approach, we can learn how our self-schemas and identities can be expanded to include *more* of reality in space and time; how there are *more* stages of growth and development than usually are recognized; that there are alternative modes of knowing, being, and doing; the importance of our profound interconnectedness with others and with all aspects of nature; the possibilities of transformation and transcendence; the usefulness of a holistic view of our personhood; and the power of the types of transpersonal inquiry approaches treated in Part 2 of this book as appropriate ways of exploring these aspects. In addition to these various inputs from different areas of psychology, we can welcome expansions informed by areas outside of psychology as well.

A fourth possibility is to *collaborate with scientists and scholars across disciplines* and to welcome and honor their methods, findings, and interpretations. Because they deal with human functioning at many levels—the findings, theories, and approaches of workers in areas of philosophy, psychology, sociology, anthropology, economics, history, literature, the arts, the natural sciences, medicine, and the newer and underappreciated disciplines of parapsychology and psychical research—are all of great relevance to anyone who wishes to develop inclusive and integrated understandings of what it means to be human. Because of their distinctive emphases, and what they choose to include or exclude from their domains of inquiry, each of these areas reveals certain things about our human nature and functioning, while concealing other aspects. By considering as many of these sources of knowledge as possible, the concealments of some sources can be balanced by the revelations of others. A researcher's interactions with other scientists and scholars can expand the perspectives and understandings of all concerned and can lead to possible transformative changes in both the researcher and his or her collaborators.

The prominent English physicist and mathematician, Sir Oliver Lodge (1910), provided an early statement about the value of attending to the works of those in other disciplines, specifically the humanities:

> If it be urged that seers are not scientific workers—that they employ alien methods—I agree that their methods are different, but not that they are alien. Science, in a narrow sense, is by no means the only way of arriving at truth— especially not at truth concerning human nature. To decline to be informed by the great seers and prophets of the past, and to depend solely on a limited class of workers such as have been bred chiefly within the last century or two, would savour of a pitiful narrowness, and would be truly and in the largest sense unscientific. . . .
>
> Truth is large, and can be explored by many avenues. All honour to those who, with insufficient experience but with the inspiration of genius, caught glimpses of a larger and higher truth than was known to the age in which they lived, and who had the felicity of recording their inspirations in musical and immortal word—words such as the worker in science has not at his command—words at which he rejoices when he encounters them, and which he quotes because they have given him pleasure. (154–55)

In an interdisciplinary or transdisciplinary context, the work of psychologist and philosopher Sigmund Koch is noteworthy. In his monumental, six-volume edited series on *Psychology: A Study of a Science* (1959–1963), Koch sought to make explicit the interrelationships of various areas of psychology and the relevance of various other disciplines to psychology. Volume 6 of that series included contributions that addressed ways in which psychology could be "bridged" with other disciplines such as psycholinguistics, sociology, anthropology, linguistics, political science, and economics. In his subsequent work (Koch 1999), Koch sought to emphasize the important roles of the humanities and the arts in enhancing psychological understanding. An updating and continuation of such work could contribute importantly to the development of a more adequate form of psychology.

It might seem that collaboration with persons in different disciplines would be difficult because of their seemingly disparate approaches. However, upon closer examination, one finds considerable overlap in the essential features of the underlying inquiry methods of various disciplines. Robert and Michele Root-Bernstein (1999) convincingly demonstrate that creative individuals in many different areas of science, humanities, and the arts use the same sorts of thinking tools in their work. These tools involve processes of observing, imaging, abstracting, recognizing patterns, forming patterns, analogizing, body thinking, empathizing, dimensional thinking, modeling, playing, transforming, and synthesizing. Using such tools in one area can facilitate their recognition and use in other areas. One of our purposes in Part 2 of this book is to help researchers and scholars become more familiar with skills such as these so that they might apply them more effectively in their own disciplines, whatever those might be, and to be able to collaborate more efficiently with persons using the same or similar skills in other areas.

Integration of Spiritual and Indigenous Insights

In times like ours, we can use all the help we can get. If the popularity of workshops, websites, blogs, and circulating emails on alternative health practices, climate changes, "green" and peace initiatives, reconciliation efforts, and gender and minority petitions for action are evidence of concern, people worldwide have increasingly begun to look to resources outside of the political, governmental, industrial, institutionalized religious, and scientific communities for answers to problems that are often personal, communal, and global. Hopefully, researchers, scholars, and the public can overcome the temptation to either dismiss or idealize spiritual masters, shamans, and priests in spiritual and indigenous communities and learn to consider and study the insights themselves, both scientifically and metaphysically, in order to distill those elements that address issues and propose solutions to local, communal, and global concerns. Perhaps those spiritual and indigenous communities, which have isolated themselves from the world culture as it is, are those that have the most useful insights.

In recent years, the popularity of Tibetan religious and spiritual insights has been epitomized in the near rock-star atmosphere that attends His Holiness, the Dalai Lama whenever he comes to town. Isolated from the world at large by the towering Himalayas and fierce weather, the Tibetan community has created unique metaphysical systems and spiritual technologies or practices that purport to cultivate mindfulness, equanimity, and compassion over time. In the last decade or so, the popularity of the Tibetan spiritual teachings is testimony to a hunger, at least in the West, for resources outside of customary sources, and a willingness to contemplate insights from cultures quite unlike our own and discern their relevance to our lives today.

The Kogi tribe of the Sierra Nevada de Santa Marta in Columbia is another isolated, mountain, and spiritual community that has received considerable public attention for their spiritual and environmental insights about the imperiled health of the Earth. In 1990, a BBC documentary directed by Alan Ereira entitled, *"From the Heart of the World—The Elder Brothers' Warning,"* was released that warned that various activities, such as strip mining and oil drilling, were killing the "flesh" of the Earth. On their mountains, heavy snows had stopped falling and the rivers were low, signaling to their priests that the Sierra Nevada mountains and the Earth were dying. For the Kogi, the Sierra Nevada is mother and heart of the world. So fierce were their elders' concerns that they broke with hundreds of years of strict isolation from the outside world for this BBC documentary. Shortly thereafter, *The Elder Brothers* was released as a book (Ereira 1992). (Further information is available on the website of the Tairona Heritage Trust, http://tairona.myzen.co.uk, a British-based nonprofit organization, that works on behalf of the Kogi, the Arhuaco, and the Assario, descendents of the Tairona civilization that flourished in the Sierra Nevada mountain range prior to the Spanish invasion of Columbia.)

The Kogi consider themselves the Elder Brothers. We are the Younger Brothers. To the extent that we despoil the Earth, we are not just younger but dead, shadows of human beings. *The Elder Brothers' Warning* offers to us a way of life in which all acts are considered in their communal, ethical, and spiritual dimensions. All life forms are interconnected. The Kogi report that their priests, called "Mamas," spend the first nine years of childhood in a cave in total darkness in order to learn the sacred rituals of inner seeing. For the Kogi, the outer physical world is first reflected in the inner world, called Aluna, which the child-priests are taught to "see" and discover her messages.

The messages from the indigenous Tibetan people and the Kogi people of the Sierra Nevada de Santa Marta are but two examples of spiritual and indigenous communities that bear witness to current global concerns. There are hundreds of such communities worldwide. We, the authors of this volume, do not suggest that any one group has "the answer," but that researchers and scholars seriously consider and study the teachings and insights of spiritual and indigenous communities that serve positive end goals and look for individual and communal solutions for the real problems facing the Earth and her inhabitants in our times.

Methodological Pluralism

The complexity of today's problems and challenges often requires methodological pluralism. Teams of researchers and scholars from disciplines throughout the human sciences, natural sciences, humanities, and arts could bring a range of methodological approaches to research endeavors as described earlier in this chapter. The parable about the elephant and a group of blind men who try to figure out what elephant might be comes to mind. Each man in his own way explores a part of the elephant and, in turn, claims a different understanding about the nature of elephant. Similarly, most experienced researchers and scholars know well that our respective disciplinary values, epistemologies, and approaches to inquiry, privilege and reveal certain types of information and minimize and eclipse the relevance of others. A reliance on quantitative methods privileges what can be counted or measured, a reliance on qualitative methods privileges what can be described well in words; a reliance on approaches in the visual arts privileges what can be represented in images, symbols, and pictures; a reliance on fiction and film for knowledge privileges what is better told in story; and so on. These same approaches minimize what can be learned from other approaches. Robert Romanyshyn (2007) states the matter eloquently:

> No, my point is not that this [empirical] method is incorrect. Rather, I am arguing that method is a way of making some things count while discounting other things. Method is a perspective that both reveals a topic and conceals it. What I am suggesting is that a method is an enacted metaphor. Just as a metaphor tells us what something is by implying that it is not what it is, this empirical method tells us that dreams are a brain function because they are also not a brain function. The metaphorical "is" is also always an "is not." (212)

Methodological pluralism would allow the strengths of various methods to offset their respective limitations. Of course, the types of methods chosen for a particular investigation would depend on the topic and its level of complexity.

In recent years, a number of researchers have proposed mixed-method approaches to research in the human sciences (Creswell 2009; Creswell and Clark 2006; Tashakkori and Teddlie 1998; Tashakkori and Teddlie 2003). These initiatives toward methodological pluralism are excellent. Our only concern is that they always do not include scholarly approaches to inquiry in the humanities and the expressive arts, the subject of the next section.

Integration of the Expressive Arts

Surely, if we wish to study and understand human experience in its vivid and various dimensions, researchers and scholars need to explore and utilize those aspects of human experience that provide us with the most meaningful, compelling, and creative aspects of our experience—including the arts, dance, drama, music, and storytelling. Therefore, using the expressive or creative arts in research has been a central theme in the content and experiential exercises of this book. The use of the arts is encouraged in Intuitive Inquiry, Integral Inquiry, and Organic Inquiry, the transformative approaches to research presented in Chapters 1, 2, and 3, and the transformation skill applications presented in Part 2. The Creative Arts section of Chapter 7 also describes and provides many examples of the use of the arts in research and scholarship and suggests how the arts might be employed in the preparation of data and data collection, data treatment and interpretation, and the communication of the findings stages of research. The use of story and storytelling is also an important feature of Organic Inquiry, the subject of Chapter 3. Therefore, in this section, we only wish to assert that we are not alone among researchers and scholars in advocating the use of the arts and the humanities in general to further our understanding about the nature of human experience.

Two well-known commentators on the use of the arts and creative imagination within science are Sigmund Koch (1959–1963) and Michael Polanyi (Polanyi 1966; Polanyi 1969; Polanyi and Prosch 1975). Earlier in this chapter, we mentioned Sigmund Koch's views on the relevance of the humanities and arts to psychological research. Koch's analyses of the limitations of the scientific method to explain human experience are well known. Not well known, however, are his studies of creative artists done toward the end of his career. This project was known as the *Artists on Arts Project* (Koch 1983–1988). The project, funded by the Ford Foundation and Boston University, is archived as videotapes at the Ford Foundation. According to Siner Francis (2008), who reviewed these archives and reiterated Koch's analytic process in her own analysis, Koch conducted a series of four two-hour interviews with fourteen accomplished artists, engaging them in dialogue about their personal history, work habits, internal process, media, and views about the problems and challenges within their artistic fields. The depth and range of these interviews attests to Koch's conviction that understanding the creative process requires interviewing those actively engaged in artistic production.

Similarly, Michael Polanyi (Polanyi 1966; Polanyi 1969; Polanyi and Prosch 1975) attest to the centrality of the arts and art-based approaches to understanding the creation of meaning. For Polanyi, all human knowledge is rooted in acts of understanding that are made possible through what he calls "the tacit dimension of knowing." That is, we always know more than we can tell or explain. Embedded in all acts of meaning is a sense of wholeness and particularity of what we know. We recognize that an unfamiliar tree is a tree because it has the wholeness or a sensibility similar to other trees. We understand the relevance of metaphor or parable to a concrete situation because of the tacit dimensions that bridge the two. For Polanyi, whether in everyday life or science, meaning is created in intuitive leaps between what is concrete and obvious and the embedded tacit dimensions of our experience. In this way, all acts of meaning making, including scientific discovery, are embedded in what we usually think of as artistic or creative processes.

Aligned with the views of Robert and Michelle Root-Bernstein (1999), throughout this book, we have advanced the notion that employing the expressive and creative arts would enrich research and scholarship. Although many researchers and scholars employ the arts in their personal lives in ways that often enrich their understanding and provide insight, these artistically-rendered promptings are not usually acknowledged in written reports. We wish to encourage researchers and scholars to directly employ the arts within disciplined inquiry and report how they used them and what they learned from them.

Practical Applications of Transformative Principles to Global Problems: The Intersections of Passions and Needs

Frederick Buechner (1973) has called attention to "the place where [one's] deep gladness and the world's deep hunger meet" (95). The most satisfying research projects, for both the researcher and the world at large, would seem to be topics where these two aspects—the researcher's greatest passions (deep gladness) and the world's greatest needs (deep hunger)—intersect. Related to this is N. Maxwell's (1992) treatment of the kind of inquiry that might best help us create a "good world."

For help in identifying some of the world's greatest needs or deepest hungers, a researcher hoping for greater global impacts of his or her work could consider the following brief listings of some of the most important world needs and of factors that could promote either their satisfaction or their frustration.

Even a brief moment of consideration reveals the following as important *world needs* (*deep hungers*): adequate satisfaction of basic human needs; adequate standards of living; values and motivations that prevent or minimize conflict; effective means of resolving conflicts that do occur; peace; sustainability of the natural environment; and values and conditions that allow life to have meaning, importance, and significance. Stated somewhat differently, important world needs (deep hungers) include increments in the health, security, peace, love, clarity, compassion, wisdom, and joy of its global citizens.

It also is easy to identify factors that interfere with the satisfaction—and even the identification and consideration—of those world needs. These factors, which also contribute to unhealthy and unsustainable world conditions, include: arrogance and hubris; greed and selfishness: intolerance of others (and their ways and values); fear; overly materialistic values; unequal distribution of wealth, goods, necessities; misplaced ambition; overemphases on growth, power, and control; proclivities toward violence, cruelty, vengeance, warmongering; and dishonesty.

Factors that can foster the satisfaction of world needs and also promote healthy and sustainable world conditions include: humility; sharing and generosity; tolerance of others (and their ways and values) and appreciation of differences; fairness (honest, just, and equitable treatment of others); compassion and caring; respect for human, animal, and plant life and for the environment; honesty, authenticity, integrity, and truth-telling (full, accurate, uncensored, undistorted information); and thoughtfulness, discernment, and critical thinking.

From a holistic and global perspective, important research projects would be those that might increase our understanding of the nature of factors that can contribute to a healthy and sustainable world, identify and promote processes—individual and societal, local and nonlocal—that can best satisfy the world's greatest needs, and help reduce the tendencies that act as barriers to the satisfaction of these needs. These considerations can help inform research projects that serve to address the researcher's most burning questions, most passionate interests, and deepest gladness, while at the same time offering possibilities for decreasing suffering and promoting the health and well-being of the entire planet and all of its inhabitants.

These considerations point to the value of meaningful and even grand studies that directly address pressing individual and social problems. However, the value of less impressive, little studies should not be neglected. Studies conducted for their own sake, performed without explicit aims of directly addressing large practical problems, often yield gifts of knowledge that, when later applied, have impacts on large social issues even greater than those of more direct and deliberate problem-fixing approaches. There is great value in both direct-and-grand and indirect-and-humble research projects. In following the principles and practices described throughout this book, the inquirer is aware of and supportive of both of these kinds of approaches.

Usually, written communications to professional audiences are privileged in "advancing the field." In transpersonal psychology, this usual means can be expanded in two ways: (a) via written communications to both professions *and to the general public* (via semi-popular and popular books and articles), and (b) by *additional means* of expressing, communicating, and presenting one's work and findings to both professionals and the general public—such as exhibits, public lectures, workshop presentations, and media presentations.

Unique Ethical Considerations

All academic disciplines have either formalized codes to govern the conduct of scholarly inquiry (American Psychological Association 1992) or mores that are shared among scholars within the discipline. As is well understood in legal and ethical circles, Western legal and ethical codes are derived historically from the values and ethics both implicit and explicit in the Torah via a succession of Middle Eastern, Roman Christian, European, and English formulations and texts. Inherent in the virtues of not killing, stealing, lying or committing adultery are values motivated toward the common good of the community as whole, understood within its cultural context. Taoist and Confucian sources and Vedic, Buddhist, and Qur'ānic sources have been the primary inspirations for the legal and ethical codes of Asia, India, the Middle East, Africa, and increasingly worldwide, formulations that also further the common good of the community or society. In the West, furthering the common good is often articulated in protection of those in the community who are the most vulnerable—be they widows and orphans in historical Israel or research participants and clients in contemporary research and psychotherapy. Without question, within the transformative paradigm of the approaches and skills proposed in this book, we adhere to and support these values and priorities as articulated formally and informally within the academic community and its respective disciplines.

In addition, the procedures embedded in the three transformative approaches to research and skills in this book involve the motive and intention to transform others in positive ways. When used in research and scholarly endeavors, skills such as intuition, empathic identification, direct knowing (via telepathy, clairvoyance, and precognition), distant mental influence, and other parapsychological processes have the potential to violate the privacy of research participants or to convey information inconsistent with participants' understanding of themselves or the ways in which they wish to be understood by others. Of course, hopefully, all researchers or scholars—whether they are working within a transformative paradigm or not—are serving the greater good. However, in using the transformative methods and skills the risks are simply higher and additional caution is required.

Therefore, we recommend that all users of the methods, skills, and experiential exercise in this book add the intention of "for the greater good" as a standard and regular research practice. Another "condition" that might be added to intentions could be in the form of "may this intention be realized in a way that does not yield any ill effects." Researchers can inform their research participants about their plan to use intentions, ask if they are comfortable with this, and include this information in their informed consent forms. One might call such a practice a "prayer that covers many a flaw in the motives or personality of a researcher or scholar." Needless to say, what the greater good might be is not always easy to discern! It is ridiculous to assume that any inquirer might know what is best for others, but he or she can care deeply. From the point of view of intention, motives matter and have a force of their own that will help keep an inquiry on course toward what is best for all.

We live in times that challenge and threaten life as we know it on Earth. If the academic community wishes to transform our world for the better, we must refine or upgrade our motives for conducting research and scholarly inquiry. Career aspirations, professorial promotion and tenure, and monetary gains that might accrue to our inquiries must become secondary motives that serve what is best for all. We must rededicate ourselves to the values of what serves the greater good: a new world in the making. What kind of world do we want to create? What values do we aver? If we want to help create a kind world, a generous world, a peaceful world, a beneficent world to all the creatures that inhabit our beautiful blue globe—as researchers and scholars we must first *become* the qualities of kindness, generosity, peacefulness, and beneficence we want. As a "tribe" of researchers and scholars, we must not follow the dictates of political and industrial agendas, but rather *lead* in dedication to the good of all that lives.

References

(ProQuest Digital dissertations can be obtained at: www.proquest.com/en-US/products/dissertations/finding.shtml.)

Aanstoos, C., I. Serlin, and T. Greening. 2000. History of Division 32 (Humanistic Psychology) of the American Psychological Association. In *Unification through division: Histories of the divisions of the American Psychological Association*, edited by D. Dewsbury, vol. 5, 85–112. Washington, DC: APA.

Abram, D. 1996. *The spell of the sensuous: Perception and language in a more-than-human world*. New York: Pantheon Books.

Aczel, A. D. 2003. *Entanglement*. New York: Plume/Penguin.

Adler, A. 1935. The structure of neurosis. *International Journal for Individual Psychology* 1 (1): 3–12.

Adler, J. 2002. *Offerings from the conscious body: The discipline of authentic movement*. Rochester, VT: Inner Traditions.

American Psychological Association. 1992. Ethical principles of psychologists and code of conduct. *American Psychologist* 47: 1597–611.

Amis, R. 1995. *A different Christianity*. Albany, NY: SUNY Press.

Amlani, A. 1995. Diet and psychospiritual development: Physiological, psychological, and spiritual changes and challenges associated with lacto-ovo vegetarian, vegan, and live food diets. Retrieved from ProQuest Digital Dissertations (AAT DP14318).

Anastasi, A., and S. Urbina. 1997. *Psychological testing*, 7th ed. Upper Saddle River, NJ: Prentice-Hall.

Anderson, R. 1996a. Interview with Miles Vich and Sonja Margulies on the early years of transpersonal psychology. Unpublished manuscript.

———. 1996b. Nine psycho-spiritual characteristics of spontaneous and involuntary weeping. *Journal of Transpersonal Psychology* 2 (82): 43–49.

———. 1998. Intuitive inquiry: A transpersonal approach. In W. Braud and R. Anderson, *Transpersonal research methods for the social sciences: Honoring human experience*, 69–94. Thousand Oaks, CA: Sage.

———. 2000. Intuitive inquiry: Interpreting objective and subjective data. *ReVision: Journal of Consciousness and Transformation* 22 (4): 31–39.

———. 2001. Embodied writing and reflections on embodiment. *Journal of Transpersonal Psychology* 33 (2): 83–96.

———. 2002a. Embodied writing: Presencing the body in somatic research, Part I, What is embodied writing? *Somatics: Magazine/Journal of the Mind/Body Arts and Sciences* 13 (4): 40–44.

———. 2002b. Embodied writing: Presencing the body in somatic research, Part II, Research Applications. *Somatics: Magazine/Journal of the Mind/ Body Arts and Sciences* 14 (1): 40–44.

———. 2004a. Guest editor, intuitive inquiry. *The Humanistic Psychologist* 32 (4): 307–425.

———. 2004b. Intuitive inquiry: An epistemology of the heart for scientific inquiry. *The Humanistic Psychologist* 32 (4): 307–341.

———. 2007. Thematic content analysis: Descriptive presentation of qualitative data, www.wellknowingconsulting.org/publications/articles.html/.

———. 2011. Anderson, R. 2011. Intuitive inquiry: Exploring the mirroring discourse of disease. In F. Wertz, K. Charmaz, L. McMullen, R. Josselson, R. Anderson, and E. McSpladden. *Five ways of doing qualitative analysis: Phenomenological psychology, grounded theory, discourse analysis, narrative research, and intuitive inquiry.* New York: Guilford.

Arao-Nguyen, S. 1996. Ways of coming home: Filipino immigrant women's journeys to wholeness. Retrieved from ProQuest Digital Dissertations (AAT DP14332).

Assagioli, R. 1990. *Psychosynthesis: A manual of principles and techniques.* Wellingborough, England: Crucible.

Athenian Society for Science and Human Development and the Brahma Kumaris World Spiritual University 1992, January. Report on the Second International Symposium on Science and Consciousness. Athens, Greece: Author.

Aurobindo, Sri. 2000. *The synthesis of yoga.* Pondicherry, India: Sri Aurobindo Ashram Press. (Original work published serially 1914–1921 and in book form 1948.)

Banks, M. 2001. *Visual methods in social research.* Thousand Oaks, CA: Sage.

Barrell, J. J., C. Aanstoos, A. C. Richards, and M. Arons. 1987. Human science research methods. *Journal of Humanistic Psychology* 27 (4): 424–57.

Bastick, T. 1982. *Intuition: How we think and act.* New York: Wiley.

Batson, C. D. 1998. Altruism and prosocial behavior. In *Handbook of social psychology,* edited by S. T. Fiske, D. T. Gilbert, and G. Lindzey, 282–316. Boston: McGraw-Hill.

Bauer, M. W. and G. Gaskell, eds. 2000. *Qualitative researching with text, image, and sound: A practical handbook.* Thousand Oaks, CA: Sage.

Behar, Ruth. 1996. *The vulnerable observer: Anthropology that breaks your heart.* Boston: Beacon Press.

Belenky, M. F., B. M. Clinchy, N. R. Goldberger, and J. M. Tarule. 1997. *Women's ways of knowing,* rev. ed. New York: Basic Books.

Benson, H. 1975. *The relaxation response.* New York: Morrow.

Bento, W. 2006. A transpersonal approach to somatic psychodiagnostics of personality: A contribution towards its development, dis-ordering tendencies, and embodied transcendence. Retrieved from ProQuest Digital Dissertations (AAT 3213075).

Binney, M. 2002. *The women who lived for danger: The women agents of SOE in the Second World War.* London: Coronet Books.

Blanck, P. D., ed. 1993. *Interpersonal expectations: Theory, research, and applications.* New York: Cambridge University Press.

Boethius. 1980. *The consolation of philosophy* Trans. V. E. Watts. New York: Penguin. (Original work written in 524.)

Bohm, D. 1996. *On dialogue.* Ed. L. Nichol. New York: Routledge.

Boyer, E. L. 1990. *Scholarship reconsidered: Priorities of the professoriate.* San Francisco: Jossey-Bass.

Bracht, H. G. and V. G. Glass. 1968. The external validity of experiments. *Journal of the American Educational Research Association* 5 (4): 437–74.

Brandt, P. L. 2007. Nonmedical support of women during childbirth: The spiritual meaning of birth for doulas. Retrieved from ProQuest Digital Dissertations (AAT 3274206).

Braud, W. 1978. Psi conducive conditions: Explorations and interpretations. In *Psi and states of awareness,* edited by B. Shapin and L. Coly, 1–41. New York: Parapsychology Foundation.

———. 1981. Lability and inertia in psychic functioning. In *Concepts and theories of parapsychology,* edited by B. Shapin and L. Coly, 1–36. New York: Parapsychology Foundation.

———. 1985. The two faces of psi: Psi revealed and psi obscured. In *The repeatability problem in parapsychology,* edited by B. Shapin and L. Coly, 150–82. New York: Parapsychology Foundation.

———. 1992. Human interconnectedness: Research indications. *ReVision: A Journal of Consciousness and Transformation* 14: 140–48.

———. 1994a. Can our intentions interact directly with the physical world? *European Journal of Parapsychology* 10: 78–90.

———. 1994b. *Toward an integral methodology for transpersonal studies.* Working Paper Number 1994-1 of the William James Center for Consciousness Studies, Institute of Transpersonal Psychology, Palo Alto, CA, www.integral-inquiry.com/cybrary.html#toward.

———. 1995a. An experience of timelessness. *Exceptional Human Experience* 13 (1): 64–70.

———. 1995b. Parapsychology and spirituality: Implications and intimations. *ReVision: A Journal of Consciousness and Transformation* 18 (1): 36–43.

———. 1997. Parapsychology and spirituality: Implications and applications. In *Body, mind, and spirit: Exploring the parapsychology of spirituality,* edited by C. T. Tart, 135–152. Charlottesville, VA: Hampton Roads.

———. 1998a. An expanded view of validity. In *Transpersonal research methods for the social sciences: Honoring human experience,* edited by W. Braud and R. Anderson, 213–37. Thousand Oaks, CA: Sage.

———. 1998b. Can research be transpersonal? *Transpersonal Psychology Review* 2 (3): 9–17.

———. 1998c. Integral inquiry: Complementary ways of knowing, being, and expression. In *Transpersonal research methods for the social sciences: Honoring human experience,* edited by W. Braud and R. Anderson, 35–68. Thousand Oaks, CA: Sage.

———. 2001a. Experiencing tears of wonder-joy: Seeing with the heart's eye. *Journal of Transpersonal Psychology* 33: 99–111

———. 2001b. Transpersonal images: Implications for health. In, *Healing images: The role of imagination in health,* edited by A. A. Sheikh. Amityville, NY: Baywood.

———. 2002a. Foreword. In J. Clements, *Organic inquiry: Research in partnership with Spirit,* Unpublished manuscript. Palo Alto, CA: Institute of Transpersonal Psychology.

———. 2002b. Psi favorable conditions. In *New frontiers of human science,* edited by V. W. Rammohan, 95–118. Jefferson, NC: McFarland.

———. 2002c. The ley and the labyrinth: Universalistic and particularistic approaches to knowing. *Transpersonal Psychology Review* 6 (2): 47–62.

———. 2002d. Thoughts on the ineffability of the mystical experience. *The International Journal for the Psychology of Religion* 12 (3): 141–60.

———. 2003a. *Distant mental influence: Its contributions to science, healing, and human interactions.* Charlottesville, VA: Hampton Roads Publishing Company.

———. 2003b. Nonordinary and transcendent experiences: Transpersonal aspects of consciousness. *Journal of the American Society for Psychical Research* 97 (1–2): 1–26.

———. 2004. An introduction to Organic Inquiry: Honoring the transpersonal and spiritual in research praxis. *Journal of Transpersonal Psychology* 36: 18–25.

———. 2006. Educating the "More" in holistic transpersonal higher education: A 30+ year perspective on the approach of the Institute of Transpersonal Psychology. *Journal of Transpersonal Psychology* 38 (2): 133–58.

———. 2008. Patanjali Yoga and siddhis: Their relevance to parapsychological theory and research. In *Handbook of Indian psychology,* edited by K. R. Rao, A. C. Paranjpe, and A. K. Dalal, 217–43. New Delhi, India: Cambridge University Press (India)/Foundation Books.

———. 2010. Integrating Yoga epistemology and ontology into an expanded integral approach to research. In *Foundations of Indian psychology,* edited by M. Cornelissen, G. Misra, and S. Varma. New Delhi: Pearson.

Braud, W. and R. Anderson. 1998. *Transpersonal research methods for the social sciences: Honoring human experience.* Thousand Oaks, CA: Sage.

Braud, W. and M. Schlitz. 1989. A methodology for the objective study of transpersonal imagery. *Journal of Scientific Exploration* 3: 43–63.

Bridgman, P. 1950. *Reflections of a physicist.* New York: Philosophical Library.

Broenen, P. T. 2006. Transpersonal and cross-cultural adaptability factors in White Euopean American men: A descriptive and correlational analysis. Retrieved from ProQuest Digital Dissertations (AAT 3221760).

Brown, L. M. and C. Gilligan. 1992. *Meeting at the crossroads: Women's psychology and girls' development.* Cambridge, MA: Harvard University Press.

Brown, S. V. and R. A. White. 1997. Triggers, concomitants, and aftereffects of EHEs: An exploratory study. *Exceptional Human Experience* 15 (1): 150–56.

Bruner, E. 1986. Ethnography as narrative. In *The anthropology of experience*, edited by V. Turner and E. Bruner, 139–56. Chicago: University of Illinois Press.

Bruner, J. 1987. Life as narrative. *Social Research* 54, (1): 11–32.

———. 1990. *Acts of meaning*. Cambridge, MA: Harvard University Press.

Bruns, G. L. 1992. *Hermeneutics ancient and modern*. New Haven: CT: Yale University Press.

Buechner, F. 1973. *Wishful thinking: A theological ABC*. New York: Harper and Row.

Burneko, G. 1997. Wheels within wheels, building the earth: Intuition, integral consciousness, and the pattern that connects. In *Intuition: The inside story*, edited by R. Davis-Floyd and P. S. Arvidson, 81–100. New York: Routledge.

Buzan, T. 1991. *The mind map book*. New York: Penguin.

Bynum, E. B. 1999. *The African unconscious: Roots of ancient mysticism and modern psychology*. New York: Teachers College Press.

Caldwell, P. A. R. 2008. Putting cancer into words: Stories as medicine for women attending the Healing Journeys Conference. Retrieved from ProQuest Digital Dissertations (AAT 3307551.

Campbell, D. T. and J. C. Stanley. 1963. *Experimental and quasi-experimental designs for research*. Chicago: Rand-McNally.

Caplan, M., G. Hartelius, and M. A. Rardin. 2003. Contemporary viewpoints on transpersonal psychology. *Journal of Transpersonal Psychology* 35 (2): 143–62.

Carlock, S. E. 2003. The quest for true joy in union with God in mystical Christianity: An intuitive inquiry study. Retrieved from ProQuest Digital Dissertations (UMI No. 3129583).

Carlson, C. 2009. On the rim of the cauldron: Exploring one community's approach to the sacred feminine tradition. Retrieved from ProQuest Digital Dissertations (AAT No. 3371950).

Carroll, L. 1962. Through the looking glass. In *Alice in wonderland and other favorites*, 113–246. New York: Washington Square Press. (Original work published in 1871).

Cervelli, R. 2010. An intuitive inquiry into experiences arising out of the Holotropic Breathwork Technique and its integral mandala artwork: The potential for self-actualization. Unpublished doctoral dissertation. Palo Alto, CA: Institute of Transpersonal Psychology.

Chah, A. 1985. *A still forest pool*. Trans. J. Kornfield and P. Breiter. Wheaton, IL: Theosophical Publishing House.

Charmaz, K. 2006. *Constructing grounded theory: A practical guide through quali-tative analysis*. London: Sage.

Chicago, J. 1985. *The birth project*. New York: Doubleday.

Chodorow, J. 1991. *Dance therapy and depth psychology: The moving imagination*. New York: Routledge.

Cioflica, D. M. 2000. The sacred search for voice: An organic inquiry into the creative mirroring process of collage and story. Retrieved from ProQuest Digital Dissertations (AAT 9971782).

Cirker, B., ed. 1982. *The Book of Kells: Selected plates in full color.* New York: Dover Publications.

Clark, J. M. 2007. The San Pedro Long Dance: Transpersonal aspects of a contemporary entheogenic ritual. Retrieved from ProQuest Digital Dissertations (AAT 3290777).

Cleary, T., ed. 1999. *The pocket Zen reader.* Boston: Shambhala Publications.

Clements, J. 1999. Riding the blue tiger: Stories of partnership with spirit. Unpublished manuscript.

———. 2002. Organic inquiry: Research in partnership with spirit. Unpublished manuscript. Palo Alto, CA: Institute of Transpersonal Psychology.

———. 2004. Organic Inquiry: Toward research in partnership with spirit. *Journal of Transpersonal Psychology* 36: 26–49.

Clements, J., D. Ettling, D. Jenett, and L. Shields. 1998. Organic research: Feminine spirituality meets transpersonal research. In *Transpersonal research methods for the social sciences: Honoring human experience,* edited by W. Braud and R. Anderson, 114–127. Thousand Oaks, CA: Sage.

———. 1999. *If research were sacred: An organic methodology,* rev. ed., www.serpentina.com.

Coburn, M. 2005. Walking Home: Women's transformative experiences on the Appalachian Trail. Retrieved from ProQuest Digital Dissertations (AAT 3221761).

Coleman, B. 2000. Women, weight and embodiment: An intuitive inquiry into women's psycho-spiritual process of healing obesity. Retrieved from ProQuest Digital Dissertations (AAT 9969177).

Collier, J. and M. Collier. 1986. *Visual anthropology: Photography as a research method.* Albuquerque, NM: University of New Mexico Press.

Combs, A. 1996. *The radiance of being: Complexity, chaos and the evolution of consciousness.* St. Paul, MN: Paragon House.

Cook, T. D. and D. T. Campbell. 1979. *Quasi-experimentation: Design and analysis issues for field settings.* Boston: Houghton-Mifflin.

Coppin, J. and E. Nelson. 2004. *The art of inquiry: A depth psychological perspective.* Auburn, CA: Treehenge Press.

Corbin, H. 1972. Mundus imaginalis, or the imaginary and the imaginal. *Spring*: 1–19, http://henrycorbinproject.blogspot.com/2009/10/mundus-imaginalis-or-imaginary-and.html.

———. 1981. *Creative imagination in the Sûfism of Ibn 'Arabi.* Trans. R. Manheim. Princeton, NJ: Princeton/Bollingen.

Costa, P. T., Jr. and R. McCrae. 1985. *The NEO personality inventory-forms.* Odessa, FL: Psychological Assessment Resources.

Creswell, J. W. 2006. *Qualitative inquiry and research design: Choosing among five approaches,* 2nd ed. Thousand Oaks, CA: Sage.

———. 2009. *Research design: Qualitative, quantitative, and mixed methods approaches.* Thousand Oaks, CA: Sage.

Creswell, J. W. and V. L. Plano Clark. 2006. *Designing and conducting mixed methods research.* Thousand Oaks, CA: Sage.

Crites, S. 1986. Storytime: Recollecting the past and projecting the future. In *Narrative psychology: The storied nature of human conduct*, edited by T. R. Sarbin. 152–73. New York: Praeger.

Cronbach, L. J. and P. E. Meehl. 1955. Construct validity in psychological tests. *Psychological Bulletin* 52: 281–302.

Csikszentmihalyi, M. 1990. *Flow: The psychology of optimal experience*. New York: Harper and Row.

Dalton, G. F. 1952. The solution of problems in dreams. *Journal of the Society for Psychical Research* 36: 645–73.

David, M. H. 1996. *Empathy: A social psychological approach*. Madison, WI: WCB Brown and Benchmark.

Deikman, A. J. 1980a. Bimodal consciousness and the mystic experience. In *Understanding mysticism*, edited by R. Woods. 261–69. Garden City, NY: Image Books.

———. 1980b. Deautomatization and the mystic experience. In *Understanding mysticism*, edited by R. Woods. 240–60. Garden City, NY: Image Books.

———. 1982. *The observing self: Mysticism and psychotherapy*. Boston: Beacon Press.

Denzin, N. K. 2001a. *Interpretive interactionism*. Thousand Oaks, CA: Sage.

———. 2001b. The reflective interview and a performative social science. *Qualitative Research* 1 (1): 23–46.

Denzin, N. and Y. S. Lincoln, eds. 2003. *The handbook of qualitative research*. Thousand Oaks, CA: Sage.

Denzin, N. and Y. S. Lincoln. 2003. Introduction: Entering the field of qualitative research. In *The landscape of qualitative research: Theories and issues*, edited by N. Denzin and Y. S. Lincoln.1–34. Thousand Oaks CA: Sage.

Deslauriers, D. 1992. Dimensions of knowing: Narrative, paradigm, and ritual. *ReVision: A Journal of Consciousness and Transformation* 14 (4): 187–93.

Dilthey, W. 1989. *Introduction to the human sciences*. Ed. R. A. Makkreel and F. Rodi and trans. M. Neville. Princeton, NJ: Princeton University Press. (Original work published in 1883.)

Donaldson, O. F. 1993. *Playing by heart: The vision and practice of belonging*. Nevada City, CA: Touch the Future.

Dooley, D. 1995. *Social research methods*, 3rd ed. Englewood Cliffs, NJ: Prentice-Hall.

Dufrechou, J. 2004. We are one: Grief, weeping, and other deep emotions in response to nature as a path toward wholeness. *The Humanistic Psychologist* 32 (4): 357–78.

Dufrechou, J. P. 2002. Coming home to nature through the body: An intuitive inquiry into experiences of grief, weeping and other deep emotions in response to nature. Retrieved from ProQuest Digital Dissertations (AAT 3047959).

Edinger, E. F. 1972. *Ego and archetype: Individuation and the religious function of the psyche*. Boston: Shambhala Publications.

———. 1975. *The creation of consciousness: Jung's myths for modern man*. Toronto, Canada: Inner City.

Eisner, E. W. 1998. *The enlightened eye: Qualitative inquiry and the enhancement of educational practice*. Upper Saddle River, NJ: Merrill.

Ellenberger, H. F. 1970. *The discovery of the unconscious: The history and evolution of dynamic psychiatry*. New York: Basic Books.

Ellis, C. 2003. *The ethnographic I: A methodological novel about autoethnography*. Walnut Creek, CA: AltaMira Press.

Emmison, M. and P. Smith. 2000. *Researching the visual: Images, objects, contexts and interactions in social and cultural inquiry*. Thousand Oaks, CA: Sage.

Ereira, A. 1992. *The elder brothers*. New York: Knopf.

Esbjörn, V. C. 2003. Spirited flesh: An intuitive inquiry exploring the body in contemporary female mystics. Retrieved from ProQuest Digital Dissertations (AAT 3095409).

Esbjörn-Hargens, V. 2004. The union of flesh and spirit in women mystics. *The Humanistic Psychologist* 32 (4): 401–425.

Esbjörn-Hargens, V. and R. Anderson. 2005. Intuitive inquiry: An exploration of embodiment among contemporary female mystics. In *Qualitative research methods for psychology: Instructive case studies*, ed. C. T. Fischer, 301–330. Philadelphia, PA: Academic Press.

Ettling, D. 1994. A phenomenological study of the creative arts as a pathway to embodiment in the personal transformation process of nine women. Retrieved from ProQuest Digital Dissertations (AAT DP14316).

Fagen, N. L. 1995. Elaborating dreams through creative expressions: Experiences, accompaniments and perceived effects. Retrieved from ProQuest Digital Dissertations (AAT DP14322).

Fern, E. F. 2001. *Advanced focus group research*. Thousand Oaks, CA: Sage.

Fisher, D., D. Rooke, and B. Torbert. 2000. *Personal and organizational transformations through action inquiry*. Boston: Edge\Work Press.

Fisher, J. 1996. Dance as a spiritual practice: A phenomenological and feminist investigation of the experience of being-movement. Retrieved from ProQuest Digital Dissertations (AAT DP14334).

Fontana, D. and I. Slack. 1996. The need for transpersonal psychology. *The Psychologist* (June): 267–69.

Forman, R. K. C. 1997. *The problem of pure consciousness: Mysticism and philosophy*. New York: Oxford University Press.

———. 1999. *Mysticism, mind, consciousness*. Albany, NY: SUNY Press.

Franklin, R. W., ed. 1999. *The poems of Emily Dickinson*. Cambridge, MA: Belknap Press of Harvard University Press.

Franks, C. M., ed. 1969. *Behavior therapy: Appraisal and status*. New York: McGraw-Hill.

Fredrickson, B. L. 2001. The role of positive emotions in positive psychology: The broaden-and-build theory of positive emotions. *American Psychologist* 56: 218–26.

Fredrickson, B. L., and C. Branigan. 2005. Positive emotions broaden the scope of attention and thought-action repertoires. *Cognition and Emotion* 19: 313–32.

French, R. M. 1965. *The way of the pilgrim and The pilgrim continues his way.* New York: The Seabury Press.

Freud, S. 1914. *Psychopathology of everyday life.* Trans. A. A. Brill. London: T. Fisher Unwin. (Original work published in 1901.)

———. 1955. *The interpretation of dreams.* London: Hogarth Press. (Original work published 1900.)

Gadamer, H. 1976. On the problem of self-understanding. In *Philosophical hermeneutics,* edited and translated by D. E. Linge, 44–58. Berkeley, CA: University of California Press. (Original work published in 1962.)

———. 1998a. *Praise of theory: Speeches and essays.* Trans. Chris Dawson. New Haven, CT: Yale University Press.

———. 1998b. *Truth and method,* 2nd rev. Ed. J. Wiensheimer and trans. D. Marshall. New York: Continuum. (Original work published in 1960.)

Gardner, H. 1983. *Frames of mind: The theory of multiple intelligences.* New York: Basic Books.

———. 1993. *Multiple intelligences: The theory into practice.* New York: Basic Books.

———. 1999. *Intelligence reframed: Multiple intelligences for the 21st century,* New York: Basic Books

Gauthier, J. A. 2003. Midlife journeys of transvaluation and meeting the feminine through heroic descent: An organic inquiry with 10 men and 8 women. Retrieved from ProQuest Digital Dissertations (AAT 3095411).

Gebser, J. 1986. *The ever-present origin,* Trans. N. Barstad and A. Mickunas. Athens, OH: Ohio University Press. (Original work published in 1949 in German.)

Gendlin, E. T. 1978. *Focusing.* New York: Everest House.

———. 1991. Thinking beyond patterns: Body, language, and situations. In *The presence of feeling in thought,* ed. B. den Ouden and M. Moen, 25–151. New York: Peter Lang.

———. 1992. The primacy of the body, not the primacy of perception. *Man and World* 25 (3 and 4): 341–53.

———. 1996. An introduction to focusing: Six steps. New York: The Focusing Institute, www.focusing.org/gendlin/docs/gol_2234.html.

———. 1997. *Experiencing and the creation of meaning: A philosophical and psychological approach to the subjective.* Evanston, IL: Northwestern University Press. (Originally work published 1962).

———. 2003. Beyond postmodernism: From concepts through experiencing. In *Understanding Experience: Psychotherapy and postmodernism,* edited by R. Frie, 100–115. New York: Routledge.

———. 2007. *Focusing.* New York: Bantam Books, www.focusing.org/gendlin/docs/gol_2176.html.

Gergen, M. and K. Jones. 2008. Editorial: A conversation about performative social science. *Forum Qualitative Social Research* 9 (2) Art. 43, www.qualitative-research.net/index.php/fqs/article/view/376.

Gershon, M. D. 1998. *The second brain.* New York: Harper Collins.

Giles, S. P. 2000. The unnested woman: An investigation of dreams of midlife women who have experienced divorce from a long-term mate. Retrieved from ProQuest Digital Dissertations (AAT 9969178).

Gilligan, C. 1982. *In a different voice: Psychological theory and women's development*. Cambridge, MA: Harvard University Press.

Gimian, C. R., ed. 1999. *The essential Chögyam Trungpa.*, Boston and London: Shambhala Publications.

Gindler, E. 1995. Gymnastik for people whose lives are full of activity. In *Bone, breath, and gesture: Practices of embodiment*, edited by D. H. Hanlon and translated by Charlotte Selver Foundation, 3–14. Berkeley, CA: North Atlantic Books.

Giorgi, A. 2006. Concerning variations in the application of the phenomenological method. *The Humanistic Psychologist* 34 (4): 305–19.

Glaser, B. G. 1978. *Theoretical sensitivity*. Mill Valley, CA: Sociology Press.

Glaser, B. G., and A. L. Strauss. 1967. *The discovery of grounded theory*. Chicago: Aldine.

Goldberg, J. 1995. The quivering bundles that let us hear. In *Seeing, hearing, and smelling the world*, ed, Howard Hughes Medical Institute, 32–36. Chevy Chase, MD: Howard Hughes Medical Institute.

Goldberg, P. 1983. *The intuitive edge: Understanding and developing intuition*. Los Angeles, CA: Jeremy P. Tarcher.

Goleman, D. 1988. *The meditative mind: The varieties of meditative experience*. Los Angeles, CA: Tarcher.

———. 1994. *Emotional intelligence*. New York: Bantam Books.

———. 2006. *Social intelligence: The new science of human relationships*. New York: Bantam.

Gopfert, C. R. 1999. Student experiences of betrayal in the Zen Buddhist teacher/student relationship. Retrieved from ProQuest Digital Dissertations (AAT 9934565).

Gribbin, J. 1995. *Schrödinger's kittens and the search for reality: Solving the quantum mysteries*. Boston: Little, Brown and Company.

Grof, S. 1972. Varieties of transpersonal experiences: Observations from LSD psychotherapy. *Journal of Transpersonal Psychology* 4 (1): 45–80.

———. 2008. Brief history of transpersonal psychology. *International Journal of Transpersonal Studies* 17: 46–54.

Grof, S. and H. Z Bennett. 1992. *The holotropic mind: The three levels of human consciousness and how they shape our lives*. New York: HarperCollins.

Grof, S., D. Lukoff, H. Friedman, and G. Hartelius. 2008. The past and future of the International Transpersonal Association. *International Journal of Transpersonal Studies* 17: 55–62.

Guba, E. G. and Y. S. Lincoln. 1994. Competing paradigms in qualitative research. In *Handbook of qualitative research*, edited by N. Denzin and Y. S. Lincoln, 105–117. Thousand Oaks, CA: Sage.

Halifax, J. 1983. *Shaman: The wounded healer*. New York: Crossroads Publications.

Hall, J. A. 1987. Personal transformation: The inner image of initiation. In *Betwixt and between: Patterns of masculine and feminine initiation*, edited by L. C. Mahdi, S. Foster, and M. Little, 327–37. La Salle, IL: Open Court.

Halling, S., J. Rowe, and M. Laufer. 2005. Emergence of the Dialogal Approach: Forgiving another. In *Qualitative research methods for psychology: Instructive case studies*, edited by C. T. Fischer, 247–77. Philadelphia: Academic Press.

Hanh, T. N. 1975. *The miracle of mindfulness: An introduction to the practice of mindfulness*. Trans. Mobi Ho. Boston: Beacon Press.

Hannah, B. 1981. *Encounters with the soul: Active imagination as developed by C. G. Jung*. Boston: Sigo Press.

Hansen, G. P. 2001. *The trickster and the paranormal*, www.Xlibris.com.

Harrington, A. and A. Zajonc, eds. 2008. *The Dalai Lama at MIT*. Cambridge, MA: Harvard University Press.

Hart, T. 2000a. Deep empathy. In *Transpersonal knowing: Exploring the horizon of consciousness*, edited by T. H. Hart, P. L. Nelson, and K. Puhakka, 253–70. Albany, NY: SUNY Press.

———. 2000b. Inspiration as transpersonal knowing. In *Transpersonal knowing: Exploring the horizon of consciousness*, edited by. T. Hart, P. Nelson, and K. Puhakka, 31–53. Albany: SUNY Press.

Hartelius, G., M. Caplan, and M. A. Rardin. 2007. Transpersonal psychology: Defining the past, divining the future. *The Humanistic Psychologist* 35 (2): 1–26.

Hartmann, E. 1991. *Boundaries in the mind*. New York, NY: Basic Books.

Havelock, E. A. 1963. *Preface to Plato*. Cambridge, MA: Belknap Press/Harvard University Press.

Hayward, J. 1997. Foreword. In *Intuition: The inside story*, edited by R. David-Floyd and P. S. Arvidson, ix–x. NY: Routledge.

Hayward, J. W. and F. J. Varela. 2001. *Gentle bridges: Conversations with the Dalai Lama on the sciences of mind*. Boston: Shambhala Publications.

Heery, B. 2003. Awakening spirit in the body: A heuristic exploration of peak or mystical experiences in the practice of Aikido. Retrieved from Pro-Quest Digital Dissertations (AAT 3095412).

Heron, J. 1996. *Co-operative inquiry*. London: Sage.

———. 2000. Transpersonal co-operative inquiry. In *Handbook of action research: Participative inquiry and practice*, edited by P. Reason and H. Bradbury, 333–40. London: Sage.

Hervey, L. W. 2000. *Artistic inquiry in dance/movement therapy: Creative alternatives for research*. Springfield, IL: Charles C. Thomas.

Hewett, M. C. 2001. "A ripple in the water": The role of organic inquiry in developing an integral approach in transpersonal research: Presented as a one-act play and video. Retrieved from ProQuest Digital Dissertations (AAT 3047961).

Hill, A. G. M. 2005. Joy revisited: An exploratory study of the experience of joy through the memories of the women of one Native American Indian community. Retrieved from ProQuest Digital Dissertations (AAT 3200238).

Hill, R. 2003. Mountains and mysticism: Observing transformation when climbing in thin air. Retrieved from ProQuest Digital Dissertations (AAT 3110309).

Hoffman, S. L. 2003. Living stories: An intuitive inquiry into storytelling as a collaborative art form to effect compassionate connection. Retrieved from ProQuest Digital Dissertations (AAT 3095413).

———. 2004. Living stories: Modern storytelling as a call for connection. *The Humanistic Psychologist* 32 (4): 379–400.

Hollenback, J. B. 1996. *Mysticism: Experience, response, and empowerment.* University Park, PA: Pennsylvania State University Press.

Hopcke, R. H. 1989. *A guided tour of the collected works of C. G. Jung.* Boston, MA: Shambhala Publications.

———. 1991. On the threshold of change: Synchronistic events and their liminal context in analysis. In *Liminality and transitional phenomena,* edited by N. Schwartz-Salant and M. Stein, 115–32. Wilmette, IL: Chiron.

Houshmand, Z., R. B. Livingston, and B. A. Wallace. 1999. *Consciousness at the crossroads: Conversations with the Dalai Lama on brain science and Buddhism.* Ithaca, NY: Snow Lion Publications.

Houston, M., and O. I. Davis, eds. 2001. *Centering ourselves: African-American feminist and womanist studies of discourse.* Cresskill, NJ: Hampton Press.

Howell, D. C. 2007. *Fundamental statistics for the behavioral sciences,* 6th ed. Belmont, CA: Wadsworth.

———. 2009. *Statistical methods for psychology,* 7th ed. Belmont, CA: Wadsworth.

Hunsley, J. and G. J. Meyer. 2003. The incremental validity of psychological testing and assessment: Conceptual, methodological, and statistical issues. *Psychological Assessment* 15 (4): 446–55.

Hunter, J. and M. Csikszentmihalyi. 2000. The phenomenology of body-mind: The contrasting cases of flow in sports and contemplation. *Anthropology of Consciousness* 11 (3and 4): 5–24.

Hurston, Z. N. 1996. *Dust tracks on a road.* New York: HarperCollins. (Original work published in 1942)

Husserl, E. 1989. *Ideas pertaining to a pure phenomenology and to a phenomenological philosophy, Book 2: Studies in phenomenology of constitution.* Boston: Kluwer. (Original work published in 1952.)

Hutter, D. M. 1999. Weaving the fabric of culture: The emergence of personal and collective wisdom in young adults participating in a wilderness rite of passage. Retrieved from ProQuest Digital Dissertations (AAT 9958679).

Huxley, A. 1970. *The perennial philosophy.* New York: Harper and Row. (Original work published in 1944.)

Jacobson, E. 1938. *Progressive relaxation.* Chicago: University of Chicago Press.

James, W. 1911. *Some problems in philosophy.* New York: Longmans, Green.

———. 1950. *The principles of psychology,* vol. 1. New York: Dover. (Original work published 1890.)

———. 1956. *The will to believe and other essays in popular philosophy and human immortality.* New York: Dover. (Original work published in 1897.)

———. 1976. *Essays in radical empiricism.* Cambridge, MA: Harvard University Press. (Original work published in 1912.)

———. 1980. A suggestion about mysticism. In *Understanding mysticism,* edited by R. Woods, 215–22. Garden City, NY: Image Books. (Original work published in 1910.)

Jenett, D. E. 1999. Red rice for Bhagavati/cooking for Kannaki: An ethnographic/organic inquiry of the Pongala ritual at Attukal Temple, Kerala, South India. Retrieved from ProQuest Digital Dissertations (AAT 9961566).

Johnson, M. 1897. *The body in the mind: The bodily basis of meaning, imagination, and reason.* Chicago: University of Chicago Press.

Johnson, R. A. 1986. *Inner work: Using dreams and active imagination for personal growth.* New York: Harper and Row.

Jones, K. 2006. A biographic researcher in pursuit of an aesthetic: The use of arts-based (re)presentations in "performative" dissemination of life stories. *Qualitative Sociology Review,* www.qualitativesociologyreview. org/ENG/index_eng.php.

Josselson, R. 1996. *Ethics and process in the narrative study of lives.* Thousand Oaks, CA: Sage.

———. 2004. The hermeneutics of faith and the hermeneutics of suspicion. *Narrative Inquiry* 14 (1): 1–28.

Judy, D. H. 1991. *Christian meditation and inner healing.* New York: Crossroad.

Jung, C. G. 1933. *Psychological types.* New York: Harcourt.

———. 1959. *The basic writings of C. G. Jung.* Ed. V. S. DeLaszlo. New York: Random House.

———. 1966. The relations between the ego and the unconscious. In C. G. Jung, *Two essays on analytical psychology,* 2nd ed., trans. R.F.C. Hull, 123–244. Princeton, NJ: Princeton University Press. (Original work published in 1928.)

———. 1969. *The structure and dynamics of the psyche,* 2nd ed. Trans. R. F. C. Hull. Princeton, NJ: Princeton University Press.

———. 1971. *Psychological types,* rev. ed. Trans. H. G. Baynes and R. F. C. Hull. Princeton, NJ: Princeton University Press. (Original work published in 1921.)

———. 1972. *The collected works of C. G. Jung,* 2nd ed. Ed. H. Read, M. Fordham, and G. Adler and trans. R. F. Hull. Bollingen Series. Princeton, NJ: Princeton University Press.

———. 1973. *Memories, dreams, reflections.* Ed. A. Jaffe and trans. C. Winston, rev. ed. New York, NY: Vintage.

———. 1993. Foreword. In E. Neumann, *The origins and history of consciousness,* xiii–xiv. Princeton, NJ: Princeton University Press.

Kalff, D. M. 1980. *Sandplay: A psychotherapeutic approach to the psyche.* Santa Monica, CA: Sigo.

Kaplan, M. A. 2005. The experience of divine guidance: A qualitative study of the human endeavor to seek, receive, and follow guidance from a perceived divine source. Retrieved from ProQuest Digital Dissertations (AAT 3174544).

Keating, T. 1991. *Open mind, open heart.* Rockport, MA: Element.

Kegan, R. 1994. *In over our heads: The mental demands of modern life.* Cambridge, MA: Harvard University Press.

Keller, E. F. 1983. *A feeling for the organism: The life and work of Barbara McClintock.* New York: Freeman.

Khan, Hazrat Inayat. 1960. *Sufi message of Hazrat Inayat Khan, gayan, vadan, nirtan.* Geneva, Switzerland: International Headquarters of the Sufi Movement.

Knowles, J. G. and A. L. Cole, eds. 2007. *Handbook of the arts in qualitative research: Perspectives, methodologies, examples, and issues*. Thousand Oaks, CA: Sage.

Koch, S. 1983–1988. *Sigmund Koch's aesthetics archive* [video recording]. New York: The Ford Foundation.

———. 1999. *Psychology in human context: Essays in dissidence and reconstruction*. Ed. D. Finkelman and F. Kessel. Chicago: University of Chicago Press.

———, ed. 1959–1963. *Psychology: A study of a science*, vols. 1–6. New York: McGraw-Hill.

Koestler, A. 1976. *The act of creation*. London: Hutchinson.

Krippner, S. and W. Hughes. 1970. Dreams and human potential. *Journal of Humanistic Psychology* 10: 1–20.

Kueppers, W. G. 2004. The practice and dynamics of authenticity: An organic research study. Retrieved from ProQuest Digital Dissertations (AAT 3129586).

Kuhn, R. 2001. Sailing as a transformational experience. Retrieved from Pro-Quest Digital Dissertations (AAT 3011294).

LaBerge S. and J. Gackenbach. 2000. Lucid dreaming. In *Varieties of anomalous experience: Examining the scientific evidence*, edited by. E. Cardena, S. J. Lynn, and S. Krippner, 151–82. Washington, DC: American Psychological Association.

Lajoie, D. H. and S. I. Shapiro. 1992. Definitions of transpersonal psychology: The first twenty-three years. *Journal of Transpersonal Psychology* 24 (1): 79–98.

Leavy, P. 2008. *Method meets art: Arts-based research practice*. New York: Guilford Press.

Leloup, J., trans. 2002. *The gospel of Mary Magdalene*. Trans. into English by E. Rowe. Rochester, VT: Inner Traditions.

LeShan, L. 1974. *How to meditate*. New York: Bantam.

Levin, D. M. 1985. *The body's recollection of being: Phenomenological psychology and the destruction of nihilism*. London: Routledge and Kegan Paul.

Lieblich, A., R. Tuval-Mashiach, and T. Zilber. 1998. *Narrative research: Reading, analysis and interpretation*. Thousand Oak, CA: Sage.

Lincoln, Y. S. and E. G. Guba. 1985. *Naturalistic inquiry*. Newbury Park, CA: Sage.

Lodge, O. 1910. The appeal to literature. In O. Lodge, *Reason and belief*, 152–55. New York: George H. Doran Company.

Loos, L. K. 1997. Sitting in council: An ecopsychological approach to working with stories in wilderness rites of passage. Retrieved from ProQuest Digital Dissertations (AAT DP14338).

Lorca, F. G. 1992. From the Havana lectures. In *The rag and bone shop of the heart*, R. Bly, J. Hillman, and M. Meade, 165. New York: Harper Perennial.

Louw, D. J. n.d.a. Ubuntu and the challenges of multiculturalism in post-apartheid South Africa, www.phys.uu.nl/~unitwin/ubuntu.html.

———. n.d.b. Ubuntu: An African assessment of the religious other, www.bu.edu/wcp/Papers/Afri/AfriLouw.htm.

Lowenfeld, M. 1979. *Understanding children's sandplay*. London: George Allen and Unwin.

———. 1991. *Play in childhood, with a foreword by John Davis*. London: MacKeith Press. (Originally published in 1935.)

Luke, H. M. 1995. *The way of woman: Awakening the perennial feminine*. New York: Doubleday.

Luna, L. E., and P. Amaringo. 1991. *Ayahuasca visions: The religious iconography of a Peruvian shaman*. Berkeley, CA: North Atlantic Books.

Lynch, K. S. 2002. Each age a lens: A transpersonal perspective of Emily Dickinson's creative process. Retrieved from ProQuest Digital Dissertations (AAT 3053917).

MacDonald, D. A., H. L. Friedman, and J. G. Kuentzel. 1999. A survey of measures of spiritual and transpersonal constructs: Part one—research update. *Journal of Transpersonal Psychology* 31 (2): 137–54.

MacDonald, D. A., J. G. Kuentzel, and H. L. Friedman. 1999. A survey of measures of spiritual and transpersonal constructs: Part two-additional instruments. *Journal of Transpersonal Psychology* 31 (2): 155–77.

MacDonald, D. A., L. LeClair, C. J. Holland, A. Alter, and H. L. Friedman. 1995. A survey of measures of transpersonal constructs. *Journal of Transpersonal Psychology* 27 (2): 171–235.

Magnussen, S. 2004. The effect of the spiritual practice of Tibetan Buddhist guru yoga on the clinical practice of psychotherapy. Retrieved from ProQuest Digital Dissertations (AAT 3110310).

Manos, C. 2007. Female artists and nature: An intuitive inquiry into transpersonal aspects of creativity in the natural environment. Retrieved from ProQuest Digital Dissertations (AAT 3270987).

Marks, L. E. 2000. Synesthesia. In *Varieties of anomalous experience: Exploring the scientific evidence*, edited by E. Cardena, S. J. Lynn, and S. Krippner, 121–49. Washington, D.C.: American Psychological Association.

Martire, G. C. 2006. Menstrual consciousness development: An organic inquiry into the development of a psycho-spiritually rewarding menstrual relationship. Retrieved from ProQuest Digital Dissertations (AAT 3215085).

Maslow, A. H. 1966. *The psychology of science: A reconnaissance*. New York: Harper and Row.

———. 1967. A theory of metamotivation: The biological rooting of the value-life. *Journal of Humanistic Psychology* 7: 93–127.

———. 1968. *Toward a psychology of being*, 2nd ed. New York: Van Nostrand Reinhold.

———. 1969. The farther reaches of human nature. *Journal of Transpersonal Psychology* 1 (1): 1–9.

———. 1971. *The farther reaches of human nature*. New York: Viking.

Mavromatis, A. 1987. *Hypnagogia*. New York: Routledge and Kegan Paul.

Maxwell, J. A. 1992. Understanding and validity in qualitative research. *Harvard Educational Review* 62 (3): 279–300.

Maxwell, N. 1992. What kind of inquiry can best help us create a good world? *Science, Technology, and Human Values* 17 (2): 205–227.

McCormick, L. 2010. *The personal self, no-self, self continuum: An intuitive inquiry and grounded theory study of the experience of no-self as integrated stages of consciousness toward enlightenment.* Retrieved from ProQuest Digital Dissertations (AAT 3397100).

McGlashan, A. 1967. *The savage and beautiful country.* Boston: Houghton Mifflin.

McMahon, J. D. S. 1998. The anatomy of ritual. In *Gateways to higher consciousness: 1998 annual conference proceedings of the Academy of Religion and Psychical Research,* 49–56. Bloomfield, CT: Academy of Religion and Psychical Research.

McNiff, S. 1998. *Art-based research.* London: Jessica Kingsley.

———. 2003. *Creating with others: The practice of imagination in life, art, and the workplace.* Boston: Shambhala Publications.

Mellick, J. 1996. *The natural artistry of dreams: Creative ways to bring the wisdom of dreams to waking life.* Berkeley, CA: Conari Press.

Menon, S. 2002. Meet the researcher II. *The Journal of Transpersonal Psychology* 34 (1): 67–71.

Merleau-Ponty, M. 1962. *Phenomenology of perception.* Trans. C. Smith. London: Routledge and Keegan Paul. (Original work published in France in 1945.)

———. 1968. *The visible and the invisible.* Trans. A. Lingis. Evanston, IL: Northwestern University Press. (Original work published in France in 1964.)

Merrell-Wolff, F. 1973. *The philosophy of consciousness without an object.* New York: Julian.

Mertens, D. M. 2008. *Transformative research and evaluation.* New York: The Guilford Press.

———. 2009. *Research and evaluation in education and psychology: Integrating diversity with quantitative, qualitative, and mixed methods,* 3rd ed. Thousand Oaks, CA: Sage. (The original edition was published in 1998, and the 2nd ed. was published in 2005.)

Mezirow, J. and Associates. 2000. *Learning as transformation: Critical perspectives on a theory in progress.* San Francisco, CA: Jossey-Bass.

Michalko, M. 2001. *Cracking creativity: The secrets of creative genius.* Berkeley, CA: Ten Speed Press.

Microsoft Research (producer) and W. Duggan, (speaker). 2008. Strategic intuition: The creative spark in human achievement. (Video), www. researchchannel.org/prog/displayevent.aspx?rlD=24503andflD=5246.

Milgram, J. 1992. *Handmade midrash.* Philadelphia: The Jewish Publication Society.

Miller, J. B. 1986. *Toward a new psychology of women,* 2nd ed. Boston, MA: Beacon Press.

Mishler, E. 1991. *Research interviewing: Context and narrative.* Cambridge, MA: Harvard University Press.

———. 2000. *Storylines: Craftartists' narratives of identity.* Cambridge, MA: Harvard University Press.

Montessori, M. 1997. *Quotes by Maria Montessori, 1870–1952.* Montessori Teachers Collective, www.moteaco.com/quotes.html.

Moran, Dermot. 2000. *Introduction to phenomenology.* New York: Routledge.

Moreno, J. L. 1993. *Psychodrama*, vol. 1. Beacon, NY: Beacon House. (Originally published in 1946.)

Morgan, D. L. 1988. *Focus groups as qualitative research*. Newbury Park, CA: Sage.

————, ed. 1993. *Successful focus groups: Advancing the state of the art*. Thousand Oaks, CA: Sage.

Moustakas, C. 1990. *Heuristic research: Design, methodology, and applications*. Newbury Park, CA: Sage.

————. 1994. *Phenomenological research methods*. Thousand Oaks, CA: Sage.

Moustakas, C. and B. G. Douglass. 1985. Heuristic inquiry: The internal search to know. *Journal of Humanistic Psychology* 25 (3): 39–55.

Muhl, A. 1963. *Automatic writing: An approach to the subconscious*. New York: Helix.

Murphy, M., S. Donovan, and E. Taylor. 1997. *The physical and psychological effects of meditation: A review of contemporary research with a comprehensive bibliography, 1931–1996*, 2nd ed. Sausalito, CA: Institute of Noetic Sciences.

Murray, K. 1986. Literary pathfinding: The work of popular life constructors. In *Narrative psychology: The storied nature of human conduct*, edited by T. R. Sarbin, 276–92. New York: Praeger.

Myers, F. W. H. 1903. *Human personality and its survival of bodily death*, 2 vols. London: Longmans, Green, and Co.

————. 1980. *Gifts differing: Understanding personality type*. Palo Alto, CA: Consulting Psychologists Press.

Myers, I. B. 1962. *The Myers-Briggs Type Indicator*. Palo Alto, CA: Consulting Psychologists Press.

————. 1980. *Gifts differing: Understanding personality type*. Palo Alto, CA: Consulting Psychologists Press.

Naranjo, C., and R. E. Ornstein. 1971. *On the psychology of meditation*. New York: Viking Compass.

Needleman, J. 1991. *Lost Christianity*. Rockport, MA: Element.

Netzer, D. 2008. Mystical poetry and imagination: Inspiring transpersonal awareness of spiritual freedom. Retrieved from ProQuest Digital Dissertations (AAT 3316128).

Nielsen, J. M., ed. 1990. *Feminist research methods: Exemplary readings in the social sciences*. Boulder, CO: Westview Press.

Nouwen, H. 1990. *The wounded healer: Ministry in contemporary society*. New York: Doubleday.

O'Fallon T., and G. Kramer. 1998. Insight dialogue and insight dialogic Inquiry. Retrieved from ProQuest Digital Dissertations (AAT 9824352).

Ogden, T. H. 1990. *The matrix of the mind: Object relations and the psychoanalytic dialogue*. Northvale, NJ: Jason Aronson.

Olge, R. 2007. *Smart world: Breakthrough creativity and the new science of ideas*. New York: Harvard Business School Press.

Olsen, A. 2002. *Body and earth: An experiential guide*. Lebanon, NH: University Press of New England.

Onwuegbuzie, A. J., and R. B. Johnson. 2006. The validity issue in mixed research. *Research in the Schools* 13: (1): 48–63.

Ormiston, G. L. and A. D. Schrift, eds. 1990. *The hermeneutic traditions: From Ast to Ricoeur.* New York: SUNY Press.

Orne, M. T. 1962 On the social psychology of the psychological experiment: With particular reference to demand characteristics and their implications. *American Psychologist* 17 (11): 476–83.

———. 2002 On the social psychology of the psychological experiment: With particular reference to demand characteristics and their implications. *Prevention and Treatment,* 5 Article 35, http://journals.apa.org/prevention/volume5.

Packer, M. J., and R. B. Addison, eds. 1989. *Entering the circle: Hermeneutic investigation in psychology.* Albany: SUNY Press.

Pallaro, P., ed. 1999. *Authentic movement: Essays by Mary Starks Whitehead, Janet Adler, and Joan Chodorow.* Philadelphia: Jessica Kingsley.

Palmer, G. E. H., P. Sherrard, and K. Ware, eds. 1979–1995. *The Philokalia: The complete text,* 4 vols. London: Faber and Faber.

Palmer, G. T. 1999. Disclosure and assimilation of exceptional human experiences: Meaningful, transformative, and spiritual aspects. Retrieved from ProQuest Digital Dissertations (AAT 9932122).

Palmer, J. 1993. Confronting the experimenter effect. In Psi research methodology: A re-examination: Proceedings of an international conference held in Chapel Hill, North Carolina, October 29–30, 1988, edited by L. Coly and J. D. S. McMahon, 44–64. New York: Parapsychology Foundation.

———. 1997. The challenge of experimenter psi. *European Journal of Parapsychology* 13: 110–22.

Pascal, B. 1941. *Pensees and the provincial letters* Trans. W. F. Trotter and T. M'Crie. New York: Random House/The Modern Library. (Original work published in 1670.)

Pennebaker, J. W. 1995. *Emotion, disclosure, and health.* Washington, DC: American Psychological Association.

Penner, L. A., B. A. Fritzsche, J. P. Craiger, and T. S. Freifeld. 1995. Measuring the prosocial personality. In *Advances in personality assessment,* vol. 12, edited by J. N. Butcher and C. D. Spielberger, 147–63. Hillsdale, NJ: Erlbaum.

Pennington, M. B. 1980. *Centering prayer: Renewing an ancient Christian prayer form.* Garden City, NY: Doubleday.

Perry, A. 2009. Does a unitive mystical experience affect authenticity? An intuitive inquiry of ordinary Protestants. Retrieved ProQuest Digital Dissertations (AAT3344550).

Petitmengin-Peugeot, C. 1999. The intuitive experience. *Journal of Consciousness Studies* 6: 43–77.

Phelon, C. R. 2001. Healing presence: An intuitive inquiry into the presence of the psychotherapist. Retrieved from ProQuest Digital Dissertations (AAT 3011298).

———. 2004. Healing presence in the psychotherapist: An intuitive inquiry. *The Humanistic Psychologist,* 32 (4): 342–56.

Piaget, J. 1929. *The child's conception of the world.* New York: Harcourt, Brace.

————. 1962. *Play, dreams, and imitation in childhood*. Trans. G. Rolfe. G. G. Gattegno, and F. M. Hodgson. New York: Norton.

————. 1972. *The child and reality*. New York: Penguin.

J. Piaget, J. and B. Inhelder. 1969. *The psychology of the child*. New York: Basic Books, Inc.

Pinard, R. A. 2000. Integrative dialogue: From fragmentation to a reverential unfolding of wholeness and mutuality. Retrieved from ProQuest Digital Dissertations (AAT 9984961).

Plotinus. 1966–1988. *Enneads*, vols. 1–7. Trans. A. H. Armstrong. Cambridge, MA: Harvard University Press. (Original work prepared circa 250 CE)

Polanyi, M. 1958. *Personal knowledge: Towards a post-critical philosophy*. Chicago: University of Chicago Press.

————. 1966. *The tacit dimension*. Garden City, NY: Doubleday.

————. 1969. *Knowing and being*. Chicago: University of Chicago Press.

Polanyi, M., and H. Prosch. 1975. *Meaning*. Chicago: University of Chicago Press.

Potter, J., and M. Wetherell. 1995. Discourse analysis. In *Rethinking methods in psychology*, edited by J. A. Smith, R. Harre, and L. van Langenhove, 80–92. Thousand Oaks, CA: Sage.

Prabhavananda, S., and C. Isherwood. 1969. *How to know God: The Yoga Aphorisms of Patanjali*. New York: Mentor.

Progoff, I. 1957. *The cloud of unknowing*. New York: Dell.

Radin, D. I. 1997. *The conscious universe: Truth of psychic phenomena*. San Francisco: HarperCollins.

Radin, D. 2006. *Entangled minds*. New York: Paraview Pocket Books.

Ram Dass and P. Gorman. *How can I help?* New York: Knopf.

Ramberg, B. and K. Gjesdal. 2005. Hermeneutics. *Stanford Encyclopedia of Philosophy*, http://plato.stanford.edu/entries/hermeneutics/.

Reason, P. 1988. *Human inquiry in action*. Thousand Oaks, CA: Sage.

————. 1994. *Participation in human inquiry*. Thousand Oaks, CA: Sage.

Reason, P. and J. Heron. 2000. The practice of co-operative inquiry: Research "with" rather than "on" people. In *Handbook of action research: Participative inquiry and practice*, edited by P. Reason and H. Bradbury, 179–89. London: Sage.

Reinharz, S. 1992. *Feminist methods in social sciences*. New York: Oxford University Press.

Rennie, D. L. 2007. Methodical hermeneutics and humanistic psychology. *The Humanistic Psychologist* 35 (1): 1–14.

Rich, A. 1979. When we dead awaken: Writing as re-vision. In A. Rich, *On lies, secrets, and silence*. New York: Norton.

Rich, B. 2000. Blowing the shofar. Unpublished manuscript.

Rickards, D. E. 2006. Illuminating feminine cultural shadow with women espionage agents and the Dark Goddess. Retrieved from ProQuest Digital Dissertations (AAT 3286605).

Riordan, L. 2002. Bringing the wilderness home: Integrating the transformative aspects of adventure into everyday life. Retrieved from ProQuest Digital Dissertations (AAT 3066242).

Rode, M. A. 2000. What is beauty? A living inquiry for the mind and heart. Retrieved from ProQuest Digital Dissertations (AAT 9969181).

Rogers, N. 1993. *The creative connection: Expressing arts as healing.* Palo Alto, CA: Science and Behavior Books.

Rogers, W. L. 1996. A heuristic inquiry into loss of fertility that occurred during the childbearing years as experienced by eight women. Retrieved from ProQuest Digital Dissertations (AAT DP14330).

Romanyshyn, R. D. 2002. *Ways of the heart: Essays toward an imaginal psychology.* Pittsburg, PA: Trivium Publications.

———. 2007. *The wounded researcher: Research with soul in mind.* New Orleans, LA: Spring Journal Books.

Rominger, R. A. 2004. Exploring the integration of the aftereffects of the near-death experience: An intuitive and artistic inquiry. Retrieved from ProQuest Digital Dissertations (AAT 3129588).

Root-Bernstein, R. and M. Root-Bernstein. 1999. *Sparks of genius: The thirteen thinking tools of the world's most creative people.* New York: Houghton Mifflin.

Rose, G. 2001. *Visual methodologies: An introduction to the interpretation of visual materials.* Thousand Oaks, CA: Sage.

Rosenthal, R 1966. *Experimenter effects in behavioral research.* New York: Appleton-Century-Crofts.

———. 2002a. Covert communication in classrooms, clinics, courtrooms, and cubicles. *American Psychologist* 57 (11): 839–49.

———. 2002b. Experimenter and clinician effects in scientific inquiry and clinical practice. *Prevention and Treatment,* 5. Article 38, http://journals.apa.org/prevention/volume5.

Rosenthal, R. and R. L. Rosnow, eds. 1969. *Artifact in behavioral research.* New York: Academic Press.

Rosenthal, R. and D. B. Rubin. 1978. Interpersonal expectancy effects: The first 345 studies. *The Behavioral and Brain Sciences* 3: 377–415.

Rosnow, R. L. 2002. The nature and role of demand characteristics in scientific inquiry, www.journals.apa.org/prevention/volume5/pre0050037c.html.

Rosnow, R. L. and R. Rosenthal. 1997. *People studying people: Artifacts and ethics in behavioral research.* New York: W. H. Freeman.

Ruumet, H. 1997. Pathways of the soul: A helical model of psychospiritual development. *Presence: The Journal of Spiritual Directors International* 3 (3): 6–24.

———. 2006. *Pathways of the soul: Exploring the human journey.* Victoria, Canada: Trafford Publishing.

Sacks, O. 1987. *The man who mistook his wife for a hat.* New York: Harper and Row.

Safken, A. M. 1997. Sufi stories as vehicles for self-development: Exploration, using in-depth interviews, of the self-perceived effects of the study of Sufi stories. Retrieved from ProQuest Digital Dissertations (AAT 9833355).

Salk, J. 1983. *Anatomy of reality.* New York: Appleton-Century-Crofts.

Salmon, Don. 2001 What if We Took Indian Psychology Seriously?, www.infinityfoundation.com/mandala/i_es/i_es_salmo_psych_frame-set.htm.

Sanders, R. E., M. A. Thalbourne, and P. S. Delin. 2000. Transliminality and the telepathic transmission of emotional states: An exploratory study. *Journal of the American Society for Psychical Research* 94: 1–24.

Sarbin, T. R., 1986. The narrative as a root metaphor for psychology. In *Narrative psychology: The storied nature of human* conduct, edited by R. T. Sarbin, 3–19. New York: Praeger.

Satprem. 1981. *The mind of the cells.* Trans. F. Mahak and L. Vernet. New York: Institute for Evolutionary Research.

Schopfer, C. L. 2010. The power of reflection: An analysis of the relationship between Nondualism and manifest reality in the written work of Swami Shantananda. PhD diss., Institute of Transpersonal Psychology.

Schleiermacher, F. 1977. *Hermeneutics: The handwritten manuscripts.* Ed. H. Kimmerle and trans. D. Luke and J. Forstman. Missoula, MT: Scholars Press. (Original text in 1819.)

———. 1998. *Hermeneutics and criticism and other writing.* Cambridge, UK: Cambridge University Press.

Schulz, J. 2006. Pointing the way to discovery: Using the creative writing practice in qualitative research. *Journal of Phenomenological Psychology* 37 (2): 217–39.

Schultz, J. H. and W. Luthe. 1969. *Autogenic methods.* New York: Grune and Stratton.

Schumacher, E. F. 1978. *A guide for the perplexed.* New York: Harper and Row.

Schutte, A. 2001. *Ubuntu: An ethic for a new South Africa.* Pietermaritzburg, South Africa: Cluster Publications.

Schwartz-Salant, N. and M. Stein, eds. 1991. *Liminality and transitional phenomena.* Wilmette, IL: Chiron.

Schwedner, D. T. 2003. Messengers from the soul: Women's shoes as instruments of psychological and spiritual growth. Retrieved from ProQuest Digital Dissertations (AAT 3095406).

Seeley, R. 2000. Sacred callings: The process of moving into vocation at midlife as seen through story and reflection in a council of nine women. Retrieved from ProQuest Digital Dissertations (AAT 9970762).

Sheikh, A. A., ed. 1983. *Imagery: Current theory, research, and application.* New York: Wiley.

———, ed. 1986. *Anthology of imagery techniques.* Milwaukee, WI: American Imagery Institute.

———. 2001. *Handbook of therapeutic imagery techniques.* Amityville, NY: Baywood.

———, ed. 2003. *Healing images: The role of imagination in health.* Amityville, NY: Baywood.

Shepherd, L. J. 1993. *Lifting the veil: The feminine face of science.* Boston: Shambhala Publications.

Shepperd, A. E. 2006. The experience of feeling deeply moved: An intuitive inquiry. *Dissertation Abstracts International,* 67 05, 2819 (UMI No. 3221764).

Sheridan, J., and A. Pineault. 1997. Sacred land—sacred stories. In *Intuition: The inside story,* edited by R. Davis-Floyd and P. S. Arvidson, 57–80. New York: Routledge.

Shields, L. J. 1995. The experience of beauty, body image and the feminine in three generations of mothers and daughters. Retrieved from ProQuest Digital Dissertations (AAT DP14319).

Sholem, J. 1999. Listening to the labyrinth: An organic and intuitive inquiry. Retrieved from ProQuest Digital Dissertations (AAT 9936945).

Simon, B. 1978. *Mind and madness in ancient Greece: The classical roots of modern psychiatry.* Ithaca, NY: Cornell University Press.

Siner Francis, K. 2008. Sigmund Koch's Artists on Art project: Archival review and single case reconstruction. Retrieved ProQuest Digital Dissertations (AAT3403404).

Skolimowski, H. 1994. *The participatory mind: A new theory of knowledge and of the universe.* New York: Penguin Arcana.

Smith, J. A. 2004. Reflecting on the development of interpretative phenomenological analysis and its contribution to qualitative research in psychology. *Qualitative Research in Psychology* 1: 39–54.

———. 2007. Hermeneutics, human sciences and health: Linking theory and practice. *International Journal of Qualitative Studies on Health and Well-being* 2: 3–11.

Smith, M. D. 2003. The role of the experimenter in parapsychological research. *Journal of Consciousness Studies* 10 (6 and 7): 69–84.

Smith, T. W. 2009. Loving and caring in the United States: Trends and correlates of empathy, altruism, and related constructs. In *The science of compassionate love: The theory, research, and applications,* edited by B. Fehr, S. Sprecher, and L. G. Underwood, 81–119. West Sussex, UK: Wiley-Blackwell.

Sowerby, D. F. 2001. The light of inner guidance: A heuristic study of the recognition and interpretation of intuition. Retrieved from ProQuest Digital Dissertations (AAT 3011300).

Speeth, K. R. 1982. On psychotherapeutic attention. *Journal of Transpersonal Psychology* 14 (2): 141–60.

Spencer, L. B. 1995. The transpersonal and healing dimensions of painting: Life reviews of ten artists who have experienced trauma. Retrieved from ProQuest Digital Dissertations (AAT DP14320).

Stanczak, G. C. 2007. *Visual research methods: Image, society, and representation.* Thousand Oaks, CA: Sage.

Stewart, D. W. and P. N. Shamdasani. 1990. *Focus groups: Theory and practice.* Newbury Park: Sage.

Strauss, A. L. and J. A. Corbin. 1990. *Basics of qualitative research: Grounded theory procedures and techniques.* Newbury Park, CA: Sage.

Stromstead, T. 1998. The dance and the body in psychotherapy. In *The body in psychotherapy: Inquiries in Somatic Psychology,* edited by D. H. Hanlon, 147–69. Berkeley, CA: North Atlantic Books.

Sullivan, G. 2004. *Art practice as research: Inquiry in the visual arts*. Thousand Oaks, CA: Sage.

Sutich, A. J. 1968. Transpersonal psychology: An emerging force. *Journal of Humanistic Psychology*, 8: 77–78.

———. 1969. Some considerations regarding transpersonal psychology. *Journal of Transpersonal Psychology* 1 (1): 11–20.

———. 1976a. The emergence of the transpersonal orientation: A personal account. *Journal of Transpersonal Psychology* 81: 5–19.

———. 1976b. The founding of humanistic and transpersonal psychology: A personal account. PhD diss., Humanistic Psychology Institute (now Saybrook Institute).

Swedenborg, E. 1963. *Divine love and divine wisdom*. London: Swedenborg Society. (Original work published in 1763.)

Taimni, I. 1981. *The science of yoga*. Wheaton, IL: Quest Books.

Targ, R. and J. J. Hurtak. 2006. *The end of suffering*. Charlottesville, VA: Hampton Roads.

Tart, C. T. 1972. States of consciousness and state-specific sciences. *Science* 176: 1203–210.

———. 1975. *States of consciousness*. New York: E. P. Dutton and Co.

———. 1986. *Waking up: Overcoming the obstacles to human potential*. Boston: Shambhala Publications.

———. 1994. *Living the mindful life*. Boston: Shambhala Publications.

———. 2001. *Mind science: Meditation training for practical people*. Novato, CA: Wisdom Editions.

Tarthang Tulku, Rinpoche. 1976. A view of mind. *Journal of Transpersonal Psychology* 8 (1): 41–44.

Tashakkori, A. and C. Teddlie. 1998. *Mixed methodology: Combining qualitative and quantitative approaches*. Thousand Oaks, CA: Sage.

———, eds. 2003. *Handbook of mixed methods in social and behavioral sciences*. Thousand Oaks, CA: Sage.

Taylor, J. B. 2008. *My stroke of insight: A brain scientist's personal journey*. New York: Viking.

Taylor, N. H. 1996. Women's experience of the descent into the underworld: The path of Inanna. A feminist and heuristic inquiry. Retrieved from ProQuest Digital Dissertations. (AAT DP14333)

Thalbourne, M. A., L. Bartemucci, P. S. Delin, B. Fox, and O. Nofi. 1997. Transliminality: Its nature and correlates. *Journal of the American Society for Psychical Research* 91: 305–331.

Todres, L. 2007. *Embodied enquiry: Phenomenological touchstones for research, psychotherapy, and spirituality*. Hampshire, England: MacMillan.

Trungpa, C. 1996. *Dharma art*. Boston: Shambhala Publications.

———. 1999. *The essential Chögyam Trungpa*. Boston: Shambhala Publications.

Turner, V. 1987. Betwixt and between: The liminal period in rites of passage. In *Betwixt and between: Patterns of masculine and feminine initiation*, edited by L. C. Mahdi, S. Foster, and M. Little, 3–19. La Salle, IL: Open Court. (Reprinted from *The Forest of Symbols*, 1967, Ithica, NY: Cornell University Press.)

Underhill, E. 1915. *Practical mysticism*. New York: E. P. Dutton and Company.
———. 1969. *Mysticism: A study in the nature and development of man's spiritual consciousness*. Cleveland, OH: World Publishing. (Original work published in 1911).

Unthank, K. W. 2007. "Shame on you": Exploring the deep structure of post-trauma survival. Retrieved from ProQuest Digital Dissertations. (AAT 3221764)

Valle, R., ed. 1998. *Phenomenological inquiry in psychology: Existential and transpersonal dimensions*. New York: Plenum.

Valle, R. S. and S. Halling, eds. 1989. *Existential-phenomenological perspectives in psychology*. New York: Plenum.

Valle, R. and M. Mohs. 1998. Transpersonal awareness in phenomenological inquiry: Philosophy, reflections, and recent research. In W. Braud and R. Anderson, *Transpersonal research methods for the social sciences: Honoring human experience*, 95–113. Thousand Oaks, CA: Sage.

Van Dusen, W. 1996. *Returning to the source: The way to the experience of God*. Moab, UT: Real People Press.
———. 1999. *Beauty, wonder, and the mystical mind*. West Chester, PA: Chrysalis Books.

van Gennep, A. V. 1960. *The rites of passage*. Trans. M. B. Vizedom and G. L. Caffee. Chicago, IL: University of Chicago Press. (Original work published in 1908.)

van Leeuwen, T. and C. Jewitt, eds. 2001. *Handbook of visual analysis*. Thousand Oaks, CA: Sage.

van Manen, M. 1990. *Researching lived experience: Human science for an action sensitive pedagogy*. Albany: SUNY Press.
———. ed. 2002. *Writing in the dark: Phenomenological studies in interpretive inquiry*. London, Canada: Althouse.

Varela, F. J., E. Thompson, and E. Rosch. 1991. *The embodied mind: Cognitive science and human experience*. Cambridge: Massachusetts Institute of Technology.

Vaughan, F. 1979. *Awakening intuition*. New York: Anchor Books.
———. 2002. What is spiritual intelligence? *Journal of Humanistic Psychology* 42 (2): 16–33.

Veltrop, M. R. 1999. *Business leaders in transition: An organic inquiry into eight transformational journeys*. Retrieved from ProQuest Digital Dissertations. (AAT 9932124)

Volling, B. L., A. M. Kolak, and D. E. Kennedy. 2009. In B. Fehr, S. Sprecher, and L. G. Underwood Eds., *The science of compassionate love: The theory, research, and applications*, 163–200. West Sussex, UK: Wiley-Blackwell.

von Bingen, H. 1954. *Wisse die wege: Scivias*. Salzburg, Austria: Otto Müller Verlag.

von Franz, M. L. 1971. Part I, The inferior function. In M. L. von Franz and J. Hillman, *Jung's typology*, 1–72. New York: Spring Publications.

Wade, J. 1996. *Changes of mind: A holonomic theory of the evolution of consciousness*. Albany: SUNY Press.

Walker, R. S. 2003. Reading differently: An exploratory study of the lived experience of reading as a praxis, based on Sri Aurobindo's Letters on Yoga. PhD diss., Institute of Transpersonal Psychology.

Walsh, R. and F. Vaughan. 1993. On transpersonal definitions. *Journal of Transpersonal Psychology* 25: 199–207.

Washburn, Michael. 1995. *The ego and the dynamic ground: A transpersonal theory of human development* 2nd ed. Albany, NY: SUNY Press.

Watkins, M. M. 1977. *Waking dreams*. New York: Harper Colophon.

White, M. and D. Epston. 1990. *Narrative means to therapeutic ends*. New York: W. W. Norton.

White, R. A. 1976a. The influence of persons other than the experimenter on the subjects' scores in psi experiments. *Journal of the American Society for Psychical Research* 70: 133–66.

———. 1976b. The limits of experimenter influence on psi test results: Can any be set? *Journal of the American Society for Psychical Research* 70: 333–70.

———. 1997. Dissociation, narrative, and exceptional human experiences. In *Broken images, broken selves: Dissociative narratives in clinical practice*, edited by S. Krippner and S. M. Powers, 88–121. Washington D.C.: Brunner/Mazel.

———. 1998. Becoming more human as we work: The reflexive role of exceptional human experience. In W. Braud and R. Anderson, *Transpersonal research methods for the social sciences: Honoring human experience* pp. 128–45. Thousand Oaks, CA: Sage.

Whitehead, A. N. 1929. *Process and reality*. New York: Macmillan.

Whitehouse, M. 1958. The tao of the body. In *Bone, breath, and gesture: Practices of embodiment*, edited by D. H. Hanlon, 241–251. Berkeley, CA: North Atlantic Books.

Whitehouse, W. G., E. C. Orne, and D. F. Dinges. 2002, October. Demand characteristics: Toward an understanding of their meaning and application in clinical practice. *Prevention and Treatment* 5 Article 34, http://journals.apa.org/prevention/volume5.

Whitley, B. E. 2003. *Principles of research in behavioral science* 2nd ed. New York: McGraw-Hill.

Whyte, L. L. 1978. *The unconscious before Freud*. New York: St. Martin's Press.

Wickramasekera, I. 1989. Risk factors for parapsychological verbal reports, hypnotizability and somatic complaints. In *Parapsychology and human nature*, edited by B. Shapin and L. Coly, 19–56. New York: Parapsychology Foundation.

Wilber, K. 1979. *The spectrum of consciousness*. Wheaton, IL: Quest.

———. 1995. *Sex, ecology, and spirituality*. Boston: Shambhala Publications.

———. 2000. *Integral psychology: Consciousness, spirit, psychology, therapy*. Boston: Shambhala Publications.

Winnicott, D. W. 1992. *Through pediatrics to psycho-analysis*. New York: Brunner-Routledge. (Original work published in 1958.)

Winter, G. 2000, March. A comparative discussion of the notion of "validity" in qualitative and quantitative research. [58 paragraphs]. *The Qualita-*

tive Report [On-line serial], 43/4. Available: www.nova.edu/ssss/QR/ QR4–3/winter.html.

Wood, R. 2010. Psycho-spiritual transformation experienced by participants of modern wilderness rites of passage quests: An intuitive inquiry. PhD diss., Institute of Transpersonal Psychology.

Wright, A. 2010. A functional interpretation of anomalous experiences associated with death: Honoring the dying and bereaved. PhD diss., Institute of Transpersonal Psychology.

Yates, F. A. 1974. *The art of memory*. Chicago: University of Chicago Press.

Yoslow, M. 2007. The pride and price of remembrance: An empirical view of transgenerational post-Holocaust trauma and associated transpersonal elements in the third generation. PhD diss., Institute of Transpersonal Psychology.

About the Coauthors
and Contributor

Rosemarie Anderson, Ph.D has studied in the fields of psychology, theology, and philosophic hermeneutics. In her graduate training at the University of Nebraska-Lincoln in the early 1970s, she was trained as an experimental social psychologist and applied the methods of experimental psychology, quantitative analyses, and feminist research methods to study the social determinants of motivation. Through data analyses, she came to understand quantitative multivariate analysis as a complex form of pattern recognition that required intuitive insights to "see" patterns embedded in statistical arrays, an understanding that was formative for her in subsequent research and influenced the development of intuitive inquiry almost thirty years later.

After graduate school, Dr. Anderson continued to conduct research in experimental social psychology at Wake Forest University, but over time, became increasingly disquieted with the limitations of experimental methods as applied to research in psychology. In the context of the influx of spiritual traditions from the East that infused American culture in the 1970s, her spiritual life was also reawakening. Keen to explore spiritual traditions worldwide, Dr. Anderson left her professorial post to teach with the University of Maryland Asian Division and lived in Japan and South Korea for two years. Still in her early thirties, the cultures and art of Asia and the monasteries visited left a strong spiritual and aesthetic impression.

Upon returning to the United States in 1979, Dr. Anderson began studies at the Graduate Theological Union in Berkeley, California in order to study life's great existential questions within her own spiritual tradition. During her seminary years, she studied ancient Hebrew and New Testament Greek and pursued advanced studies in Biblical exegesis and hermeneutics. After receiving her M. Div. in 1983, she returned to the University of Maryland and served as a university dean for the European Division for four years. She was ordained a priest in the Protestant Episcopal Church in the United States in 1987. Thereafter, for several years, she served as a parish priest and university chaplain, applying her knowledge of Biblical exegesis and hermeneutics to pastoral responsibilities and sermon preparation.

In 1992, Dr. Anderson accepted a position on the core faculty at the Institute of Transpersonal Psychology (ITP, Palo Alto, California), an appointment that encouraged her to integrate her interests in psychological research and spirituality. Training herself in qualitative methods, she acquired expertise in case study, narrative research, heuristic research, hermeneutical approaches, and phenomenological psychological approaches to research. In the late 1990s, Dr. Anderson and ITP colleague Dr. William Braud developed transpersonal approaches to research in response to the research needs of their doctoral students, who studied transpersonal and spiritual phenomena and who needed methods that approached "the farther reaches of human nature" of the topics studied.

Dr. Anderson has published numerous articles, chapters, papers, and has written three books: *Transpersonal Research Methods for the Social Sciences* (coauthored with William Braud; Sage, 1998), *Celtic Oracles* (Random House, 1998), and *Five Ways of Doing Qualitative Analysis: Phenomenological Psychology, Grounded Theory, Discourse Analysis, Narrative Research, and Intuitive Inquiry* (coauthored with Frederick Wertz, Kathy Charmaz, Linda McMullen, Ruthellen Josselson, and Emalinda McSpladden; Guilford Publications, 2011). She has also developed a Body Intelligence Scale (BIS) and a developmental model that details the role of the body and myth in psycho-spiritual development called The Body Map.

Dr. Anderson is currently Professor in the ITP's online Ph.D Program and serves as a member of the advisory and editorial boards for several professional journals and associations dedicated to transpersonal and spiritual endeavors.

Additional information about Dr. Anderson's research can be found on her website www.rosemarieanderson.com or on her ITP faculty web pages at www.itp.edu.

William Braud, Ph.D has a variegated research-methods background. He absorbed natural science methods and viewpoints in undergraduate physics studies. In his doctoral work in experimental psychology at the University of Iowa, he was trained in the behavioral and hypothetico-deductive approaches of the Hull/Spence learning theory and motivation tradition, and he studied the philosophy of science, epistemology, and ontology with Gustav Bergmann, who had been a member of the Vienna Circle of logical positivists. Later, through university and medical center appointments in Houston, Texas, he supplemented behavioral approaches to learning, memory, and motivation with clinical, psychophysiological, and pharmacological methods. At a private research laboratory (Mind Science Foundation, San Antonio, Texas), he developed new research methods for exploring topics in areas of biofeedback, physiological self-regulation, altered states of consciousness, and parapsychology; and with collaborators at several health science centers, he conducted studies in the then-new field of psychoneuroimmunology. During his seventeen years of teaching at the Institute of Transpersonal Psychology. Professor Braud expanded his research expertise to include not only established quantitative methods, but also more newly developed qualitative methods, mixed methods, and transpersonal inquiry approaches.

As Professor, Director of Research, Dissertation Director, and Co-director of ITP's William James Center for Consciousness Studies in ITP's Residential Ph.D Program, and later, in its Global (distance learning) Ph.D. Program, Dr. Braud taught research-related graduate psychology courses, supervised dissertations, and carried out quantitative and qualitative research studies in areas of exceptional human experiences (mystical, intuitive, peak, transformative) and their interpretations, meanings, and life impacts; personal and spiritual change and transformation; alternative ways of knowing; the development and promotion of more inclusive and integrated inquiry approaches for transpersonal studies and science in general; and the examination of some of the underlying assumptions of science, psychology, transpersonal psychology, and certain spiritual and wisdom traditions.

Dr. Braud has published his methods and findings in over 250 professional journal articles, book chapters, and books, and has made many national and international conference presentations. He coauthored, with Rosemarie Anderson, *Transpersonal Research Methods for the Social Sciences: Honoring Human Experience* (Sage, 1998), and authored *Distant Mental Influence: Its Contributions to Science, Healing, and Human Interactions* (Hampton Roads, 2003). He is a member of the advisory and editorial boards of several professional journals. Dr. Braud now is Professor Emeritus, Institute of Transpersonal Psychology.

Additional information about Dr. Braud's background and research can be found on his website http://inclusivepsychology.com or on his ITP faculty web pages at http://itp.edu.

Jennifer Clements, Ph.D is a Guest Contributor for Chapter 3. She began her career as a practicing architect and also was employed as Lecturer at the University of California at Berkeley, teaching graduate design. She received her Ph.D in transpersonal psychology at the Institute of Transpersonal Psychology in 1992, staying on as adjunct faculty to teach classes in organic and feminist research, clinical practice, and feminine issues, as well as advising students' doctoral dissertations. She also had a private psychological practice in San Francisco. She currently lives on an island in Maine, where she continues to advise ITP students on organic inquiry while developing her new career as a writer of nonfiction and fiction that explores and supports the notion of working in partnership with Spirit.

Index